G-Forces

Frank Feather

The 35 Global Forces
Restructuring Our Future

William Morrow and Company, Inc.
New York

Library of Congress Cataloging-in-Publication Data

Feather, Frank, 1943–
    G-Forces : the 35 global forces
  restructuring our future /
Frank Feather.
        p.   cm.
    Includes bibliographical references (p.
    ISBN 0-688-08962-3
    1. Economic history—1971–   2. Economic forecasting.   3. World
politics—1945–   4. Forecasting.   I. Title.
HC59.F4   1990
330.9′001′12—dc20   90-5715
                                                         CIP

Printed in the United States of America

First U. S. Edition

1 2 3 4 5 6 7 8 9 10

To all geo-strategic change agents :
those who recognize that the future
is not a spectator sport; rather,
it is something in which we must
invest most of our thought and action,
because destiny is something we create —
and we are building a global civilization.

Contents

ix   Lists of Charts, Maps and Diagrams

x   List of Tables

xi   Acknowledgments

xiv   **Preface:** The Geo-Strategic View

1   **Introduction**
Re-Visioning the Future: The Dynamic "4-STEP" Process
of 35 G-Forces Reinventing the World

13   **Section "S"**
G-Forces of Social Motivation: Satisfying Psychological Drives

G-Force S-1	Stabilizing Global Population	23
G-Force S-2	Feeding the Future — And Lots to Spare	35
G-Force S-3	Piping Clean Water for All	45
G-Force S-4	Creating Global Wellness	53
G-Force S-5	Providing Meaningful Work	59
G-Force S-6	Housing the Future in Super-Cities	65
G-Force S-7	Achieving Sexual and Racial Harmony	73
G-Force S-8	Globalizing Values, Beliefs and Culture	87
G-Force S-9	Educating the Future: 10-Billion Super-Brains	95

103   **Section "T"**
G-Forces of Technological Innovation:
Creating the Info-Rich Leisure Society

G-Force T-1	Eliminating Hard Work — Creating Leisure Society	117
G-Force T-2	The Drive for Productivity and Efficiency	123
G-Force T-3	Sharing Information and Technology	129
G-Force T-4	Micro-Powered Expansion	137
G-Force T-5	Real-Time Info-Globalization	143
G-Force T-6	Techno-Leadership of Japan	151
G-Force T-7	Pushing Back High-Tech Frontiers	161
G-Force T-8	Creating an Info-Rich World	169

175 Section "E"
G-Forces of Economic Modernization: Redistributing Planetary Riches
G-Force E-1   Atlantic "Sunset," Pacific "Sunrise"   185
G-Force E-2   Industrializing the Third World   191
G-Force E-3   Reinventing the Global Financial System   199
G-Force E-4   Building the "Planetary Information
                    Economy" (PIE)   213
G-Force E-5   Eliminating Global Energy Shortages   225
G-Force E-6   Ensuring Resource Self-Sufficiency   235
G-Force E-7   Restoring the Planet's Environment   243
G-Force E-8   Reinventing Capitalism and Communism   257
G-Force E-9   Converting Military Waste to Earthly
                    Eco-Development   271

279 Section "P"
G-Forces of Political Reformation: Restructuring Political Power
G-Force P-1   Disarming the Planet   285
G-Force P-2   "Amexicana": Traumatic Rebirth of America   293
G-Force P-3   *Perestroika*: Gorbachev's Global "Check-Mate"   309
G-Force P-4   Soviet Unification of Europe   319
G-Force P-5   *Ichi Ban*: Japan's Global Role   327
G-Force P-6   Modernizing China for Super-Stardom   335
G-Force P-7   Third World Solidarity   349
G-Force P-8   Informed "Partocracy"   365
G-Force P-9   Globalized Governance   375

391 Conclusion: Grasping the Promise
401 Bibliography
417 Index
437 About the Author

List of Charts, Maps, Diagrams

Fig. 1   Global Post-Industrialization   2
Fig. 2   North America's 6-Wave Economy   4
Fig. 3   6-Wave Satisfaction of Needs and Aspirations   17
Fig. 4   Population "Spike" Growth Rate   25
Fig. 5   Declining Birth Rates (Selected Regions)   26
Fig. 6   Aging Population (Selected Countries)   28
Fig. 7   Global Population Imbalance   31
Fig. 8   Global Urbanization Trends   69
Fig. 9   Effects of Computer-Communications Technology   108
Fig. 10   6-Wave Bursts of Technology   112
Fig. 11   Third World's Share of Global Industrial Output   126
Fig. 12   End of 2nd-Wave in West   128
Fig 13   ISDN: Integrated Services Digital Network   145
Fig. 14   High Mass Knowledge Creation Society   174
Fig. 15   Global Economic Imbalance   192
Fig. 16   Developing Economies Growing Fastest   193
Fig. 17   The 57-Year Long-Wave Economic "Mega-Cycle"   200
Fig. 18   Micro-Model of Planetary Information Economy (PIE)   214
Fig. 19   Information-Related Industries   215
Fig. 20   Macro-Model of Planetary Information Economy (PIE)   217
Fig. 21   Global Governance and Economic Growth   220
Fig. 22   New Global Economic Ranking   223
Fig. 23   Estimated Proven Oil Reserves   227
Fig. 24   G-Forces of Political Participation   283
Fig. 25   U.S. Cycles of Rebirth   300
Fig. 26   Superpower Foreign Aid Competition   353
Fig. 27   Incipient Global Multi-Polarity (1965-90)   381
Fig. 28   Global Multi-Polarity by 2000   381
Fig. 29   Existing State-Centric World Disorder   383
Fig. 30   Proposed Geo-Centric 4-STEP World Governance Order   388

List of Statistical Tables

Table 1   Potential Household Water Savings   48
Table 2   University Degrees Earned by Women   75
Table 3   Work Performed by Women in Africa   77
Table 4   Shifts in Global Steel Production   125
Table 5   Forecast Average Rates of Economic Growth, 1987-2050   222
Table 6   Global Energy Sources   228
Table 7   Declining Energy Intensity in the West   229
Table 8   Global Mineral Resources   236
Table 9   Industrial Waste Reduction   251
Table 10   Investment for Sustainable Economic Development   276
Table 11   Increasing Third World Self-Reliance   352

Acknowledgments

Shaped by Global Minds

In the current knowledge explosion of the Information Age, all authors owe an incalculable debt to all previous writers and thinkers. The ideas in this book have been shaped by many global minds, particularly those of pioneer geo-strategic thinkers such as Buckminster Fuller, Herman Kahn, Alvin Toffler, Marshall McLuhan and Yoneji Masuda. The Bibliography provides a more complete acknowledgment of my debt.

The reactions of various audiences to a multitude of papers, articles, conference speeches, corporate seminars and international presentations helped inestimably in the book's development. The manuscript would not have been initiated without the urgings and inspiring encouragement, thoughout the 1980s, of various mentors among a global network of friends and colleagues in multinational corporations, government ministries, education and various other institutions, as well as several strategic planners and futurists. I thank especially Hazel Henderson (for urging me to jump in and set up my own consulting company in 1981) and Ramesh Sakaria and Rashmi Mayur for helping me do so. Others among many I must thank are Roy Anderson, Jay Bell, Cabell Brand, Noel Brown, Lynn Burton, Cai Qi-Xiang, Bob Carman, Raul Carvajal, Chen Ling-Zhu, Keshav Chandaria, Richard Clark, Harlan Cleveland, Martin Connell, Ed Cornish, Jim Dator, Christian de Laet, Chuck DeRidder, Maurice Dubras, Henry Evering, Orville Freeman, John Gilbert, Ian Graham, Willis Harman, Barrie Haverluck, Ivan Head, John Hilliker, Enrique Iglesias, Alexander King, Liang Feng-Cen, Lin Min, Liu Dong-Sheng, Lu Cong-Min, Lu Hong-Jun, John McLeish, Norman Macrae, Christina Baumann Massie, Roy Megarry, Jay Mendell, Morris Miller, Norman Palmer, Perry Pascarella, Lewis Perinbam, Marlene Preiss, Pauline Price, Lilya Prim-Chorney, Qin Ling-Zhen, Tim Reid, Erika Rimkus, Ray Rouse, Rodger Schwaas, Satish Seth, Clive Simmonds, Stuart Smith, Robert Stanbury, Maurice Strong, Fred Thompson, Cosmo Torisawa, Eric Trist, Garth Turner, Mahbub ul-Haq,

André van Dam, Cesar Virata, Kayleen Watson, Ponna Wignaraja, Keith Wilde, Zhang Bao-Gen, Peter Zuckerman and many others I cannot name here, but they know who they are. The book has been "hatched" over seven years as a result of gentle "heat" from these friends of the global future.

Others have had a more immediate influence by reading and criticizing all or part of the manuscript. In particular, I thank Gordon Montador and Jim Williamson at Summerhill Press, for insisting that "we get it right" and challenging me to strengthen my arguments, Ed Greathed for his extensive but constructive criticisms and suggested revisions, Shaun Oakey for polishing the final copy, and Jim Landis at William Morrow & Company for publishing the U.S. edition. The manuscript would never have been produced without the tireless wordprocessing expertise of Jane Lush, Janet Reid, Lucy Black and Dianne Proulx, to whom I am ever grateful.

Only I, however, can claim and accept the blame for the book's remaining failings. I do so gladly and welcome suggestions from my readers so that I may continue to learn and understand the global future.

Finally, I deeply appreciate the unfailing support and understanding of the entire Feather family, especially that of my daughters, Alison and Joanne, and particularly the extensive, direct assistance and loving support of my best friend, intellectual companion and wife, Tammie M. Tan (Tan Min). Their own love and concern for the future of the world is reflected throughout this book.

A heartfelt "Thank You!" to you all.

The Geo-Strategic View

"Results are gained by exploiting opportunities,
not by solving problems."
— *Peter F. Drucker*

It is time for some straight talk and fresh ideas about the exciting prospects for the future of the world. We have all been misled by gloom and doom predictions about the future. In truth, our prospects are much brighter. Unfortunately, the very complexity of persistent global problems, fragmented analyses, widespread disinformation, myths and human prejudice have all combined to form a dense fog of misunderstanding. This fog obscures the massive global opportunities staring us in the face and creates confusion about the variety of constructive options open to us. Consequently, all too often there is a pervasive conditioned negative reflex that stems from parochial, short-term and shallow understandings — a blindness to the planetary sweep of positive progress.

Fortunately, our accumulated knowledge of the process of global change during the past century and a half, coupled with a geo-strategic view of unfolding current events, make it possible for us to see clearly what is really happening, to look into the long-term future with reasonable accuracy and to realize what needs to be done. Adopting such a geo-strategic view, this book aims to blow away the fog and bring the real global future into focus — and within our grasp — by objectively and comprehensively separating future fact from misinformed opinion and by describing the global forces of change at work. Many readers will be disturbed by some of my prognostications and provocations. It is my intention to disturb — and to change some minds. Only by ridding ourselves of preconceived and outmoded ideas can we look realistically at "what on earth is going on" and understand what is geo-strategically probable and possible in the decades ahead.

To those who cannot grasp the ongoing realities of global change, this book may strike them as unrealistically utopian. Some are always pessimistic, and it is indeed easy for them to marshal evidence to support their gloomy outlooks. I reject their doomsday attitude — an essential prerequisite to proving it wrong. It is not necessary for me to redocument or discuss in detail in this book the litany of problems that humanity must solve. However, none has been ignored or brushed aside. Rather, my prescriptions implicitly consider the obstacles to progress even though my emphasis is on broad solutions and specific recommended strategies to maximize opportunities.

I am neither an optimist nor a pessimist; I am a pragmatic businessman. Born into a Yorkshire farming family in War-depressed England, I am "frank" by nature as well as by name. Conditioned by the business pragmatism of a 22-year international banking career, my ideas have been refined and honed by lecturing to the world's top academics and professionals as well as by eight years of consulting to multinational corporations, national governments and international institutions.

This book is based on geo-strategic studies carried out since 1981 at the Toronto headquarters of the Geo-Strategic Opportunity Development Corporation (GEODEVCO) through our Global Management Bureau. For major international clients, we gather and analyze information from around the world on global trends affecting business, government, education and society at large. The material in this book thus forms the basis for much of our clients' organizational strategic planning and management efforts for the 1990s and beyond. In other words, this considered outlook for the next 60-years on Earth has already gained wide currency as a realistically thought-through and in-depth study of global trends. The future we envisage is not utopian but managerially pragmatic and distinctly attainable.

I challenge my readers, reviewers and critics to think as geo-strategically as our clients. By wearing a truly realistic set of fog-proof lenses, may you too perceive the long-term global opportunities now within our grasp. I invite you to read the entire text, give it careful and objective consideration — and then join the exciting task of "reinventing the world."

May the G-Forces be with you!

Frank Feather
Toronto, Canada
September, 1989

Introduction

Re-Visioning the Future:
The Dynamic "4-STEP" Process of
35 G-Forces Reinventing the World

*"The task is nothing less than
to reinvent the world."*
—*Jonathan Schell,*
The Fate of the Earth

The prospects are dazzling. The world has within its grasp the potential to change — and progress — like never before. The outcome is in our hands. We need to rewrite and re-vision the course of our collective destiny — to re-invent the world with a geo-strategic agenda that will take us to an affluent and peaceful future. That this future is possible, and that humankind must pursue it, underlines everything in this book. We can and must re-invent the world.

The major agents of change are not a few nation states, political leaders, business executives or scientists working on scattered, individual projects. They are what I call G-Forces, 35 global forces of change that are restructuring the world. And fundamental to these driving forces of globalization is the overriding behavior of ordinary people: their needs, their aspirations and their ideas. Little improves in the world unless people decide to change things, either consciously or subconsciously. The power of the "masses" — all 5-billion of us — is the most powerful G-Force of change on the planet.

Beyond the "Third Wave"

These 35 G-Forces provide a much more powerful, global and long-term structure for understanding change than so-called "megatrends"; they also help us make sense of the world's progression far beyond what has become known as the "third wave" of societal development. Alvin Toffler referred to the Agricultural and Industrial Ages as 1st-Wave Society and 2nd-Wave Society respectively. Third-Wave Society is the Post-Industrial Revolution already underway.

The first bar chart (Fig.1) shows the shift of employment between the 1st, 2nd and 3rd-Waves in various groups of countries between 1960 and 1980. In developing countries, which are mostly agrarian societies, people still work on a labor-intensive basis, just as people in Western countries did in the Agricultural Age. But we are seeing a continual shift of employment from the labor-intensive agricultural sector into the industrial and service sectors as national economies modernize across the path of socio-economic development. As machines take over agricultural tasks, the rural population moves to the cities, where they form industrial labor pools for the manufacturing and service sectors. Even the most backward countries show some growth in the 3rd-Wave sector, and the most advanced countries of the Third World are moving strongly towards 3rd-Wave society characteristics.

Fig. 1 Global Post-Industrialization

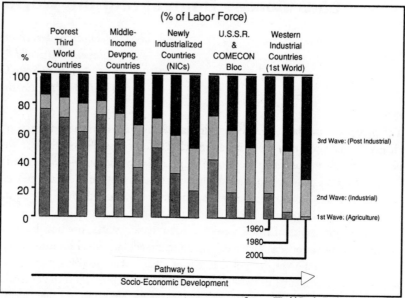

Source: World Bank; Forecasts GEODEVCO

Western nations have already moved beyond the 3rd-Wave, which is now so large that it employs almost 80% of North America's work force. Indeed, Toffler's "Third Wave" must now be divided into four distinct waves:
- 3rd-Wave: Services (financial, health, personal, etc.);
- 4th-Wave: Information (including knowledge and high-tech);
- 5th-Wave: Leisure (and tourism); and
- 6th-Wave: Outer-Space.

These waves exist simultaneously in individual countries, though at any one time one wave predominates. The old waves rarely disappear; rather, the new waves complement them. For example, machines built in the 2nd-Wave manufacturing sector helped modernize agriculture and increased crop production. Today, the 4th-Wave information sector is not just spawning the information economy; it is helping to modernize all other sectors of the economy so that computerized information is essential to modern industry, be it a farm, factory, office, hospital or hotel.

The six waves manifest themselves in varying strengths and speeds in different countries and regions around the world. Hawaii, for example, has been primarily a 5th-Wave leisure economy for many years. Its original agricultural base has virtually been eliminated, and the other sectors are insignificant. The six waves also have cross-impact effects among regions and countries — for example, the high-tech career couple in Toronto who has a nanny from the Philippines whose income helps to educate her children in Manila so that they can qualify for high-tech jobs. Likewise, major American banks (3rd-Wave) in New York employ keypunch operators in the 5th-Wave Caribbean who "telecommute" to Manhattan via 6th-Wave satellite technology.

In North America, the white collar service sector became the largest employer in 1950. This was the real 3rd-Wave revolution. The next wave, the 4th-Wave information sector (of computers, robotics, information, knowledge, media), began to rise to supremacy in the 1980s. As we enter the 1990s, this wave is the predominant job creator in the United States, Canada and Japan. By the year 2000 or so, it will the largest contributor to the Gross National Product (GNP) in these countries. Already, however, the fastest-growing employment area is the 5th-Wave leisure sector, that is, the travel, tourism, hospitality, recreation, entertainment and cultural industry. This sector will be the largest employer in North America by about 2020.

As Western society has moved from an agriculture-based 1st-Wave society through to a 4th-Wave information-based society, employment has shifted to an almost upside-down reversal of the earlier situation. Fig. 2 illustrates this, as well as the strong growth of the 5th-Wave leisure society and the emergence of the 6th-Wave outer-space sector.

As the new waves pile on top of the previous ones, they build the economy and enhance socio-economic development. But the fortunes of individual nations vary depending on their drive to change and their degree of innovation. China, for example, was an innovator that created paper, printing, gunpowder and rocketry and, before the Industrial Revolution, was the world's largest manufacturer, thanks mostly to its domination of the world silk market. Then, suffering internal political misdirection and external attempts at colonization, China faltered and declined, and it failed to take part in the Industrial Revolution at all. Since 1978, China has changed directions and is now pursuing an active 6-wave modernization strategy. Britain, which has failed to innovate since World War II, is now a second-rate economic power. In 1988 it even postponed indefinitely its space plane program, thereby potentially forgoing any effective participation in the 6th-Wave outer-space sector of the world economy.

By the year 2000, the leading nations — including many developing countries — will be those that have strongly growing 4th- and 5th-Wave sectors. Indeed, some Third World countries, such as China and India, have ambitious 6th-Wave space programs already in place.

Fig. 2 North America's 6-Wave Economy

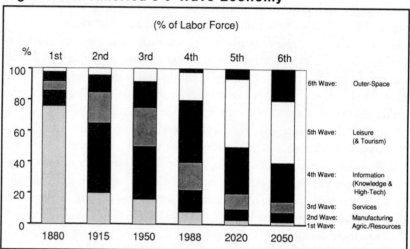

Source: U.S. Dept. of Labor, Statistics Canada; Forecasts GEODEVCO.

"4-STEP" Global Restructuring

The world's future is being dramatically influenced by the G-Forces of change that interact in a "4-STEP" long-wave cycle of global social development. 4-STEP is my acronym for the Social, Technological, Economic and Political process of change, described as follows:

Step 1 — Social Motivation

The first STEP in the cycle of social development is initiated by human G-Forces. As we progress upward through the human hierarchy of needs and satisfy our evolving aspirations, we generate new ideas to sustain our progress. To further satisfy our changing needs, we apply these ideas to technological innovations. As the information wave spreads across the world, ideas and innovations travel like lightning, changing needs and aspirations worldwide and tuning humanity to the same wavelength on an increasing array of global issues such as disarmament and environmental protection.

Step 2 — Technological Innovation

Human innovation therefore spurs research and development to push back the frontiers of scientific knowledge and spawn further G-Forces of new generations of technology. The more efficient and productive the new technologies, the greater the economic and social benefits for us to enjoy. We can increase our economic well-being and clean up our environment. We can switch investment away from space weapons to high-tech economic modernization.

Step 3 — Economic Modernization

The third STEP, therefore, is the effective management of technological G-Forces to restructure and modernize the planet and the use of its resources — including its natural environment — to orchestrate the production of worldwide economic wealth on a long-term sustainable basis.

Step 4 — Political Reformation

Finally, to ensure that the people benefit from all this technological innovation and economic modernization, the social development process must be elevated to a higher level of human aspiration. Therefore political processes and government systems are inevitably reformed — preferably by consensus, but by social upheaval and revolution if necessary. Recent global agreements to collaborate on disarmament and environmental protection are solid examples of what can be achieved. In this way, we can continue to re-invent the world.

The core of this book is organized into four parallel Sections that describe the next "4-STEP" mega-cycle, which is already underway, by analyzing the effect of the G-Forces of change within each of these four stages.

Geo-Strategic Mind Understands G-Forces

To understand why and how the world is changing — and to know what to do about it — we need a geo-strategic mindset. As Marshall McLuhan's global village evolves, information is creating a world with no national, political, language or other boundary. It is thus becoming possible — and essential — to deal with problems and opportunities from a global perspective. As Japanese information guru Yoneji Masuda has discerned, the spirit of the future and the single concept characterizing the thought of the new Information Society must (and will) be globalism. The major feature of globalism is Buckminster Fuller's "space-ship thought" (looking at the world as a space station) and Masuda's consequent suggestion that this will bring about a symbiosis of humankind and nature. This perspective is gradually coming into its own, thanks to the increasing information networks that enmesh the global village and deepen our understanding of our world. In turn, the spirit of globalism will become broadly and deeply rooted in human minds, which will become geo-strategic in outlook — and will re-invent the world. Again, the recent disarmament and ozone agreements are indicative both of this trend and of its promise.

According to Harlan Cleveland, former dean of the Hubert Humphrey Institute of International Affairs, five attitudes are the key to understanding and reinventing the global future:

- a genuine interest in what other people think and what makes them tick;
- a highly developed intellectual curiosity;
- a passionate interest in the future;
- a belief that risks are to be taken and not avoided; and
- the courage to reconcile personal power (which knowledge confers) with personal responsibility (which it requires).

It is within this spirit that I have written this book. The geo-strategic mind unlocks human creativity, and its widespread application — by all of us — in business, government and education will release unbounded innovation, global understanding and the solution of all major world problems. It will allow us to leap away from self-interest and an obsession with short-term solutions to achieve long-term results that benefit us all. Every one of us must adopt geo-strategic thinking. Only then can we understand the global social development process and realize the fantastic opportunities being presented by the G-Forces of change already in action.

The first essential of geo-strategic thinking is the ability to think globally, to observe and understand the dynamic patterning in the entire global environment, from the micro to the macro (that is, from deep inner-space to deep outer-space).

To begin to understand the nature of global change, it is essential to think about all aspects of life on Earth in its micro dimensions. We must use our geo-strategic mind to consider the direct and indirect long-term global impacts of our frontier developments in such fields as microelectronics, microbiology and the tiny details of system functioning at the organic level. Exploration of human inner-space increases our understanding of our psychological and neurological functioning. These discoveries, in turn, are starting to give us a greater understanding of the human motivations and behavior (Social G-Forces) that drive the world. Geo-strategic thinking at the micro inner-space level thus reveals the major driving force of global change: the constant striving by every one of the 5-billion people on this planet to move from misery and despair to happiness and contentment.

At the same time, just as humanity is exploring outer-space, so we must allow our global mind to explore Earth from a solar perspective — the macro dimension. To understand what is going on down on our planet, and to anticipate how the pattern might change, we must "mentally sit on the Moon." Once we allow the global mind to circle the Earth via the Moon, we gain a completely new perspective of the human condition and our place in the overall scheme of things. This phenomenon has struck every astronaut sent aloft by the U.S.A. and the U.S.S.R. When we mentally go into orbit, we can see all the problems, all the chaos, all the human idiocy; but we can also see all the order, all the human genius, all the opportunities.

Global thinking thus requires us to venture beyond our own front yard. By looking at what management expert Peter Drucker calls the "planetary production site" and the "global supermarket," for example, we can see that the North American market is stagnating — it is saturated with material goods — while the mass market of the developing countries (on the other side of the planet, where almost 80% of the world's people live) represents the real growth opportunities of the future. The geo-strategic view also reveals that this new mass market is too far away to be effectively served with material goods shipped from the developed countries.

No situation is static, and we need to see the world in motion over the long term. The second essential of geo-strategic thinking is, therefore, futuristic thought. But to simply think futuristically is not enough to anticipate the future. Futurists tend to identify only isolated trends in everyday life. Geo-strategic thinkers do much more: they perceive the long-term multifold global trends, they anticipate global changes and they analyze the interactions of the different G-Forces. Geo-strategic thinkers see the whole picture — inner and outer, micro and macro.

Prevalent long-term global cycles abound, yet we know almost nothing about them. As we swiftly approach a time when we may be confronted with the basic scientific secrets of nature, there is mounting evidence that we are surrounded by long-term planetary forces. Many cycles in nature seem to have the same wavelength as cycles in human economic affairs, and many of the cycles found on Earth seem to have the same wavelength as cycles found in the Solar System. This is an unsettling concept. It ranks with the realization that Earth is not the center of the Universe, that humanity is not a special creature and that many of our actions result from subconscious forces about which we are ordinarily ignorant. To admit the existence of these cycles demeans our self-esteem, so we tend to resist any suggestion that our life and our Universe vibrate in regular rhythms caused by forces still unknown and possibly uncontrollable.

But can all these cycles, some of them recurring since the beginning of time, be merely chance phenomena? When a cycle has repeated with enough regularity and with enough strength, it cannot reasonably be dismissed as mere accident. Earthquakes occur at rhythmic intervals, as do volcanic eruptions. Wildlife populations fluctuate in regular cycles. Water levels in rivers and lakes rise and fall in cycles. As meteorologist Raymond Wheeler has documented, the weather shows rhythmic cycles, often over as long as 500-years.

I believe these rhythms have a universal source, the force of which reflects itself in human behavior and thus in the very evident 50- to 60-year long-wave cycles of social, technological, economic and political affairs worldwide — that is, in the G-Forces at work in our world. I am not saying that world events are predetermined. Although a cyclic force may be inevitable, its result is often subject to our will — if we know in advance about the force. Once we know about these cycles, we can transform their effects and create new cycles of change. This is particularly important, for example, as we face the urgent need to restructure the global financial system or to better manage the planet's environment. "Trend is destiny" — but only when we make it so.

The future also contains many so-called wild-card events, which threaten any concept of a truly stable future. However, a geo-strategic view demonstrates that some of these wild-card events are not so wild-card at all. For instance, OPEC should have been no surprise to anyone who was geo-strategically alert. OPEC was formed in 1962, yet most people had not heard of it until oil prices suddenly tripled 11-years later. In any event, OPEC is a normal part of the restructuring of global energy needs in response to the 6-wave modernization of world economies.

Similarly, most observers will be surprised by the apparently sudden impact of the Third World debtors' cartel which was formed in 1985 (itself presaged in 1982, when Mexico threatened to default). While this cartel goes unnoticed and the debt default has not yet officially happened, the default will occur soon and it will extend to all Third World countries. Most people were also surprised by the overthrow of the Shah of Iran. Yet it could have been anticipated — as could the consequences. This was no wild-card event. Any social scientist will tell you that it is dangerous to technologically advance a society as quickly as the Shah tried (especially without real economic benefit to the masses or any political reform) and that — as I shall explain — all dictatorships and absolute monarchies are doomed anyway. What Iran needed was economic and political reform before initiating more technological change. In other words, the Shah ignored the orderly 4-STEP process of development.

New developments always have wide-ranging effects, which can be foreseen. For example, if we apply futuristic thinking to the micro issues, we can anticipate the long-term ramifications of microelectronic technology and biotechnology. The geo-strategic futurist can foresee, sooner or later, the twinning of biogenetic life forms with electronic computers to produce biological computers with human "intelligence" sufficient to run most of the world for us. We can also see a parallel development in human cognitive functioning: the increasing prevalence of whole-brain, or holistic, thinking. We are witnessing the evolution of a "planetary consciousness" that awakens and fuels the latent "global mind" in all of us. Japan is already trying to foster this phenomenon internationally.

Futuristic thinking requires an openness to such new and unconventional ideas. Human minds are like parachutes: they work best when they're open! Effective futuristic thinking requires, then, that you constantly scan the environment for little bits of information that, like in a kaleidoscope, change the big picture in a dynamic way.

We must creatively integrate this information to discern interrelationships among the social, technological, economic and political G-Forces and, in turn, their effect in furthering collective interest rather than self-interest. For example, a reduction in the population growth rate is directly dependent on the provision of nutrition, healthcare and education, on the availability of birth-control technology, on the economic shift away from 1st-Wave society (where children are an essential part of farm labor), and on the politics of population management systems.

The third essential of geo-strategic thinking is opportunistic thought. This is much more than the ability to creatively solve problems. It is the ability to create not only brand-new opportunities but fresh opportunities out of old problems, and to do so without creating more problems. Opportunistic thinking is the ability to spot strategic opportunities presented by global changes and to develop strategies for their implementation. True geo-strategic opportunistic thinking is not a linear (left-brain) reaction to information, it is a whole-brain harmonic function that often comes as an intuitive flash, originating from insights that are somehow beyond the reach of conscious analysis.

Geo-Strategic Action Leadership

Geo-strategic thought, then, is a combination of global, futuristic and opportunistic thinking skills that are *applied* in understanding and reinventing the world. The key word is *applied*. All the thinking in the world is of no use unless it finds application, unless the ideas are transformed into action. To take action in a complex, fast-changing world, where it is all too easy to cling to the status quo and do nothing, you need the courage to *take* — not *make* — decisions. Any fool can *make* a (wrong or irresponsible) decision — witness all the problems in the world today. But to *take* a decision is to take full responsibility and accountability for its long-term positive results. That is called pro-active leadership. This is easier said than done, for to take a decision — no matter how pro-active or sound — also means to take risks. We therefore need to overcome our fear of failure. Decisions must be taken if results are to be achieved. Geo-strategic thinking must be integrated into geo-strategic action leadership, the pivotal force behind any successful long-term organizational effort.

Yet the only effective economic leadership in the world today is in Japan, China and (since Gorbachev) the U.S.S.R. These are the only major nations in the world that have a geo-strategic vision and a specific long-term plan to take them to the threshold of the 21st-Century and beyond. They have realized that times of rapid change place a premium on visionary leadership. Maintaining the status quo does not impose the heavy demands on leaders that change does; change requires both intellectual and political innovation. Effective leadership in a time of rapid change also demands not only a vision of the future but the capacity to communicate that vision. Therefore, in 1978, Japan articulated its plan to become the "Information Utility of the Planet" by 1995. In 1978, China outlined a plan to quadruple its economic output between 1980 and 2000. Both nations, as of 1989, are well ahead of their agenda. In 1985, the U.S.S.R. set itself the goal of doubling its economy by the year 2000.

Neither the United States, Britain, France, Germany, Canada, India, Brazil nor any other major world nation has such a plan — while the world cries out for such visionary leadership. Nationalist ideology is a weak substitute for informed, responsible geo-strategic policy-making. Successful leadership requires a fusion of positive self-regard with optimism about a desired future for the world. Learning about global change is the essential task of the leader. Those who do not learn will not survive as leaders in tomorrow's world.

Global Governance Essential

As well, in a world with "nobody in charge" but many nations scrambling to stay in charge of diverse elements of world affairs, elite collegial structures and summit conferences among the select few are no basis for global governance. International geo-strategic management and planning cannot be done by a few nationalistic politicians who are advised in secret by parochial experts. Together they have neither the global mandate nor access to the required global information and knowledge to produce effective geo-strategic blueprints for the 21st-Century. Geo-strategic planning has to be a dynamic improvisation by the many on the general direction that is announced by geo-strategic leaders only after genuine consultation with those who will have to improvise on it — i.e., their global constituents.

The threats to — and opportunities for — the progress of the world today are of such magnitude that people from all walks of life will have to participate in any meaningful planning. More participatory decision-making implies a need for more information. Information is thus transforming international relations and national politics. As information — stemming from education and innovative ideas — takes on this primary role in geo-political affairs, it becomes at once our savior and our benefactor.

Above all, we need to bring into being new or re-invented institutions capable of meeting the challenge of the future. The institutions that succeed will be those that effectively and geo-strategically manage information.

Reinventing the World

Information is reinventing the world through a process of "info-globalization." At center stage are people and their ideas. Within a generation, the world will be as different as today's is from a century ago. What is certain is that the future belongs to *we the people* — all armed with the power of new ideas in a world "globalized by information." If we recognize how today's world is being turned on its head by G-Forces, we will reap the satisfying rewards of having tapped into the greatest economic renaissance in human history.

As innovative change agents, our manifesto of change is:
- Every problem represents an opportunity via change;
- Every change is directed by human values — it involves a trade-off between individual and collective values, between self-interest and collective interest;
- The common denominator of change and wealth-creation is information; and
- To occur, any change must be:
  — technologically and economically feasible;
  — socially and politically acceptable;
  — in the interests of the planet itself; and
  — managed with geo-strategic action leadership.

In the final analysis, its not so much what will happen but what we do about it. If we take the necessary steps, global order is achievable out of today's apparent chaos. All we need to do is marshal our collective resources, manage our creative processes, diffuse the technology and the information, and get in league with the G-Forces of change. Above all, we must be headstrong yet humbly confident that, together, by 2050 we can re-invent the world.

Section "S"

G-Forces of
Social Motivation

Overview
Satisfying Psychological Drives

"People are the moving force of history."
- I.E. Petrov

Today, more than ever, an understanding of human behavior is the key to geo-strategic pursuits. The future is not something impersonal, imposed upon us from "somewhere out there" by mysterious forces. People create their own future. The power of "the masses" is the most powerful G-Force of change on the planet.

As we search for clues to identify technological, economic and political trends, we find that everything always comes back to people. For example, notwithstanding religious doctrines and government policy, it is people who decide how many children to have and thereby dictate the size of the average family. Technology is not thrust upon us; it is people who create scientific breakthroughs and technological applications. It is people who cause pollution — and decide to clean it up. No matter how strong the seduction of people-created advertising, it is people who decide how much they will spend and borrow and invest in the future to satisfy their economic needs and aspirations. It is people who create layers of bureaucracy — and learn how to break through them. It is people who elect politicians — and then decide to replace them with genuine leaders. It is people who act out of self-interest — and then learn that the counterpoint of self-interest is individual responsibility for the collective interest. It is people who change society and reinvent the world.

In short, human behavior creates social, technological, economic and political change. To understand the social future and its impact on technology, economics and politics — to understand the future of the world — we need to understand what makes people tick.

The major driving force of social change is the constant striving by every human being to move from misery and despair to happiness and contentment. Whereas it is easy to despair, even the most dejected can be shown rays of hope, and we all somehow keep striving to achieve a better tomorrow. Though the vast majority are still at the basic survival level, most of us — rich or poor — try to improve our daily lot — for ourselves, our families and our organizations.

Hierarchy of Needs

The renowned psychiatrist Abraham Maslow identified a basic hierarchy of human needs. However, the geo-strategic view reveals that these needs become aspirations, and that both have different levels of emphasis for each of us, depending on the stage of socio-economic development and social class in which we find ourselves. Some of the obvious human driving forces, expanding Maslow's hierarchy and extending it across the six waves of social development are shown in Fig. 3.

At the bottom of the hierarchy are the basic survival needs of food, water, and air. As our socio-economic level rises, we slowly climb across the axis of the matrix to a new set of needs and aspirations. As we progress, our values change, but while basic needs must still be met, some of them start to be taken for granted, being readily available in a reasonably developed society. Other aspirations, perhaps previously considered unattainable, assume larger importance and further condition our behavior to move in new directions. We gain confidence and, in turn, we are motivated to achieve progress more quickly. Social change accelerates.

The overall goal of human motivation is to move diagonally across the matrix, along the "axis of social change" from the bottom left to the top right corner. The bulk of the world's people (mostly poor and living in the Third World) are still struggling to escape the bottom left corner, concerned with basic survival. As their socio-economic circumstances undoubtedly will improve, they will want to be fed well rather than being limited to a bowl of rice. They too will demand sophisticated food served in a nice restaurant, with appropriate ambience and a sprig of parsley on the plate. While it may take an enormous leap of faith to believe such progress is possible by 2050 for the 4-billion underdeveloped people of today's 5-billion world population, yet we must not forget that the West has achieved similar progress in only a century.

Humans everywhere are driven by the aspiration to achieve a 5th-Wave leisure society and the 6th-Wave society of global freedom that lies beyond — at the top right-hand corner of the matrix. A leisure society is one in which nonphysical labor becomes the pre-eminent human activity and where leisure forms the predominant sector of the economy in terms of employment and economic output. Western countries are currently becoming 4th-Wave information societies and will fully achieve 5th-Wave leisure status by about 2050. Despite thousands of years of human misery, despite the billions who are still struggling today, the whole world now has the remarkable potential to achieve leisure society status.

Fig. 3 6-Wave Satisfaction of Needs and Aspirations

AXIS OF CHANGE	(Up to 1880) 1st-Wave Society (Agriculture)	(1880-1935) 2nd-Wave Society (Manufacturing)	(1935-1990) 3rd-Wave Society (Services)	(1990-2045) 4th-Wave Society (Info/Knowledge)	(2045-2100) 5th-Wave Society (Leisure)	(Beyond 2100) 6th-Wave Society (Outer Space)
LIFESTLYE	Tribal Serfdom	Work Ethic	Lifestyle Ethic		Leisure Ethic	Global Freedom
VALUES	Survival of Fittest	Selfishness/Competition		Cooperation	Trans-Culturalism	Global Family
SPIRITUALITY	Will of "God"	Basic Faith	Diverse Beliefs	Search for Meaning	Monism	Global Conciousness
WEALTH	Poverty Stricken	Materialistic/Aquisitive, Possessions & Status		Surplus Income	Superfluous Wealth	"Common-Wealth"
EDUCATION	Illiteracy	Basic Literacy	Literacy/ Education	Higher Education	Lifelong Learning & Pursuit of Knowledge	
HEALTH	Short Lifespan	Free of Basic Disease	Physical Fitness	Psychological Fitness	Complete Wellness & Extended Lifespan	
EMPLOYMENT	Slave Labor	Secure Job (60 hr/week)	Meaningful Work (40-hr/week)	Stimulating Work (30-hr/week)	Sufficient Work (20-hr/week)	Global Freelance
SEX DRIVE	Reproduction of Species	Large Family	Smaller Planned Family	Small/No Family Supra-Sex	Recreational Super-Sex	Cosmic Sexuality
SHELTER	1-Room Shack, 1-set Clothes	Small House, Basic Wardrobe	House/Apt., Full wardrobe	Big House/Condo, Stylish Clothes	Villa, Leisure Wear	Super Cities, Space Wear
FOOD/WATER	Bowl of Rice, Water, Air	Increased Nutrition	Well-Nourished Clean Air	Sophisticated Nutrition, Clean Environment		Global Cuisine

The drive to overcome basic needs and achieve a leisure society results from two fundamental human traits: we are at once physically lazy and intellectually energetic. We constantly use brains over brawn to overcome deprivation, improve efficiency, generate wealth and get rid of unpleasant, mundane, laborious tasks. All new wealth comes only from improved productivity. Western affluence stems mainly from the application of intellectual (not so much physical) energy to create technological innovations that are more productive and thereby make life physically and economically easier. This intellectual drive has led to every technological innovation from the creation of the wheel to the splitting of the atom and the probing of the very essence of biological life, and the exploration of the frontiers of the solar system. We constantly aspire to learn more, and today's explorative innovations across the entire spectrum of knowledge from the micro level (inner space) to the macro level (outer space) are reinventing our world.

As we progress, our values and attitudes change. We redefine work. When we are concerned about basic needs, any job will do. The better off we become, however, the better and more secure the job we need to maintain our improved economic standing. We also look for a certain amount of status from our job. Above a certain income level, basic needs are easily met and increased income tends to be surplus. This point is where Maslow identifies the need for personal achievement and fulfillment that meaningful and stimulating "work" (not necessarily a job) might bring. Most of us aspire to work fewer hours, in order to have more time for further education, the arts and leisure.

As the 4th-Wave of social development proceeds in the West, people are concerned not so much with the material world and their survival, which for most can be taken for granted. Instead, the emphasis is increasingly on higher values concerned with improvements in the quality of life. As the 5th-Wave leisure society unfolds, the leisure ethic is also increasingly evident. Work will again be redefined. Indeed, as a 20-hour work week will become sufficient to maintain an improving quality of life, the leisure ethic will start to replace the work ethic as a predominant value. This is not to deny that "work is good for people." What this phrase really means is that a disciplined organization of life's activities and an appreciation of where wealth comes from is an essential component of human development. In the future, these qualities will not need to come from back-breaking work. Future wealth will come from sensible self-management of our intellectual work habits, which will underpin the ability to create and enjoy leisure.

Beyond leisure, the primary aspiration of human motivation is freedom. But in today's global village we are living in close quarters as members of a single tribe and, as the "spaceship Earth" mindset brought by the 6th-Wave outer-space society becomes the emerging reality, we see that we are all passengers and crew. In such a situation, freedom cannot mean a self-interested individual license to simply do as we please. Rather, the only freedom open to us is global.

Global freedom is surely to be prized much more than individual freedom. It will represent freedom from the past: freedom from technological need, from work and economic want, from political nonparticipation, from nationalism, from weapons and war. Global freedom offers an escape from present predicaments and opens up abundant opportunities to grow and to be truly human. In contrast, widely professed individual freedoms (of speech, to bear arms, and so on), actually imprison people in hopeless personal cul–de–sacs of lost freedoms, where human growth is grotesquely deformed and limited. Apartments in New York, for example, have numerous locks and bolts to keep undesirables out. But these security devices also lock the resident in, imprisoned and shut away from human community. It is the same with nationalism. Global freedom will allow us to break the locks and chains to the individual and nationalistic cul–de–sacs of nonprogress.

The Global Imbalance

When we consider the extent to which the basic needs and wants of the bulk of the world's population are *not* being met, we see that the global social milieu is dangerously out of balance. Despite great strides in curing disease, in rapidly expanding school enrollment, in reducing birth rates and in modernizing agriculture, the Third World is mired in debt and economic depression and is essentially still trapped in the 1st and 2nd Waves of social development. This drastically slows our collective progress and could even halt it.

When viewed on a global scale, therefore, and in spite of the basic human values and concern for the well-being of others that we profess, any social system that remains so out of balance will sooner or later experience increasing degrees of discontinuity and socio-political crises that could lead to civil chaos and war. At the very least, we could expect these social dynamics to result in massive economic and geo-political shifts. Such revolutions can be peaceful or not. They can enhance human social development, delay it or retard it. In Iran, for example, the Shah tried to compensate for his lack of political reform by giving his people advanced American military and other technology. The people rebelled and installed in power an opportunistic fundamentalist who promptly plunged the nation into war and further retarded socio-economic and political development. In 1988, Iran began to change its course, and a more mature level of political leadership will ultimately set the country back on the way to socio-economic modernization. In the Philippines, President Marcos' similar lack of political reform eventually led to his removal by a wave of "people-power" that, in utter despair, was prepared to lay its life on the line in order to restore social progress. The Third World is similarly excluded from participation in global politics and governance. Nonparticipation, by people and nations, brings political change to redress imbalances.

Just as individuals progress across the hierarchy of needs and aspirations at different speeds and with shifting priorities, so do nations. Sometimes, progress can be set back or, at the very least, major adjustments are required. Individuals and nations can make errors in judgment, take wrong decisions and fall into traps, often under the hypnotic trance of media hype, advertising, propaganda and myths. But, as individuals and nations constantly show, we have an extraordinary resilience and an ability to eventually "see the light" and to get back on course. We may be brought back to our senses through the opportunity created by a technological breakthrough, through sheer economic necessity (say, the unaffordability of weapons) or political maturity and change.

Clearly, then, if a few countries (or elites) remain so much more affluent than others, there will be strife because those people who do not have what they need (the majority) will try to take it away from the minority who has. To avoid conflict, people in affluent and poor countries alike must re-evaluate and redirect their joint aspirations. In short, for us all to prosper, the developing countries must be provided with all the means necessary to help themselves so that the global economic pie continues to grow.

New Mindset Will Change Things

This ability to refocus our minds on our collective long-term needs and aspirations underlies progress. Unfortunately, if there is one thing about human nature that is universally true, it is that — at least until now — people tend to act from self-interest. Hence, it is said, if people are involved, change is difficult. But I believe it is possible to move beyond stalemate to a world where the collective interest will overwhelm self-interest and be seen not to impinge on self-interest but to enhance it. As mentioned earlier, the collective interest around such issues as nuclear arms has led individuals (even "enemies" like Reagan and Gorbachev) to come together to solve problems.

All kinds of international systems and arrangements are working the way they are supposed to — in our collective interest. They include World Health Organization campaigns to wipe out diseases, civil aviation flight control and security systems, allocation of air waves for radio, television and satellite transmissions, and collaboration on world weather forecasting. They work because there is a consensus on desired outcomes where sovereignty is pooled, and not only does no one lose but everyone wins. These and other examples of successful global co-operation are building a momentum for collective action to become easier.

We can therefore anticipate a 6th-Wave world society in which people will live together without quarreling. Indeed, I will show that we can easily produce all the food, shelter and clothing we need. We will be able to consume a more reasonable part of the resources of the world, and add less and less to its pollution. Such a world is possible, as major trends are now showing us.

For this to occur, the entire world must be revisioned and redesigned to encourage people to behave in ways that ensure a better future for the whole human family. Above all, we require a contextual shift in our way of thinking about the future and our individual roles in it, about how we can become self-sustaining and thereby create a win-win situation for all. In short, the existing global situation, seen in the light of the G-Forces of change, confirms that our individual self-interest now lies in optimizing the common interests of humanity.

This is an old message, and one to which much lip service has been paid. But it has clearly been much ignored, because of the fear of having to give something up — a fear that drives people into self-protection. The effects of the Information Age and the global village, on the other hand, will make it easier to convince the world that we are all part of both the problem and the solution — and, more important, that we have huge opportunities within our collective grasp. It is no longer effective to frighten people back into their basic individual survival mode. This futile technique unnecessarily traps people in old problems — which in reality can only be solved by creating future opportunities. The Club of Rome's report about "limits to growth", published in the early-1970s, and other more recent pessimistic studies such as "Global 2000", probably did scare some people into some worthwhile changes in behavior. Some people only change when their backs are against the wall.

However, it is difficult to build on negatives. A belief that nothing can be done to improve a situation dooms us to mental anxiety, stress, depression and outright fear. Fear alone produces irrational, often aggressive, defensive behavior, which is short-sighted. Conversely, too much hope alone produces good-hearted, well-intentioned advocacy but unrealistic aspirations and expectations of early results. Co-operation is best motivated by what the international affairs expert Harlan Cleveland calls "a cocktail of fear and hope" — may I add, shaken down over an ice-cool base of pragmatic, long-term realistic planning. I am neither optimist nor pessimist; I am a pragmatist. And I have found that human achievement is better stimulated by an understanding of the long-term outlook and of what it is possible to achieve. We humans fare much better when our environment is predictable; we then have a sense of being able to exert some control over important events in our lives — over our future. The biggest initial change required is a relatively small, mental one: to open our minds to the realization that we can create a happy future for all. With a realistically positive mindset, we can achieve almost anything we put our minds to. Practically, there are no limits.

As individuals, this long-term view is often difficult to reconcile with our short-term, mortal existence because, we say, "in the end, we are all dead." Such an individualistic mindset denies our own children. Though death is at the core of our private lives, our death is simply part of the continuum of our biological and social world. We live forever through our children. The species — and world society — literally regenerates itself with each new generation of people. Edmund Burke described this regeneration of humanity as not just a social contract but as a "partnership" of the generations (between those who are dead, those who are living and those still to be born) to achieve "perfection." Each new generation thus aspires to progress beyond the level attained by its predecessor by progressing further and faster across the hierarchy of human needs.

This is the only way to build a civilization. And now we are building a global civilization. While we know our individual lives will end, we also know we live as part of a single species that lives on. As Jonathan Schell advised, we can thus plan for a common future that is unharmed by individual death. To be human is to participate in human ventures that outlive us. Now, our personal responsibility as citizens in the common world is to be a partner in the perfection of human life and global social development. Global society overarches each of us and summons us to act in favor of something larger than all of us. We must become allies in reinventing the world — allies of life itself.

G-Force S-1

Stabilizing Global Population

> *"[Population growth] will be one of the strongest forces*
> *shaping the future of human society."*
> — *Brandt Commission on*
> *International Development Issues*

Our sex drive — the demographic G-Force of our basic desire to reproduce the species — has a phenomenal influence on world affairs. Global population passed the 5-billion mark in mid-1987 and is forecast to increase to 6.2-billion by the year 2000. By 2050, it will climb to 10-billion.

Most people presume that this increase is a major threat to our collective well-being. They believe that the world does not have sufficient resources to support even today's population, never mind the billions still to be born. I disagree. The carrying capacity of the Earth is at least 30-billion — six times present levels. The world does not lack resources; it lacks imagination about how to manage and allocate its resources. Meeting the needs of the growing world population will generate a vast amount of economic activity. This unprecedented increase in world population thus presents the greatest economic opportunity ever afforded to humanity. Such a large and rapidly increasing population is a major G-Force for change. Population pressures will create food shortages, mega-cities, health and education challenges, illegal migrations, refugee problems and other troubles that will change the world in ways that few have yet imagined. More than anything else, I believe that these pressures can — and must — have a positive effect by coalescing us into the single human family from which none is excluded.

Population Dynamics

Current population growth rates are unique in world history. At the end of the 18th-Century, there were only 1-billion of us. The second billion was added in little more than a century. But the third, fourth and fifth billions all arrived in the last 60-years. The sixth billion is expected to accumulate during the 1990s.

Five more billions will be added during the first half of the 21st-Century, before the population eventually stabilizes at 10-billion.

Most of the expected increase in population will take place in the same geographic areas that have already experienced the largest increases since 1950 — Asia, Africa and Latin America. Unfortunately, these regions are also economically poor. In 1950, about two-thirds of the world's population lived in developing countries. That proportion has now reached almost 80% — and about 90% of the future population growth will occur in these same countries.

This situation is often posed as an economic problem: "What is the maximum number of people the world can feed, clothe, house, etc., to the best Western standards?" But perhaps that isn't the appropriate question. The issue is how quickly the world's population grows, not its ultimate size. The total number of people that the world can adequately support depends not only on lifestyle and consumption patterns but also on the invention of technologies and the substitution of different resources as global society develops across the 4-STEP process of modernization. As economist Lester Thurow points out, if the world's population had "the productivity of the Swiss, the consumption habits of the Chinese, the egalitarian instincts of the Swedes and the social discipline of the Japanese, then the planet could support many times its population without deprivation for anyone." Economic analysis tells us not so much about the ultimate level of population that the world can sustain but about the speed at which the world can reach that limit. If a given country desires economic development, it must learn that its population growth cannot increase by more than about 2% a year — half the rate of population growth now experienced in many of the least-developed regions, especially Africa — and institute population control programs to achieve this rate.

The worldwide population growth rate is already declining rapidly. The pace of growth peaked around 1960, at about 2% per year. This was more than double the average rate of world population growth during the first half of the 20th-Century and four times the estimated average growth of the 19th-Century. Since 1960, a significant slackening in growth rates has been recorded by the United Nations. While the global population is still increasing rapidly, the U.N.'s projections of growth rates each year since 1980 have indicated a continuing and gradual reduction to about 1.5% annual growth by the end of the 1990s.

The overall pattern of world population growth rates over 16,000-years is depicted in Fig. 4. The recent growth rate is indeed dramatic: a single sharp "spike" in an otherwise stable trend. This "spike" is estimated to be quite narrow — about 100-years at the 1% mark — and illustrates the unprecedented and relatively short population transition we are now going through.

The late futurist Herman Kahn was fond of pointing out that we can legitimately refer to the "before-spike" and "after-spike" phases in population history and that the extraordinarily sustained high growth rates that characterize the

Fig. 4 Population "Spike" Growth Rate

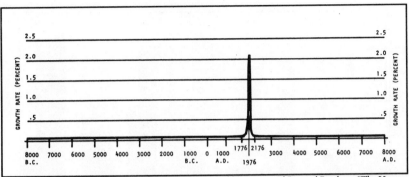

Source: Adapted by Herman Kahn from Ronald Freeman and Bernard Berelson, "The Human Population," in *Scientific American*, September 1974.

current period are unique; we will probably never see them again. Growth rates have already started to head down the rapid decline on the right-hand side of the spike. This is because many crucial growth processes are responsive to social — as distinct from physical — limits. Over the long run, natural forces tend towards an equilibrium, not the collapse that is conjured up by the fear of exponential growth. By 2050, the world population growth rate, according to this "spike" theory, is expected to drop to less than 0.5% a year, and world population will then stabilize at about 10-billion.

One of the major reasons this will occur is the declining birth rate. In 1973, the U.N. Fund for Population Activities, the world's acknowledged expert organization on matters of population, estimated that the annual average birth rate during the last half of the 1970s would be 1.95%. This estimate has since been successively lowered; to just more than 1.0% in 1986. Fig. 5 illustrates the declining birth rates around the world from 1950 to date, with a forecast through to 2025. UNFPA has concluded that the human race possesses an innate capacity for adjusting its growth and that the recent downward trend in birth rates marks the beginning of a new population epoch.

Reductions in family size are not restricted to small isolated population groups such as Western two-career families, but occur across entire national entities (say, China) and in diverse regional and cultural circumstances. The socio-economic determinants of reduced birth rates in all cultures include family planning, delayed marriage, the education of women, the increased participation of women in economic activity and greater access to advanced healthcare and nutrition. The latter leads to a decline in infant and child death rates and hence less need for large families. The economic shift away from 1st-Wave society, in which more children are required for farm labor, also results in less need for a sizable family. U.N. figures indicate a global decline of 22% in the average size of the family between the early-1970s and the early-1980s, from 4.5 to 3.6 children per family. The decline in the developing countries was 26%, from 5.5 to

Fig. 5 Declining Birth Rates (Selected Regions)

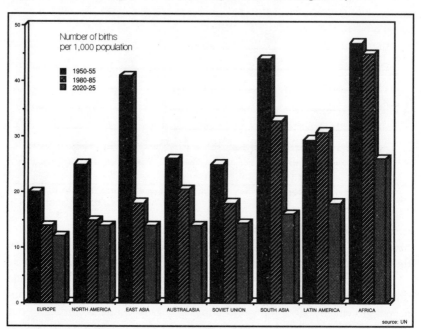

Number of births
per 1,000 population

■ 1950-55
▨ 1980-85
■ 2020-25

EUROPE   NORTH AMERICA   EAST ASIA   AUSTRALASIA   SOVIET UNION   SOUTH ASIA   LATIN AMERICA   AFRICA

source: UN

4.1 children. Though much of this global decline arises from a large reduction of birth rates in China (with a population over 1-billion), 26 other developing countries (with a combined population of another 1-billion) also experienced declines in excess of 20%.

The outlook for world population may be even more optimistic than these figures indicate. The U.N. forecasts indicate that if population growth continues under current assumptions, world population will reach 8.2-billion in 2025. However, if lower birth rates continue to occur, population in 2025 will be only 7.3-billion, because the annual rate of population growth will be reduced from 1.7% in 1980 to only 1.3% (instead of 1.5%) by the turn of the century. The U.N. concludes that to achieve this reduced rate of 1.3% should not be an overly difficult task. Should it be attained, the global population in 2025 will be 900 million lower than otherwise — as much as the present-day population of India. Indeed, at a 1988 conference that included the heads of the World Bank, UNICEF, WHO, U.S.-AID and a dozen health ministers from various countries, officials unanimously agreed that the number of births will peak sometime between 1996 and 2000, or by 2005 at the latest. Under this timetable, the global population will stop growing by 2050 (at well below 10-billion) and will stabilize instead at about 8-billion.

Accompanying the spectacular changes in its size, growth and distribution, the age structure of the world's population is being profoundly modified. The most significant implications of a given population's age structure are socio-economic: the level and composition of society's collective demands, the size and type of educational institutions, the number and form of employment opportunities, the type and scale of healthcare, and the degree of "economic dependency" (the number of workers versus nonworkers) are only a few examples. Generally, a higher rate of population growth is the result of a high level of fertility and a moderate-to-low level of infant mortality. These conditions initially generate a very young population. As the population ages, the proportion of children decreases, there is a small expansion in the proportion of the aged, and a considerable increase in the proportion of young and middle-aged adults.

Tremendous variations exist between developed and developing countries in the ratios of their age structures. In 1980, for instance, in most developed countries 25% of their populations were under 15, and only 10% were over 65. The remaining 65% were 16-64 years old. By the end of the century, the developed countries will experience increasing numbers of older people and a further reduction in the proportion of children. Life expectancy in developed countries increased from 49-years in 1900 to almost 75-years in 1987. It is continuing to rise. In the 21st-Century, the average life expectancy will go into the 80s, and for women may even reach 90. With our increased knowledge about the aging of human organs, we will be able to devise ways to prevent bodily functions from deteriorating. The very old population — people 85 and older — will be the fastest–growing segment of the population for the next 30-years in Western countries, rising from 9% in 1980 to about 20% in 2050, when 5% of all people living in the West will be 85 or older. In contrast, the developing countries will see a welcome 25% reduction in the proportion of dependent children and a large increase in the proportion of working adults.

The Social Security Issue

All countries have "aging" populations. The developing countries can anticipate a substantial rise in the number of people 60 and over by the middle of the next century. But in the short term the increase in the proportion of their aged will be moderate because of their essentially "young" populations. Most developed countries, however, have begun to voice serious concerns about the aging trend of their populations. They are examining the looming effects of aging on their social security and healthcare systems and trying to determine how to care for the elderly. Fig. 6 shows that the elderly segment of the population will almost double by 2050 in such countries as the U.S.A. and Canada.

The burden of outlays on pensions and medical care could lead to a 70% increase in social expenditure. Yet when viewed in relation to the growth in GNP, these increased expenditures appear modest. According to a 1986 study by the International Monetary Fund (IMF), the ratio of social spending to GNP will in fact decrease in Canada, France, the U.K. and the U.SA. In other words, the growth in government social spending implied by demographic factors alone is manageable; it is a matter of adjusting government budget allocations relative to economic growth.

27

Fig. 6 Aging Population (Selected Countries)

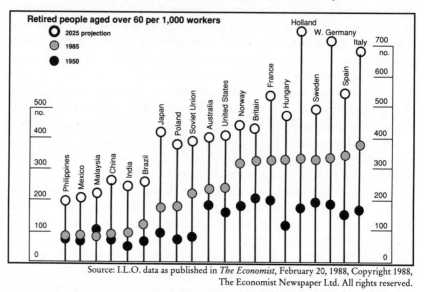

We must also remember that in many existing pension schemes, real benefits are limited to real earnings — both of which increase with productivity. As well, increases in real wages in the albeit labor-intensive health sector will not exceed the long-run increase in productivity at large, and hence the economy's ability to finance them. Consequently, the IMF finds, social expenditure in a country such as the U.S.A. (as a percentage of GNP) will remain essentially unchanged during the entire period of 1980 to 2025. In fact, the ratio of pension spending in some nations (e.g., Canada) will fall before it increases. Thus, while the potential demand for social spending in the West is still likely to grow, the incremental cost is effectively limited by tying increased benefits to productivity improvements. This would effectively shift the financing burden to the private sector (away from the assets of the elderly and the incomes of their families) and might also induce a higher savings rate by the present working generation. Indeed, there is every reason to believe that today's baby boomers will be the richest pensioners ever. The pension/healthcare problem is not anywhere near as serious as panic-mongers would have us believe.

Increasing Life Expectancy

The progress made in the betterment of health and the reduction of mortality rates in the Third World has been spectacular since World War II. Life expectancy in these regions increased from about 42-years in 1950 to over 60 today. In some countries such as China, longevity equals the West's. UNFPA estimates that these gains are at least as great as what was achieved during the entire century before 1950.

Nevertheless, the average gap in life expectancy between developed and most less-developed countries, although narrowing dramatically, is still wide at about 18-years. A large number of developing countries continue to suffer from widespread infectious and parasitic diseases and poor health and malnutrition, which result in high rates of infant mortality and lower life expectancy. These conditions trap people at the subsistence level of existence and adversely affect their productivity and, hence, their economic progress. Interestingly, an extended life expectancy is one of the keys to escaping this trap. Declines in birth rates often come about only after increases in life expectancy are seen to have occurred. Life expectancy in developing countries has now reached 61-years, and the U.N. projects that it will rise to 65-years during the 1990s. Birth rates will then drop further.

Life expectancy is also determined by child mortality rates. The child death rate for the world declined from an annual average of 19-per-1000 births during the 1950s to 10-per-1000 during the 1980s and is projected to fall to 9-per-1000 by the year 2000. In the Third World, high death rates frequently persist throughout early childhood. Infant mortality is very high in African countries, especially in tropical sub-Saharan regions: the most recent estimates exceed 200-per-1000 births. That is to say, more than one out of five babies die before their first birthday. Nevertheless, for the developing countries, the death rate declined from 24-per-1000 to 11-per-1000 in the 1980s and will decline to the present world level of 9-per-1000 by the turn of the century.

This reflects the dramatic progress made in the struggle to improve the lives and health of millions of the world's children. In 1986 and 1987, according to UNICEF, several nations have doubled if not trebled their levels of immunization. In 1985, world demand for vaccine was almost three times the 1983 level, and the annual number of child deaths prevented by vaccine is now estimated at 1-million per year. This is a result of the determined efforts of such organizations as WHO, UNICEF, and smaller volunteer groups such as the Foundation for International Development in Toronto. This people-driven, low-cost child survival revolution lengthens lifespan and thus is an important step in reducing world population growth rates. Of course, the development of children is closely related to the development of nations. Mortality is an important indicator of social welfare, since it best reflects the prevailing economic conditions.

As death rates decline and family affluence increases, we see a distinct trend towards smaller families. This has been the case in Western countries since the Agricultural Age. Other countries, such as China, have brought about one-child families — at least in urban areas— through regular family-planning programs. In 1970, China was faced with the prospect that even if each couple was to have just two children, the nation's population would have grown by another 400-million by 2000. Recognizing that this would further strain resources and slow down the increase in living standards, the country launched its one-child family-planning program. Thus, while two-child (and larger) families still are common in the rural areas and a baby boom is now occurring, China's average family size declines every year.

Like China, Third World countries such as India and Nigeria are waiting too long in tackling their population problems. Eventually, they will discover that they are forced to choose between a one-child family program and stagnant living standards. Though it will take years to achieve — given the unprecedented numbers of young people who will reach reproductive age in the next few decades — a couple of generations of one-to-two-child families will be the key to restoring a sustained improvement in their living standards. In sharp contrast to the aging populations in the Western world, small families of young growing populations in developing countries will provide an important impetus for major economic growth.

Population Redistribution

Population (and resultant socio-economic) pressures frequently lead to a considerable migration of people, both internally and between countries and regions. Within the developing countries, the general movement of population has been from rural to urban areas, to seek employment. International migration in recent times has flowed predominantly from poorer to richer countries (from British colonies in the Third World to Britain), from less developed to more developed neighboring regions (from Ireland to Britain), and especially towards those regions experiencing rapid economic growth (from Europe to North America).

The world is now divided into two severely imbalanced population blocs: the developed countries of the Northern Hemisphere, where the population is relatively small, where population growth is slow or nonexistent and where living standards are generally high and improving; and those countries where, by and large, population growth is rapid and living conditions are deteriorating or in imminent danger of doing so — that being in the poorest parts of the Third World (see Fig. 7). Such a demographically (and hence economically) divided world is simply not sustainable.

This global population imbalance combined with the changing age structures of populations will probably spur mass migrations from the Third World. The rise in the proportion of old people in the industrialized countries — and the resulting fall in their economically active population — will favor the need for expanded immigration from the Third World. Indeed, the potential economic decline of the industrialized world may already be signaled by the aging of its population. For example, without increased immigration, Canada's population will plunge from 26-million today to only 13-million by about 2030. The demographic pressure from the high birth rate countries, together with the manpower requirements of the industrialized countries like Canada, U.S.A., U.K., West Germany and so on, could lead to these countries becoming increasingly dependent on the developing countries for a labor force. Though there exists a grave

Fig. 7 Global Population Imbalance

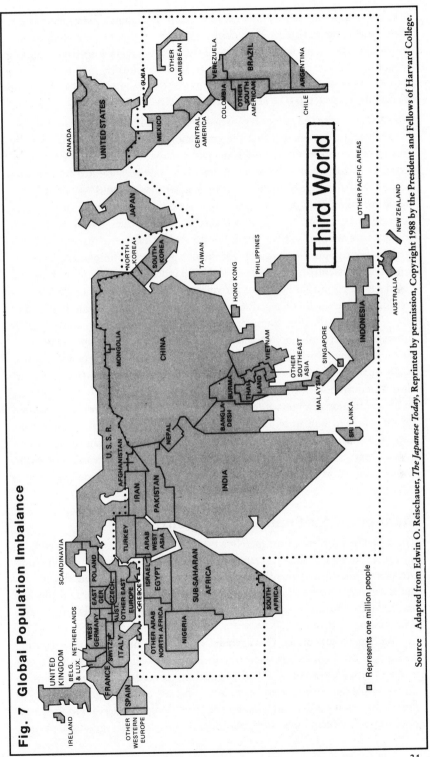

■ Represents one million people

Source   Adapted from Edwin O. Reischauer, *The Japanese Today*, Reprinted by permission, Copyright 1988 by the President and Fellows of Harvard College.

risk that racism and xenophobia could develop in the aging West, its member states must come to realize that a closed society with diminishing youthfulness will decline economically. Only open, zestful societies will prosper in the global economy.

Misleading Population Implosion

We must also raise the question of whether the world really is too crowded. As Marshall McLuhan pointed out, the population "explosion" is not what really creates our concern even though doomsayers present that as the problem. Rather it is that we all have to live in the close proximity created by our electronic ("global village") involvement in one another's lives. This we call electronic crowding. Rice-growing peasants in rural China do not notice the world population explosion. Technical "peasants" in front of their TV sets in Western countries are alarmed — their senses bombarded by a negative myth about what is in fact not a population explosion at all but a population "implosion."

There is essentially no shortage of physical space. In reality, all of the world could reside comfortably in one province of China, and the rice grower still wouldn't be crowded out. Startling as it may seem, any sizable state or province could house us all. For example, Texas has 262,134-square-miles (728,000-square-kilometers) of land, or about 1500-square-feet (136-square-meters) per person for each of 5-billion persons. A family of four could thus be allocated 6000-square-feet (545-square-meters) — enough to accommodate an upper-class American home (including its front and back yards), and all of us could be so housed in Texas. While we could not bear to live that way, there is also room for the whole of humanity to comfortably stand indoors in greater New York City — with more room for each human than at an average Manhattan cocktail party! Clearly, we must better manage our physical space, since there are many areas of the world that are crowded. But I repeat, the population explosion is not a problem.

Managing the Population Resource

The so-called problem is not merely a question of birth rates, or birth control, or smaller families, or life expectancy, or migration patterns. It involves the comprehensive question of managing population as a global resource, through an understanding of the following aspects: population dynamics; natural physical and technical resources; environment and the quality of life; and future socio-economic imperatives.

As Satish Seth of the Government of India's Futurology Commission points out, developments in science and technology will lend considerable support to the management of global population, its needs and its aspirations by lifting people out of the poverty zone and imparting to them a greater quality of life. We have not yet realized what modern technology can do to turn the global population "problem" into an opportunity. No amount of legislation, primary health services or family-planning education — though essential — will be sufficient. Rather, we need technical and economic progress to moderate population growth and create prosperity. The focus should be on providing education to transform the population into its own best resource, and providing meaningful work opportunities for people "as they are, where they are." This, says Seth, can solve many of the problems of both mass unemployment and mass migration, diminish the all-pervasive poverty and significantly enhance the quality of life.

UNFPA's World Population Plan of Action states that the principal aim of social, economic and cultural development, of which population goals and policies are integral parts, is to "improve levels of living and the quality of life of the people." We have learned that the combination of out-of-control population growth, slowly growing income and inadequate technology lead to over-exploitation of land and resources used for food and fuel. The result is a deteriorating human and natural environment. Conversely, managed population growth, increasing incomes and advanced technology are what will achieve our goals.

A major objective of national and international socio-economic development must be to increase per-capita income living conditions. Increased economic well-being fosters improvement in the demographic variables associated with the quality of life — longer life expectancy, lower mortality rates for all age groups, lower death rates through disease, and lower birth rates — variables that the United Nations forecasts will continue to improve well into the 21st-Century as the population level stabilizes. In other words, as far as the purely demographic G-Force is concerned, we are heading towards an improved quality of life for everyone.

Nearly half the nations of the world, including the industrial countries and China, have completed or nearly completed the demographic transition to a stabilizing population base; in these countries, the birth rate is close to or at the replacement level. As incomes begin to rise and birth rates begin to decline, the 4-STEP process of development will feed on itself, and other countries will quickly achieve the same demographic transition. These self-reinforcing trends will lead to global economic revitalization and growth, and by the middle of the 21st-Century, the world population "problem" will essentially have solved itself. We will all be living longer and healthier lives, with an extraordinarily increased quality of life worldwide and — rather than being viewed as a liability — people will have become their own greatest asset.

G-Force S-2

Feeding the Future — And Lots to Spare

"To plant is to prophesy."
— Robert G. Ingersoll

From the moment we are born we need to eat. Feeding the future is a critical G-Force; every day, Westerners are confronted with obesity at home while the television portrays skeletal famine victims abroad. The truth is that while politicians, scientists and concerned citizens have agonized for years over whether the world will be able to feed its growing population, and while photographs of famine victims reinforce this concern, agri-food technology is more than keeping pace with per-capita food and nutrition requirements. The world has more than enough food for its growing population, and crop yields and nutrition levels are increasing constantly.

The problem is that while some countries — the United States and Canada, for example — have exceeded food self-sufficiency, most of the world's population growth is taking place in the Third World, far from the traditional food supply areas of North America and Europe. Even though world food prices are low, hunger and famine are high in the poorer Third World countries due to their shortage of foreign currency to buy food and, more important, a lack of new investment in their own agriculture. Consequently, international food markets are economically depressed (production of food is greater than the amount of money available to buy it), and these soft markets are eroding the investment in research and development that is essential for achieving long-term gains in agricultural self-sufficiency worldwide.

Successful "Green Revolution"

We clearly have more than enough food in the world today. The Organization for Economic Cooperation and Development (OECD) — the Paris-based economic planning organization of the major industrialized Western countries — has concluded that "if the world population stabilized at about 12-billion in the

35

year 2075 the resource base will be adequate to sustain that population." And remember, a world population of 12-billion is 2-to-4-billion higher than current forecasts.

Another study, by the International Wheat Council, concluded that only a 3% annual increase in overall grain supply between 1985 and 2000 would satisfy most Third World needs. But this would be far lower than the growth rates already attained between 1975 and 1985, when the Third World's grain output increased by 40%. More than 80 Third World countries have ended hunger since 1900, half of them since 1960. This Green Revolution, as it is called, was achieved largely through the use of better-yielding seeds, mechanization and increased use of fertilizer and pesticides; the planted land area was increased by only 2%.

As a result, the annual global grain harvest is approaching 2-billion metric tons, and world grain stocks normally average nearly 300-million metric tons. The world's ability to feed itself, despite periodic droughts in the most important grain-growing regions, is proof that the food supply is secure. Farmers are more capable than ever of keeping up with the rising world population. India, for example, tripled its wheat harvest between 1965, the start of the Green Revolution, and 1983 and is now virtually self-sufficient in grains. The rise in output in China has been equally dramatic: in good years this nation of 1.1-billion people can now feed itself and export surplus grain. China and India, together accounting for 40% of the world's population, have thus shown that we now possess the agricultural, technological and financial resources to eradicate hunger forever.

As with other global issues, what is still missing in many countries is commitment. We also need a commitment to stop fighting each other, because civil wars can devastate food production —as in much of Africa, where the most severe food problem exists. In 1976, for example, the U.S. Central Intelligence Agency forecast that Angola could produce enough to feed 250-million of Africa's 600-million people. Today, though, after a decade of civil war, Angola has to import fully half the food it needs to feed its small population of 9 million. Experts at the United Nations Food and Agriculture Organization (UNFAO) say that not only should Africa be able feed itself but it could also become the granary for some land-starved Asian countries (such as Japan) by early in the 21st-Century.

Once our basic food needs have been met, of course, the drive for improved nutrition takes precedence. Yet, if the world's current economic order and food policy continue unchanged, UNFAO estimates that the number of undernourished people will surpass 600-million in the year 2000. Today's chronic state of malnutrition, affecting nearly one-tenth of humanity, is directly responsible for the deaths of 50-million people a year, including 17-million children. At least 10% of Third World children have some form of nutrition deficiency, and 80% of these (120-million children) do not have access to medical rehabilitation facilities.

Nutrition is a matter of improved diet. Diets — given regional and ethnic variations — fall into one of two categories: animal products supplemented by grains and vegetables; and grains and vegetables supplemented by animal products.

The Western animal-product diet is rich in protein but has long food chains (that is, food is available only when the animal has grown large enough to be eaten) that consume a lot of food energy — it wastes food. For example, the production of only 1-kg of beef, pork or poultry requires 4, 3, and 2-kg of animal feed concentrates respectively. Consequently, as of 1981, the annual per-capita consumption of grain in the developed countries was 583-kg (175-kg of grain plus 408-kg of animal feed grain), but 2.3-times more grain was eaten via the meat of grain-fed animals than was eaten as grain. This excessive consumption of animal foodstuffs makes little if any contribution to improved nutrition. Moreover, it may lead to heart disease, hardening of the arteries and obesity. Nutritionists in the West have long been arguing that this high consumption of animal foods must be reduced and replaced with vegetables and grains.

The second type of diet may not be ideal either. Many believe that the grain, vegetable and fruit diet of the Third World suffers from a lack of animal protein and nutrients. But this diet's short food chain makes it cheap and efficient to produce. Moreover, a proper combination of grains, vegetables and seeds — as in Mexico — can provide a good, healthy and protein-complete diet. Elements of both diets need to be balanced and adopted by both the under- and over-nourished segments of the population if global nutrition is to improve. This has been happening, albeit slowly. In the West, increased healthcare concerns are gradually leading to healthier diets, and we are moving away from wasteful meat production. Nutrition in the Third World is improving by a gradual switch to grain-fed beef to supplement the vegetarian diet.

More Research Funding Needed

Food shortages and malnutrition in the Third World are not caused just by a lack of agricultural production or protein-deficient diets. Inadequate distribution, storage and packaging results in as much as 50% of the food supply being spilled or spoiled. To solve such problems, the World Bank estimates that investment of $30-billion per year for 20-years is necessary in the developing countries. This is not a particularly large sum. Each year the world spends $1.2-trillion on armaments but only $15-billion on food production. James Grant, former executive director of UNICEF, is convinced that with a total of only 2% of what is spent on weapons — with only an additional $10-billion per year — hunger and malnutrition can be eliminated from the world. This paltry sum is equal to only a few days' worth of the world's expenditure on weapons and equals what the United States spends on alcoholic beverages in just one year. Until the money is found for much more agricultural research, periodic critical shortages are bound to occur. Until improved global food management systems (harvesting, storage, distribution, planting, and so on) are in place, emergency food aid will still be needed. But this need must eventually be overcome. Emergency aid perpetuates dependency and tends to turn people into beggars by diverting support away from longer-term self-help initiatives.

Instead, new technologies must continue to be developed so that people can farm without destroying the environment. We need to discover different kinds of fertilizer, pesticides, herbicides and new crop varieties — some of which might not even need fertilizer. Undoubtedly we will have to devote much less cropland to growing cereals for livestock in favor of more cropland for cereals for humans to eat. We are already seeing the use of new biological technologies (such as single cell proteins) to create both human and animal foods and the application of computers and satellites in agriculture. And we need to rethink the very basic methods of farming — from low-tech to high-tech.

Low-Tech Agro-Solutions

UNFAO forecasts that if the present destructive forms of farming practice continue in some parts of 64 countries — 29 of them in Africa — they will be unable to feed their populations by the turn of the century. The solution lies in adopting a form of agriculture that is both ecologically sound and affordable to farmers who work marginal lands, a method combining traditional farming methods with the modern know-how of biology and technology.

A major problem is that most Third World farmers grow a single crop on land cleared by burning. Millions of hectares of forest are destroyed annually in this way, as we are seeing in Brazil. Such cleared land produces decent crops for only three-to-five-years, however, and then will not provide a satisfactory yield for perhaps another 25-years. Farmers move on, clearing more forests, leaving desert-prone lands behind them.

In contrast, systems that use more than one crop — in sequence, in combination, or both — boost productivity and conserve resources because they increase the soil's organic matter (which is plowed back in). In Mexico, land planted with a traditional mixture of maize, beans and squash produces 70% more food than land planted with maize alone and continues to produce high yields year after year. In China, rubber and tea grown together produce much higher yields and reduce soil erosion by 70%. In the Nile Valley, farmers have adopted new multiple cropping practices to increase the yield of broad beans by up to 100% on large scale production plots.

Multiple cropping has other advantages. Because of different growing periods, something is always being harvested. This spreads labor demand throughout the year, ensures that a crop is always coming to market for sale and reduces the risk of seasonal weather damage to a single crop. Trees, instead of being chopped down, are planted among the crops to provide not only shade but, when leaves fall, nourishing compost. The trees also help to retain nutrients, which otherwise drain from the soil through leaching and soil erosion. As well, trees restore nutrients by drawing them up from the lower levels of the soil strata towards the roots of the crop plants. And mature trees provide edible seeds or beans, and fodder for animals.

This form of agroforestry is starting to restore semi-arid areas of Africa to productivity. In the Sudan, farmers are leaving trees in the fields and growing millet continuously for up to 20-years instead of only three-to-five. In Senegal, agroforestry is supporting up to 60-persons per hectare of land — several times the traditional average — with no loss of soil productivity. In Rwanda, agroforestry is replacing inappropriate, intensive Western agricultural techniques, which are more preoccupied with what can be extracted from the soil than with what should be restored to it. As a result, a typical farm family can produce 50% more fuelwood than it needs, and the new multicrop method provides 54% more calories, 31% more protein and 62% more carbohydrates than single-crop systems.

A major problem in the Third World is food storage. Refrigerators are a rarity there, so there is no choice but to leave large amounts of food to rot. In Zimbabwe, most families use local, nontoxic methods to preserve vegetables and grain and are developing improved granaries built of traditional materials. But this is not a solution for the 21st-Century. The availability of low-tech 20th-Century refrigerators, although consuming valuable energy, would more than offset the cost of wasted food.

High-Tech Farming

Despite these low-tech solutions, future agricultural success will also depend on the application of 4th-Wave high-tech solutions. Advanced forms of aseptic packaging (now used in the West for juices) and atmospheric/vacuum packaging (used for fresh vegetables) may someday enable us to do away with the refrigerator entirely. This would be a big bonus for the Third World, avoiding energy use and preserving foods that would otherwise rot.

With genetic engineering, we are starting to breed plants capable of thriving under adverse conditions or in salty soil. Salination threatens the fertility of 1.2-million-square-miles (3.3-million square kilometers) of soil around the world. Salt-resistant breeds of oats and other cereals are already being nurtured by scientists. Herbicide-resistant plants are also being developed. Herbicides destroy weeds, but very often also damage valuable crops.

Farmers in developing countries find it difficult to afford the fertilizers that would improve their crop yields, so scientists are developing breeds of plants that virtually produce their own fertilizer. Nitrogen is essential to plant growth and health, but ineffective unless it operates in conjunction with other elements. Many fertilizers are produced by combining nitrogen with hydrogen, but this energy-intensive process is costly. Certain bacteria perform the process naturally, and some plants (such as legumes) have a symbiotic relationship with these bacteria — the plants benefit from the fertilizers these bacteria produce. The range of plants that are capable of forming this union is expanding. Soon, plant species able to manufacture their own fertilizer will, in one stroke, reduce the costs of cultivation and increase crop yields.

Today, only a few products of genetic engineering are on the agricultural market, including vaccines to prevent diseases in calves and piglets. But this is just the beginning. Scientists are also exploring ways to improve plant protein and thereby solve malnutrition. The grain crops such as wheat, rice and corn that form the dietary staple of millions of impoverished people around the world lack certain essential amino acids and hence provide incomplete protein. The result for those who depend on these grains — often as their only food — is malnutrition. Geneticists are trying to incorporate genes into plants that will allow them to manufacture the missing amino acids. Should these efforts succeed, by the late-1990s such grains as wheat and rice will be as satisfactory a source of protein as meat.

We are also producing new strains of plants using isotope (radiation) technology. In China during the last 30-years, scientists have used isotope technology to develop 194 strains of vegetable and fruit crops, accounting for fully one-third of the world's new strains developed in this way. China's crop strains of rice, soya beans, wheat and corn have produced an annual increase of 4-million metric tons of grains and 0.3-million metric tons of edible oil. Isotope technology is also being used in the study of crop metabolism and fertilizer absorption, helping to improve plant cultivation and manuring techniques.

Within the next 20-years we will also see developments in tissue culture (the breeding of hybrid plants through grafting of one plant onto another), which will lead to the development of yet more hardy, robust plant strains. These strains will increase crop yields, grow in currently unplantable soils and significantly decrease the need for pesticides and fertilizers. "Cloned" vegetables, the result of isolating the genetic makeup of superior seedlings and mass-producing them through biotechnologies, will soon be on the market. A Japanese plant-culturing company has established mass-multiplication technology for ten types of vegetables, including celery, lettuce, asparagus and sweet potatoes. These cloned vegetables are germless, take less time to mature (two-years instead of three) and are more nutritious than common varieties. In 1988, tens of thousands of cloned seedlings were introduced to Japanese growers. In the United States, scientists working on a project for NASA are using plastic growth chambers and carefully selected varieties of lettuce, rice, soybeans, wheat and potatoes to produce crops much faster than ordinary. Started from tissue culture instead of seed, and grown in nutrient solution instead of soil, crops of lettuce are harvested in just 19-days, rather than 60-days in the farmer's field.

Detractors of such biotech breakthroughs claim that the processes have long been available but have failed, as yet, to fulfill their promise. Thus a number of developing countries are wary of what they perceive as "biohype" and are adopting a wait-and-see attitude. This is a serious mistake. Even though the full agricultural effect of biotechnology may well be some years away, the potential socio-economic benefits to developing countries are so wide-ranging, and have such a magnitude and significance, that neglect of biotechnological research today could dramatically narrow their food policy options tomorrow. While the Third World must continue to push ahead with its low-tech Green Revolution, it must also start its own research in high-tech agricultural techniques.

Even if none of these high-tech food solutions come to fruition, there is still a huge reservoir of untapped agricultural abundance. Of the nearly 500,000 types of vegetables grown in the world, only about 300 have yet been developed commercially, with wheat, rice and corn varieties accounting for the majority. In other words, 99.9% of the planet's potential supply of vegetables have not been exploited agriculturally. Even then, an estimated one-half of the world's good arable land is not yet being farmed. To be sure, most of this unused land does not have the necessary infrastructure (irrigation, roads, and so on) and opening it up will require major capital investment (and a solution of foreign debt problems). Nonetheless, the potential is there. A recent study by the University of Waginingen in the Netherlands, based on new UNFAO/UNESCO world soil maps, concluded that the Earth could produce 32-billion metric tons of grain each year — almost 20-times current levels. Much of this would be grown in nontraditional growing areas in the Third World. Productivity also can be further improved. In most of the Third World, productivity is at a level of only one-third of demonstrated potential. If agri-food technology and resources around the world were employed at a level comparable with that of a typical North American corn farm, probably enough food could be produced to sustain a world population of up to 48-billion.

"Blue Revolution" Needed

In discussing food and nutrition potentials, we tend to focus on land-based crops and animals and overlook water-based sources. The development of giant ocean farms, which could supply as much as 10% of the world's agricultural production — feed for cattle, fish for people, plus kelp (seaweed) for energy — is considered inevitable within the next fifty years.

Various estimates have been made of traditional ocean fish resources. The oceans are not being overfished. Rather, most fishing takes place fairly close to land — where relatively few fish live — and it is these resources that are getting scarce. The most generally accepted estimate (UNFAO and others) of the total conventional fish availability is about 100-million metric tons per year. Given that the ocean fish catch in 1982 was only half a million metric tons, it is highly unlikely that the fish supply will ever be threatened. The potential ocean yield of unconventional sources (that is, fish that are not yet a major part of conventional diets, such as krill and squid) is also substantial.

We make poor use of our land-based freshwater resource as well. The solution may be a "Blue Revolution", recently proposed by the Guizhou Futures Research Society in China. The Blue Revolution would focus on aquatic production and water conservancy reforms to fully utilize rivers, lakes, reservoirs and rice fields to develop fish production. China already easily leads the world in efficient freshwater use and aquatic production. In addition, intensive aquatic farms (saltwater and freshwater) developed in Scandinavia and Scotland are already making a substantial contribution to the world's food supply.

Space Age Agriculture

The 6th-Wave outer-space economy will also play an increasing role in the modernization of 1st-Wave agriculture. When combined with meteorological data, remote sensing satellite data can be used to predict crop production and health. The United States already uses satellites to predict annual corn, soya bean and wheat yields (of both itself and other countries) with over 90% accuracy. By participating in the meteorological satellite programs, some Third World countries can now plan and manage their agriculture more efficiently. This participation is essential to their food future. After all, at present, 80% of Chinese and Africans, 70% of Indians, and 60% of South Americans still depend on agriculture for their livelihood and survival. Half of India's national income flows from the agricultural sector, which must endure the vagaries of the monsoon rains.

Satellites forecast weather, water tables and pests. Agriculturalists in India estimate that more precise rainfall predictions would save $3-billion a year in crop damage and agricultural planning costs. Similarly, the increasing size of desert in the Sahel of Africa probably could have been controlled by examining the data available through remote sensing and then planning irrigation and planting programs accordingly. With the proliferation of satellites and the creation of the Global Environmental Monitoring System by the U.N. Environment Program, such applications will not be overlooked from now on. Satellite data has already been useful in recent years in managing forests in Thailand, in agricultural development in the Upper Volta and in crop surveys in Brazil. In Africa, satellite-derived maps monitor "greenness" levels (the rate at which vegetation responds to rainfall) to track the hatching and development of grasshoppers and locusts, which lay their eggs in the greenness areas. Farmers then spray the identified areas with pesticides.

Computer-based systems are also being used to help detect locust-breeding areas in Africa. Personal computers can provide earlier warning than the satellite greenness maps alone. The computer identifies rain-producing clouds and transmits its readings to the satellite, which relays the information, with the greenness maps, to mobile, solar-powered weather stations. Three of these stations can cover most of North Africa and they cost only $20,000 each, an investment that could eliminate pesky grasshoppers and locusts from the continent forever.

Computer technology is also helping to make barren areas fertile. For example, in the deserts of Israel's Negev and the Arabian Gulf area, it is now possible to farm in sandy and rocky soil. Under huge plastic covers that prevent evaporation, crops are irrigated drop by drop by a computer-controlled network of specially designed pipes that ensures maximum-efficiency water use. With an investment of only 5-cents per farmer in various types of computer applications, the long-term benefit in Third World countries would be in the order of 40-cents in food production — not counting better health.

Lastly, computer technology is making the choice and preparation of crops more practical and helps gauge the interplay of market supply and demand in a more rational way.

Crops and the Greenhouse Effect

It would be remiss of me not to discuss how a huge buildup of carbon dioxide in the atmosphere, causing what is called the greenhouse effect, impacts on crop growth and yield. (Later on I discuss the overall greenhouse effect and argue that it will not have the detrimental result that worry-mongers will have us believe.)

Be that as it may, if the global temperature does rise — even for a few years or decades — the increase would be far greater in the higher latitudes. Temperatures near the equator are projected to change very little, if at all. While it is true that much of the world's food is currently produced at higher latitudes, this will not necessarily be the case in the future, as we have seen. An increasing proportion of the world's food will be produced in the Third World, centering on the equator.

Even while North America and the Soviet Union would lose soil moisture and yields could be reduced, perhaps even eliminating some crops (and farmers) in many areas, the wheat-growing season in Canada and the Soviet Union would lengthen and the more northern areas of these countries would be able to grow wheat for the first time. U.S. Agriculture Department experts have forecast that, if the wheat belt shifted northwards, yields could increase by as much as 35% and more crop areas would be opened up. In addition, these experts believe that the three major global foods — wheat, rice and corn — would all benefit, because a carbon dioxide-enriched environment would improve crop productivity. For example, if levels of carbon dioxide doubled, the yields of such grains as wheat and rice would increase by 36%, while corn production might rise by 16%.

Therefore, the greenhouse effect would not necessarily impair, but could even enhance, our ability to feed ourselves — with plenty to spare.

G-Force S-3

Piping Clean Water for All

"Dig a well before you are thirsty."
— Chinese proverb

There is no shortage of clean water. Enough rain and snow falls over the continents every single year to fill Lake Huron 30 times, to magnify the flow of the Amazon River sixteenfold, or to cover the Earth's total land area to a depth of 83-centimetres (32-inches). Yet millions die thirsty, and the lack of water to grow crops periodically threatens millions more with famine. We can survive without food for as long as a month, but each of us needs 2-litres (half a gallon) of water every day or we will dehydrate and die. Water tables in southern India, northern China, the Valley of Mexico and the U.S. Southwest are falling precipitously, causing wells to go dry. Fresh water for drinking and irrigation, and for use in industry and for air cooling and so on, has long been taken for granted. In many areas of the world, however, lack of water (or its poor management) is becoming a constraint on economic growth and food production. Water is an essential ingredient in virtually every human endeavor. Its availability is a vital G-Force for our future well-being. As our family continues to grow and our social aspirations extend across the 6-wave hierarchy of needs, attaining a secure water supply is essential if we are to reinvent the world.

Global Water Cycle

Fresh water everywhere is linked to a vast global cycle. Its viability and adequacy as a resource are determined by the amount available locally and by the way it is used and managed — or mismanaged.

Each year, the sun's evaporative energy lifts some half-million cubic kilometres (264-billion gallons) of water from the Earth's surface. An equal amount falls back to Earth as rain, sleet and snow. Moreover, because considerably more falls onto the land than is evaporated from it, about 40,000 cubic kilometers (21-million gallons) of water are annually transferred from the oceans to the conti-

45

nents. By virtue of this cyclical flow, fresh water is a constantly renewed resource and we have just as much water in the world today as when civilization dawned. Fresh water is abundant: for every human there is a renewable supply of 8000 cubic metres (40,000 gallons) per year, several times the amount needed to sustain a reasonable standard of living.

However, water is not always available when and where it is most needed. Asia, for instance, has proportionately less water than it has people. As well, much of the global run off flows away rapidly in floods, often bringing more destruction than benefit. Even though the growing world population will diminish the supply available to each person, especially in some drier or over-populated regions, there will still be a sufficient and reliable source of water for drinking and irrigating crops year–round — at least in the short term. While we now waste enormous amounts, fortunately for the long-term we are learning to use water in much more effective ways — in agriculture, in industry and in our homes.

Agricultural irrigation claims a 70% share of the world's water. Since irrigation was first developed in the Middle East, the world's irrigated area has been increased by almost 200-million hectares (500-million acres). The conditions conducive to irrigation are concentrated in Asia, where population is high relative to available water but where many of the world's great rivers flow — the Indus, the Ganges, the Brahmaputra, the Chang-Jiang (Yangtze) and the Huang-He (Yellow). These rivers originate at high elevations and travel long distances, providing numerous opportunities for irrigation before they reach the sea. Thus one reason that Asia can support half the world's population is that it has two-thirds of the world's irrigated area. Unfortunately, in other parts of the Third World, silting is reducing the storage capacity of surface reservoirs, making it difficult to extend irrigation to new areas. And the engineers who design irrigation systems frequently pay little or no attention to the deforestation of watershed areas. As trees are cut down, the soil erodes and silt fills the reservoirs. In addition, growing Third World cities are diverting water away from farmers.

Another problem is that farmers the world over still irrigate the way their predecessors did 5000-years ago — by flooding or channeling water through and across the fields. Because very few fields are perfectly flat, this technique fails to evenly distribute water, and creates heavy runoff, which wastes water and harms crops. About half the water used in U.S. agriculture is wasted, and in almost every Western country it would be cheaper to save water by upgrading irrigation methods than by building more dams, reservoirs or canals. Modern technology can solve this problem. At the University of Oregon, experimental laser systems are being developed to ensure that a field is absolutely flat at planting time. Laser scanners in satellites can also identify, with the precision of a few hectares, where crops are too dry and where they are being overwatered. This system can literally save billions of gallons of water every year in the flat, prairie, wheat belt areas of the world.

Computers can help save water in other ways. Israel has pioneered the development of automated irrigation, where the timing and amount of water applied are controlled by computer. The computer sets the drop-by-drop flow of water — often salt water — to individual seedlings and plants, detects leaks, adjusts water application for wind speed and slow moisture absorption and optimizes fertilizer usage. The average volume of water applied per hectare, using this system, declined by nearly 20% between 1967 and 1981, allowing Israel's irrigated area to expand by 40% while the use of water for irrigation rose by only 13%. The systems thus pay for themselves in about four years through water and energy savings and higher crop yields.

Industry is another big waster of water. In Sweden, industrial water use increased five times between 1930 and the mid-1960s. Since then, strict environmental protection requirements of the pulp and paper industry, which accounts for about 80% of Sweden's industrial water usage, have fostered widespread adoption of recycling technologies. Despite more than doubling production between the early-1960s and the late-1970s, the industry cut its total water usage by half, a fourfold increase in water efficiency. Largely because of these savings, Sweden's total water withdrawals in the mid-1970s were only half the level that had been projected a decade earlier. Recycling systems in other developed countries are similarly helping to curb manufacturing water use. Between 1954 and 1983, for example, U.S. manufacturers doubled their efficiency of water usage; in some states, daily water use in industry declined, despite an increase in the number of factories, from 213-billion gallons (almost 1-trillion litres) per day in 1970 to 129-billion gallons (580-billion litres) per day in 1985. Building water-efficiency and pollution controls into new plants is vastly less capital-intensive than renovating old ones. As Western industries become less and less water-intensive, more and more water is saved. Developing countries, of course, are in a prime position to take advantage of these new recycling technologies as they industrialize.

Even though Western families are notorious for wasting water, household and other municipal water demands rarely account for more than 15% of a Western country's water budget, and worldwide they claim only 7% of total water withdrawals. Yet storing, treating and distributing this water, as well as collecting and treating the resulting waste water, is increasingly expensive, so ways must be found to use less. Many Western household fixtures and appliances — which the whole world naively strives to copy — use much more water than necessary. The average U.S. citizen uses 155-gallons (700-litres) of water every day. Most toilets in the United States use as much as 5-gallons (22-litres) per flush; water-conserving varieties average only 13-litres (see Table 1). A typical West German toilet requires only 9-litres per flush, and a new model that meets government standards uses about 7-litres — less than one-third the American norm. In Japan, new toilets can be flushed either full or half, simply by turning the lever in the opposite direction. These toilets also incorporate a

Table 1   Potential Household Water Savings
(With Available Water-Efficient Household Fixtures)

Fixture	Water Use	% Savings Over Conventional Fixtures
Toilets	(litres/use)	
Conventional	22	—
Common low-flush	13	32
Washdown	4	79
Air-assisted	2	89
Clothes Washers	(litres/use)	
Conventional	140	—
Wash recycle	100	29
Front-loading	80	43
Showerheads	(litres/min.)	
Conventional	19	—
Common low-flow	11	42
Flow-limiting	7	63
Air-assisted	2	89
Faucets	(litres/min.)	
Conventional	12	—
Common low-flow	10	17
Flow-limiting	6	50

Sources: *Residential Water Conservation Projects* (U.S. Department of Housing and Urban Development); *Journal of the American Water Works Association*.

small hand basin, the waste water from which drains into the toilet cistern ready for the next flush. Water-efficient dishwashers and clothes washers can also reduce water use by as much as 30% over conventional models. With simple conservation measures such as these, household water usage in the West can easily be reduced by a third.

Third World Water Problems

Although the Third World has lots of water, it is not readily available. Many women in developing countries have to trudge up to 10-kilometres (6-miles) every single day to reach the essential water supply for drinking and cooking. In many places, not enough is available for washing. One-quarter of the world's people lack clean drinking water and sanitary human waste disposal.

After sufficient food, a clean water supply and adequate sanitation system are the most important factors in ensuring good health in a community. This is why village water supply systems have been favorite Third World development projects of many government and international agencies for several decades. These measures have been considerably more important than curative medicine in contributing to improved health, increased life expectancy and lower infant mortality — just as they have been in the West.

The World Health Organization (WHO) estimates that a sanitary water supply would eliminate 50% of diarrhea-related diseases (for example, 90% of all cholera, 8% of sleeping sickness and 1% of guineaworm infestation) because much water is often obtained from unclean rivers and swampy areas, from which people can contract these and other illnesses. And because water is often too valuable for washing, an important defense against such infections is lost. According to WHO statistics for 1983, 26% of urban and 61% of the rural Third World population lacks regular access to safe drinking water. By 1990, an estimated 1.2-billion people will be in that situation. For them, piped water is still a dream, and water wells are scarce. Even where available, most wells are open to contamination. Frequently, animals are watered from the same wells that humans drink from. The water bucket itself is also a major source of contamination. Held in dirty hands or placed on filthy ground, it can quickly spoil all the water in a well.

Water supplies need not be such an all-or-nothing phenomenon. The solution lies in matching people's needs and cultural patterns with their given water supply potential and a much broader range of technical choices than is usually offered by foreign governments and development agencies. Local solutions are often required and are frequently better. For example, foreign-made hand-pumps often fail to work properly and village water systems sometimes break down faster than they are built. The ease with which water pumps can be locally manufactured is therefore an important consideration. While many types of water pumps can be made, countries are learning that standardization of pump types eases the distribution of spare parts, improves manufacturing quality control and eases the training of installers and village repairers. Thousands of low-cost, locally made hand-pumps using plastic pipe are now irrigating small plots in Bangladesh. The farmer can do simple repairs, and the cheaper pumps pay for themselves in one crop. A surprising number of such innovative and unique pumps have been made in large numbers. In China, in Hebei Province alone, about 3-million human- and animal-operated pumps are being used.

Another kind, the hydraulic ram pump is powered by the flow of stream water. It pumps only a small percentage of the stream water that flows through it, but lifts that water to a level much higher than the source — such as to a house on a small hill above a creek. Its many advantages over pumps powered by hand, animal, wind or motor are: since it does not need an additional power source, there are no operating costs; it has only two moving parts, both simple and cheap to maintain; it works efficiently over a wide range of water flows; and it can be made with simple workshop equipment.

The purification of water is another major Third World problem. Villagers often reject chlorinated water because the chlorine is not always available, calculating the amount needed to purify each well is tedious and the taste of chlorinated water is not always to their liking. Fortunately, simple, low-cost purification is now possible through the Slow Sand Filtration method, which percolates water through a sand bed system. Applications in such countries as India, Colombia, Kenya, Thailand and Jamaica show that this technique can remove up to 99.9% of pathogenic bacteria and reduce water murkiness by about 70%, thus requiring only a minimal amount of chlorination for final disinfection.

Slow sand filters have been in use in Western public water supplies for almost 150-years. Even though some European cities still use them on a large scale, they tend to be dismissed as old-fashioned or out of date. However, many people are once again realizing that slow sand filtration is very effective and deserves more widespread use, particularly in rural and urban fringe areas of developing countries. Filter sand of good specifications is readily available in most countries, and optimal use can be made of locally available bricks, mud-blocks and mass concrete. Operation and maintenance are relatively easy for semi-skilled operators. Operational costs are minimal, and no chemicals are required.

Solar distillation is another elementary purification process. Salt water or even polluted water can be placed in a container under a transparent plastic cover, which traps solar energy to heat the water. The water condenses on the underside of the cover, and the impurities are left behind. This condensed water can be piped to households for drinking and cooking. Units producing anywhere from 4-to-4000 litres (1-to-1000 gallons) per day can operate unattended for long periods in isolated locations. No auxiliary power source is needed, other than some means for feeding the water into the unit.

Purification would obviously be aided by better means of sanitary waste disposal. But just as the flush toilet has not solved the sanitation problem in the rich part of the world, neither can it solve the problem in the poor countries where waterless waste treatment systems such as compost privies and pit latrines are often much more effective. A compost toilet can be a sanitary and efficient waste treatment system. The main question, as usual, is whether users are prepared to take the time to manage the system efficiently. Once the correct liquid and carbon/nitrogen balances are maintained, however, the toilet will function properly with an impressive long-term economic benefit. In Zimbabwe, for example, 20,000 ventilated pit latrines have been built for less than $10 per person, and it takes a family of six as long as 35-years to fill a pit. Such systems clearly would go far to solve the current problem for the 1.8-billion people who lack any form of sanitation.

Between the pit privy and the waterborne sewage system is a range of effective sanitation systems that do not demand heavy use of water. Human wastes are high in nitrogen and other nutrients and can be a valuable source of fertilizer. Chinese farmers use simple composting methods to convert human waste into safe fertilizers, and in a number of countries, aquaculture (fish cultivation) ponds also use human waste as a valuable nutrient supply. The economic benefits of such systems far outweigh the recycling costs, and there is little serious risk of pathogens returning to human food or drinking water.

Water Management

It is clear that the so-called water shortage problem can only be met through more efficient water storage, management of water usage and sewage disposal. By understanding the links between these elements, we can truly secure a sustainable and plentiful water supply. The U.N. Water Conference (1977) and the resultant International Drinking Water and Sanitation Decade (1981-90) have already created the impetus needed to formulate and implement long-range water planning. Many initiatives have since been taken in countries as diverse as Argentina, Egypt, Mexico, Romania and Nigeria. Numerous water laws have been passed in both developed and developing countries; at least one-third of nations have revised their administrative and statutory arrangements for regulating water resources, water pollution and waste water treatment. Research and education capabilities have also been enlarged through the creation of such institutions as the Water Research Centre in the U.K. and the Institute of Water Economics, Legislation and Administration in Latin America. As a result of these activities, since 1980 an additional 540-million people will have gained access to clean water and another 360-million will have sanitation by 1990.

But this progress has not kept pace with population growth. As population grows and natural water supplies threaten to become inadequate to meet some countries' demands, water planners and engineers must respond by building dams to capture the runoff that would otherwise flow — unused — through the water cycle and into the oceans. They must also consider diverting rivers to redistribute water to areas of greater need.

Dam construction in the Third World is now in its heyday and two-thirds of the world's biggest dams (more than 150-metres high) slated for completion are located there. Designed also to generate hydro-electric power, such large dams and reservoirs promise clean water, greater energy independence, and irrigation to help attain food self-sufficiency. For example, China has completed the feasibility study for the world's largest hydro-electric dam, on the Chang-Jiang (Yangtze) River. As well, China plans a major diversion of water from the Chang-Jiang through the old Grand Canal system to expand or improve irrigation on 4-million hectares (1.6-million acres) and to meet municipal and industrial water demands in drier northern regions.

These projects, of course, require money. Sadly, the World Bank has allocated less than 5% of its funds to water projects since 1980, compared with 6% allocated in the 1970s. Unlike other international agencies, UNICEF has not increased its budget for water projects for several years and the U.N. Development Program, which co-ordinates the work of other U.N. agencies, still allocates only 3% of its budget to water and sanitation. Much more is required if proper water reserves are to be made available in the 1990s and beyond.

Such mega-projects are unlikely solutions for the water needs of the West, where daily water use is declining. At any rate, many industrial countries are finding that the list of possible dam sites is growing shorter and that the cost of such facilities is rising rapidly. It simply does not make sense to spend $1-billion to build another dam when for only $25-million you can do some redesigning that will provide a lot more production. In the United States, for example, scores of alternative ideas are being considered. These include plans for relining old aqueducts to reduce seepage, rewiring hydro-electric generators instead of building new ones, using computers to better manage water flows and improve power production, and applying engineering skills to complex environmental problems.

Before the West is able to balance water supply and demand, however, there will be severe water shortages in many countries and regions. In the United States, the shift of people and industry (albeit high-tech) to the sunbelt, plus the wasteful use of tap water for irrigation, is causing reduced water-table levels throughout the Southwest.

But the crisis will be temporary. By the middle of the next century, there is no reason why we should all not be able to drink safely from any tap, stream or river, anywhere on the globe. This is essential if we are to reinvent the world.

G-Force S-4

Creating Global Wellness

"Health is the first of all liberties."
— Henry F. Amiel

Medical marvels abound, continuing the overwhelming historical trend in healthcare to achieve cures and treatment for disease. There is no reason to assume that this successful track record will suddenly stop. As each disease is cured or controlled, scientists will continue to devote their attention to the next most dangerous on the list as they tirelessly seek to satisfy our G-Force aspiration for total wellness. Progress made in the betterment of health and the reduction of mortality rates in developing countries has been outstanding, particularly since World War II. The 21st-Century promises to be one of astonishing achievement, not just in healthcare but in every scientific endeavor, because 90% of all scientists who have ever lived are alive today, and in the next 30-years, the pools of both working scientists and scientific knowledge are expected to double again, just as they have during the past 30-years. And the result: people will live longer, healthier and more leisured lives — invigorated as they continue to re-invent the world.

Healthier Children

If we are to re-invent the world, it must be for our children's benefit. And the health of our children both results from and contributes to socio-economic development worldwide. Improvements in child health over the last 20-years stand as an impressive achievement, even in the poorest countries of Africa. The Third World has cut infant deaths from 24% of live births in 1960 to only 11% in 1986. China has reduced its infant mortality to a rate close to that of some American cities — despite family income levels that are among the lowest in the world — to achieve the World Health Organization (WHO) goal of 5%. But 17-million children still die worldwide each year from poor nutrition, diarrhea, malaria, pneumonia, measles, whooping cough and tetanus. Virtually all these deaths occur in the Third World. Half to two-thirds could be prevented with the implementation of simple measures like access to clean water and basic health education.

Malnutrition caused by poor child feeding practices claims more than ten times as many lives as actual famine or poor healthcare. A major step in the fight against malnutrition is female education, in primary schools and through maternal education. Across the Third World, female education is essential for effective hygiene, immunization, breast feeding and family planning — in short, child health. Countries where female literacy rates are high achieve lower birth and child mortality rates. In 1960, 26% of the world's girls did not attend primary school; this figure has now been reduced to 14%. WHO and UNICEF have also launched major campaigns to combat the decline of breast feeding. Parents are being taught that baby milk powder can be used only when there is an available supply of clean water with which to mix it. As well, educational campaigns are underway to improve weaning practices in many underdeveloped parts of the world.

High-Tech Medicine

Telecommunications and computerized diagnoses have already prevented health disasters around the world. While some "people problems" and environmental constraints still need to be overcome, "tele-medicine" of the future will assist in providing emergency and routine healthcare to even the remotest areas or centers with inadequate healthcare facilities or medical personnel. Pictures of X-rays, EKGS, skin lesions, pages of text and charts can all be stored on computer tape and sent to major medical centers in about 60-seconds, at the same cost as a long-distance telephone call. With the addition of satellite and microwave links, tele-medicine has considerably improved 24-hour emergency service to rural areas in several parts of the world. As well, new computer-based diagnostic tools will provide doctors with unsurpassed cross-section images of body tissues, thus eliminating much exploratory surgery.

In 1986, more than 2-million North Americans received medical laser treatments. Laser therapy will have increased fourfold by 1990, according to Health and Welfare Canada, and laser care will have a significant effect on almost every surgical specialty and healthcare center in Western countries within the next decade. Lasers were first used in the 1960s in opthalmology, and during the 1980s the laser has been used to successfully treat the eye disease glaucoma without the need for an incision. Lasers are now commonly used in gynecology, and there is a 97% cure rate in treating precancerous lesions of the cervix, vagina and vulva. Because laser therapy eliminates the need for conventional surgery, it is less physically traumatic for the patient and reduces hospitalization costs since it usually requires a shorter hospital stay, less anesthesia and less use of expensive procedures and equipment.

Improved healthcare also requires a constant stream of new vaccines. Today, China and Southeast Asia are the first to begin widespread testing of a new vaccine against the deadly Hepatitis B virus , carried by more than 200-million people worldwide. Hepatitis can lead to chronic liver disease, now the most widespread form of cancer in Asia, where 70% of the world's carriers live, and in sub-Saharan Africa. If all children could be vaccinated at birth, hepatitis would be eradicated, like smallpox before it, within two generations. The new vaccine, derived from ordinary baker's yeast, will soon be produced for as little as 10-cents per shot. It will also be produced in developing countries, not only to keep the cost low and create local employment but to make it readily available to those who need it most.

Biotechnology is advancing so rapidly that breakthroughs of tremendous potential to healthcare occur almost weekly. This field of science can provide new and improved treatments for major killers in the West as well as better and cheaper antibiotics and vaccines to protect against diseases in developing countries. Examples include the control of sickle cell anemia, a hereditary and frequently fatal disease; the pending production of a vaccine against malaria, which kills more than 1-million children each year in Africa alone; the application to multiple sclerosis, a crippling nerve disease, of an experimental therapy that cures mice; the reduction of heart disease, North America's leading killer, not just by increased understanding of nutrition and lifestyle but also as a result of current commercial biotechnology research.

Other "gee-whiz" medical breakthroughs that can be expected in the future include a cure for dental caries, male contraceptives, control of asthma, a perfection of allergy relief, memory-recall drugs, disease immunities for newborn babies, the conquering of autoimmune illnesses, artificial blood, and the development of anti-aging medications and therapies. Biotechnology will give us artificial limbs and organs and transplants of various kinds, ultimately including the implant of bioelectronic chips into various parts of the body. For example, minuscule computers implanted in the bloodstream will monitor body chemistry and automatically correct imbalances. A combination of microelectronics and microsurgery may eventually make it possible to restore feeling and use to deadened limbs. The use of artificial eyes and ears will be widespread by the late-1990s.

Biotechnology can facilitate rapid tests to help doctors make accurate diagnoses. In India, for example, where the number of cancer cases is forecast to triple by the year 2000, and where cancer occurs at a considerably younger age than in the West, there is a possibility that up to 40% of patients could be offered a cure if the disease was diagnosed earlier and proper treatment was provided.

Curing Cancer and AIDS

Biotechnologists are creating monoclonal antibodies for the diagnosis of infectious diseases and immunotoxins as a new approach in cancer therapy. There is a growing belief among radiation and biotech scientists that a cancer cure will be available by the mid-1990s. Researchers at the University of Nebraska School of Medicine may have found a cross-linking agent in a species of chemical known as free radicals, which link proteins, DNA and other long molecules. Free radicals harm body cells in radiation sickness and may even begin the transformation of normal cells to cancer. Free radicals are easily generated from food, water and air; tobacco smoke is filled with them.

The cancer breakthrough may already have happened. Scientists have discovered that all cancer cells produce a substance known as chorionic gonadotropin (CG). This protein is also manufactured by the fetus to prevent the mother's immune system from rejecting fetal cells as foreign; it may perform the same function in a tumor. If this research proves productive, it may be possible to make a vaccine that could trigger the body to produce antibodies against all CG-producing cells, automatically destroying any future cancer and perhaps wiping out existing tumors.

A few vaccines against specific cancers are already in the works. A scientist at George Washington University has developed a vaccine against four types of lung cancer. In experiments, only 17% of immunized patients died of the cancer, compared with more than half of those who did not receive the vaccine. New drugs produced by genetic engineering provide the most hope for significantly reducing cancer deaths. A leading Japanese company claims that if the new genetic protein "tumor-necrosis factor" lives up to its early promise, a mere 25-lbs (11-kg) of it will suffice to treat every cancer patient in the entire world.

Similar technological breakthroughs may enable us to cure AIDS (Acquired Immune Deficiency Syndrome) fairly soon. In a recent poll of 250 U.S. medical scientists, 46% anticipated that a safe and effective vaccine against AIDS would be generally available sometime in the 1990s, and 26% expected an effective cure by the year 2000. U.S. scientists have since discovered a protein that destroys cells that produce the AIDS virus. Developed at the U.S. National Institute of Allergy and Infectious Diseases, CD4-pseudomonas exotoxin is more effective than the earlier genetically engineered protein now being tested.

In the meantime, the U.S. Center for Disease Control agrees there is no evidence that AIDS will ever reach epidemic proportions, except perhaps among high-risk homosexuals and intravenous drug users. They say that the threat of AIDS has been exaggerated and that sexually active heterosexuals are at greater risk by not wearing automobile seatbelts than they are from AIDS. In early 1988, the *New York Times* confirmed this when it reported that a wide array of data amassed in 1987 shows that the virus has stopped spreading in the U.S.A., even among gay men (where 20% to 25% are infected) and that only 0.02% of the heterosexual population has been infected.

The outbreak and resulting fear of AIDS is nevertheless encouraging stronger global co-operation on public health measures to combat it. In 1987, the Public Health Foundation in the United States created an electronic network linking

700 AIDS-program co-ordinators and public health professionals. The database stores time-critical information on the latest AIDS cases, AIDS statistics, articles on AIDS from 65 major journals and abstracts of AIDS literature from around the world. Plans are underway with both WHO and the Pan American Health Organization to create an international AIDS electronic network. The AIDS phenomenon is thus helping foster a new sense of planet-wide interdependence and responsibility for healthy human survival in general.

Stress as a Disease

Not all diseases are new. Stress is a disease that has affected people worldwide for centuries. In the Agricultural Age of Western countries, individuals gave up their rights to a feudal chief in exchange for unquestioned paternalistic protection and the provision of basic survival needs. In the Industrial Age, psychological illnesses reflected the mechanistic, isolationistic, materialistic "crowding" of an urbanized, impersonal society that spawned them. The Post-Industrial Revolution has progressively accelerated the change. In the group-oriented, seemingly more "crowded", post-industrial future, some values that were once positive — individualism and nationalism, for instance — often take on negative connotations. People and nations who rigidly adhere to such old individualistic values, while resisting new global and pluralistic ones, tend to be overwhelmed and left behind.

As we enter the 4th-Wave Information Age, many stress-related health problems stem from the so-called information overload. As the quantity of new information and knowledge explodes, it implodes on our senses: we are "crowded" by information. We need to know what not to read as much as what we should read. Yet, if we are to adequately comprehend the complexity of change, information overload is a necessary precondition that is forcing us to learn to differentiate between valuable and nonvaluable information. At that point, complexity becomes more simple and stress starts to evaporate. Geo-strategic thinkers understand this but many others, unable to distinguish between types of information do not. They suffer what Alvin Toffler called "future shock."

Future shock tends to be a generational problem. The generation that grew up in the old 2nd-Wave industrial environment has a more difficult time adjusting to the rapid change of the post-industrial world. Children born of the current age do not suffer greatly from future shock. They are born literally into the "space age", into the age of Moon landings, of test tube babies, biotechnology, cloning and the breathtaking pace of computer development. Though these children may have been poorly prepared to manage information, they are generally more adept than their parents at realizing its value and relevance. And by growing up with such unprecedented "living the future" training, they are much better equipped than their parents to manage the future — their future. We should learn from them that the antidote to future shock is to immerse ourselves in the future — to literally live the future. Then there would be fewer surprises and much less future shock.

From Sickness to Wellness

None of the foregoing, no matter how spectacular, will be enough to satisfy our G-Force aspiration for wellness. An agenda for a healthier world must include basic health education as a recognized aspect of general medical practice for all the people of the world, coupled with new and closer working relationships between health professionals (of all kinds, not just doctors), their technologies, voluntary workers and families. An increasing share of health budgets needs to be spent on the promotion of good health practices, on education about the effect of lifestyle on health, and on community care and self-help. For example, the current development of simple medical technologies that we can use for ourselves (say, do-it-yourself diagnostic kits that are computer-linked to medical offices and hospitals) will greatly reduce our dependence on the medical profession and hospital medicine worldwide.

We also need to re-invent our concept of healthcare. Today's healthcare system is really a "sickness" system, not a "wellness" system. It rewards sickness: the more frequently a patient goes to the doctor, the more money the doctor earns. Prevention and curative medicine need to take priority over simplistic and short-term diagnostic medicine — the outright prevention of illness rather than the treatment of symptoms. And we need to explore ways for families to take on more responsibility for their own healthcare by adopting healthier lifestyles.

The fundamental problem is that the very practice of so-called modern medicine is scientifically behind the times. Much of medicine still uses the dualistic concept of the patient as a divided body and mind. This leaves us with the mistaken belief that disease is a physiological disturbance that can be corrected only by chemical or physical means. While science has since gone through quantum conceptual leaps, healthcare has responded only with behavioral medicine.

"Holistic" health concepts come the closest to keeping up with science, but they have failed to dislodge the biomedical model of treating "sickness." Holistic health needs to incorporate knowledge from the new sciences of biotechnology, genetic engineering, neurology and information technologies. An "informed" holistic health process must itself be transformed into what I would call an "info-global wellness" system that is capable of meeting the health aspirations of the global family. By 2050, basic wellness should be able to be taken for granted by almost everyone worldwide as they live increasingly healthier and longer lives. That opportunity is now within reach — if we re-invent medical practice.

G-Force S-5

Providing Meaningful Work

"Jobs are the true source of human welfare."
- Leo Tolstoy

Productive jobs create wealth, which in turn creates leisure, and the globalization of labor is a major G-Force of socio-economic development. In the developed countries, the human race is succeeding magnificently at reducing its working hours and heading towards a 5th-Wave leisure society by the middle of the 21st-Century. On the other hand, while the Third World is now faced with "forced leisure" (read unemployment), as it becomes self-sufficient in meeting the needs of its burgeoning population this self-sufficiency will satisfy the accompanying need to create 2-billion new jobs in those economies by 2050. The demand for basic consumer needs in these countries is automatically stimulating massive job creation. These trends do not mean that one part of global society is going to be at leisure while the Third World plays catch up — at least not for long. The entire world is constantly moving towards the same kind of 5th-Wave leisure economy that is being created in the West. But it will still be a society of full employment except that work will have been redefined, reduced and redistributed in various ways.

Global Redistribution of Work

The International Labor Organization (ILO) predicts that the world's working population will increase by 1.5-billion before 2030; the working population in the least developed regions will grow by 95% by then. To cope with these massive increases in the available work force and to absorb the estimated 90-million now unemployed, the world faces the challenge of creating 47-million jobs in *each* of the next 40 years.

For North America and Western Europe, on the other hand, the ILO predicts the work force will grow by only 1.9% and 0.2% per year respectively. This is a modest gain of only 2-million workers per year in each of the next 40-

years. The ILO suggests that this could lead to a shortage of workers and slow economic growth in the West, but their analysis is faulty. Balanced employment will be maintained because, thanks to technology, working hours in the West will continue to be reduced. Economic growth and higher incomes will come from increased productivity generated by the ongoing information explosion (as I explain later). Moreover, through concerted global economic development policies, which recognize the new international division of labor made possible by the worldwide information technology revolution, the economies of the Third World will take off spectacularly. Thus we now have an opportunity to provide meaningful participation in economic development for all the people now needing work — in the West and the Third World — and those millions yet to be born.

The argument is often made that Third World countries need labour-intensive industry so they can create enough jobs for their surging populations. This is a short-sighted prescription. Concentration on labor-intensive (that is, obsolete) technology would be economically disastrous for these countries. Their resulting low productivity in an otherwise high-tech world would severely impair their ability to meet essential domestic material needs. In turn, such poor economic performance would make it even more difficult to provide productive labor for each successive wave of workers. Unless they join the Electronic Age, the Third World countries will be left behind. They must adopt the latest non-labor-intensive work processes to the maximum extent possible.

Neither would providing low-tech jobs close the international rich-poor gap. India's annual per-capita income, for example, is only $240. In the richest developed countries it averages about $20,000 — fully 80-times higher. If an annual economic growth rate of 5% per year could be sustained across the Third World, while the developed countries held steady at 2.5% per year, it would take 300-years for Third World incomes to catch up! The people of the developing countries are patient people, but they are not *that* patient. They have already lagged behind for centuries. Now, with today's technological compression of the time needed to accomplish just one cycle of the 4-STEP process of socio-economic development, they might rightfully expect to bridge this time warp. Only high-tech work environments will provide the wealth-creating opportunity to leapfrog the development process.

Most developing countries are still agrarian societies, yet there is a distinct shift of employment from the agricultural to the industrial and post-industrial sectors of their economies. Employment will be created in the new sectors of their economies as these countries go through successive phases of the 4-STEP process. Jobs are created in response to the full G-Force spectrum of human needs and aspirations. For example, in a feudal village society, where the family farm is a self-sufficient economic unit, the work is shared among the family members. Each contributes to the success of the economic unit and is rewarded for his or her labor through the collective provision of food, clothing and shelter. In this way, the basic needs of each member are met and all are fully employed. Each is the servant of the others and, hence, of his or herself. This model persists at every phase of the 4-STEP process. Each one of us, in varying degrees, is the servant of everyone else in society. Employment is created to meet the needs of society's members — ourselves included.

The number and type of jobs required is thus fundamentally dictated by the number and location of people to be served and their changing needs and aspirations as society modernizes. The number of people to be served is forecast to double by 2050, and the bulk of them will be living in the Third World. Hence, most jobs will also be created in the Third World. As well, almost all of the peoples' needs are still to be met — so an abundance of work waits to be done. Food for up to 10-billion people has to be grown, harvested, processed, distributed and sold. Water has to be purified, stored and piped into houses, 2-billion of which are still to be built, furnished and maintained in towns and cities yet to be constructed. Clothing, healthcare and education have to be constantly provided to a several-billion-strong population that replenishes itself every third generation or so. All these people need increasingly sophisticated means of transportation and communication so they can effectively go about their daily lives.

These phenomenal job creation opportunities are difficult to appreciate when, as now, the world is caught up in a mega-transition to a globalized economy with new technologies. Technological changes of such magnitude as the electronic revolution, like the textile machine of old, cloud the transition and breed a fear that perhaps more jobs will be eliminated than created.

This fear begins to fade when a geo-strategic perspective is brought to bear. New technology does eliminate some jobs, reduces and changes others, and inevitably reduces humanity's need to work. However, while major technological revolutions cause major disruptions in labor markets, they also create a massive expansion in the new sectors of the economy. Every computer or robot, for example, requires people to design it, to program it, to market it, to deliver and install it, to service it, to operate it — and to develop a newer model to replace it. Such technologies create thousands of spinoff jobs in companies making components and supplies such as microchips, electric wires, disk drives, printers, paper and ribbons. As new technologies replace old tasks they enable society to do things that were not previously possible. Airplanes replaced ocean liners but carry many more passengers, through an expanding network of international airports, creating yet more jobs in the transportation and hotel systems — the supporting infrastructure of the 5th-Wave leisure sector.

Sharing the Work in the West

As it de-industrializes, the West is faced with fairly serious problems of structural unemployment — especially in certain sectors of the "old" economy. This is a temporary phenomenon of post-industrialization, though it tends to raise the familiar "exporting jobs" argument — that cheap imports from developing countries cause unemployment in the West. On the contrary, as of 1985, Third World purchases from the West were directly responsible for sustaining some 3.5-million jobs in the industrialized countries. At the same time, the so-called dumping of cheap Third World products on the Western markets contributed to the loss of only about 850,000 manufacturing jobs. In other words, the West was able to find and sustain employment for about 2.7-million workers, thanks to the fact that the productive output of these people was being bought up by the poor developing countries. So, for example, while jobs may have been "lost" in such sectors as textiles, others have been "gained" in the electronics sector. These figures in fact probably underestimate quite considerably the extent of the West's dependency on the developing countries for job creation. Protectionism, therefore, would be a foolish answer to the persistent unemployment problem in the West.

Job-sharing, part-time employment, shorter working hours and earlier retirement may all sound impractical now, but they will eventually create full employment in the West by sharing the work. Only 17% of U.S. firms yet allow one or more people to "share" a single full time job and 60% of companies still persist with the 40-hour workweek. Instead of sharing work, we have so far largely elected to use various forms of unemployment insurance and welfare programs to effectively pay about 10% of the Western European and North American work force to stay at home. This is the worst possible kind of investment decision because these millions of "forced" unemployed are missing out on any form of work experience and career development, and their skills are becoming increasingly obsolete.

As Adam Smith pointed out in 1776, a country that in any way fails to invest in its human resources (what I call the intellectual capital of its future economy) will not create new real wealth and hence will not prosper. By paying people to stay at home, North America and Western Europe are failing to invest in their people — in their own long-term future. After the last Depression and the subsequent economic restructuring, the return to economic growth was accompanied by full employment at lower amounts of time worked. This will again happen during the next 25-years as the world comes out of the 1990-93 "Mini-Depression" (discussed later). When the next real economic boom comes, in the late-1990s and the early part of the 21st-Century, those Western countries will be poorly equipped to take advantage of it unless they provide themselves today with an appropriately trained and futuristically educated work force.

In the West, the phasing out of a mandatory retirement age, though an expression of people's desire for more leisure, does create job openings for others. Abolishing the retirement age altogether, said the U.S. Department of Labor in 1982, would prompt as many as 200,000 Americans to keep on working beyond the traditional retirement age. Yet this is not happening. Rather, retirement ages have continued to drop. In 1977, 37% of all American retirees were aged 62 or under. By 1982, this had increased to 51%, and it is now estimated that more than 60% of U.S. firms have adopted a retirement age of between 55 and 60, both in an attempt to rejuvenate their work force and as a reflection of a mature population's desire for leisure.

Globalized Labor

With the globalization of labor comes parallel changes in the economic advantage of various parts of the world. Western countries are being pushed towards an economic growth pattern that is increasingly intensive in capital, research, innovation and skills — in parallel with the creation of a 4th-Wave economy. Global labor is also being divided in complex ways. For example, 4th-Wave telecommunications technologies are changing where and how work is done not only in the West, but internationally. Many multinational corporations own or rent satellites, to enable them to communicate internally as well as globally, and also to employ people internationally. This kind of "remote working" allows service companies and manufacturers to gain access to the cheaper labor pools in developing countries. Many big American banks, for example, employ people in the Caribbean to do keypunching, working electronically by satellites hooked into a central data bank in the United States. Much of the routine accounting work for a bank or major international corporation could be done in, say, Nairobi, or even in remote Third World villages — in fact anywhere that computers can be linked with global satellite networks.

There is nothing exploitive in this approach. On the contrary, in global terms, rather than capital being invested to create few, short-term jobs in Western economies (for a small improvement in the standard of living of a small number of people), the global return on investment is much better when a manufacturing plant or a service center is established in a developing country. There the potential long-term economic gain for a much larger number of people is proportionately much greater. New jobs in the Third World increase the purchasing power of millions of people, who then become marginally better off. Moreover, they then reinvest their new disposable income in the local economy, creating more wealth and fostering their further economic development. In turn, these countries can then do more business with the developed world and acquire the 4th-Wave technology and expertise that the West is producing, thus creating long-term jobs in the West.

These measures need to be taken on an international scale to spur the needed creation of jobs and wealth. The malnourished and hungry cannot buy from the West. As the Japanese are showing us, we need a much increased flow of investment from the developed to the developing world and greatly improved access for Third World exports to the markets of the West. Above all, nations need to abandon inward-looking policies and recognize their own enlightened self-interest in creating global employment.

The West also needs to invest in its own human resources. What could be simpler than to use the enormous sums of money now spent on unemployment benefits and other social security payments to give people the chance to prepare themselves for the future labor market? Such money should be paid to employers as hiring and training incentives. Work experience and education would be gained by those now unemployed who could again become consumers and taxpayers. As well, accounting and taxation policies should be changed to create a human capital allowance so that the costs of training by corporations, rather than having to be absorbed out of the current year's profit, can be amortized over the working career of employees. This would spur business investment and expand the local economy. The generation of greater wealth would allow working hours to be reduced yet again across the economy.

A Future for Trade Unions?

Trade union movements in Western countries gained tremendous strength as a result of the Great Depression and reached their peak in the 1950s. Since then, union membership in Western countries has experienced a long decline (from 29% of employed workers in 1975 to 18% by 1985 in the U.S.A.) and will soon revert to pre-Depression levels. Does this mean the end of unions? Clearly the employment environment in the West has improved considerably, and, with the notable exception of the mining, construction, chemical and nuclear industries (all employing relatively few people), most employees are now working in cleaner, healthier conditions and much tedious work has been eliminated.

On the other hand, a tremendous amount of mundane paper-shuffling is done in the service and information processing sectors. We also expect a Mini-Depression from 1990 to 1993. While these conditions could enable the trade union movement to make a comeback in the 1990s, further automation, post-industrialization, enlightened management approaches and various forms of employee ownership will negate unionization. As First World unions achieve a greater global awareness, they may temporarily be strengthened by action in solidarity with Third World workers, who will certainly be exploited over the next few decades. But they will be brought up to 4th-Wave standards far more rapidly than western workers have been over the past few centuries. Ultimately, however, wage rates will increase in developing countries in response to the supply and demand of labor, and these economies will continue to introduce yet more new post-industrial technologies to improve working conditions.

As Third World economies take off, working hours will constantly be reduced, incomes will constantly increase, and management will be more enlightened. Consequently, while trade unions may grow worldwide in the short term, as the 5th-Wave leisure society unfolds they could disappear from the West by 2025 and from the whole world by 2050.

G-Force S-6

Housing the Future in Super-Cities

"A house measures the degree of civilization."
— *Moritz Alsberg*

"The city is the fireplace of civilization."
—*Theodore Parker*

Providing the expanding human family with adequate housing certainly represents a major challenge. About a quarter of the world's 5-billion people are either homeless or live in slum settlements; 100-million have no shelter at all. By 2050, more houses will need to be replaced and the population will increase by 5-billion. Assuming four people per family by then, the world needs to build more than 2-billion "houses" of various types if everyone is to have proper shelter. That represents one new house every second of every minute of every day for the next 60-years. This mammoth task alone will create millions upon millions of the full-time jobs that I forecast in the previous chapter.

Some people claim that this task of housing the future is bleak. They say that more and more people will have to crowd into less and less space, regardless of socio-economic, technological or political circumstances. They tell us that we must lower our standards of space and of municipal service, and reduce our urban environmental expectations.

Such claims are nonsense. We know how to house everybody but have failed to do so. We know how to organize and plan our urban environments but, all too frequently, bureaucracy and lack of political will prevent the necessary collective resources from being marshaled. The future must be housed. The rapid change in human settlements throughout the world cannot wait for yet more U.N. conference resolutions about what to do. In most communities, local or national, housing needs are well known and the resources to meet these needs are available. Housing the future requires political courage. Disputes about zoning and types of housing miss the point. Meeting the needs of the future does not depend on more research or more analysis. As noted already, there is no shortage of land in the world. There is no shortage of materials or labor. Housing the future also requires little further technological innovation. It simply needs doing.

High-Tech Housing

Technological innovations around the world promise to make the task even easier. Many analysts predict that within a few years, more than half the residential units built in the United States will come from factories. Housing trends in the American sunbelt are leading this drive. Many firms now manufacture modular apartments, single family homes, and motel units. The improved quality of construction and insulation are changing the negative image we have of such prefabricated housing and mobile homes. Prefab housing is not necessarily cheaper, but the quality is better and construction is faster, thereby reducing labor costs. The technique also permits home builders to erect accommodation anywhere in the country — simply shipping the home rather than establishing an on-site construction facility.

The Japanese companies are even starting to build houses like they build cars and computers. Japan's manufactured-housing industry already accounts for over 15% of its housing construction. Their computer-designed houses include high-tech materials and techniques such as floor panels that contain tiny hot-water pipes for heating and precast wall panels made of aluminum and foam or ceramic instead of concrete. The bathroom of the house is a single precast waterproof unit made of plastic, with everything from toilet to washbasin molded into it.

Since 1985, Japan has been using robots on construction sites to improve productivity and reduce costs. One type of remote-controlled robot travels up and down wet concrete floors of new apartment and office buildings, using trowels on the ends of its rotor arms to smooth the concrete. This robot can smooth 400-square-metres (500-square-yards) of concrete per hour, the equivalent of five human workers. Other robots erect steel columns and beams while a separate robot manipulator aligns the two pieces and inserts the bolts. With these innovations, building construction in Japan between 1982 and 1986 increased 43% more than normal.

Japan has also developed two new structural materials. The first, called ultra-high durability concrete, slows down the neutralization of concrete and the rusting of reinforcing rods by ten times. Under normal environmental conditions, it is claimed that this concrete will last more than 500-years, thus essentially eliminating the need to replace buildings. The second material, super-concrete structure, has three to ten times the strength (for only one-third the thickness) of traditional ferro-concrete. Used in the support pillars for warehouse floors where heavy cargo is stored, this new material is made by packing concrete inside steel tubes, which check the normal tendency of concrete to spread horizontally under pressure. When used in the support pillars of a 50-

story building, the cost is 40% lower than that of steel frames and 20% lower than ferro-concrete. This material will make it possible to build ultra-highrise buildings of more than 100-stories, previously considered near impossible in earthquake-prone Japan.

The Japanese are also pioneering airdome (canvas roofing) architecture, which economically creates huge enclosed spaces that use air pressure to support the walls and roof. It is being used for amusement parks and baseball stadiums in Japan and airport terminals in desert areas of the Middle East. In northern climates, architecture is taking on a different shape. The University of Minnesota's Civil/Mineral Engineering Building is a mammoth structure extending 100-feet (30-meters) below ground and a mere 20-feet (6-meters) above. In such a layered-city concept, function and climate determine which buildings go underground. Minnesota's climate varies by 130°F (55°C) but, 25-feet (7-meters) underground, the temperature remains at about 50°F (10°C) all year round. The energy savings in such an underground building are close to 80%.

Low-Tech Housing

In developing countries, it is a somewhat different story. In the next 60-years, these countries will be faced with the problem of not only meeting the housing needs of existing urban populations but also of providing new housing, infrastructures, and municipal services for 4-billion more urban dwellers, many of whom — at least initially — will be poor and unemployed rural migrants. The existing living conditions in the large cities of the developing world — growing slums and squatter settlements, overcrowding, and deteriorating transport and sanitation services — will probably prevail until at least the year 2000.

But this depressing scenario does not take into account the present low-tech solutions that are available. In parts of China, for example, some houses are being made of rigid panel boards manufactured from waste rice and wheat straw, using a process developed by a British firm. Other factories are producing fiberboard for construction out of waste sugarcane materials. In Brazil and Bolivia, a simple, portable, hand-operated hydraulic press is used to make cheap, high-quality building blocks to improve housing and reduce disease. (Poor housing is a leading cause of those diseases transmitted by parasites living in cracked walls and earth floors.) The Brepak press produces building blocks (from lightly stabilized soil) as durable as cement or kiln-fired bricks, and does so without energy consumption and at half the cost. A team of six people can produce 3000 hard, dense, weatherproof bricks and construct a house in two weeks. The press has already been so successful that Kenya and Jamaica have agreed to include such building blocks in their draft building regulations. Another affordable, low-tech alternative to cement is rice husk ash (RHA). Rice mills accumulate enough husk waste a year to produce 24-million tons of RHA-cement. Made from a mixture of the burnt husks, lime and water, this cement can be used as mortar, wall-rendering or to make floors.

In Mauritania, West Africa, a "self-house" project is turning destitute former nomads into skilled masons who, using local building materials and innovative techniques, are transforming the small town of Rosso. Inspired by the achievements of Egyptian architect and urban planner Hassan Fathy, a team of architects, technicians, sociologists and economists studied the architectural traditions of the area, its capacity for absorbing technology, and the availability of local building materials. Most important, the team gained the confidence of the dwellers by listening to their requests. A prototype house was built in 1979 to train the masons and to test local materials and equipment with a variety of housing styles. Bricks made of stabilized earth, using only 6% cement, were produced at a small, on-site brick-making plant. Instead of employing wood or metal for roofing, brick domes were devised, as was an ingenious ventilation system. The first dozen houses were built in 1980. The response of the people was enthusiastic. Self-help brigades sprang up and, for the first time, women were integrated into a building scheme. Within three years, 750 houses of one to three rooms each were built at a cost of about $1,000 per house — the equivalent of only four years' per capita income.

This low-tech/high-tech approach demonstrates that a graceful mudbrick structure can be economic to build, admirably suited to the local climate and architecturally attractive. The technique is now being adopted in other parts of the world. With this kind of ingenuity, resourcefulness and continued technological innovation — coupled with futuristic skills in settlement and community planning and infrastructure management — there is no reason why the challenge of housing the future masses of the world cannot be met.

Global Mega-Cities

People tend to gravitate to the commercial centers, and the rapid growth of cities, especially in the developing countries, has been conspicuous since about 1950. In 1950, there were only six cities in the world with populations over 5-million, and their combined population was only 42-million. Now there are 29 such cities with a combined population of over 250-million. By the year 2000, there will be 58 such cities, with an estimated total population of nearly 650-million.

Such unprecedented expansion of cities will have far-reaching consequences. If most of the world's people move into the cities, it follows that most of the world's human problems — and the greatest opportunity to advance human potential — reside in the cities. The shift to the cities is greatest in Latin America (see Fig. 8). Its urban population rose from 40% of the total in 1950 to 71% in 1988, and is projected to reach 84% in 2025, when Latin America will be the most urbanized region of all.

Fig. 8   Global Urbanization Trends

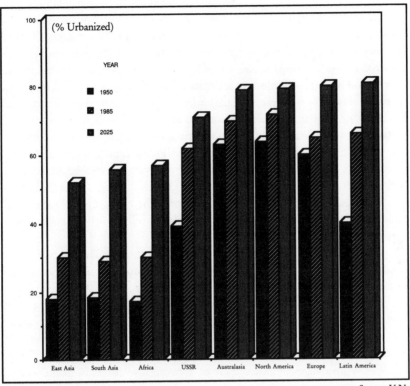

Source: U.N.

Most Third World governments have encouraged the growth of large cities in order to create links to the international economy. One city, usually the capital, often dominates a country, controlling its trade with international markets. As a result, such cities as Manila or Mexico City often have more in common with Tokyo or New York than with their own rural hinterlands. This magnet draws too many people to the city, chasing too few jobs, and results in sharp income stratifications. In metropolitan Manila, for example, 16% of the labor force is unemployed and 43% is underemployed. Due to lack of planning and political will, at least two-thirds of all new housing being constructed in the city is illegal and uncontrolled. Though many people are at least building their own shelters, huge slums are being created.

Undoubtedly, the poorer countries are going to have poorer cities, but they need not be inefficient and inequitable cities. Inadequate provision of housing, sanitation and public transport are lamentable given what is possible with our resources. It is possible to have large but efficient and humane cities if social, economic and environmental forces are appropriately mobilized. The urban crisis is not merely a matter of too many people concentrated in one place. As demonstrated by Mexico City and Manila, it is also the failure of political and economic systems to meet the minimum requirements of urban habitation.

Third World cities are growing not only as a result of industrialization or proximity to resources. Their growth is also led by domestic market demand factors (such as population increase, rural poverty and hyperinflation), city-centered public investments and a proliferation of international representative offices (and other paper-shuffling activities). They also serve as global trade and service centers, often a branch-plant carbon copy of New York, where local franchises of transnational corporations go about their business. As centers of global commerce, finance and communication, the exciting lure of the city further spurs the rural exodus like never before. Public expenditures and foreign loans generate a bigger flow of money and precipitate yet more demand for consumption, which in turn stimulates the growth of more trades, industries and services. Third World cities have become the consumption capitals of national economies where a continuous population influx further stimulates this perpetual cycle by increasing demand.

World Bank and U.N. experts forecast that most of the Third World urban transition will peak in about 2025 (see Fig. 8). A slowdown of city growth began in the late-1970s, and these cities need not continue to grow at the same exponential rate as we have just seen. The experts conclude that alarmist forecasts have exaggerated the effects of land density, foreign capital inflows and population growth on Third World urbanization. More critical are the realignment of productivity advances across the 6-wave sectors of the economy and the changing relative advantages of global trade as between raw materials, manufactured products and services. Further, as discussed later, the computerized 4th-Wave information society will restructure urban forms, reversing the centralization phenomenon of the 2nd-Wave manufacturing society.

The enormous problems of managing cities include the provision of food and water, the removal of human waste, and the provision of housing, urban transit, education, healthcare and employment. Most experts agree that China is doing the best job of population and urban management. The Chinese have decided that the development of medium-sized cities (with populations between 200,000 and 1-million) will best help the country achieve its overall economic goals for the year 2000 and beyond. Most of these medium-sized cities are evenly distributed throughout the country, close to both a supply of natural resources and a ready industrial and/or consumer market demand. Cities with populations of 500,000 people account for 36% of China's urban population, half of the large enterprises, and two-thirds of the total industrial and agricultural output. Small townships that are close to resources will be the bases for producing primary goods for industries, leaving the medium-sized cities to be the backbone of the country's manufacturing and processing and the large coastal cities to be the business, financial, foreign trade and technologically oriented centers. This approach contrasts totally with that taken in other countries, where single cities such as Manila and Mexico City have grown up to try to serve all these purposes. Medium-sized cities are more flexible, and can better adapt themselves to economic modernization. As the Chinese saying goes: "It is easier for a small boat to turn around."

China is also trying to make its mega-cities self-sufficient. The city limits of larger centers, such as Shanghai, have been expanded, not to create more urban sprawl but to take in and preserve some of the surrounding agricultural countryside, so that the city can grow its own food. (This shift of nearby land to city management also greatly facilitates waste disposal, because human wastes can be used as fertilizer.) As a result, by 1986 Shanghai was self-sufficient in vegetables and produced most of its grain and a good part of its pork and poultry.

As China modernizes its economy and attempts to move half of its 1st-Wave peasant laborers from the land into the 2nd-Wave sectors and beyond, it is also decentralizing industry. Small factories and enterprises are being established in rural areas so that farmers and their families do not have to go to a city to find other work. This keeps cities much smaller and more manageable. In other Third World countries, the rural exodus has led to the hideous development of huge shantytowns in Caracas, Lagos, Calcutta and dozens of other megalopolises. As in China, rural villages, if given authority, could be transformed into development enterprises, creating a local decision and management network for national economic modernization.

Modern technology can help this process. Microcomputers are the essential tools of any decentralized urban vision. A village committee can help its people if it is connected to data banks and telecommunications networks that provide information, knowledge, education and medicine. Access to such technologies makes the gloom-and-doom scenarios about the prospects of squatter settlements premature. Today's poor housing conditions do not indicate that the situation will remain the same or become worse in the future — unless governments fail to implement forward-looking housing and city management strategies using the best means available.

The way forward for the Third World has at least three components: institutional reform, with emphasis on revived local government; political reform, with emphasis on a greater community participation in the design and delivery of village and mid-sized urban facilities and services; and planning reform, with emphasis on adopting a global approach to mega-city management and rural land management, using the latest technological applications. Unfortunately, since about 1950, local governments have suffered decline and neglect, even abolition, in many parts of the world. Yet local governments have more knowledge and understanding of local needs than the central government many hundreds of miles away. Local government needs to be seen and built up by national and provincial leaders to be the major provider of services in towns and cities all over the world.

Exurban Communities

Decentralization is happening even in developed North America. Since about 1960, and especially during the 1980s, many a North American metropolis has been transformed into something new and different. Suburbs, once dependent on the central city, have grown into vast independent satellite cities that rival and often surpass the traditional big-city downtown as the center of economic power and vitality. The outer city has become an urban entity all its own: an evolving landscape of skyscrapers, office parks and retail palaces, arranged in clusters that create a sense of presence in the suburban sprawl. It is in the outer city where employment is now being generated, and where the labor shortage has developed.

The outer city or decentralized workplace phenomenon is a physical expression of the 4th-Wave information economy. The first real surge of Western city growth occurred 100-years ago, with the onset of the Industrial Revolution. With the arrival of the automobile, cities mushroomed again. The personal computer reverses this process: information workers do not need to travel to work in the downtown core; now the work can travel to them electronically. We are creating decentralized networks of economic activity. Regional and national headquarters of major corporations are even moving to the suburbs, as are hotels, restaurants and such specialized functions as banking, accounting services and legal offices, once thought to be geographically immovable bastions of downtown enterprise. The evolution is towards more urban amenities in the outer cities which, once all the elements are put together, spell what a sense of community is all about.

Meanwhile, historic preservation of cultural heritage is providing a new vision for the future of downtown, the central locale of the major educational, cultural and entertainment assets of society. New historic districts provide a sense of place and history that the outlying centers cannot match. The old downtowns can thus become revitalized gathering places at the center of a network of decentralized exurban forms to create an uplifting "super-city" of genuine community spirit.

With high-tech housing and the electronic decentralization of socio-economic activity, city planners and managers have the opportunity to create healthy habitats across the global village. Urbanization is slowing down and there is no reason why innovative patterns of urban development, as are now occurring in North America and China, cannot spread all over the world to create networks of such "super-cities" by the early decades of the 21st-Century. While the hideously huge megalopolises will take longer to modernize, they are becoming major "nodes" along the global electronic highway. This will ultimately make them major centers of new wealth, as economically powerful as many of today's nation states, and hence able to modernize. By 2050, the world should be agleam with pulsating "super-cities."

G-Force S-7

Achieving Sexual and Racial Harmony

> *"The relation of the sexes is the invisible*
> *central point of all conduct."*
> — *A. Schopenhauer*

> *"There is but one race — humanity."*
> — *George Moore*

Until very recently, most women and "non-white" people have been excluded from the power centers of society and kept on the economic and political margins. This is now changing rather dramatically, particularly in the West. Because the new 4th-Wave society is based on information and knowledge, as many more women gain access to education we are seeing a rapid change in their status. With the emergence of post-industrialism, women are coming into their own and making a significant contribution to society that will continue to gain in strength and importance. In many ways, women are better adapting to the changes in Post-Industrial Society because, unlike men, they are less likely to carry the stereotypical values of the preceding Industrial Age. Similarly, "non-white" people are more attuned to the emerging global values of the essentially "non-white" and non-Western global village. Together, women and "non-white" people will be more and more visible and become the primary builders of the future.

Western Women's Movement

The women's movement in Western society is a natural outgrowth of post-industrialism that has moved women away from the margins of society. The move from labor-intensive 1st-Wave agriculture and 2nd-Wave manufacturing to 3rd-Wave services activity has changed the family structure such that there is less need for child-bearing. This has allowed women to gain access to higher education, which in turn has equipped them with the ability to leave the home to develop careers and become financially independent of a male "bread winner." Large numbers of women are now moving into the central corridors of power: in business, the professions, politics, and even the military and all-male clubs.

The business graduates who tomorrow will be running most of North America's corporations graduated from college in the 1980s. Close to half were women. In fact, 1982 marked the first year that American graduate business schools enrolled more females than males. Apart from the mathematical implications of this phenomenon, which is plain enough for anyone to grasp, it has subtler psycho-social implications. The business schools are providing an atmosphere wherein young business students of both sexes can learn to work effectively together, without stereotyping, and to complement each other's strengths and weaknesses. As these graduates move into male-dominated institutions they are working together as change agents to modify the predominant macho, 2nd-Wave industrial pattern of organizational behavior. This will emerge more strongly as they reach higher levels of decision-making freedom in the business world.

The movement of women into positions of power in business since 1970 is dramatic. In 1970, only 1% of business travelers were women. Today, working North American women make up 35% of the frequent-flying group on airlines and spend $3-billion annually on business travel. The number of North American women holders of American Express cards, for example, increased from a mere 70,000 in 1972 to over 5-million in 1986. By the year 2000, half of all business travelers will be women.

Women have proven that they can run small companies capably — more capably and profitably than men, several surveys show. In the 1980s, women have begun entering the management ranks of major corporations in unprecedented numbers. For example, 64% of the Bank of America's officers are female (though only 20% of the top 3500 executive posts are now held by women). Progress towards the executive suite is slowest in the big technology firms such as IBM, where only 500 women, or 7%, were among the top 6700 managers in 1986.

The more an organization internally reflects the real-life situation of its external environment (52% of the population or marketplace is female) the more successful it is likely to be as an enterprise. Both sexes working together in management will be enriching. It is critical that both sexes have opportunities to develop their careers and manage their organizations in environments free of sex-role constraints. This is starting to happen in what I call supra-sexual management: team management that transcends gender but twins the unique intellectual capabilities of the sexes in genuine executive partnerships.

By 1982, women earned 49% of the bachelor degrees, 51% of the masters degrees, and 33% of the doctoral degrees awarded in the United States — that's close to their 52% share of the population. In the 1970s, North American women had more than doubled their share of many types of university degrees; this is expected to almost double again in most categories by 1990 (see Table 2).

Table 2

University Degrees Earned by Women

Type of Degree	% of All Degrees		
	1970	1980	1990
Accounting	10	41	60
Business	14	34	55
Law	12	37	53
Medicine	15	28	48
Computer Science	24	30	40
Agriculture	7	29	35
Architecture	21	28	35
Engineering	1	9	25

Throughout the post-industrial world, women are catching up with men in education, income and decision-making power. As a result, they have made substantial inroads into what have been traditionally male-dominated professions. It is also worth noting that women now fill more than 40% of university teaching positions in North America. With 80% of elementary school teachers and 50% of secondary school teachers already being women, North America's next generation is the first to receive a supra-sexual higher education.

Women are also moving into political life in developed countries. In Canada in 1885, women could not vote. A century later, in 1984, they comprised the majority of the electorate. In the same election, a record number of women were elected to the House of Commons: 27 of 214 female candidates. Until 1974, there had never been more than five female MPs in Canada. Their number increased again in 1988. Next time, there is a good possibility that 50 or 60 women MPs will be elected — and 240 men. Most women first enter politics at the municipal level, and there are now several women mayors of large cities in the U.S.A. and Canada. Then they graduate to the provincial or state legislatures before seeking federal office. There are thousands of women moving up through the political system in the West. The number of women in the U.S. state legislatures has grown in every election since 1960 to reach 16% of senators and representatives. In some states it is over 30%. The U.S. Congress now has 5% female membership. It therefore won't be long before another woman runs for the American presidency — and wins. Several women have become national leaders in various countries in recent years; in the 21st-Century there will be dozens of them worldwide. Whatever their ideological bias or personal style, these women are potent symbols of changes in societal power structures.

Women are also moving into the previously all-male preserve of military decision-making positions, particularly in the United States. In 1973, the U.S. military had no women officers. By the end of 1987, it had 40,000. While there are only 10 women in the general/admiral ranks, and all of those are at the junior level, the sheer mathematics of promotions from the expanding ranks below (where women already fill about 14% of officer positions) will significantly increase women's representation in future years.

As a result of these female incursions to the center of societal power, many old bastions of all-male tradition are breaking down, either voluntarily or as a result of legal decision. In 1987, the U.S. Supreme Court ruled that the male service organization of Rotary Clubs must allow local chapters to admit female members in states that guarantee equal rights in public accommodations. In addressing the Toronto Rotary Club in 1980, I had told them that this would be the inevitable course of events. Few listeners agreed with me. Although many Rotarians apparently welcomed the Court's decision as belated recognition that times had changed, others have greeted the ruling with outright hostility. Human inertia is a powerful force. Sometimes change takes weeks, other times it takes years. In early-1989, Rotary's International Legislature Council voted by a 75% majority to open their doors to women, ending the 84-year tradition of male-only membership. Clearly a trend is afoot to end the West's tradition of female exclusion.

Third World Women's Movement

In 1st-Wave developing countries, of course, the male-female situation is much different. Basic survival is the priority of the day. According to some estimates, women account for two-thirds of the world's working hours, though they constitute only one-third of the world's labor force, receive only 10% of its income and own less than 1% of its property. For example, as shown in Table 3, women in Africa do almost all the work.

Much of the women's food growing and processing tends to be overlooked because, like housework, it is unpaid; even when taken into account, the amount of women's farm work is often underestimated. The proportion of women par-

Table 3

Work Performed by Women in Africa

Task	Share (%)
Farming	
Growing Food	70
Storing Food	50
Selling, Exchanging Produce	60
Grinding, Processing Food	100
Caring for Animals	50
House Work	
Child Care	100
Cooking	100
Fetching Water	90
Cleaning	100
Community Work	
House Building	30
House Repair	50
Community Projects	70

Source: U.N. Economic Commission for Africa, 1985.

ticipating in paid 2nd-Wave manufacturing employment has increased (which ends their damaging isolation), but a substantial wage gap persists because the majority of jobs in which women predominate are badly paid. In Islamic countries such as Iran and Saudi Arabia, women have been virtually left out of the development process because of their supposed inferior status, their invisibility in national economic reckonings and a traditionally small voice in decision-making. In the long run, as Pakistan under Bhutto has demonstrated, these nations will not find their natural progress impaired if they move away from such obsolete paternalism.

Third World women also have poor access to healthcare. Although they are the major healthcare providers, they primarily have support roles and are more likely than men to be malnourished and to have less access to medical facilities. Nevertheless, much progress is now being made in providing primary healthcare and in learning more about women's health. Literacy in developing countries is estimated at 52% for men and 32% for women; throughout much of the Third World, boys are still brought up to be served and girls to serve them. The education gap between boys and girls in primary school is closing, but it is the poor quality as well as the low quantity of girls' education that prevents them from advancing. Still, education is the area in which Third World women have made the greatest gains in recent decades, and laws requiring compulsory school attendance are now widespread in many developing countries. In countries as diverse as Uruguay, Iraq and Lesotho, women even have a higher literacy rate than men and poor and isolated countries such as Chad and Nepal show strong gains in female literacy.

Women are making most gains where economic modernization is most advanced. In many industrializing developing countries, women are starting to behave in accordance with the emerging 4th-Wave nonstereotypical global society, not in the typical ways of the 2nd-Wave Western industrial era. They are starting to provide support to each other in small groups, recognizing that education and the capacity to work in several different jobs are basic elements in their progress. These women are also developing horizontal support networks rather than traditionally male-designed hierarchical organizational relationships.

Even a paternalistic society like China's is progressively opening up senior career positions to women who, in the 1980s, have begun to reach high levels of decision-making in government, business and institutions. In 1988, both the president and vice-president of the People's Bank of China were women; the president also sits as one of 14 women ministers and vice-ministers on the State Council, China's chief administrative body. There are 10 female provincial governors or vice-governors and almost 1000 women heads of prefectures and counties. In municipal politics, two of the seven vice-mayors elected in 1988 in Beijing are women — an unprecedented event in the history of the capital city. Women also hold many senior positions in Chinese industry. The general manager of the huge Beijing-based Capital Iron and Steel Company is a woman and over 30% of its senior staff positions are held by women. The Soviet Union compares just as favorably. Women constitute one-third of the Supreme Soviet, 49% of provincial and local deputies, 44% of judges, 69% of medical doctors, 74% of teachers and 40% of scientific and research professionals.

Beyond Patriarchy

Although one of the slowest societies to lose its paternalism is Japan, where there still is a pervasive negative response to female leadership, the number of Japanese women company presidents is rising dramatically. According to the Teikoku Research Data Bank, their number has grown by more than 10% annually since 1975 and, by 1985, 4.2% of companies had female presidents. They are predominantly in the retailing, hospitality, real estate, civil engineering and transport sectors. Though the majority of Japanese women presidents inherit the post from their deceased husbands, growing numbers of women are founding their own businesses to overcome the patriarchal system and lead "the age of women" in Japan. Whereas male formal values were once exclusively dominant, female informal values are increasingly emphasized as Japan tries to build a society where men and women can work and share society's affairs together.

Clearly, the end of patriarchy is a major G-Force of social change. At the First Global Conference on the Future held in Toronto in 1980, we conducted a "global opinion poll on the future" among the 5400 attendees. The poll found that 80% would like to see a major transformation of society. The respondents — two-thirds were male — unexpectedly predicted that this transformation would not be technologically driven but would be characterized by a reduced force of masculine/exploitive/manipulative values and patriarchal institutions. Increased influence would come from feminine nurturing/intuitive/spiritual values.

Many international futurists have since written about how this transformation is now happening. Eleonora Masini, past president of the World Future Studies Federation, believes that women will have supremacy in some aspects of the new society. She says this supremacy is already evident where women have different perspectives about what is important, particularly in developing countries, and she believes these perspectives are better adapted to the evolving new society. But women's perspectives and capacities conflict with the still prevalent but limited Industrial Era thinking. Masini believes that women can stimulate futuristically sound policies and directions simply by permeating society with their own different value systems and behaviors. Women must concentrate on their own higher education and foster an understanding of nonstereotypical sex-role models.

This theme is taken up by Barbara Marx Hubbard, an outside candidate for the U.S. presidency in 1984, who claims that women are achieving power while we are witnessing a species-wide shift of feminine function. Until recently, says Hubbard, women's primary role has been to reproduce the species. Most women had to have as many as eight babies to ensure a few would live. In some developing countries this is still the case, because until they achieve basic industrial, scientific and technological progress — disease and early death will be rampant. Concurrently, Hubbard points out, men's energy has been bound to the necessity of sustaining family life as the economic bread-winner. Today all this has changed. Women are having fewer babies — and not only because the species no longer needs more children. Since a rapidly decreasing percentage of a woman's life is invested in procreation, Hubbard believes the feminine energy is now for "co-creation," consciously participating in the process of evolutionary change. Sex moves from being procreational to recreational and, rather than nurturing babies, the energy of women is increasingly available for nurturing the Planet's evolution.

Supra-Sexual Family Revival

These sex-role changes are in turn altering the family structure. We have seen escalating divorce rates in many Western societies in recent decades, with as many as three-quarters of marriages breaking down in some countries. This has led many alarmists to predict the decline of the family. They are wrong. Rather we are reinventing the family in Western society, reconstituting the structure of human partnership on a basis more suitable to the Post-Industrial Age.

The post-World War II generation blindly married into the Industrial Era status quo family arrangement, its values reinforced by the Great Depression and the economic effects of the war. Jobs were scarce, it was still a man's world, and women did not yet have access to higher education. Consequently, the man was the bread-winner: he had to find a secure job, work for 40-hours a week until he was 65-years-old, earn a gold watch and retire. His wife was to keep house, raise children, cook and sew. These couples married for two main reasons: sexual lust and the economic security of "two can live as cheaply as one." The family was an economic unit with a domestic division of labor with the focus on production.

The economic boom of the 1950s and 1960s brought the onset of 3rd-Wave Post-Industrial Society, with access to education for all, brain work in offices rather than manual work in factories, increasing leisure time and a realization that large numbers of children were now a liability and, hence, there was less need for mother to stay at home. The family became a unit of economic consumption and growing affluence. Consequently, in the 1970s, these couples began to realize that the 2nd-Wave arrangement they married into was not for them: there was less and less need for individual economic security (especially for two-career families), and enduring sexual compatibility increasingly depended on intellectual compatibility — a factor hardly considered when they had married. A majority of these marriages ended in divorce.

Yet the family institution has not declined. The human need for partnership bonding still exists; 75% of those who divorce remarry. But post-industrial marriages — at least among well-educated Westerners — are what I call supra-sexual partnerships: intellectual intercourse is "hot" and of primary importance; sexual intercourse also then becomes hot (in a "cool" sense, becoming recreational super-sex) and reinforces the couple's co-creativity. In addition, their intellectual growth is fostered by the increasing financial independence flowing from the 4th-Wave information-rich economy.

As a result of this re-invention of the family, the divorce rate has started to decline, dropping from 23-per-1000 marriages in 1980 in North America to 21-per-1000 in 1985. It will fall further into the 21st-Century as the economic "Super-Boom" of the next long-wave cycle brings knowledge-intensive marriages and makes financial worries disappear forever. The new supra-sexual family is alive and well and prospering in the West.

Supra-Sexual Partnerships

As people learn to develop supra-sexual relationships in their lives, the new empowerment of women need not be at the expense of, or in competition with, men. To achieve power, women must aim at co-creative relationships with men to do chosen work with shared purpose and common goals. When such couples unite, Hubbard believes, we will experience the greatest emancipation of genius the world has ever seen. Women achieving power will foster new links of whole men and women, creating together through shared intent rather than biological and economic necessity. They will emerge as supra-sexual (as well as super-sexual) beings, leading the way — through sexual and intellectual attraction — to the co-evolution of an unlimited future.

The formation of these supra-sexual intellectual partnerships will be reinforced by unique complementarities that stem from inborn differences between male and female brains. Brain researchers have found that visual-spacial skills (in which men are generally superior) are organized in the male brain's right hemisphere; verbal skills (in which women are generally superior) are in the left side of the brain. The male brain is thus highly differentiated between the two hemispheres and highly structured. The female brain, on the other hand, is more symmetrically organized and less tightly structured. Research shows that she can shift back and forth between the hemispheres much more easily. She is more sensitive to context (geo-strategically global), good at picking up incidental information (geo-strategic futuristic scanning) and better at combining perceptual with verbal skills (geo-strategically opportunistic).

Clearly, if organizations are to find excellence, they must foster better male-female executive team-work. Indeed, our research has shown that a co-creative coupling of the male-female geo-strategic thinking capabilities offers distinct advantages. We have conducted several experiments in basic creative problem-solving and opportunity-identification. We tested all-male groups, all-female groups and mixed groups. The all-male groups performed identically as well as the all-female groups. The mixed groups, however, always did at least 25% better than the single-sex groups.

Clinical research reveals that these mixed-sex groups are, as Hubbard surmized, channeling their sexual energies into intellectual creativity. This joint male-female creativity ("co-creative supra-sexual team-work") has tremendous implications for the way global societies and organizations are governed and managed. Women simply think differently than men and — together with the new breed of men — will bring a new set of values to organizational life. Paternalistic and rigid organization structures will be transformed into fluid and organic networks for decision-making and the effective management of change for the future. As the 4-STEP process of socio-economic development proceeds worldwide, there is no reason why these trends cannot unfold internationally.

End of "White Man's World"

Not only are we witnessing the end of male dominance over females, we are also witness to the coming end of white racist power. Until World War II, the modern world was ruled by white male Europeans. In 1950, Europe and North

America accounted for about 25% of the world's population. That figure is now less than 12% and will plunge to about 6% by 2050. In some societies an elite can often control the destinies of many, but in the world at large it is inconceivable that such a small percentage of world population will be able to continue to control world affairs as we have witnessed during the past few decades. It is no longer a white man's world — even in America. By 2000, the United States will be the second-largest Spanish-speaking country in the world, and early thereafter Hispanics will outnumber blacks. Whites are already a minority in New York City and will be in California by about 2005.

In such a polyglot world it is heart-breaking to witness ongoing racial and ethnic conflicts. Though many such differences have been eroded by time or eradicated by education, they persist in many, if not most, countries. Extremist racial and ethnic political movements progressively undermine and swamp what should be the overriding political issues of socio-economic development. The most prominent current example today, of course, is South Africa, where group antagonisms not only trap the majority in servitude and poverty but sap the energy of the minority. Such antagonisms, as sociologist Thomas Sowell has suggested, stem from fear based on unfounded myths, misunderstandings and arrogant claims — perpetuated and institutionalized by white colonialism — that people of different ethnic background are inferior. Whites may be enlightened to learn that more than 75% of blacks in the United States have at least one white ancestor, while tens of millions of whites have at least one black ancestor.

Racial discrimination also persists when one group of people becomes prosperous. Virtually every portion of the human species excels at something. Geostrategically, this means that mutual benefits should result from cooperation among different racial and ethnic groups, whether through domestic markets, international trade or the migration of peoples. In reality, excellence at something often creates a pervasive level of discrimination. Yet this discrimination does not necessarily blunt the success of the prosperous group. For example, no major country in Southeast Asia has granted equal rights to its economically prosperous Chinese minority — meanwhile the numerical and political majority has remained poor. This has also been the story of the affluent Jews in Europe, where governments have sporadically reduced them to destitution by confiscating their wealth. But governments are unable to confiscate the skills and traits that produced that wealth in the first place. Jews and Chinese thus are often resented around the world because their ability to constantly excel — and succeed — is seen as threatening. Even where a whole group has been considered genetically inferior — blacks, for instance — it is often the demonstrably capable members of that group who are particularly resented. While in America this is predominantly the case in politics and business, it does not extend to sports or entertainment, where black stars attract great adoration and public support — but only until they are rumored for a managerial position. The prevailing bias seems to be that it is okay for black — or other so-called minorities — to entertain us but not to manage, control or govern us in any way.

It has been more than a century since Abraham Lincoln espoused a slave-free (supra-racial) future in America. It is almost 30-years since supra-racialism was "shot" with John F. Kennedy, Malcolm X and Martin Luther King. Following a period of intensive care, however, and even in the 1984 heyday of Reaganism, it became legitimate for the descendant of a black slave to run for president of America. Sooner rather than later a black (or other non-white) will occupy the White House.

The surging influence of black leaders in American political life is quite astounding. The 1980s saw a 52% increase in the number of black managers, professionals, technicians, government officials and politicians. Black members of Congress have risen to heights of power and prominence scarcely imagined a few decades ago. Congress has more than 20 black members — all House Democrats — and they chair about 20% of its standing and select committees as well as several important subcommittees. A black became chairman of the House Democratic Caucus in 1989, after serving four-years as chairman of the House Budget Committee, and another black was elected chairman of the Democratic Party itself. In 1989, several of America's largest cities had black mayors — among them Washington, Los Angeles, Atlanta, Baltimore, Detroit and Philadelphia. Political movements always start at the grassroots like this, then, as the movement grows, move up to the state legislatures and finally to the federal level. More than 7000 U.S. blacks were elected to office at all levels of government in 1988, compared with only 1500 in 1970.

This political surge is the result of greater political participation. Fully 58% of all black adults voted in the 1988 U.S. elections, up from 50% in 1980. The biggest gains in black voter registration and turnout occurred among young adults: in 1988, 56% of 18-to-24-year-old blacks registered, and 41% voted; in the 1980 election, 47% registered and only 30% cast ballots. By contrast, the polls showed little or no difference in voter registration and turnout for white voters in the same period. America's black population is therefore gaining increased political influence and can be expected to hold a significant proportion of power positions within a few short years.

America's large black churches have also taken steps to forge a united front. Their leaders seek to build a movement from already-evolved black institutions — a network of 65,000 churches and 20-million black Christians. This movement could establish a solid base for the civil rights and black self-help movement, which will very rapidly work itself into the political sphere. Indeed, while most U.S. blacks remain undereducated, unemployed, unhealthly, poor and angry, black leadership is maturing fast. There already is a passing of the baton from former civil rights leaders to a generation of blacks who have been professionally trained in government. They are consensus builders who have come up through the system on equal terms with whites.

As a result of these many trends, Americans are being forced by socio-economic reality (not idealism) to find a higher degree of co-operation in which all societal groups can benefit. If whites continue to attempt to dominate non-whites in America today, the latter will use their increasing power to potentially overthrow the economic system. On the other hand, if non-whites strive for control over whites, they will only isolate themselves from the economy and from political power. On the international stage, it is the same between the white West and the non-white Third World. Both need each other. The only outcome — the only solution — is a supra-racial future.

Human Rights ... Or Duties?

Only if we genuinely feel ourselves to be equal and only if political, judicial and bureaucratic decisions start to override existing processes, can we move significantly beyond bigotry. Clearly linked to the concept of relations between the sexes and the races are human rights. Western society, which once took its cue from the Ten Commandments, has replaced these with various human rights declarations. Canada, for example, has enacted the Charter of Rights and Freedoms, which has spawned a whole accumulation of rights claims and counterdemands. As a typical product of our time, such legislation is well-meaning and desirable, but it simply misses the point and will not achieve the desired goals.

In all their provisions, such declarations, like the U.N.'s Universal Declaration of Human Rights before them, mention only the rights of people, not their duties. This one-sided stress on individual rights ignores the need for duties as their essential counterpart. A civilization that emphasizes rights without duties is doomed because it destroys personal dedication and responsibility. An emphasis on rights alone, as practiced since the 1960s, creates undesirable clashes between the rival demands of individuals and groups. Only by shifting our focus onto the duties of the individual that accompany our rights in the world community can individual rights be preserved.

As John Kennedy urged: "Ask not what your country can do for you, ask what you can do for your country." It's the same in the world at large. What we really need is a declaration of planetary rights that places the planet, its environment and our global culture — rather than individuals — at the center of our concern. Once the necessary duties to the planet are carried out by us all, then individual rights will fall automatically into line and be achieved.

As we move into the 21st-Century, the crucial issues will focus on human ethics and humanity's relationship within the global community, with much less interest in individualism. We are coming to recognize that each branch of humanity and each nation has something valuable to offer human progress. Rather than disdaining the "inferior" values of other cultures, Westerners — and Americans in particular — are starting to feel indebted to them and learn from them. Collaboration — not self-interest — is the key.

We are about to embark on a new Pacific "spring" of cultural restoration. The coming pre-eminence of Japanese and Chinese/Southeast Asian

Confucianism will shift the global mindset towards a world where the truly rich and heroic societies are those that do not distinguish between men and women or their race but celebrate our supra-sexual and supra-racial oneness; societies that re-invent their political and social institutions so that all people can fulfill their duties and achieve their rightful potentials; societies where the greatest joy stems from the establishment of genuine relations between the sexes and the cultures — from our common humanity.

G-Force S-8

Globalizing Values, Beliefs and Culture

"Culture is always a product of mixing."
— Friedrich Hertz

Fatalism (the fundamental belief in the will of some mysterious "God") and individualism (a selfish emphasis on the survival of the fittest) comprised the basic value and belief systems of 1st-Wave tribal culture and were the basis on which the modern world evolved as a mostly 2nd-Wave Western European, individualistic, capitalist, Christian culture. The new actors on the world stage come from movements and cultures that did not participate in forming the rules of today's international social system. It is not surprising, then, that they feel little obligation to maintain those rules and rather seek something new, as do growing numbers of people in Western society. This common search for higher values and beliefs and the aspiration for a truly global culture is a major G-Force of social change. These aspirations are fundamentally challenging the conventional wisdom of ruling elites who dogmatically insist on the primacy of their outmoded values and beliefs — to which people can no longer relate because in the modern world they are intangible, illogical and incongruous. Instead, core human values such as a respect for life, responsibility towards future generations, protection of the environment, an obligation to aid those who need help in our family and community — if not the nation and the world at large — are widely if not universally acknowledged in at least some form. These moral elements are the foundation on which a wider consensus of global values can now be built.

Values Change Slowly

Unfortunately, values and beliefs are deep-rooted and change slowly. At all levels of human behavior, deeply held values assign a relative worth to optimal conditions and articulate a preference for one state over another — say, health is better than illness. Values thus do not specify what is, but rather what ought to be. That is, they try to perpetuate the past, whether or not it is relevant for the future. Similarly, a belief is a conviction that something is true, proven or known, absolutely beyond dispute. Often it is based on incomplete or distorted information that is rationalized into a dogmatic conclusion — for instance, abortion is inhuman. When a deeply held value or belief is challenged by new facts or a new belief, these are often rejected as preposterous and the old value or belief is protected and sustained. One of the strongest impediments to change in values and beliefs is religious dogma.

Religious beliefs were once the major source of personal identity and basic security, and they continue to play a leading role in world affairs. Today, though, the personal value accorded to religion varies greatly around the world. Of twenty values rated in a 1987 survey (by Futuribles of Paris) of social scientists around the world, religion ranked in the top seven in only Latin America/Caribbean (that being Catholicism) and the Arab States (Islam). Religion reached the eighth position in Africa, was ranked only fifteenth in both North America and Asia/Pacific, and did not appear at all among the top twenty values of either Eastern or Western Europe.

The low value assigned to religion in Europe, the seat of modern Western culture, is revealing. The effective numerical — if not the ideological — power base of Roman Catholicism, for example, has essentially shifted from Europe to Latin America, which today embraces the largest single segment of the world's Catholic population. Nevertheless, though the bulk of the Latin American population has been baptized as Catholics, this does not necessarily signify their commitment to Catholic values, practices and structures. Industrialization, massive urbanization and the changing patterns of rural socio-economic organization have eroded much of the basis of that traditional social order within which the Catholic church was once so firmly embedded. This erosion reveals the extent of the Church's failure to deeply penetrate the lower strata of Latin American society. Equally, social and political change was accompanied by a significant degree of secularization that was both the cause and effect of a growing ideological pluralism.

While the Catholic Church still stands against a Communist regime in Poland, its influence across the Western world is otherwise waning. Its hard-line papal opposition to birth control and abortion and its espousal of economic sharing are diametrically opposed to each other in terms of prevailing global economics. While opposition to birth control is not an espousal of large families, they are the result of futile attempts to adhere to the so-called spiritual virtues of will-power and self-denial. The resultant large families simply run against the 6-Wave 4-STEP process of modernization. Throughout the Western world, and in many developing countries such as the Philippines and in Latin America, this is causing millions of Catholics to seriously question whether this is the kind of institution from which they want to draw their values in a post-modern world.

Yet the Church is awakening to its inconsistencies. In 1988, the Pope made a sweeping social pronouncement that the Church should sell some of its "superfluous holdings and ostentatious ornaments" (his words) to help the world's poor. In a refreshingly candid statement he said: "It could be obligatory to sell these goods in order to provide food, drink, clothing and shelter for those who lack these things." The Church does teach mothers to stop getting pregnant once their family size is unsustainable. Yet it is unlikely that the Vatican will ever acknowledge that, in practice, its birth-control dogma is swelling the rosters of people who lack food, clothing and shelter. To do so would mean to acknowledge that its dogma is inconsistent with available family planning science and technology (developed by God's will) and with the socio-economic dynamics of population management.

As documented by Marilyn Ferguson, author of *Aquarian Conspiracy,* Western society is increasingly yearning for something truly spiritual because dogmatic religion (Catholic, Anglican or otherwise) has proven unsatisfying. Formal religion in the West has been shaken to its foundations by defections, dissent, rebellions, loss of influence and diminishing financial support. While many people, especially in the middle class, are becoming more spiritual in their daily lives, there is nevertheless a growing popular movement away from the traditional forms of Judaism and Christianity. This is reflected in the number of inter-faith marriages. In 1957, only 6% of Americans had a spouse of a different faith. By 1988, that percentage had climbed to 17% of Protestants, 22% of Jews and 38% of Catholics. In a 1983 *Time* magazine survey, 60% of North American churchgoers agreed with the statement: "Most churches have lost the real spiritual part of religion." Instead, Western people are looking to some Eastern traditions to see what they might offer. They are finding that no single religion provides the answer to their quest — and that religion is not the same as spirituality — and are concluding that dogmatic religious beliefs are often the most divisive of elements in a world searching for global spiritual unity. How many Gods are there?

Fundamentalist Islam is both the most dogmatic and most divisive of belief systems; many Muslims think of the world not as divided into first, second and third, but as split between Muslim and non-Muslim. The basic reason for the fervent revival of the Islamic religion — and the splits it has produced — was the introduction into Muslim communities of Western technology and education. To make effective use of this technology and Western methods generally, many citizens had to be educated in the West. Even when the teachers were Muslim, the curriculum was inevitably permeated by secular Western ideas and values. In many Muslim countries, the outlook of the great majority of the better-educated citizens has consequently become more Western. But the introduction of Western technology also led to social disruption, such as we saw in Iran, and a loss of old securities. When combined with the wide acceptance of Western secular ideas, it was not surprising that many people, even those with a Western outlook, felt a loss of traditional Muslim identity.

The Islamic resurgence is primarily a reassertion of that cultural identity to the exclusion of others. Islam thus has problems adapting to what is an evolving global culture. The split between militant traditionalism and evangelical Islam will continue to widen. The former, as in Iran, could spread to Iraq and Syria in reaction to economic reform and Soviet (socialist) interference. On the other hand, evangelical Islam, as in Egypt, achieves a balance between public law (often semi-Westernized), private religion and family life. This reformed Islam is conducive to devotion to family, community, brotherhoods and societies, not outright devotion to Islam itself. Ultimately, therefore, the Islamic fervor of Iran must moderate if it is to retain any credibility in the global community.

Beyond Materialism and Individualism

Values finally come down to a matter of identity. Each person, group or community has a tendency to assume that their paramount values are shared by human beings everywhere. Clearly this is not the case. We are a plurality of distinct communities and civilizations; each has its own substructure of paramount values. While this is all too obvious, it bears repeating to remind us that Western ways need not, and probably will not, prevail in the 21st-Century.

Instead, there is a growing sense that there does exist a universal common logic shared by all people — one metaphysical pool of universal human thought upon which we can all draw. This cosmic consciousness seems best manifested in Asian societies, which derive their cultural and political strengths, and thereby their primary sustaining values, from religious or quasi-religious belief systems that comprehensively address life in its entirety. Hinduism, Buddhism, Confucianism, Islam and Shinto all converge in not viewing the individual as separable from the group he or she belongs to or represents — be it the family, the caste — or the human race.

With the strong global emergence of Asian value systems, we are coming to the end of an age in which problems have been exclusively defined in Western materialistic terms. Instead, people are beginning to assert that it is impossible for them to realize their full humanity in a totally secularized world where no value is assigned to immeasurable qualities such as rectitude, sharing, mutual obligation, inner peace, and harmony with nature.

The progression towards individualism — the all-American trait — seems to be reaching a point of diminishing returns. As Western society industrialized, values were increasingly influenced by materialistic and economic factors. Transcendent spiritual values and goals became steadily less influential. In 2nd-Wave society, knowledge about wholesome human values, ethics and behavior became neglected, and economic rationality substituted as a pseudo-ethic. It was assumed that fulfillment came from the consumption of scarce resources, and the goals of the economy became the goals of society. We were taught to think of employment as a by-product of economic production — keep production rising and people would have jobs. Thus, meaningful work became a scarce commodity, and a job was the individual's primary way of relating to society, of making a personal contribution and receiving affirmation in return.

As Stanford University social scientist Willis Harman has often noted, the most basic, tacitly held premises of industrial society are increasingly questioned, marking this as a period of fundamental transformation in world affairs. Every previous world transformation has rested on a new metaphysical and ideological base; or rather, as Lewis Mumford said, "Upon deeper stirrings and institutions whose rationalized expression takes the form of a new picture of the cosmos and the nature of man."

Today, there are encouraging signs that global society is starting to enter a new cultural phase that will be dominated by values oriented to life and vitality and by the strongly intensified values of togetherness and community. Numerous studies show that high on our value scale now is a delight in vital and healthy lives, enjoyment of physical fitness, co-operation between the sexes, and general well-being. The strongest rising values relate to togetherness and community, to co-operation between people, both locally and globally.

Cultural Mixing

Such new world relationships are readily discernible in our culture. Cultures change in many ways, but essentially they are a product of social mixing — and now we are mixing like never before. As we acquire knowledge and ideas from each other, we reduce the differences between our diverse cultures. Global cultural integration is being strongly brought about by a global flow of information, technology, money and people across national boundaries. As economic boom times come again in the 21st-Century, international population flows will become easier and easier — as has always occurred in boom times. As more large geographic common markets like Europe are created, the free movement of people across borders to live, work or play will become increasingly commonplace.

As long as human communities have existed, there have been places where people have done well and where innovation and effort were rewarded by increase in numbers, growing strength, comparative stability and general social and economic progress. The most dynamic economic area today is East Asia at large. The circulation of not only goods but ideas intensifies in such areas; their traditions and ways of life become examples for other areas far and near. These "cultural hearths" are the sources of civilization, from where radiate the ideas, innovations and ideologies that eventually change the world. As this occurs, the self-feeding spiral of migration and inter-racial mixing will continue. Inter-racial marriages will increase, and families will be scattered across different countries in the ultimate extended cultural family of the global village.

Cultural mixing is thus yet another manifestation of the 4-STEP process:

1) Socio-psychological processes: the tendency to "do things the way your new neighbors do" and to resist the conservatism of traditional societies;
2) Technological processes: these open up boundless opportunities presented by new ideas and innovations;

3) Economic processes: as cultures gain affluence and well-being, their values and aspirations shift; and

4) Political processes: highlight new ways in which society can be governed.

As a result of these processes internationally, 4th-Wave communication across the globe is constantly increasing the quantity of knowledge and information available. For better or worse, these exchanges and contacts, propagated by the uniform dissemination of instant news, the same television series, and the same musical rhythms, tend to be accompanied by a growing standardization of tastes and behavior and a homogenization of certain patterns of life, thought and action, and of production and consumption. As we move into the Information Age, the diffusion of culture becomes contagious and spread over wide areas at a rapid pace. In the past, when cultures of different strength made contact, the stronger culture usually swallowed up the weaker. Stronger cultures still impose many of their attributes on weaker ones but, in today's world, each culture serves as both source and adopter of different values, ideas and innovations.

In other words, we are increasingly witness to the transculturation of world affairs. Today, for example, a total of 400 satellites encircle the world. These "tom-toms" of the electronic global village will bring the world together as never before. Satellite telephone links, multinational business and satellite TV are an instantaneous and ever-present, constantly switched-on, form of trans-global cultural interchange and entertainment. Increasingly, people are encountering other cultures in their everyday lives, discovering other values, observing attitudes unfamiliar to them, and thereby coming to know the many faces of humanity. Cultural groups cannot exist in total isolation in the electronic global village. The eruption of other cultures into every home becomes a permanent fact.

Globalization of the media will speed up through the 1990s and into the 21st-Century, with enormous implications, influencing the way people around the world feel about each other. Global television, representing another step towards a single, unitary global society, is already bringing many countries and groups together. The Chinese have watched Hong Kong broadcasts for years. In Europe, many Hungarians, East Germans and Czechs watch West German and Austrian TV, even though their governments disapprove. Global television thus can break through barriers of misinformation, propaganda and myth. It can change people's perceptions by exposing them to other values, beliefs and cultures. We will gradually move away from Western monoculture towards an ecology of diverse global cultures. Rather than gawking at the essentially uncultured "plastic" of cheap Hollywood movies and trashy soap operas, North Americans can learn to appreciate the facets of a hundred other truly rich cultures. Its the same in other countries. In this way, we can grow closer together as we develop our global cultural mosaic — something that Americans, thankfully, have failed to "melt" down within their own nation state. Global television involves all of us, simultaneously.

Electronic speed brings social and political functions together to heighten human awareness. The Olympic games or political summits are media events, slotted into prime-time viewing hours in New York — or Moscow. The world is a stage and we are all part of both the program and the audience. This implodes or fuses together our cultures and the way we feel and understand about each other.

As this occurs, humanity will finally complete a total transition from 1st-Wave food gatherers to become 4th-Wave "information gatherers" and 5th-Wave "culture gatherers." As Alvin Toffler observed, in 1st-Wave society, cultural knowledge was stored and updated — live — in the heads of the elders of the tribe. In the manufacturing age, our information bank took on a new form, in libraries full of books. Now, with the microcomputer connected to satellite, the members of the new global tribe are global information nomads, searching the global village for information and cultural nourishment. Electronic speed, as Marshall McLuhan told us, thus mixes the cultures of pre-history with those of the so far uncultured Post-Industrial Age. The whole world is temporarily suspended between two technological revolutions and consequently is suffering a cultural lag. Eventually, however, our social and cultural data bank will synthesize across ideologies and cultures. Information is the global integrator. For example, several hundred students at Tufts University in Massachusetts and at Moscow State University are linked once a month to discuss issues such as the 1962 Cuban missile treaty, global environment, disarmament, and relations between developed and developing countries.

Language is another predominant factor in transculturation. In the modern world, the universal language of trade, commerce, science and technology and general communication is English, suitably modified by technical buzzwords and computerese. Apple Computer is designing a "Global Education Network" which uses English as the language of instruction. As different computer languages evolve, with different systems of artificial intelligence, and as global economic and political activity grows, the planet will increasingly be united by the English language. Not that everyone will have to learn English; computerized translation systems will smash the language barriers that now keep us culturally isolated.

Another global common language is music. Musical ideas — melodic, structural, rhythmic, stylistic, from many cultures rapidly reach receptive audiences around the globe. Transistor radios as far afield as the Pacific Islands and African villages are links in the worldwide system of musical dissemination, another transcultural phenomenon. As well, through increased tourism, thousands upon thousands of people are being exposed to different styles of clothing, music, art and food. The internationalization of taste is widespread as restaurants serving a wealth of the world's cuisines spring up everywhere providing many with a taste of other cultures in a very direct way — yet another subtle but large-scale cultural "learning" process with immense global ramifications.

Cultures, guided by values and beliefs, are ultimately ways of building civilizations. Civilization grows from richness of culture which itself begins in the cult. But today the cult is globalism and we are building a global civilization. People are growing tired of dogmas that mean less and less to increasingly intelligent humans in a science and technology driven world. With the rapid rate of these trends, transglobal culture should reach maturity well before 2050. The present search for spiritual meaning will probably culminate in the latter part of the 21st-Century in a surge, not yet of religious monism, but of what I call "harmonic globalism" as people realize they are all part of a single global community consciousness.

G-Force S-9

Educating the Future:
10-Billion Super-Brains

"Education is the answer for all the problems of the world."
— Lyndon B. Johnson

Education enables people to do what they have never done before. The world's biggest single requirement, bar none, is to maximize its human potential. People are our greatest resource, and we must therefore invest in their brain-power — the "intellectual capital" with which our genuinely rich future will be built and sustained. The world already has 5-billion of the finest "computers" that will ever be developed — human brains. During the past hour, 12,000 children have been born around the world, and every one of them has a potential intelligence greater than any genius alive today. By the year 2050, there will be close to 10-billion such brains. The vast majority of them are waiting to be given intelligence. This untapped capability by far represents the strongest G-Force for reinventing the world. Educated people will overwhelm any other force.

"Growing" People
In his book *The Wealth of Nations*, published in 1776, Adam Smith observed that "the skill, dexterity and knowledge of a nation's people is the most powerful engine of its economic growth." This "intellectual capital" — not the energy, forests, cropland or other physical properties of the Earth — is our most important economic resource, the untapped wealth that will be decisive in meeting the aspirations and needs of the world. Investments in improving the quality of people through schooling, work skills and work experience are the best possible way to ensure our own future personal satisfaction. As the Chinese proverb teaches us: "If you are planning for a year, grow rice; if you are planning for 20 years, grow trees; if you are planning for a century, grow people."

We must focus on the "growing" of people. Increases in the acquired abilities and knowledge of people hold the key to future economic well-being in both developed and developing societies. Successful industrial growth in the West is the direct result of higher education. Unfortunately for the Third World, knowledgeable human beings have been relatively immobile on the globe, unlike Western financial capital, which travels far. But Western information and knowledge are increasingly mobile and, in the 4th-Wave society, become globalized, not just by people coming to the West to study but, more importantly, by the transfer of knowledge to the Third World.

Students in the Third World leave school with far fewer skills than their counterparts in the West, who are exposed to schools of substantially higher quality. The West has discovered that exposure to education does not guarantee literacy, but it is generally true that the poorer the country, the fewer the cognitive skills its people acquire by the end of primary school. Yet, because education is so critical for development in these countries, even a poor education (in basic mathematics, science and reading) develops better farmers and administrators, and mothers with healthier children. School enrollment in the Third World has increased dramatically in recent decades. Though the worst situation is in Africa, where only 36% were enrolled in 1980 (versus 29% in 1970), Asia achieved 71% enrollment (up from 28% in 1970) and Latin America stood at 81% (up from 37%). By 1990, about 90% of Third World children should be attending school.

Educational quality is another matter. Schools in the poorer countries generally have few resources, so they cannot effectively pass on the increasingly complex skills required in today's world. Better-quality teaching methods and tools are needed if education is to have a significant effect on pupils' achievement. For a start, government spending must be refocussed. For example, India spends nearly $4-billion a year on education, but this is still less than it spends on defense. Even though the national literacy rate has more than doubled from a mere 16% at Independence in 1947 to over 40% today, with redirected greater spending the rate would be much higher. In China, educational spending has increased from 5.9% of GNP in 1978 to 9.5% in 1986, while in the same period military spending declined from over 14% of GNP to less than 8%. Even then, many programs are still insufficiently funded and many schools are inadequately staffed and poorly equipped.

In the Third World, investments in primary education yield bigger economic returns than investments in higher education. World Bank studies indicate that farmers with four years of primary education produce 13% more, on average, than farmers with no schooling. As part of its economic modernization plans, China has thus mandated a phased-in nine-year compulsory program of education for all citizens. Junior secondary school education will be universal in all urbanized areas by 1990 and for 50% of the country's population by 1995. Education for girls and young women is also one of the best investments a country can make towards its economic growth and human welfare. As already discussed, when mothers are educated, families are better fed, children are less likely to die and fewer children are born. Education therefore determines trends in mortality and population growth. Consequently, an increase in the school-age population and the quality of its education will increase national economic growth — and hence the funding available for yet more education in the future.

Mass education does not require the building of expensive schools. Rather, modern technology makes mass education in the Third World inexpensive. Television educational programs beamed in by satellite can provide "class-rooms" in even the remotest areas. A single village TV set can serve as a means of education for up to about 100 people at a time. The traditional infrastructure of classrooms is not required, and the equipment costs less than $1 per student per year. In India, just such a program was launched in 1976, and it has vastly improved both the quality and the quantity of education in the villages. It would be a mammoth task to bring conventional education to all 560,000 vil-lages in India, but the creation of a Third World "space education" system could expedite the process at the lowest cost of any form of educational delivery. Teachers will still be necessary but the placing into orbit of a few satellites would make mass education via television commonplace across the Third World in the 21st-Century.

We therefore need to establish an international "educational order" to close the knowledge gap between the developing countries and the West. The first priority is to guarantee a basic education for all. Increased co-operation among countries and regions, perhaps creating centers of excellence in science and tech-nology, would also help countries in their efforts to modernize education. Many more exchanges of teachers and students between the regions and the provision of transnational inter-cultural educational courses through telecommunications systems would also move things along much faster. Perhaps this all needs to be done through the creation of a "Global Education Council," with national counterparts, and an experimental "International University of the Future" — a university without walls, operating through electronic networks and focussing on the permanent study of how education can be adapted to the world of tomorrow.

Futurizing the Curriculum

The next priority is to improve teaching methods and the curriculum to provide an education that is constantly geared to a changing future. Above all, we must place an emphasis on "learning to learn," whereby people can find their way through ever more complex labyrinths of information. There is too much to learn. We need, as a basic principle, to know where to find knowledge (not to know it "off by heart"), to learn to differentiate good (valuable, relevant, up to date) information from poor information, and to learn to manage and apply knowledge in long-term planning and decision-making. The prime objective of teaching this new curriculum should be to develop the students' ability to adapt as quickly and easily as possible to a constantly changing world. The teacher becomes a "facilitator" of learning (not a teacher) and the student becomes a "learner" (not a student) such that education becomes the promotion of learning to learn. Those who do not learn will become the peasants of the Information Age. Societies that do not give all their people future-related education will be left behind. As Winston Churchill observed: "The empires of the future are the empires of the mind."

The future, of course, is automatically built into the education system — the kids who enrolled in kindergarten in 1986 (at least in the West) will graduate at the dawn of the next century. In a very real sense "the future is now," and yet we have only a vague idea about what these graduates will need to know. Like so many Western institutions that have served us well in the Industrial Age, education fell behind the times in the late-1970s and is now scrambling to find a new future for itself in the Information Age. With higher education paramount to future success, paradoxically it is the universities that are most seriously behind. They have generally failed to make their course offerings future relevant or to update their mode of delivery, thereby allowing teacher training to fall behind. As T.S. Eliot once asked, "Where is the wisdom we have lost in knowledge? Where is the knowledge we have lost in information?" We must re-invent education: bring it into phase with new social aspirations, the new technologies, the new information/knowledge economy and the new politics of 4th-Wave society — a thorough reform of the curriculum and its delivery.

The core curriculum hasn't changed for years. In the West, it is still founded on the basic building blocks of reading, writing and arithmetic. Under stress and spurred on by alarmed parents, who recognize that their children are poorly equipped for the modern world and ill-advisedly blame their child's unpreparedness on poor basic skills, the education system is trying to go "back to basics." This knee-jerk reaction, if carried out, would condemn our children to backwardness. We cannot simplistically go back to old basics. Instead we need to ask: "What needs to be learned by students who will be productive citizens in 2050?" In short, we need to identify the "future basics."

The new basics will include some of the old basics but much of the old content and way of teaching will be changed. We are living in a different world, which demands new skills. For example, we do not need to spend so many months of a child's schooling on rote learning of mathematical tables, which in everyday life a machine will calculate for them. Nobody does math in the real world of work except by calculator or computer — at least in the West. Moreover, voice-activated technology will make even keyboarding skills obsolete in the late-1990s. What we need to understand are math calculation concepts, how they are applied, and to know when the machine is providing a correct answer.

Computers are also changing how we read and write. As Marshall McLuhan told us, "electronics reverses all process." Experiments with thousands of preschool children across the United States have demonstrated that students who use computers can learn to write before they can read — the reverse of what happens in traditional education. These children can write down (that is, type onto the computer screen) anything they are able to say and are significantly more literate than their peers in traditional schools. New technology also changes language structure. Like the telegraph, telex, telephone and television before it, the computer changes sentence structure, grammar and forms of expression. Business sentences get truncated, political concepts shortened into 30-second sound bites. This will change again with voice-activated machines, because we all speak quite differently than we write. The traditional rules of language are in for a shake-up.

Consequently, the basics of education must always change in parallel with the 4-STEP process of change. Future educational basics must therefore be supplemented to include:

1) Social skills, especially family studies, multicultural studies, communications/human relations skills of all kinds, negotiating skills, and a capacity for self-analysis and identity;

2) Technological skills, especially the ability to understand the capability of modern technology, to be able to function with computers (but not necessarily to program them);

3) Economic skills, especially information synthesis and management, economic management, generalist skills and the management of change; and

4) Political skills, especially civic education about important social issues, goals and purposes, costs and benefits, and the ethics of citizenship and political leadership.

The citizens of the future must have additional basics in their tool kit if we are to build a better world. These comprise the three elements of geo-strategic thinking skills: a global and futuristic perspective; creative/opportunistic thinking abilities; and risk-taking/entrepreneurial/action-leadership skills. Each of these needs to be incorporated into the curriculum from kindergarten through to PhD. Only by learning to understand the future do people lose their fear of it. Only by learning to take risks do people become able to make decisions about the future. And only by learning to think creatively can people turn problems into opportunities.

The curriculum must also recognize that knowledge becomes obsolete rather quickly in the 4th-Wave Information Age. The curriculum (and the educational system itself) must therefore be geared to update knowledge throughout people's lives. This concept of lifelong learning gains importance when the continuing educational needs of an aging population are taken into account. More and more "retired" people are seeking new knowledge to keep up with the changing times. In 1983 in China, the world's first university for the elderly was established in Shangdong Province. By the end of 1987, China had established 221 such universities with a total of 70,000 students, plus 188 schools for the elderly where 40,000 people have finished their high school studies. This novel concept, which to my knowledge has not yet been taken up elsewhere, enables the elderly to further enrich their lives and enhance their social roles.

Computers: Stopping Factory Schooling

The Industrial Age spawned the still prevalent mass-production model of education — factories of learning. Today's students are hungry for information relevant to the future. Mass education with rote learning bores them to death and drives them to frustration, if not right out of the system. While boredom is not the only reason, all studies show it to be predominant. In Toronto, 32.4% of students drop out before they reach Grade 12. It is much the same across North America. Instead, many watch television, which is far more entertaining. Even those who stay in high school watch an average of 28 hours of TV a week — about the same amount of time spent in the classroom — and only 4 hours doing homework. To try to overcome this dropout problem, in the 1960s and 1970s Western education debated the best pupil-teacher ratios to guarantee quality education. In the 1980s, it started debating pupil-computer ratios (now one for every 22 students in the U.S.A.) in an attempt to achieve individualized learning. Computers turn kids on; they don't drive them away. The computer is the ideal tool for individualized learning: you can learn at your own speed, review material, synthesize information and get feedback. Yet you can still learn in a group setting.

A wide range of educational software is currently available for teaching elementary- and high-school-level skills and concepts. The supply of pedagogically sound software has improved dramatically in recent years. You no longer see factual or logical errors in programs, or ill-suited graphics. Soon there will be exciting software that moves beyond multiple-choice drill and practice routines to offer training in a variety of skills or advice of a tutorial nature. New technologies thus give us an added margin of flexibility in teaching and research, and represent one of the greatest opportunities for change in the history of education. They reduce costs and provide wider access — the basis for profound and pervasive changes in education not only in the West but all over the world.

It has been suggested that the only significant boost to instructional productivity since the time of Socrates was the introduction of large lecture halls and lecture-recitation courses. It still took the educational community 200-years to adopt the textbook as a teaching mechanism. Let's hope we don't take 200-years to get rid of it and adopt computerized learning. We now find that the new technology boosts the efficiency and productivity of the education system. In some cases computerized learning has halved education costs within five-years and significantly speeded up the educational/learning process.

Computers break the time barriers marked by the ringing of the school bell, allowing 24-hour learning, in school, in learning centers or even at home. Students can thus also learn according to their own biological clocks (morning people, evening people). And with remote electronic learning, or "distance education" learning can take place at any time or place in the electronic global village — instantly. Using the old correspondence-school model, the Open University in the U.K., using BBC-TV, pioneered electronic learning. Now, distance education commonly delivers education to remote parts of such countries as Canada and Australia.

Several major universities and corporations in the U.S.A. have teamed up to create the first electronic university — National Technological University (NTU) — which broadcasts 150 graduate-level courses via satellite to some 20,000 working engineers and scientists at more than 80 corporate office locations. Now widely recognized and accepted, NTU awards masters degrees in computer science, electrical engineering, engineering management and manufacturing systems. About one third of the broadcasts are "live-interactive"; the rest are delayed broadcasts of live classes. Students can view videotapes at their convenience; if they still have questions, they can call the professor — electronically. As well, tests and homework are transmitted through an electronic mail system.

In the Netherlands, the major institute responsible for distance education recently introduced electronic mail capabilities to speed assignments between students and tutors who use the system for 48 courses. Such systems allow courses to be shared between other universities or with students in other regions or countries. Hundreds of American campuses already have satellite facilities and hundreds more have access to satellite technology through local TV stations. In the United States in 1988, there were over 50 educational networks and an individual course can be received via satellite by a school or university anywhere in North America for an institutional cost of only $12,000 per year. By 1993, an estimated 500 such educational networks will be available to North Americans. Apple Computer's "Global Education Network" aims to link at least one school in every nation by 1991 and to have 1000 schools on the system — from New York to Moscow to Beijing — by 1993.

This network will break down cultural and geographic barriers and demolish classroom walls and educational jurisdictions. Everywhere, students of the future will "telecommute" into databases. These database "schools" will attract several millions of learners who will have access to the best in global education at minimal cost. Agriculture students in Zaire could learn pest control from Iowa State University. Economics students in America could exchange information with finance officials from Buenos Aires. Ultimately, the computer will have the capacity to reach every individual in the world and provide better access to up-to-date knowledge that will both enrich their personal lives and provide a consensus of views that will give them more control over their collective destinies.

As we re-invent education, so will we re-invent our world. The most abundant and prolific natural resource — the unique human resource of brain and mind — remains essentially untapped. This untapped human potential, once turned loose, will toss a host of global problems into the blackhole of history by the year 2050 and beyond.

Section "T"

G-Forces of
Technological Innovation

Section ???

Causes of
Technological Innovation

Overview

Creating the Info–Rich Leisure Society

"Technology not only relieves us of a crushing weight of physical and mental labor but it constantly increases the scope and clarity of our perceptions, satisfying our instinctive craving for the maximum of consciousness with a minimum of effort! Having embarked upon so profitable a path, how can mankind fail to pursue it?"
— Teilhard de Chardin

How *can* we fail to pursue technology's benefits? Technology has become part of humanity's evolution. Technology is us: it is our know-how, extending our range, taking us to a constantly better future. Stemming from the basic human G-Forces that aspire to satisfy the 6-wave hierarchy of human needs, a new burst of technology is starting to pave the way for the creation of the new 4th-, 5th- and 6th-Wave societies we all crave. Technology is redistributing global manufacturing activity to, and generating new wealth in, the Third World. Technological innovations are transforming and globalizing the economy through planetary telecommunications networks that operate 24-hours-a-day, making international transactions instantaneous and building a "real-time" (constantly switched-on, never-sleeping) global information economy. We are developing previously inconceivable fields in high-technology that will solve old problems and create new opportunities. In short, the world is being reinvented as we push back the frontiers of technological research, all the way from the micro (inner-space) to the macro (outer-space) levels. As the second step in the 4-STEP process of global social development, this scientific and technological reinvention process is transforming society and the economy, and will ultimately transform political structures.

Understanding Technology's Unlimited Potential

Many people are skeptical about the potential of technology despite its widespread daily use, because they know little about it. To most human beings, advanced technology is essentially indistinguishable from magic, particularly when innovations first appear. Indeed, each breakthrough tends to make most people think that we have reached the limits of scientific and technological advance. Whereas this mixture of disbelief and intellectual smugness is nothing new, it is unfounded. There are no technological limits. Scientifically, almost anything is possible. Old technologies are almost always replaced by newer and better ones. The following quotations illustrate how technology's potential is always underestimated, even by experts:

"The advancement of the art of invention from year to year seems to presage the arrival of that period when further improvement must end."
   - Henry Ellsworth, U.S. Commissioner of Patents (1844)

"Everything that can be invented has been invented."
   - Director, U.S. Patent Office (1899)

"Heavier-than-air flying machines are impossible. Radio has no future. X-rays will prove to be a hoax."
   - Lord Kelvin, President, Royal Society (1890-5)

"The energy produced by the breaking down of the atom is a very poor kind of thing. Anyone who looks for a source of power in the transformation of the atom is talking moonshine."
   - Sir Ernest Rutherford, Atomic Physicist (1923)

"I think there is a world market for about five computers."
   - Thomas Watson, C.E.O. of IBM (1943)

These and many more false predictions prompted Arthur C. Clarke to come up with this maxim regarding the phenomenon of expert misprediction:
   "When a distinguished but elderly scientist states something is possible, he is almost certainly right. When he states that something is impossible, he is very probably wrong."

Understanding Technology's Impacts

Even though it is obvious that anything is technologically possible, lots of people have negative feelings about the effects of technology. Technology is not infallible, but the fear and caution it inspires reveal a shortsighted misunderstanding about its essential major role in global human development. Forecasting the long-term cycles of technological development and its socio-economic effect is very complex. Nevertheless, only three simple criteria must be met in order to implement technological innovation:

- Social Criteria: The technology must be socially acceptable (it must satisfy people's aspirations and they must enjoy using it);
- Technology Criteria: The technology must be technically feasible (it must function efficiently in performing tasks and in relation to other technologies); and

- Economic Criteria: The technology must be economically viable (it must generate real gains in wealth for the greatest number of people possible).

By the same token, we need to understand that technology has social, technological and economic effects.

Social Impact of Technology

Technology's social and environmental effects are so complex that they have become the main subject of many books. The most famous is Marshall McLuhan's brilliant and farsighted classic, *Understanding Media*, which taught us that "the medium (the technology) is the message." Every technology serves as an extension of human capabilities and behavior. The screwdriver (or any other hand tool) is an extension of the human arm and hand. (This is why weapons are called arms or armaments.) The automobile (or any other form of transportation) extends our ability to move about.

Every technology affects its environment and its users. Automobiles created the need for highways, spawned shopping centers, and have dictated the urban design of North America so as to suit — at least initially — the human demand for convenience and economic efficiency. This design superstructure also changed work patterns and job locations, and often created deserted downtowns that people feared to visit. The automobile itself became a symbol of status and a haven for personal refuge. It provided the means to a rural escape from the increasingly congested urban environment and virtually eliminated walking, which had a negative effect on health — as, of course, did exhaust fumes.

Clearly, technology has positive and negative social and environmental effects. In general, however, it should be noted that the new wave of high technologies (such as microelectronics, artificial intelligence, super-computers, communications and biotechnology) does not deplete resources, uses energy extremely economically and has a lower impact on the natural environment than do old technologies.

By and large, these new technologies are highly socially acceptable, because we are inventing them in order to further satisfy our collective social needs and aspirations. Fig. 9, adapted from the work of Japan's information-age mastermind, Yoneji Masuda, plots the effects of computer-communications technology on social development. The emerging wave of biotechnological developments (not shown) will have other economic and socially regenerative capacities. For example, in industrial microbiology, the efficient use of abundant microbial resources will produce energy and food, process waste and other materials and cure numerous diseases.

In Third World societies, more and better technology is essential. Their choice is not between adopting "alternative" or "appropriate" technologies on the one hand and Western-style industrialization on the other. Rather, the Third World must adopt elements of both. Technology is not socially benign; I do not dismiss the need for cultural sensitivity in its transfer. But excessive concern in this regard will trap the Third World in 1st- and 2nd-Wave backwardness. There

107

Fig. 9 Effects of Computer-Communications Technology

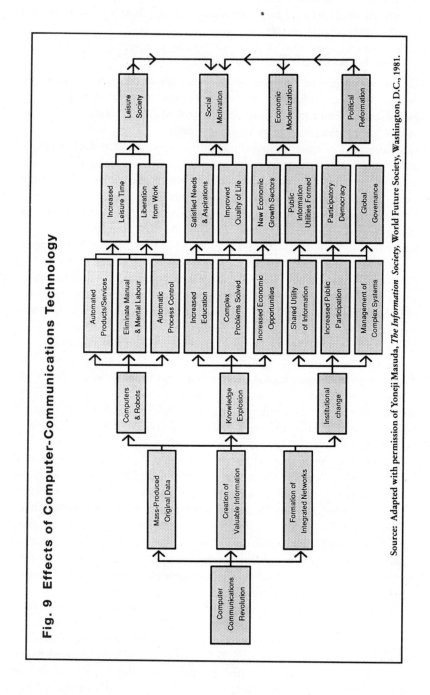

Source: Adapted with permission of Yoneji Masuda, *The Information Society*, World Future Society, Washington, D.C., 1981.

is but one 4-STEP process of social development, and its optimal success demands the application of the latest technologies available.

But, as Iran demonstrated, without economic benefit or political reform, there will, at best, be limited social benefit and hence no developmental progress. When progress is retarded, society rebels. The Shah of Iran focussed his efforts almost exclusively on military technology. While there is much evidence to support the argument that the drive for military supremacy spurs innovation, in the long run military innovations must prove themselves economically viable if they are to recoup their heavy initial investment and create a positive social benefit. Military technology must meet social criteria. Because of the basic human need for security, people will support the development of military technology during wartime or when threatened during peacetime. However, if military spending is seen to be detracting from people's basic economic security, and/or is not producing any readily apparent spin-off benefits into the civilian economy, people will demand a redirection of such investment to restore the overriding socio-economic progress that best meets their real aspirations for security. Hence, we see in the global village the recent momentum to forge a disarmament treaty and continuing worldwide public concern over Star Wars spending.

Developing countries face two dilemmas as they attempt to achieve socio-economic progress and statehood. They are aware of the negative social, economic and environmental effects of military and other technologies in the West. However, being anxious to develop and to catch up with the West, they must choose between military and civilian technologies, and also between financially affordable old technologies that are labor-intensive and pollute, and more expensive new ones that are not labor-intensive and are less environmentally damaging. Globally, much will be achieved to overcome this latter dilemma by transferring information and advanced technology (along with primary fabrication and manufacturing activity) to the Third World — that is, closer to the needed raw materials, labor and markets. The technologies transferred must be the latest available if they are to generate enough economic activity to foster national pride. Only in this way can the Third World stop feeling the need to concentrate on military technologies.

Ripple Effects of Technology

Any technology has a direct effect on, and also interacts with, other technologies or production processes. This effect is purely task-oriented and simple to understand: "hammer hits nail, nail sinks into wood." An individual piece of technology may also evolve further (the development of better airplanes or computers) or may be replaced by another generation of technology (facsimile copiers replacing telex machines). By discovering what is being developed in research laboratories, and anticipating how social aspirations might converge with new innovations, we can identify those future technologies that are likely to emerge and become widely used. We can also anticipate the interaction between disparate technologies. Microelectronics and biogenetics, for example will combine to produce biological computers with a human "intelligence" so advanced they will likely be capable of independently operating most of our technological infrastructures.

It is more difficult to understand a technology's indirect or "ripple" effects on industrial structures, consumer behavior and the economy at large. New technologies cannot normally operate economically unless an infrastructure is also put in place to adapt them to the needs, aspirations and capabilities of industry and potential customers. Computer hardware, for instance, is useless without software. Automobiles need highways; airplanes need airports. The value added (economic contribution) by the entire technology system often produces a greater ripple effect than that of the value added by the manufacture of the initial technology hardware. Simple computer software modernized the financial services sector in the 3rd-Wave services revolution. Sophisticated computer software and electronic networks are an even more valuable part of computer technology. They are spawning the 4th-Wave information sector, in which industrial firms can interconnect their telecommunications infrastructures and individuals with personal computers can send electronic mail and tap into global information banks.

Other ripple effects are more subtle and convoluted. Microwave ovens, for example, first appeared as a piece of "magic" that could cook very quickly, in an oven that did not get hot. In the 1960s, they were used only in restaurants. Their application spread with the growth of fast-food outlets that catered to consumers' demand to save time in food preparation and dishwashing. Many households formed by the baby boom generation make no time for cooking. Today in North America, 70% of households have a microwave oven. Ultimately, advanced versions of this technology will replace the old convection oven and further change industrial structures and employment levels.

The microwave is also changing the nature of the food we eat and our methods for preparing it. For example, the fact that metal objects cannot be placed in the microwave oven has spawned the production of new kinds of cookware, and is leading to the elimination of the metal soup can, since it cannot be placed in the oven to heat the soup. More importantly, baby boomers do not want to waste time opening the can, finding a saucepan to cook the soup in, diluting the soup, waiting for the stove to heat up, stirring the soup and washing up the saucepan, dish and spoon afterwards. This is why the soup manufacturers are producing soup — in a disposable plastic bowl, with a disposable plastic spoon attached — that is already diluted and ready to "heat and eat."

The ripple effects of microwave technology do not end there. The soup manufacturers are converting their production lines to make plastic bowls instead of metal cans. This not only changes the nature of jobs and necessitates different machinery; it also reduces the demand for metal and increases the demand for plastic. It changes the way soup is packed in cartons for shipping and the way it is displayed on store shelves. Finally, it worsens the garbage disposal problem: nonbiodegradable plastic bowls are taking the place of metal cans that will rust away.

Economic Impacts of Innovation

The pure economic effects of a technology usually depend on the magnitude of its innovation. Technological innovation comes from applied ideas. While innovative applications occur almost daily, major technical innovations seem to come in periodic bunches or waves, which spawn G-Forces of change. (The major bursts of technological innovation of the last century or so are shown in terms of their impact on the economy in Fig. 10, modified from economist Gerhard Mensch's concept.) When such a cluster of radical innovations occurs, it gives rise to a series of technological and related economic revolutions.

The so-called 2nd-Wave Industrial Revolution actually stretched over three "long-wave" technological cycles that began about 1760 and ended in 1933, at the lowest point of the Great Depression. The last of these technological cycles — which created what I call the 2nd-Wave manufacturing society — began in the mid-1870s, also a time of economic depression. It was based on a cluster of innovations, particularly in transportation (with the development of crude motor vehicles followed by that of rudimentary airplanes) and in communications (with the development of the telephone). It also gave rise to simple production-line processes and the widespread use of light metals, which found their way into the various products of the "modern" manufacturing society that lasted until about 1933.

World War II interrupted technological progress to an extent but spurred innovations in computing, microwaves and rocketry. By the 1950s and 1960s, a new technological revolution was coming to full strength on the basis of these and other commercially viable inventions. While the automobile came to full economic fruition during this period, the new revolution was characterized by new sources of energy (nuclear as well as oil substitutes) and by electronics, mainframe computers and jet airplanes. These innovations spurred the growth of the 3rd-Wave service sector of the economy, creating opportunities in computer manufacturing, which allowed increasing sophistication in the banking and financial–services industries.

As can be seen from the chart, technological (and hence economic) revolutions tend to overlap in a wavelike sequence. The beginning of the wave, when innovation first occurs, requires a great deal of investment in research and development and productive effort to generate economic results. For example, billions of dollars are spent in trying to develop advanced automobiles and tool

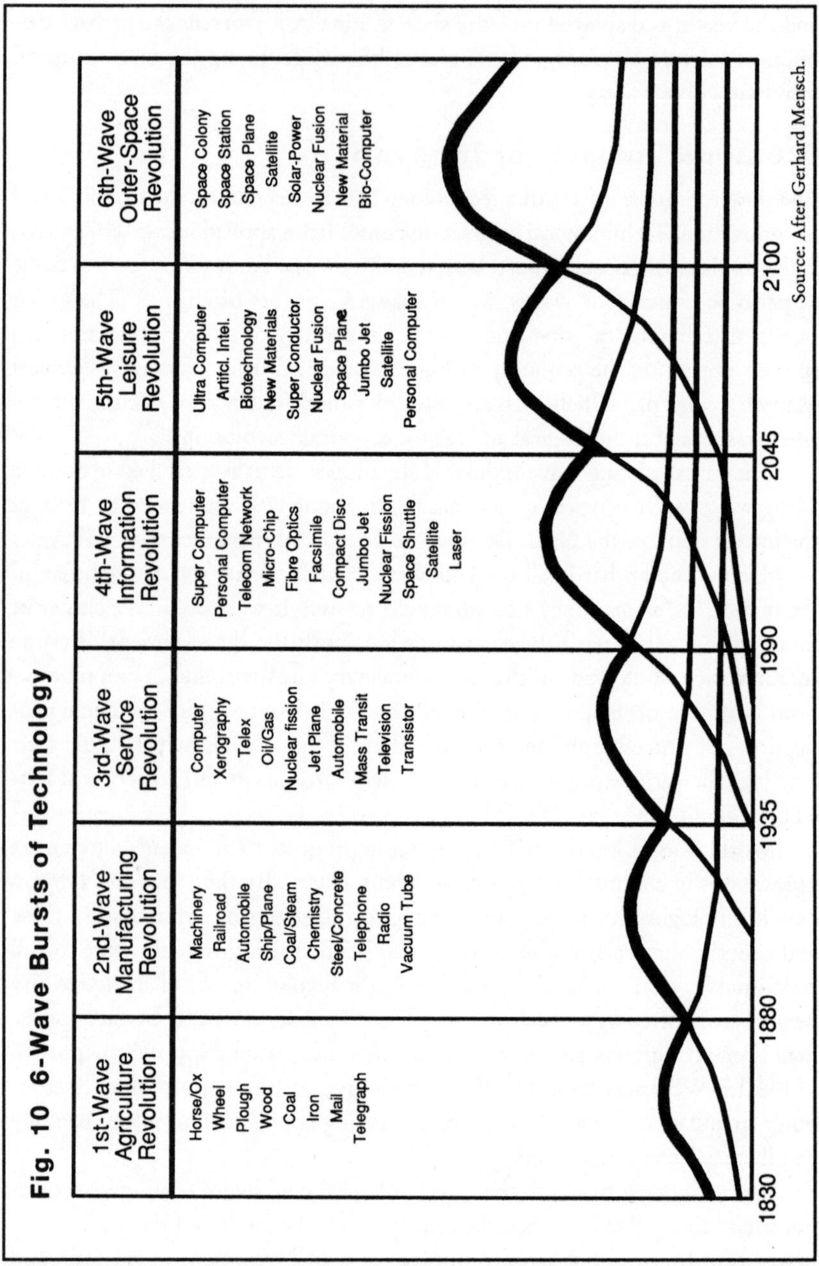

Fig. 10 6-Wave Bursts of Technology

1st-Wave Agriculture Revolution	2nd-Wave Manufacturing Revolution	3rd-Wave Service Revolution	4th-Wave Information Revolution	5th-Wave Leisure Revolution	6th-Wave Outer-Space Revolution
Horse/Ox	Machinery	Computer	Super Computer	Ultra Computer	Space Colony
Wheel	Railroad	Xerography	Personal Computer	Artifcl. Intel.	Space Station
Plough	Automobile	Telex	Telecom Network	Biotechnology	Space Plane
Wood	Ship/Plane	Oil/Gas	Micro-Chip	New Materials	Satellite
Coal	Coal/Steam	Nuclear fission	Fibre Optics	Super Conductor	Solar-Power
Iron	Chemistry	Jet Plane	Facsimile	Nuclear Fusion	Nuclear Fusion
Mail	Steel/Concrete	Automobile	Compact Disc	Space Plane	New Material
Telegraph	Telephone	Mass Transit	Jumbo Jet	Jumbo Jet	Bio-Computer
	Radio	Television	Nuclear Fission	Satellite	
	Vacuum Tube	Transistor	Space Shuttle	Personal Computer	
			Satellite		
			Laser		

Source: After Gerhard Mensch.

1830   1880   1935   1990   2045   2100

them for production, but the technology involved has little economic effect until cars start rolling off the production line, are sold, and put to economic use. Once technological development, learning and application are completed, however, a greater economic effect is generated with less investment or productive effort. But solid economic progress does not necessary last. After about 25-years, the wave of most technologies peaks and economic gains start to moderate. This is the point of diminishing economic returns; too much effort and expense are required to achieve minimal economic improvement. The wave turns downward as the technology wanes — or until it is upgraded or replaced.

The gap between two curves represents a period of technological and economic discontinuity. This occurs when one group of technologies is being replaced and/or supplemented by another, as we see today in the automation of factories and the rapid obsolescence of computers (as increasingly advanced models replace their predecessors). Because of this G-Force cycle of discontinuity, the best time to enhance or replace a technology is when it is working most successfully — just before its economic effects peak. However, this does not seem to happen. During an economic boom, we are lulled into expecting the good times to continue forever and tend to overinvest in existing productive capacity. Worse still, much of this investment comes from money borrowed against expected earnings. Then, when the economy turns down, a huge unserviceable debt "overhang" ensues — as, for example, in the North American "smokestack industries," which, by and large, have failed to innovate. Instead, they have resorted to excessive borrowing to stay competitive and maintain profits — and have become technologically noncompetitive. The best example of this disastrous strategy is the steel industry.

Government bailouts of dying, uncompetitive firms also have not helped them modernize and compete in the global economy. Even the seemingly successful bailout of Chrysler, because it took business away from General Motors and Ford and presented them with unfair competition, has weakened the U.S. auto sector's collective global competitive strength and has created unnecessary overcapacity in the North American auto industry. Chrysler should not have been bailed out. Investing in new technologies and firms, before the discontinuity stage in the economy is ever reached, is better than throwing good money after bad through last-ditch investment in maturing technologies and firms. Another problem is that investment is often misdirected into military spending (as we have seen in the 1980s in particular), which, except in the long run through possible spin-offs, produces no economic benefit.

Without farsighted resource allocation and investment in new technologies, the previous generation of technologies falls into maturity and economic nonproductivity before the new innovations reach full economic fruition. The overall result is that the total economy rides the "crest of the wave" (along the top of the consecutive waves of innovation in the chart). This creates a long-wave cycle

113

of economic booms and downturns. The industrialized world now faces a painful transition; the 4th-Wave information economy will not start to emerge in full strength until after the mid-1990s.

Information Technology as Wealth-Creator

Nevertheless, information is already coming into its own as the overwhelming source of improvement in economic productivity. It is fast becoming the essential component of all economic input (raw material) and output (products and services) in all six waves of the economy. You cannot operate a modern farm, factory, office, hospital or hotel without advanced and timely information. Information is what distinguishes superior products and services from poor ones. In the 4th-Wave information economy, information is the major raw material. Information-based technologies will be the major source of economic prosperity during the next long-wave cycle.

The late futurist John McHale observed that a key effect of current technological change, of considerable importance to the development of the global economy, is this emergence of information and organized knowledge as the basic economic resource — now reinforced by the integration of computers and telecommunications. This technologically driven shift in the economic resource base will change many aspects of global society. It used to be that one side had to lose if the other gained, because resources were too scarce to be shared. While resources such as raw materials and energy are still scarce and decreasing, information is inexhaustible: it is not depleted by wider use. True, it can become obsolete or lose economic value through its competitive application as a component of end products (as in bringing about rapid reductions in the price of personal computers). But information as a raw product gains value when it is widely distributed and exchanged. While most products depreciate in value, information appreciates the more it is used. When more information becomes accessible to people, albeit at reduced cost, the total volume of activity in the information economy expands exponentially and knowledge explodes to new levels of advancement; its value is enhanced yet again, which more than offsets any diminished value of the old information.

Human survival and prosperity will be predicated on the sharing of abundant information and information-based technologies — on everyone winning — through co-operation in generating knowledge, rather than competition for information resources. Otherwise, a massive "information gap" between rich and poor would severely retard economic progress across the world — even in nations that attempted to keep their information to themselves. Information is of limited use and diminishing value to them unless they sell it in the wider global market — and create in that market the purchasing power with which to buy it.

Regardless of the orientation of economic policy towards information and technology transfer in specific nations, the planet as a whole must and will move towards economic modernization and global economic interdependence. We are learning that information is the common denominator of this change and of the creation of wealth. Information and other leading-edge technologies offer the opportunity to build a global information infrastructure and, through it, to distribute wealth worldwide.

This is the essential second step in the 4-STEP process of creating global prosperity and furthering social development. Its success depends on the speed of diffusion of new technology and information throughout the global economy.

G-Force T-1
Eliminating Hard Work— Creating Leisure Society

"Leisure is the last product of civilization."
— Malcolm Muggeridge

The driving force for all technological advances is based on the human penchant for finding easier and more efficient ways of doing things in order to provide time for other activities (mostly intellectual and recreational pursuits) or for doing nothing at all — that is, to create leisure time, however people choose to define it. Western economies are succeeding magnificently at putting themselves out of work. They have reduced the number of hours devoted to human labor from 12-hours-a-day, 7-days-a-week (mostly on the land) to 7-hours-a-day, 5-days-a-week (mostly in the office). Every major technological revolution brings about a major reduction in working hours. As the 4th-Wave electronic revolution takes firmer hold, we are racing — at electronic speed — towards the "leisure society" that we have craved for the last 2000 years. We will see working hours reduced drastically — to 24-hours or fewer per week by the end of the 1990s — for most Western populations.

Eliminating Work

As explained in the Social Section, human beings are at once physically lazy and intellectually energetic. While we say we subscribe to the "work ethic," we constantly use brains instead of brawn to improve efficiency. Our highly developed intellectual curiosity leads to the route of least physical effort. While we have built the pyramids of Egypt and the cities of Athens and New York, least physical effort is the maxim which determines the criteria for the intelligent planning of our enterprises. In the 4th-Wave information society, this process will be accelerated, bringing the 5th-Wave leisure society more rapidly within our grasp.

Every technological revolution in human history has reduced the number of hours during which human beings are required to work, whether the labor be physical or mental. For example, automation in the Western textile industry has continuously reduced its human labor input to a mere 0.1% of what it was two centuries ago. The latest technological revolution — microelectronic technology — has yet to have a significant effect on working hours in Western countries. Although computers have handled an increasing volume of work without the need for more humans, the reduction in working hours during the 1970s and 1980s has been modest. But the introduction of artificial intelligence systems in the 1990s will eliminate the laborious, production-line, paper-shuffling, clerical tasks in today's 3rd-Wave "paper-factories," just as robots transformed the 2nd-Wave manufacturing production lines. Recent studies show that the intensive use of automation in the West over the next 20-years alone will allow significant economies in labor. In one Carnegie-Mellon University scenario, for example, at least 20-million fewer workers than today will be required in the United States by the year 2000. This represents a reduction of 12% in the economy's overall labor requirements, mostly in the clerical sector, that will more than offset any potential labor shortage arising in the aftermath of the baby boom.

Workers in industrialized countries already work significantly fewer hours each day than their parents did, and they enjoy longer holidays. Reductions in working hours depend on the influence of short-term business cycles and the long-term 4-STEP dynamics of social, technological and economic change. Over the long-wave economic cycle, standard working hours are reduced — but overtime work tends to rise in a boom and fall in a recession. The recession of 1981-83, however, was an exception to the rule. Many workers were laid off, and the rest were asked to work longer and harder. In other words, there was no reduction in standard working hours for the working population in total. Work was not shared and unemployment increased to levels unknown since the Great Depression of the 1930s. Western societies simply failed to adjust to the creation of the leisure society spurred by the latest wave of technological change. The goal of innovative techniques is to create wealth and have the leisure to enjoy that wealth. Why, then, do we stubbornly cling to 35-hour and 40-hour work-weeks? Society must learn to share the work savings that it can achieve through increased productivity.

The desire to work less is reflected in the massive shift towards part-time employment, which is making a mockery of the traditional workweek. Since 1973 — the year of the first oil-price shock — the number of part-time employees has increased significantly in all industrialized countries. For example, the part-timer's share of all jobs in Sweden increased from 17% in 1973 to 25% in 1986. Sweden is regarded by most futurists as a reliable bell-wether of global trends: it often leads the world in social innovation in response to technological trends. We can expect other countries to follow suit in the shift towards part-time workers. Projections show that 22% of work in North America will be performed by part-time workers by the year 2000 (up from 16% in 1988).

The shift to part-time work is a reflection of the electronic revolution, changing lifestyles, and socio-economic values. The reduction of working hours, through a reduced full-time workweek or an expansion of the part-time work-force, provides the social benefits of allowing available work to be shared more equitably, and producing more leisure. Part-time workers and work-sharing improve the efficiency and flexibility of the new information economy, because two fresh minds are better than one tired one. And part-time work creates the opportunity for re-education and retraining as the work environment continues to change rapidly. Leisure time also boosts economic spending and job creation (particularly in part-time work) in the 5th-Wave sector of the economy. The Japanese government has estimated that a 1% reduction in the national workweek would produce a 0.9% increase in labor productivity and boost GNP by 1.3% due to increased activity in the leisure sector.

More and more employees place a higher value on nonworking hours. Many are even willing to forgo benefit packages and accept lower wages if they can have more time for themselves. For example, a 1985 survey by Statistics Canada and the Conference Board of Canada showed that 31% of employees would be willing to take a cut in pay (or forgo some of their pay increase) for more time off. In total, 2.6-million Canadians (a quarter of the work force and more than one-tenth of the country's population) would give up as much as 20% of their pay to have equivalent time off. Japanese firms are now finding that they cannot recruit young people if they don't offer a 5-day workweek, because the 6-day week impinges on workers' quality of life. The general human preference is to work fewer days each week to allow time for leisure activities and family matters.

The desire to spend more time with one's family is a driving force for the work-at-home movement. The Industrial Revolution concentrated work in the mass production facilities of factories. The Electronic Revolution is reversing this process. In 1985, the U.S. Chamber of Commerce reported that 10-million American businesses listed home addresses as their place of business. At that time, 18-million Americans worked at home. Today, 25-million do so. By the year 2000, the number will have reached 40-million. These workers have eliminated commuting time and gained freedom to arrange their own schedules to allocate more time for the things they really want to do. There are even more electronic workers in facilities specially built to accommodate cottage industries, and some people both live and work in one condominium/office building. Many such buildings, villages and communities are springing up across North America. Blue Cross, the American medical insurance company, has a pilot program called "Cottage Keyers" under which a number of claims processors work at home with computers.

Beyond the Work Ethic

The desire to work less time for less pay makes a mockery of the work ethic. Many are prepared to give up paid work in order to pursue education and enjoy more leisure — for which they pay handsomely. In other words, we value these things so much that we are happy to pay for them. Thus, whether we admit it or not, or whether we can yet afford it or not, we all prize leisure more than work. Henry Ford believed that prosperity depended on the ability of workers to "have the leisure to enjoy life and the wherewithal with which to finance that enjoyment." In 1926, Ford became the first major U.S. employer to introduce the 5-day, 40-hour week and give his workers the same pay for five days' work as for six. This gave workers more money and time to purchase, among other things, automobiles. Ford stated that "the short workweek is bound to come because, without it, the country will not stay prosperous since it will not be able to consume its increased production capability." Nevertheless, old-fashioned economists still believe that overtime is a good thing because it expands production and tax revenues. They have not realized that people need the time to purchase and enjoy those extra goods. Nor has it dawned on them that one worker's overtime keeps another unemployed and, hence, nonproductive.

We must learn that leisure is no longer only for the affluent, the lazy, and the retired (who have "earned" it). Leisure can provide the same personal satisfaction as work. Indeed, leisure can be defined as encompassing work — and you do not have to be a workaholic to think so. Leisure encompasses:

- Work (new careers — part-time or full-time);
- Hobbies and games (skills and interests);
- Sports (observing or participating);
- Social activities (with spouse, family and/or friends);
- Education (courses, workshops, lectures); and
- Community involvement (voluntarism, politics).

Sounds like life itself! We are achieving what we have always craved: a quality life of leisure. We had better get ready by sharing the work.

Yet most Westerners remain wedded to a work-oriented society in which a person must be encouraged, persuaded, coerced, enticed or otherwise inveigled to work. This thinking permeates our institutions, and conditions the way we govern ourselves. For example, curing Japanese workers of workaholic attitudes is a difficult task. In November 1987, Japan's parliament approved a 40-hour workweek — down from 48-hours — to be implemented by 1993. Recognizing that it will take years for average working hours to fall to the new level, Japan has created the Leisure Development Center to encourage a leisure ethic among the working population.

To return to the U.S., extensive public opinion research by Stanford Research International shows that the five most important American status symbols in the next 15-years are likely to be:

- Self-directed free time;
- Unity of work and play;
- Recognition for one's creativity;
- Non-monetary rewards; and
- Social commitment.

Clearly, many managerial systems and incentives are out of sync with these changing values and attitudes. The broad cultural shift towards personal growth and self-development is redefining success in terms of intangibles, such as "fulfilling one's potential."

In developing countries, of course, most people still work on a labor-intensive basis. However, there is a continual shift of employment from the labor-intensive agricultural sector into the industrial and service sectors of Third World economies as they modernize. At the same time, as in the West, the number of working hours in the Third World is constantly being reduced by the introduction of technological change. For example, China has announced a shift from a 6-day week to a 5-day week, to be implemented by 1992. As developing countries continue to gain access to the latest technologies, they will skip many stages of the traditional economic development process to arrive at the worldwide 5th-Wave leisure society of the 21st-Century.

The Emergence of the Leisure Ethic

Futurists have been predicting since the 1960s that tourism would become the largest industry in the world by the year 2000. Tourism is already the second largest industry in Toronto, for example, and became the second largest retail sales industry (after automobile sales) in North America in 1981. In 1969, there were about 150-million international arrivals at national frontiers (not including excursions) and world tourism receipts were less than $20-billion. By 1985, the number of international arrivals had doubled, and tourism receipts ballooned to well over $100-billion. The planetary playground is well on its way to becoming the world's number one industry, and a corresponding "leisure ethic" is fast emerging.

Central to all definitions of "leisure" is the idea that it is free time, not devoted exclusively to work, allowing the exercise of choice. The traditional Greek view was that leisure was an end unto itself and included such activities as scholarship, contemplation, self-expression, self-realization and self-development. In ancient times, leisure was viewed as the most desirable form of "being" for a citizen with high social status. Work was identified as an inferior activity — to be performed, as much as possible, by slaves. With the coming of the Industrial Revolution, the Protestant work ethic stressed the primary importance of work, and the functions of leisure came to be seen as therapy, rest and relaxation. That is, leisure rested the individual so that he or she was able to work harder and more efficiently. This interpretation was broadened by economist Thorstein Veblen to include leisure as a symbol of wealth.

Since then, leisure has changed from the exclusive domain of the wealthy elite into a mass phenomenon. Technology is the new "slave"; indeed, world tourism could not have grown to the extent that it has — increased leisure time notwithstanding — without the new technology of jumbo-jet transport. Technological innovation will continue to make it possible for computers to perform more and more work now done by humans. One of the goals of artificial intelligence is that computers will eventually be used for work that currently requires such complex human cognitive skills as judgment, decision-making, relational thinking and creativity. Such systems will begin to emerge, at least in a rudimentary fashion, in the late-1990s.

Once achieved, a 5th-Wave leisure society will continue — through the self-feeding cycle of technological innovation and the generation of real wealth — to foster the 4-STEP process of economic development towards yet more leisure. By the turn of the century, the "leisure ethic" of the 5th-Wave Economy will have replaced the "work ethic" in Post-Industrial countries. By 2050, the developing nations will stand on the threshold of the same utopia.

G-Force T-2
The Drive for Productivity and Efficiency

*"The choice that confronts Western industry is to
automate, emigrate or evaporate."*
— *James Baker,*
General Electric

We are living on a giant ball, not the flat Earth depicted in a world map. And with 80% of workers and consumers living on one side of the ball, it does not make economic sense to extract, fabricate and market resources and products (except for information-intensive items) on the "rich" side of the ball and then ship them all the way around to the other ("poor") side. On the contrary, products are increasingly made in the developing countries and shipped back to the developed ones. As Western management guru Peter Drucker has been telling us for a couple of decades, we are living on a "planetary production site." Only the multinational corporations have so far been geo-strategic enough to understand this new reality. They are both automating and emigrating as they strive to meet the G-Force of improvement in productivity and efficiency.

Geo-Strategic Corporations

Historically, many companies viewed each of their businesses around the world as an independent entity that served the market in which it was located. Today, however, a company with a global strategy tends to sell a fairly uniform product worldwide and co-ordinate its activities accordingly. It may buy components on three continents, ship them to a country with cheap labor for partial assembly, and then finish the products in countries close to the customer. These companies are always looking for sources of global competitive advantage.

From a manufacturing standpoint, as William Lee of Touche Ross Management Consultants has pointed out, geo-strategic advantage stems from relatively few factors:

- classical comparative advantage (a country or region with significant cost advantages tends to become the site of production, and exports flow from it);

- production economies of scale (through centralized production);
- global marketing (as applied technologies become constantly less cost-competitive, production volume is increased by selling in many national markets, thereby maintaining an overall cost advantage);
- logistical economies of scale (the economic co-ordination of shipment of goods around the planet); and
- purchasing economies of scale (bulk purchase bargaining power through centralized worldwide buying of materials and components).

As industries become more global and as international competitiveness increases, simply becoming a more efficient manufacturer is not sufficient. Rather, a company must perform better in its own economy than an international competitor. As a result, wherever possible, factories are placed in countries whose industrial infrastructures may have relatively low productivity levels, but where costs have little bearing on production.

Bata Limited, the world's largest shoe manufacturing and retailing concern, is a good example of a geo-strategic corporation that "looks beyond borders" to become an integral part of the changing global dynamic — a strategy it has effectively pursued since World War II. This giant corporation sees itself not as a multinational but as a "multidomestic," looking beyond the current structure of international, political and economic borders to find opportunities. Bata operates about 100 factories worldwide from a tiny headquarters in Toronto, using electronic communications networks to oversee the 30% of the world shoe market that it has thereby captured. As C.R. Hickman and M.H. Silva point out in *The Future 500*, multinationals are already moving through the phase of globalization to one of global strategy implementation.

By the 21st-Century, multinationals will face globally homogenized yet specialized markets. Technology is driving the world towards global markets for standardized consumer products. Such corporations as Bata, geared to this new reality, benefit from enormous economies of scale in production, distribution, marketing and management. The new global corporation sells the same things everywhere, but does so in different ways. This is enhanced, as Bata has shown, by worldwide communications that carry the constant drumbeat of new homogenized market possibilities everywhere.

Third World Takes on Production

The global steel industry provides a good picture of the planetary production site in action (see Table 4).

Steel is no exception. In the planetary production site, the developing countries are taking on a larger share of the world's manufacturing activity in many sectors (see Fig. 11). Since 1970, manufacturing production has grown by an average of 5% per year in developing countries. In 1988, according to the United Nations Industrial Development Organization (UNIDO), developing countries accounted for more than 14% of world manufacturing output — up

Table 4   Shifts in Global Steel Production
(% global market shares)

	USA	EEC (W.Europe)	Japan	Other West	Third World	COMECON (E.Europe)
1950	47	26	3	4	2	19
1960	26	28	6	5	3	31
1970	20	23	16	6	5	30
1980	14	18	16	7	10	36
1985	11	17	15	6	12	38

Source: American Iron and Steel Institute (1987)

from less than 9% in 1970. Much of this gain is due to the "emigration" of manufacturing from the West.

There was a time when being a multinational company meant finding ways to sell domestically made products abroad or, at most, to make and sell a product in a foreign country. Global manufacturing in the new planetary production site is immensely more complex. Technological diffusion is faster and new competitors spring up everywhere. World manufacturing activity is being restructured. Products now have components made all over the world. For example, it is not uncommon to find a German car made of Swedish steel, with French tires and an interior of Argentine leather, which operates on gasoline made from Saudi Arabian crude oil shipped in a Liberian tanker with a Filipino crew to a refinery on the island of Aruba.

Entire industries are on the move. Notwithstanding new plants opening in the West, even global automobile production is shifting from the industrial countries. In the long term, the outlook for some Third World producers — particularly those with large and growing domestic markets, such as Brazil — could be even brighter. Such Third World countries, for example, could successfully set up their own automobile industries. According to a study by the Massachusetts Institute of Technology, as a whole Third World countries now meet about 60% of their own automotive demands domestically (up from 20% in 1960 and 40% in 1970).

Since the early-1970s, such Third World nations as India, Nigeria and Mexico have generated their own multinational corporations; China is investing heavily to build up global corporations. Third World multinationals tend to have advantages in labor-intensive, adapted-process technology, as well as in cheap, standardized products. Most Third World multinationals are state-owned. And 90% of the approximately 1000 manufacturing subsidiaries in

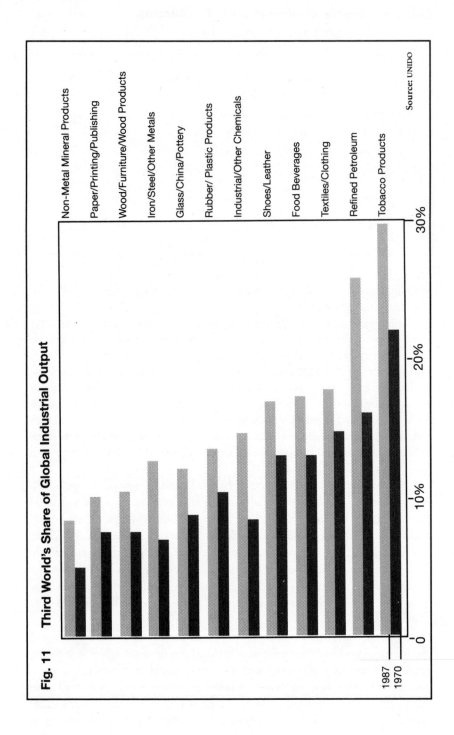

Fig. 11   Third World's Share of Global Industrial Output

Non-Metal Mineral Products
Paper/Printing/Publishing
Wood/Furniture/Wood Products
Iron/Steel/Other Metals
Glass/China/Pottery
Rubber/ Plastic Products
Industrial/Other Chemicals
Shoes/Leather
Food Beverages
Textiles/Clothing
Refined Petroleum
Tobacco Products

0   10%   20%   30%

1987
1970

Source: UNIDO

Third World countries are now of the joint-venture variety, not wholly owned subsidiaries of foreign companies. As Third World multinationals grow, we are likely to witness an even greater geographic shift in global manufacturing.

Western De-Industrialization and Robotization

With manufacturing being decentralized to the low-cost operating environments in developing countries, the West's share of output is declining (see Fig. 12). Those manufacturing entities that survive will have to be as highly automated as possible in order to achieve optimal levels of efficiency, productivity and quality control. The 2nd-Wave manufacturing age saw mechanical engineering and machine power replace muscle power in the factory. Since about 1970, the factory has begun to be transformed by a new generation of electronic machines in the form of robots. In the coming decades, robots will become widespread, and "flexible manufacturing systems," that is, fully automated production processes — will eliminate virtually all human labor from Western factories.

This electronic factory revolution, will not be restricted to Western manufacturing centers. For example, as economies of scale change, it defies logic that China, which has 400,000 factories in need of modernizing, will not adopt the latest available technology. China's robotics program, although still far behind the West's, is progressing rapidly; one of several planned robotics research and development centers has been set up. China's aim is to build cheap robots for raising worker efficiency and reducing labor-intensity; special-purpose robots are being developed to work in dangerous environments.

By 2025, robots could be handling virtually all manufacturing chores, according to many expert studies. Laser technology is expected to give robots almost human touch and sight capability in the early-1990s. (A robot para-surgeon has already performed about 20 brain surgery procedures at Long Beach Memorial Hospital in California.) A recent study by Carnegie-Mellon University predicts that, by the year 2000, robots will have supplemented at least 20-million factory workers (90% of today's complement!) in the United States alone.

In 1986, General Motors had roughly 40,000 programmable devices in its factories, and some 4000 robots that perform a variety of fabrication and assembly tasks. By 1990, the company plans to have expanded its inventory of programmable devices to 200,000 including about 14,000 robots. By then, it hopes to have more than half of its programmable devices communicating with each other. The goal is for the system — called Manufacturing Automation Protocol (MAP) — to link every aspect of an automobile's manufacture, from design to assembly.

In the global drive for productivity and efficiency, any company which produces a material, product, or service that will be rendered even partially obsolete by technological change is facing a dim and rapid decline. Those that go high-tech and/or go global will survive and prosper— and play their part in the reinvention of the world.

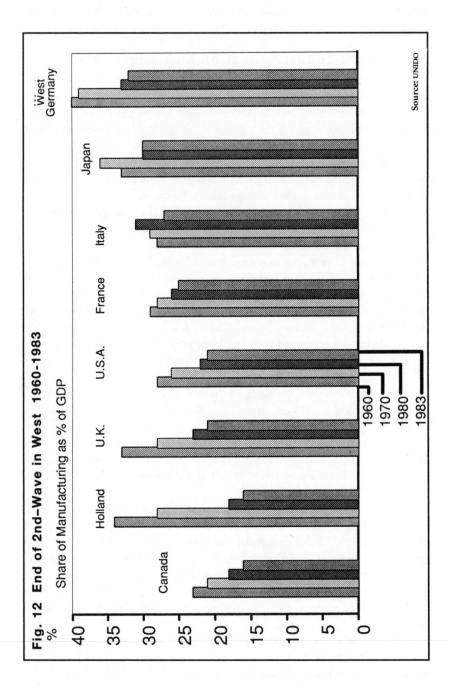

Fig. 12 End of 2nd-Wave in West 1960-1983

% Share of Manufacturing as % of GDP

Source: UNIDO

G-Force T-3

Sharing Information and Technology

*"Copyright protects the knowledge monopolies of the 'haves'
against the real needs of the underdeveloped for access
to knowledge which is an international commodity."*
— *John Stuart Mill*

Humans are territorial beings. But in the shrinking global village, they are being forced to shed this prehistoric trait. Within 60-years, they will lose it forever, despite futile attempts to place territorial limits and ownership rights on information and knowledge. In a real-time electronic world, information knows no boundaries. As Japan's Yoneji Masuda has pointed out, the utility of information will become more and more oriented towards the public interest because of the ever greater number of people who will be able to use the information. In the information society, he concludes, "the right of usage is predominant, not the right of ownership," and synergy rather than competition will be the basic societal principle of information usage.

Copyright Law Becoming Obsolete

In the face of this G-Force trend, copyright laws and attempts to protect intellectual property are becoming obsolete. Individual intellectual property rights will become absurd once collective knowledge is shared in a single electronic global brain, accessible to all. Only in books can the ownership of ideas still be pinned down. And with 60,000 new books now published each year just in the U.S., even that is becoming impossible. (Increasingly expensive, books will become obsolete, once electronic technology is cheap enough and "reader-friendly" enough to replace them — probably by 2010.) Ironically, such developing countries as Singapore, Malaysia, South Korea and China have acquiesced, or are acquiescing, to Western pressure to install copyright practices, contrary to their East Asia cultural tradition, in which knowledge is shared.

Laws protecting the right of individuals to intellectual property cannot be upheld, as is evident in futile struggles to stop U.S. college teachers and students from the "fair use" photocopying of books and articles (and similarly stupid quibbles over non-accredited quotations by a U.S. presidential candidate in 1988). Plagiarism is one thing, but surely we all have a right to "profit" from collective human wisdom. Copyrights do not protect ideas, procedures, discoveries or facts. Authors are entitled only to protect their particular expressions of ideas. No one disputes an author's right to study and build on the work of others; progress depends on this principle. The free flow of ideas cannot be legislated out of existence. Ideas must be allowed to flow freely from our collective consciousness to the collective knowledge bank to which we all have equal access.

Efforts to restrict technology transfer are similarly futile. With the rapid diffusion of technology, copying has become so rampant and universal that it cannot be stopped by any police or customs officer or jurisdictional body. In the electronic global village, protection of intellectual property is legally impossible. Any effective policy would have to overcome three major obstacles:

- •The peculiar characteristics of information as a commodity (cheap to produce, costly to synthesize yet inexpensive to copy; an economic commodity with value added, yet a societal resource);
- •The increased complexity of the intellectual property system (problems of identifying authorship and infringements, enforcing rights, private use, functional works, derivative use, intangible works, educational priorities); and
- •The changing nature of technology (text, sound and images will all be interchangeable under international networking systems).

No judiciary is suited to make such policy. In the electronic global village, ideas are akin to fresh air and universal access to knowledge becomes a birthright. Indeed, this comparison was made by the Supreme Court of Canada, which, in its 1987 decision that confidential information that is copied or memorized cannot be considered stolen property, stated that "no conviction for theft would arise out of a taking or converting of the air we breathe, because air is not property." The court went on to say that "one cannot be deprived of confidentiality, because one cannot own confidentiality. One enjoys it," and that society's best interests have to be considered ahead of those of a victim who loses confidential information, because society's interests tend to include the free flow of information.

As with copyrighted information, we must realize that global knowledge is a common economic good. In Japan, while patent law exists, intellectual property is already considered a common good, rather than something to which one has a right of exclusive possession. This cultural norm operates to widely disperse the scientific and artistic products of human ingenuity throughout Japanese society. Realistic legal rules depend on such a social consensus about acceptable behavior. Even in the United States, the fundamental goal of intellectual property rights (as drawn from the Constitution) is not to benefit the creators of works but to further the public good — any legal protection is conditional on public disclosure.

The more speedily knowledge is diffused throughout the world economy, the better off we will all be, thanks to the value added that such diffusion will create. The potential effect of ideas applied in a 10-billion-person economy (as opposed to, say, a 250-million-person economy in the United States) is phenomenal. To restrict access to information, then, is to restrict economic development for everyone. Ideas are only economically valuable once they are applied in economic activity, and their value can be increased only through their widespread diffusion.

Technology Transfer — Essential to Prosperity

The irrational fear of sharing knowledge puts developing countries at a disadvantage in trying to promote economic growth and industrial diversification. This seriously slows down the progress of the global economy. All developed country technical knowledge is now patented, and all equipment bears a trademark. Never before have ideas been made so subservient to the wishes of mercenary authors. These days, you must buy ideas or do without them — unless you succumb to piracy and counterfeiting. The West wants the Third World to pay for every new idea it develops. On that basis, the Chinese, who invented the wheel, could claim a fee from everyone using anything vaguely resembling a circular moving object. The problem today is that world competition has become intensely threatening. The fear of this threat is impeding our collective progress.

When countries acquire the technical means to imprint their word on the globe instantaneously, they must surely realize that this ability carries with it some responsibility. They are no longer dealing with a domestic audience to which they have traditionally been accountable; they are reaching out for the respect of a global audience to which they must make themselves accountable. Technology now takes the word and the image far beyond national boundaries. If the global economy is to prosper, technology transfer must become universal.

The West is slow to learn that technology transfer is a game for two players. The apparent industrial decline feared in the West is really a high-tech transition to a new era of productivity, profitability and prosperity — in all sectors of the 6-wave economy. This transition is occurring at a time when economic interdependencies are growing among companies, industries and nations. Mature industries are looking to microelectronics and other new technologies to improve their products and boost productivity. Manufacturers are looking to their suppliers for new ideas and technology. The growing interdependence of industrial nations is evident in the recent flurry of international joint ventures and co-production arrangements.

"We all gain from a spirit of convergence," notes Harry Gray (former chairman of United Technologies Corporation), "and in an interdependent world, we can benefit from uniting in a common interest." Unfortunately, says Gray, countries faced with stagnating economies have fallen back on unilateral actions to protect their narrow interests rather than seeking multinational opportunities. This shortsighted parochialism undermines the universal, long-term, enlightened self-interest made possible by sharing ideas. While industrial countries must revitalize their troubled economies and developing countries must get theirs moving faster, the development of high-technology products is becoming too complex, expensive and time-consuming for any company or country to "go it alone." This means, says Gray, that companies around the world must turn more and more to technology transfer — what he calls "the sharing of information about the science and engineering behind the product."

This is the only way to promote worldwide industrial revitalization. Third World application of new technology and new production equipment will create new business opportunities worldwide. When a Third World country strengthens its technological base through transfers, it raises its standard of living and boosts its economy. Although this makes it a stronger competitor, it also makes it a better customer for yet more high-technology products on the global market. In an interdependent (and nonprotectionist) world, both transferors and transferees of technology would have a lot to gain. While such sharing is unlikely in the present tough economic times, those trailblazing companies that lead the way will reap the greatest rewards in the coming decades. Those who resist technology transfer and impose tough intellectual property rights to protect themselves will find themselves hostage to their own laws once ideas start to come from elsewhere.

Growing technical complexity, Gray points out, also means that research and development (R&D) will have to be done co-operatively by groups of companies — both within a particular country and across national borders. The high costs of research and the rapid pace of product obsolescence neccessitate cost-sharing. Some countries — notably Japan and the U.S. — have already recognized that companies can co-operate in R&D and still compete in the production, marketing and servicing of their products. Individual companies such as General Motors and Toyota have been able to find ways of co-operating internationally.

This requires a worldwide environment of business and intellectual property unfettered, as far as is possible, by government and legal interference. As Napoleon said, "When trade no longer crosses international borders, armies soon will." Global trade protectionism in the 1930s helped bring about the biggest war in history. Global trade and technology transfer have since grown immensely. Shutting them off will bring economic malaise and major confrontations around the world.

Global trade in engineered products has grown by 154% since 1970, surpassing $900-billion by 1988. About one-quarter of this total is for high-technology products, including aircraft, transit systems, computers, nuclear reactors, microchips, machine tools, medical equipment, instruments, telecommunications systems, office machines and gas turbines. Almost 90% of all technology exports originate in the West.

This upsurge in the global technology market relates to the easy portability of technology. High-technology can be developed anywhere: it is not restricted to on-site development near large ore deposits or seaports. R&D skills that enable technologies to be readily adjusted to meet changing global needs offer much long-term economic promise. Western studies have shown, for example, that high-technology industries average more than $100,000 per employee in annual output. Thus, while every 2-million high-tech workers in America generate $200-billion in economic output, 2-billion high-tech jobs worldwide would expand the global economy by $200-trillion, which is 50-times the size of the U.S. economy today!

Despite the positive potential of widespread high-technology for its own domestic economy, the United States is concerned about the increasing technical sophistication of the developing countries. Asian component suppliers of personal computers, for example, produced 5-million units — one-third of the world total — in 1987. According to Dataquest, a market research company, only three weeks elapse between the introduction of a new U.S.-made electronic computer product and its duplication (in violation of patent or copyright), manufacture and export to the U.S. from Asia. "Unauthorized" third-party use of intellectual property "costs" U.S. manufacturers $8-billion to $20-billion a year, according to claims by the U.S. International Trade Commission and the U.S. Chamber of Commerce. In 1984, Congress shortsightedly ordered that a foreign country's record on protecting intellectual property would be a major consideration in the granting of preferential trading benefits. The U.S. also recently succeeded in placing copyright issues on the agenda at the ongoing negotiations of the General Agreement on Tariffs and Trade. The U.S. goal is the creation of an international joint patent system. At present, patents have extraterritoriality only in Europe, which set up a joint system in 1978. But if a global system of patent protection were instituted, the Western countries would be the biggest losers. In 1987, the U.S. already had a trade deficit of $3-billion in its high-technology sector, and this could double or triple every year that such protective laws were in effect, thereby limiting U.S. exports.

Virtually the only technologies legitimately available to the poor countries are those that are more or less obsolete in rich countries because of their intensive use of labor, capital and energy. Lathes, machines and old production lines demand elaborate servicing and support systems. Their transfer from rich to poor countries — often at inflated prices — is a major cause of Third World indebtedness (which now threatens the Western banking system) and mass unemployment — and, hence, of worldwide economic stagnation.

For more than two decades, social scientists and international "do-gooders" have exacerbated this problem by advocating the use of "appropriate" technology for the Third World. The technologies they have in mind are, in fact, totally inappropriate; they are recipes for backwardness in developing countries. While low-tech applications can be a useful stepping-stone to progress, to maintain that a people should not adopt the most modern technology but must make do with obsolete instruments and appliances is to commit the whole world to retarded development. History shows that those countries that turn their backs on technological advancement are left behind. When large parts of Asia failed to adopt the printing press, for example, calligraphy nevertheless declined, and is now only a small part of the Asian economy. Technology that is transferred must be the most modern available — and it must be diffused throughout the local economy as quickly as possible.

The real key to avoiding "copying", "loss" and debt-burdened, inferior economic performance is joint-venture technology transfer — as transferors like Japan and transferees like China are demonstrating. Joint-ventures preserve "ownership" and create "win-win" partnerships. It is no fluke that the economies of Japan and China are performing better than those of any other country.

There is still only a trickle of information reaching developing countries other than China about technologies that promote self-reliance and are suitable to their real needs. More than 2-million scientists work in R&D in Western countries and the Socialist bloc, while the number in the Third World is less than 300,000. The Third World accounts for only 2.9% of the worldwide production of technology and only 4% of global R&D. North America annually invests $331 per worker to improve productivity; Japan invests twice as much. Third World countries invest only $3 per worker per year.

This both perpetuates the gap between rich and poor and causes a "brain drain" from the Third World to the West. For example, the total monthly overhead and salary cost of an engineer is now estimated at $15,000 in the West — at least 10-times higher than in the Third World. To simply import the West's expensive technology, instead of creating engineering jobs in the Third World, perpetuates this typical per-capita-income differential. This is a recipe for each party cutting the other's throat, because the Third World struggles to buy the technology but then floods the West with cheap goods produced with that technology. Technology transfer, on the other hand, brings benefits to both sides and expands trade at higher prices.

The impossibility of continued Third World production of the same old thing with the same old technology for Western markets has led to inverse technology transfer, wherein Third World countries become a source of trained scientific personnel for the West. In 1985, for example, almost four-fifths of all highly skilled immigrants to the West came from Third World countries. These scientists tend to represent the Third World's technological elite. Their departure is often decisive in the future development — or collapse — of a series of technological activities at home, which again retards global economic growth. Clearly it is not in anyone's long-term interests that this kind of imbalance continue. Joint-venture technology-transfer projects will reverse these negative trends.

Management of Technology

The key is management. Global opportunities for technology transfer will expand dramatically in the coming years. The response of business management must be both geo-strategic and multidisciplinary. Meeting the aspirations of a growing world population requires four kinds of technologies:

- Basic needs technologies (in the fields of food, water, housing, clothing, healthcare);
- Material needs technologies (in the fields of education and consumer products and services);
- Infrastructure needs technologies (to build and operate air, rail, road and telecommunications networks); and
- Pure technologies (to modernize the 1st-, 2nd- and 3rd-Waves of developing economies).

The transfer of technologies must be geo-strategically managed. Since it is technology-intensive firms that generally obtain the greatest marketplace success, most of the planning for technology development and its global marketing focusses on R&D and quality issues. Major benefits of globalizing R&D efforts through collaborating with Third World countries include cost savings to both sides, engineering advantages (assuming skilled technicians are available) and ease of communications (using such means as global telecommunications networks and facsimile transmission).

Finally, the Third World itself needs to greatly improve its ability to manage the technology-transfer process. The ability of developing countries to achieve potential economic goals will depend on the capacity of local civil servants and business managers. Many Third World technology-transfer projects fail because of inadequate planning and decision-making, improper training and a managerial attitude that often rejects any technology offered, regardless of its suitability. Even where good management capabilities exist in the Third World, Westerners often assume otherwise, which usually results in a self-fulfilling prophecy of failure.

Managers in developing countries must view the technology-transfer process in light of the criteria of the 4-STEP process. First they must set socio-political objectives for the technology transfer being contemplated, considering such factors as the technology's effect on national security, environment and the society as a whole. Second, they must set technological objectives. These must address the cost of acquiring the technology, their right to use the patents involved and, especially, the "life-cycle" of the technology transfer (from sale to transfer to technological self-sufficiency to re-export of the technology). Finally, the transfer's economic objectives must be established and managed. These must take into account: overall economic productivity and growth; the generation of exports; the technology's effect on foreign debt, foreign exchange and domestic prices; and the direct creation of jobs.

135

To the degree that they are labor-saving, technologies will contribute to the short-run unemployment problem. But to the degree that they are resource-saving — capable of maximizing the productivity of land, capital and scarce management skills — technologies will both improve the overall utilization of these factors and promote national welfare. The resource-saving factor is much more important than the labor-saving factor. In the majority of technology-transfer arrangements, increases in productivity allow more efficient control of available resources, which cannot be obtained simply by increasing the number of managers or staff.

The introduction of modern technology alongside modern management increases managerial and technological effectiveness and boosts the creation of wealth. In the long term, this generates more employment than does focussing on short-term labor-creation. It also will create mutual global economic prosperity of immense magnitude.

G-Force T-4

Micro-Powered Expansion

"The world stands on the threshold of a second computer age. New technology is changing the computer from a fantastically fast calculating machine to a device that mimics human thought processes."
— *Business Week magazine*

Humans have always sought to improve their communication and decision-making processes. Until inscriptions began to be carved on clay tablets, all of society's knowledge was stored, "alive", in the heads of the elders of the each tribe. With the invention of writing and then of the printing press, knowledge was captured in books — "dead" — and became outdated increasingly soon after its publication. Computer data banks bring knowledge "alive" again; they are interactive, always up-to-date and much more reliable than human brains ever were. New methods of communication foster further advances in civilization. The rise of civilization itself is linked to the evolution of language. The establishment of the great civilizations paralleled the development of writing or innovations in written communication techniques. The rise of printing was simultaneous with the Renaissance. The machine energy and steam power that fueled the Industrial Revolution enabled the development of high-speed printing, cheap paper and book publishing. The telegraph, the telephone, the phonograph, the radio and television all marked the beginning of post-industrial civilization.

The scope of communications systems has historically shaped social order. Societies formed and maintained without writing were ultimately restricted in space and time. A society with the power to proliferate the written word can extend itself infinitely in distance and time. With modern electronic technology, communication is no longer restricted by the speed of humans or animals, or even by the speed of light. Electronic technologies such as audio and video tapes, personal computers and movies allow us to bypass the printed word and to expand our communications capabilities directly. The speed of this post-industrial expansion is unprecedented, often occurring as much as six-times faster than in the Industrial Era.

Speech Technology

Initially, information was transmitted vocally. Then, with tablets and ideograms, it was transmitted in an objectified form. This separation between people and what they communicate was reinforced by the printing press. The computer has not simply advanced this objectification of information by another step; rather, computers completely separate the production of information from its human subjects: a critical qualitative leap. Operating as a mechanical brain, the computer substantially amplifies human capacity for memory, calculation and control. With the impending addition of artificial intelligence capabilities, the computer will take on the old function of "word of mouth" transmission of information.

Once the stuff of science fiction, computers that take voice dictation are nearly here. The new "NeXT" personal computer (PC) is a major step towards workstations in which computers will perform secretarial functions, taking dictation and reading your morning mail. In the next decade computers will begin to mimic — but will not yet replicate — human knowledge-processing capabilities, starting with hearing and speech. An IBM electronic typewriter (called a voice-writer) already recognizes and types up to 20,000 spoken words — enough vocabulary to accommodate the dictation of entire letters. In this kind of environment, the voice box replaces the keyboard; in the event of error, the user simply tells the machine to "try again." Voice recognition will become standard for controlling computers by telephone and allowing callers to have the computer read back the day's (electronic) mail or file a report. In 1989, Apple Computer introduced a voice-recognition device that can operate a PC from across the room or from a telephone on the other side of the world. The new PCs will also be able to verbalize while performing another task. They will look up phone numbers (already one compact disk can store entire city telephone directories) and automatically dial the phone.

Speech technology makes it easier for people to use computers, and it will find widespread use in such fields as factory and office automation, telephone services and education. Environments ranging from hospital operating rooms to fighter planes are being fitted out with computers that simulate human speech and understand voices. U.S. airforce pilots can adjust their radar by voice command instead of removing their hands from the controls. Surgeons doing exploratory surgery can "speak" to a computer instead of relying on an assistant to enter third-hand information about a patient. There is even a machine that can scan a book and read words aloud to people who are blind. Though speech technology is expected to evolve slowly in the 1990s, it will simplify the tasks of thousands of workers who now use the telephone to take orders, make reservations and do other routine jobs.

Whereas current systems use the English language, future single-language systems will work in Japanese, Chinese, Spanish, German, French and Italian. And computers will not be restricted to single-language operation. There are more than 5000 languages and dialects spoken in the world and, although some people still believe that machine translation is not viable, it is becoming increasingly evident that all major languages will be translatable by computer by the late-1990s. Already, millions of words a year are routinely translated (partly or completely by computers) by large global companies such as ITT, Xerox and General Motors and by such organizations as the European Economic Community (EEC) and the United Nations. While such translations currently focus on specialized scientific, technical, legal and administrative texts, translation is a burgeoning service industry and, with software companies writing sophisticated packages for PCs, the prospects for automated translation are very exciting.

Computer translation is possible because every language has a grammatical and syntactical structure that can be logically analyzed. Machine translation at the EEC, for example, now starts with text being keyed into a word processor, where it is stored, and then sent by telephone line to the computer. The computer translates the text and returns it to the word processor, where the raw translation can be copy-edited by a skilled translator to remove any errors and improve stylistic quality. Each year, about 1-million pages of text are translated in this way by computers all over the world. Raw computer translation costs, even allowing for final editing, are still about 60% lower than those of manual translation. Of course, this dynamic will change once computers become voice-activated. Fujitsu, the leader in the field, introduced its commercial English-Japanese and Japanese-English translation system in 1984. The company has already sold more than 140 of its mainframe-based Atlas systems in Japan. The system's voice-input method is four-times faster than keyboarding. It translates two English words per second and can be connected with an artificial intelligence system to answer questions.

Japanese companies are already using computer systems to translate technological articles, news reports and product documentation and specifications. The Japan Information Center for Science and Technology maintains what is probably the world's largest database of international scientific and technical information. Today, the only obstacle to widespread automatic translation is its high cost. While we wait for the cost to decline through wider application of the technology, developments in artificial intelligence promise translation comparable to that performed by humans. The Japanese are already exploring this possibility in their widely publicized Fifth Generation computer project, designed to develop a new order of super-computers in the 1990s.

Growing Computer Power

Super-computers and ultra-computers will become a reality as new microchips are developed. The worldwide market for computer memory chips is almost infinitely elastic. Since the beginning of the era of integrated circuits in the early-1970s, each drop in the cost of storing computer data has created new demand. Prices have been dropping at an average of 35% a year, and the world market has been growing at an annual rate of 36%. By 1984, four Japanese chip makers had announced the creation of the one-megabit (1-million-bit) chip. A four-megabit chip was announced by both IBM and the Japanese in 1987. Portions of a 16-megabit chip have already been tested. Researchers are devising a 64-megabit chip and are looking even further ahead to a 256-megabit chip incorporating circuit lines only several hundred atoms wide. In 1985, there was less than one 64K-chip (64,000 bits) for each person on the planet. By the year 2000, 64k-chips will be obsolete, and Hitachi expects there will be one hundred 64-megabyte (512-million bits) chips per capita. (One bit of information is a single digit or character; one byte is eight bits.) A personal computer will have at least one gigabyte (8-million bits) of main memory. Most experts believe that even this is nowhere near the physical limits.

The expansion of chip power dramatically speeds up processing. Speech and natural-language systems require billions of logical steps per second, but all experts believe that such systems will evolve to maturity by the early-1990s. Vision systems require computing at 1-trillion instructions per second, and yet are already being developed. The speed-up in electronic technology is phenomenal. The word "instant" has lost its meaning, because shorter and shorter intervals of time are measured in tiny segments of a second. As a result of this exponential acceleration, experts in computer technology are forecasting a sixteen-fold increase in chip power between 1988 and 2000, with several chips built into each product. Some PCs already have 20-megabytes of computing power. Fiber-optics communication capacities of more than 300-million bits per second (bps)are now being developed compared to present telephone dial-up transmission capacities of only 1200-bps. Photonics, or lightwave, technology will be about 100-times faster than that of today's computers, and overall power could potentially be 1000-times greater. Super-conductivity (which overcomes electrical resistance to avoid the loss of electricity during transmission) will have dramatic effects in further increasing the power and speed of all forms of computer technology.

The Power of Miniaturization

Computer power is also being enhanced by miniaturization. Virtually all kinds of electronic consumer and industrial goods are affected by the worldwide movement to miniaturization of technology that electronics and biotechnology permit. Already, much office and auto equipment and scores of newly compact medical devices, telephones, industrial controls, household appliances and entertainment systems are reaching the marketplace. Many other miniaturized products are on the drawing boards, and miniaturization is prompting the rapid sales of microsensors, computer chips that measure pressure, heat, speed and sound. Small robotic instruments capable of inserting transistors, resistors and microchips inside miniaturized electronics components are also evolving. These robots reach into places that human fingers cannot penetrate.

Miniaturization is also showing up in the phenomenon of plastic cards. A plastic identity card that can display nearly half-a-million words now allows Americans to carry their complete medical histories in their wallets. The cards store up to 800-pages' worth of medical data — including X-ray and EKG records, drug prescriptions, lab test results, allergy alerts and surgical history — for instant access by hospitals and doctors. This is all made possible by laser-optics technology. This same technology can be used to create audio and video disks, which in a few years will lead to foolproof passports, social security cards, and credit or debit cards for vending machines, transit systems and telephones. Some publishers envision entire books encoded on cards, at a cost of only $1.50 each, for reading on video screens. At least 20 companies worldwide — including four in the United States and 11 in Japan — are now developing this technology.

Engineers are using other techniques to shrink mechanical devices to dimensions almost invisible to the naked eye. For instance, a robot the size of a flea could travel through the human body's blood stream to correct a heart defect. In a handful of laboratories around the world, scientists are already creating devices that will soon undertake such fantastic voyages. By etching patterns on silicon chips, they are creating gears, turbines and motors so small that 10,000 such devices would fit in a single square centimeter (60,000 in a square inch). AT&T is developing silicon-chip processing techniques to make similar turbines. And working gears that are only one to five microns in diameter with gear teeth a mere 15-microns wide (less than one-fifth the thickness of a human hair) are being produced. In West Germany and Japan, scientists are working with slightly different processes to achieve the same ends. Some of these machines are so small they will operate on static electricity!

The Japanese are also trying to build a machine to decipher the human genetic code. Government planners enlisted a watch manufacturer, a computer-software house, a maker of photographic film, an electronics concern and a soda-ash firm to develop a piece of micropowered technology that will read the body's internal blueprint. They are designing machines that will decipher DNA, the genetic material that determines the development of every living organism. Biologists talk of compiling a catalogue of all 3-billion pieces of genetic information in human DNA. Such data holds many clues about how the body works (which could allow us to treat and probably cure various currently incurable diseases) and also how the mind works. Eventually, the Japanese want to find a way to link biotechnology with miocroelectronics to produce a biologically operated computer. The new super-computer chips being developed are what researchers exploring artificial intelligence have been waiting for.

The awesome power of increasingly miniaturized microchip technology and the development of human-like machines are and will continue transforming human society worldwide. We can now expand ourselves almost without limit, across national boundaries and the old barriers of language. By the early

141

decades of the 21st-Century, all societies will be able to communicate in a common language and by mid-Century micromachines will run the world at our common command.

G-Force T-5
Real-Time Info-Globalization

"Computers are becoming global society's central nervous system."
— *Tohru Moto-oka*

The planet Earth is becoming more and more enmeshed in a complex, pulsating web of wires, cables, fiber-optics, radio airwaves, TV broadcasts and satellite transmissions. These communications links are increasingly becoming integrated, forming a tightly woven lattice of electronic impulses carrying vital information throughout the world. The network is as complex — and as important to socio-economic development — as the human nervous system. The brainpower, or neural intelligence, of this new global electronic system has become possible through the integration of technologies and massive computer data banks around the world, all humming quietly, 24-hours-a-day, to meet the needs of a world population hungry for knowledge. People's appetite for information is a major G-Force for change, which is creating a real-time info-globalized network of "information utilities" that every world citizen will ultimately have access to — and cheaply.

Building the Global Electronic Highway

Recent advances in computer telecommunications technology have brought the world enticingly close to the global village that Marshall McLuhan predicted in 1964. The main difficulty in achieving instantaneous worldwide communication is that the various telephone and data transmission systems around the world operate with different technologies, each requiring its own set of elaborate, expensive, specialized hardware.

Starting in the mid-1980s, however, a sophisticated universal system is being introduced that will not only replace some existing technologies but will, in the coming decades, dramatically expand the communications services available to businesses and households worldwide by integrating disparate technologies into a common system. This integrative G-Force is literally reinventing the telephone and the computer.

143

The Information Age is based on the highly segmented marketplace of the storage, manipulation, retrieval and communication of information and knowledge. Just as 2nd-Wave society demanded networks of roads and railways to haul mass-produced goods, telecommunications requires a comparable infrastructure to move information around. This "digital highway" is already being built worldwide. Because the key to success in the Information Age is a sound technological base for the processing of information and knowledge, the infrastructure must be an integrated network much like the communication/information-processing system of the human brain/mind. Telephone companies the world over are thus joining forces under the banner of the Integrated Services Digital Network (ISDN) — the key to linking all the communication elements of the Information Age (see Fig. 13).

At least ten international telephone companies are already conducting ISDN field trials. They will determine the world's telephone network of the year 2000 and beyond. Eventually, ISDN will be a single network that carries voice, data, text and image traffic along the global digital highway that is already unfolding, with operating links from London to New York to Tokyo. Soon to link up will be Hong Kong, South Korea, Taiwan, Australia, the Philippines, China and other Pacific Rim countries. China itself is developing a massive domestic information network linking all its centers with the world. The two information "ports" of China are Guangzhou (Canton) and Shanghai, its traditional major seaports. The Chinese recently hooked up (via Hong Kong) with the world-wide I.P. Sharp Network (centered in Toronto) which is part of the Reuters digital network — just one of many such global networks in operation.

Real-Time "Tele-Prosperity"

Faced with intensified global competition, many business leaders are grasping the geo-strategic profit potential of communications networks. North American companies spent about $500-million on electronic-data interchange in 1988. As the industrial rationalization process continues worldwide, there is increasing demand for links both within and between individual companies. The U.S. auto industry, for example, has found that it is wasting $2-billion per year shuffling paper. In an effort to eliminate this waste, General Motors (GM) alone has four major integrated networks — involving hundreds of offices and warehouses, 18 assembly plants and 80 data centers. In addition, some 13,000 GM dealers access the system via telephone. Expert industry observers say the information networks of the 1990s, like that at GM, will encompass tens of thousands of intelligent devices. The trend will go much further than linking the "islands of automation" now in place in many organizations into enterprise-wide networks. In fact, the 1990s will see whole enterprises and other users linked by networks that span the globe.

Anything less will not meet emerging business requirements. The linking of computer and communications products and services to operate together within

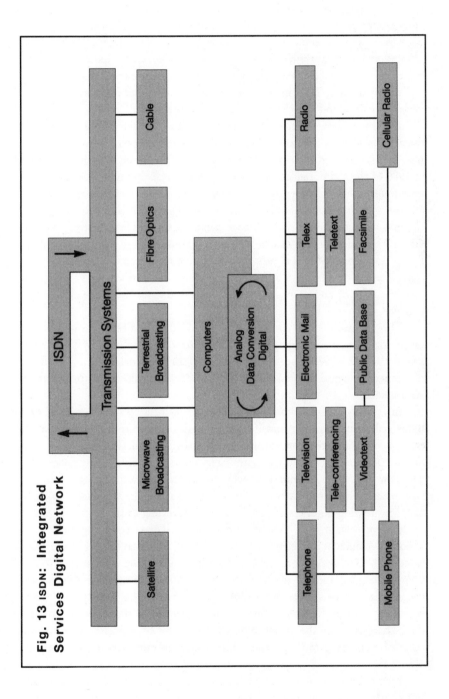

Fig. 13 ISDN: Integrated Services Digital Network

a universally accessible, international telecommunications network is a fundamental requirement for the success of almost any business in the emerging global economy of the 21st-Century. The rationalization of industry in Western countries, transnational corporate growth, corporate decentralization and intrapreneurialism, turbulent economic times, cost pressures and changing customer markets have created a changing corporate environment that demands a real-time response. Total integration and the flexibility to cope with complex decision-making and fast-changing conditions are essential.

For this reason, early in 1985, senior executives of the 20 leading international computer and telecommunications companies met to find ways to solve inter-connection and inter-operability problems. The result was the formation in 1986 of the Corporation for Open Systems (COS), an unprecedented global coalition that now includes more than 60 of the world's top industry suppliers and users worldwide that is shaping the future of global ISDN networks. To date, COS has attracted more than 20 user companies, including Boeing, Kodak, General Electric, GM and VISA, as well as companies from the United Kingdom, France and Japan. ISDN is clearly the way of the future, and those who understand it and adopt it will go on to "tele-prosperity." Those who don't will suffer "tele-frustration" and decreasing effectiveness in the new real-time global marketplace.

The integration of traditional computer, office and telecommunications technologies is also changing the work environment profoundly. The central product of this convergence is the personal electronic workstation. The effects of this technological integration on both productivity and the nature of work are dramatic.

In 1st-Wave society, work was traditionally done at home. Then 2nd-Wave industrialization brought massive centralization in common places of work (such as factories) to achieve economies of scale. The 3rd-Wave service revolution perpetuated this trend by centralizing work in offices ("paper factories"). The new 4th-Wave information technologies reduce the need for traditional workplaces. The workplace of the future can be anywhere we want it to be — and, for growing numbers of people, work is reverting to the home. An AT&T study found that, in 1985, 13% of Americans did all or a large part of their work at home — much of it electronically. By 1988, this had risen to 18% of the work force. By 2000, as many as 40% of North America's workers may work at home. The integration of telecommunications and computers thus permits the decentralization of a great deal of information-processing. Employers benefit because workplace flexibility enhances productivity. For the economy at large, these changes create the opportunity for more jobs by reducing the overhead costs of employing more people, which results in more sharing of work for more pay.

Electronic technology permits households to become self-sustaining and lets workers abandon institutional settings. Of course, working at home demands new skills. Employers need to learn how to supervise "remote" workers, assess their prospects for career development and socialize them into the "total workplace" environment. "Remote" employees (and freelancers) need to learn self-management skills and must be able to socially integrate with the "total workplace" and/or family or local community environments. Programs for managing these human factors are being implemented by several large North American companies (including Control Data and Blue-Cross). People with home computers also find that they spend more time studying and being with their families. In what Toffler called the "Electronic Cottage," the computer is binding families together again and is enabling people to network with others at home and abroad. The technology is spawning a rapidly growing popular subculture. Many users of personal computers belong to specialized groups within a network of thousands of electronics clubs that appear whenever and wherever they are needed.

Computers are also being used for shopping and banking at home. Electronic shopping is coming soon to North America's department stores, supermarkets, convenience stores, banks and malls. The economics of this are simple: a giant retailer like Sears can buy 10,000 terminals for what it costs to renovate one store. By the early-1990s, retailers predict, 50,000 terminals will rack up annual in-home shopping sales of $5-billion to $10-billion across North America. It is predicted that electronic shopping will account for 5% of North American retail sales by 1990 and 20% by the year 2000. Japan's Science and Technology Agency predicts that integrated audiovisual systems will become "living necessities" in Japanese homes by 2010, if not sooner. As of 1988, almost one third of Japanese homes already had facsimile (FAX) copier machines and this figure is expected to rise to 80% by the year 2000. News will be perused on electronic "newspapers" customized to individual reader specifications, articles will be copied onto optical disks, and international telephone conversations will take place by means of automated simultaneous interpretation at the in-home relay station. Electronic mail and FAX systems threaten all popular modes of communication: the postal service, cables and telex. ISDN will work even faster than current electronic-data-transmission facilities. At top speed, for example, a 1000-page book could be transmitted over ISDN in only 7-minutes — with existing equipment, it takes 7-hours. By 2010, there will be no more conventional, door-to-door mail or newspaper delivery, either in North America or in Japan.

Third World "Tele-Frustration"

In the developing countries, of course, the story is very different. An efficiently functioning telephone system is taken for granted in the West. In Toronto a man was fined $50 for ripping the handpiece from the public phone booth and throwing it on the ground "in a moment of frustration" at not being able to place an important call while he was between flights at the airport. It's a good thing he wasn't in the Third World. A Parisian passing through Bombay recently used the term "tele-frustration" in describing the telephone system there. After a full two days of grueling efforts to call from one area of the city to another, he gave up and left the city, distraught and disappointed. His experience is commonplace for thousands of telephone users in India and other Third World countries. It is an annoying paradox of the communications era that we can talk instantaneously and clearly with a person on the Moon, yet we cannot get a simple connection from a Bombay suburb to downtown.

The telephone is one of the most important technologies for the conduct of affairs in the modern world. Life without telephones is just not conceivable in the West. Indeed, everyday commercial activity would grind to a halt without telephones. For example, a 1975 fire in a downtown New York telephone exchange left some 250,000 telephones out of order for one month, leading to total chaos and great financial loss. But this pales in comparison with the situation in developing countries, where down-time of the telephone system is commonplace. In 1984, for example, it was estimated that 15% of Bombay's telephones were permanently out of order. During the monsoon season, the figure rises to 25%, and as many as 70% of the telephones can be out of order on any single day. Repairs can take hours, days or even months — and telephones often go out of order again soon after repair. (In comparison, less than 1% of New York's telephones are out of order at any one time.) Even when you find a working telephone in India, half the time you will have difficulty hearing the other party or get cross-connected lines. On 40% of your calls, you will get either a wrong number, no dial tone, a dead line, or no connection at all. It has been computed by Dr. Rashmi Mayur of the Urban Development Institute, Bombay, that more than 40 person-years are wasted every single day by the people of Bombay unsuccessfully trying to make telephone calls.

As if this were not frustrating enough, long-distance telephoning in a large Third World country like India is costly and impractical. Often, it is simply not possible to place a call, even if you can afford it. To call from Bombay to New Delhi is difficult at best. In Africa, when you dial from one country to another, just a few miles away, calls often still have to be routed through operators in London, England. Consequently, important or urgent messages in most cities of the Third World have to be delivered by bicycle, not by telephone.

Another serious drawback of telephone systems in developing countries is poor citizen access. More than half of India's telephones, for example, are in a few large urban centers where only one-fifth of the total population resides. In contrast, almost everyone in Canada and the United States has a private telephone and often there are several telephones in a single-family dwelling. Canada alone has more than 60-million telephones for a population of 26-million, and North Americans can buy an extra telephone off the shelf at the telephone store for about $30, take it home and simply plug it in. In India, there are only 2-million telephones for 800-million people, and new subscribers have to wait several months for a telephone to be installed, and often it breaks down immediately thereafter. In China, private access to a telephone is virtually impossible due to lack of infrastructure and costs that are still too high for families to afford. How, then, can socio-economic development take place?

The telephone — with or without computer integration — is a vital force for global economic development. Even in countries whose telephone systems are plagued by inefficient management, defective equipment and poor mainte-nance, the telephone plays a pivotal part in economic development. At first glance, the obvious solution to Third World "telefrustration" is to improve and expand the telephone system. Unfortunately, installing a telephone system using present-day technology is an enormously expensive undertaking. To reduce the cost per user requires the rapid addition to the system of many new subscribers. Building such a large user-base, particularly in rural areas where line costs are high, is a slow process.

As the telephone is reinvented, however, fiber-optic and satellite transmis-sion will change the cost equation. Small, newly developed receiving stations will lower the cost of using satellite communications for developing countries from $5-million to $50,000 per station. Satellite networks to be operated across the Third World by the International Maritime Satellite Organization (INMARSAT) will link into other fixed telecommunications systems anywhere in the world. INMARSAT, which was set up jointly by various governments in 1982 as part of the International Telecommunications Earth Satellite Organization (INTELSAT), had three satellites in operation by 1988. This system will enable much of the Third World to bypass a whole generation of telephone technolo-gies, skipping radio-based and wire systems to move straight to satellite com-munications.

By about 2010, all of the world's major nations will be plugged into the global information utilities network envisaged by Yoneji Masuda of Japan, whose "global information utility" — which projects an infrastructure using a combination of computers, communications networks and satellites — is now being created. By the middle of the 21st-Century, this infrastructure will allow any ordinary citizen in the world to obtain all necessary information readily, quickly and at low cost, at any time and place.

In the West, the cordless telephone is sprouting up everywhere, from auto-mobile to pool-side. It is now technologically possible for every individual in the world to be given a wrist-watch telephone at birth, with a single telephone number that he or she will keep for life. Satellites and reduced costs will make it possible for such devices, formerly the stuff of comic strips and science fiction, to be universally available by 2050. This will create the ultimate real-time global telecommunications network.

In the interim, the global "electronic highway" now being built will solve most of the telephone–access problems in the Third World by about 2000. Indeed, as the number of world telephone subscribers expands from 700-million to 10-billion (a 14-fold increase), the potential socio-economic benefit of this

G-Force over the next 60-years is so profound that it is impossible to imagine. What is certain is that information equates with abundant wealth creation and economic power.

G-Force T-6
Techno-Leadership of Japan

"We thought they could never catch up, but they tried harder
and here we are — to paraphrase an old American slogan:
A Sony in every house and two Toyotas in every garage."
— George A. Keyworth II,
former National Science Advisor,
Reagan Administration

More than any other country, Japan is providing the world with a much-needed new model of long-term global technological development. Realizing in the early-1970s that supremacy in high-technology was the key to economic progress and leadership, Japan developed an ambitious six-pronged strategy to become the world's technological leader, setting up parallel-track research and development (R&D) projects. America, the world's technological champion in the 1960s and 1970s, has been forced to give up that title as we prepare to enter the 1990s. What motivated Japan, more than anything else, was the publication of *The Limits to Growth*, the influential Club of Rome study in 1970 that used computer models of the global economy to predict environmental and resource constraints on economic growth. This report, soon followed by the 1973 oil crisis and the subsequent global recession that battered the Japanese economy, triggered near-panic in Japan. Although it turned out to be unfounded, the report did the Japanese — whose economy is dependent on external resources — a favor by making them focus on a new future. Japan's techno-leadership (in collaboration with its Southeast Asian neighbors and with China) is a major G-Force that is restructuring world economic and political affairs.

"Technopolis" Strategy

In a long-range planning document called "Visions for the 1980s", (produced in 1980) the Japanese Ministry of International Trade and Industry (MITI) recommended a major shift in investment, from resource- and energy-intensive heavy industries and petrochemicals to high-tech and "knowledge-intensive" industries that would consume less energy and fewer raw materials. This

"Technopolis" strategy, as it is now called, is a plan to build a network of 15 high-tech cities throughout Japan. The basic infrastructure of this network is almost complete. Japan has set up several research projects, including its super-computer project, in these technopolis centers. Projects are also being mounted in other fields predicted to be the main engines of economic growth in the 21st-Century, including those of semiconductors, aerospace, lasers, biotechnology, pharmaceuticals, ceramics and solar energy. Some 30 such projects are underway in the Tokyo area, and Japan now challenges the United States in most fields of basic research and advanced technology. Japan also plans to pursue strategic international alliances (with developed and developing nations alike) of joint research ventures and technology exchanges, in order to ensure a continuing flow of new ideas into the country. Notably, foreign scientists now make up about one-tenth of Japan's huge program of exploratory research for advanced technology.

The "Technopolis" strategy is being implemented through a four-pronged approach. First, to modernize the 2nd-Wave industrial sector, Japan has taken the lead in bringing microelectronic and laser controls to the production process and continues to introduce as many industrial robots as does the rest of the world combined. Second, to modernize the 3rd-Wave services sector and the 4th-Wave information sector, the standardization of telecommunications net-works, facilitated by the rapid accumulation of capital and by technological breakthroughs, is providing a sound basis for economic growth. Third, the pro-portion of GNP devoted to R&D has risen from 2% in 1980 to 3.5%. In the early-1990s, Japan will surpass the U.S. in non-military R&D spending. Finally, Japan is geo-strategically driving into world marketplaces.

The Japanese are reluctant to call world attention to the full scope of their planned international technological and economic success. Conversely, North Americans and Europeans find it difficult to acknowledge the extent to which their global technological and economic power is declining. They also tend to console themselves with the belief that the Japanese still depend on the West for new ideas. This arrogance, coupled with Japan's quiet modesty, is helping Japan achieve its goal of world high-tech leadership. Consequently, Japan will over-take North America in global high-tech exports in the 1990s. Indeed, Japanese firms constantly study the global chess-board to identify technological opportu-nities at an early stage. In contrast, according to a recent study by the Global Competitiveness Council in Washington, only one in eight American high-tech firms actively study what is happening in Japanese technology. Despite evidence to the contrary, many U.S. companies obstinately continue to believe both that the superiority of American technology obviates the need to monitor techno-logical progress abroad, and that Japanese research is not as creative as that in the West.

American technology, of course, is still first in the development of big sys-tems, software, computing and aerospace. But nobody can approach Japan's manufacturing technology. Also, U.S. technology is geared mainly to the manufacture of domestic products (such as phones and cars) while Japan looks to commodities with huge export markets (such as continuous steel casting, emission control for cars and optical coatings for camera lenses) and is also making gains in all fields in which the U.S. now leads.

With its former glory fading, high-tech industry in the U.S. is scrambling to compete. A new offensive is being launched in the software industry, but, as discussed later, we can expect the Chinese to become the world's software leaders in the 21st-Century. Some American companies hope to overcome the current malaise by moving into new materials and into sensor and laser technology. However, these are areas in which Japan (and Germany and Sweden) is also moving fast.

Biotechnology perhaps holds the greatest promise of growth in the United States and the world at large. But here, too, Japan is leading the way. Some Western biotech experts privately concede that Japan now conducts more than half of all world research in biotechnology. The 1988 "JTECH" report — a U.S. government evaluation of Japanese technology compiled by senior U.S. scientists from, among others, Bell Labs, Bellcore, IBM and the Universities of California, Cornell, Maryland and Michigan — concludes that Japan is leading the world in many areas of high-tech research including those of crystallography (for use in semiconductor chips) and prostaglandins (hormone-like compounds for pharmaceuticals).

From Manufacturing to Informatics

Japan's technological progress in manufacturing has been astounding. Back in 1960, Japan's struggling auto makers could barely produce 70,000 vehicles a year, but the country is now the world's top manufacturer. In 1985, Japan produced 12.3 million vehicles (while the U.S. made 11.7 million) in a staggering range of models for a fast-changing domestic market as well as the very diverse export markets of North America, Europe, the Middle East, Southeast Asia, Africa and Latin America. Moreover, Japan's production engineers are exporting their techniques to develop automated assembly plants to more than 40 countries, including the United States, Canada, and Britain.

Indeed, Japanese production concepts — such as the just-in-time inventory control method developed by Toyota and now used in most Japanese auto plants — are being avidly adopted by the usually conservative car makers of the U.S. and Europe. Japan's motor industry has been much quicker than its competitors to adopt such innovations as numerically controlled machine tools and industrial robots. Production engineers have taken advantage of the programmability of robots to develop "mixed-model" assembly lines that can produce several hundred variations of a few basic models. As a result, Japanese car makers can change the production mix quickly in response to market demands, and can accommodate year-to-year model changes without extensive plant shutdowns and retooling. Even the current opening of Japanese markets and the recent and ongoing devaluation of the dollar against the yen will not resolve America's poor competitive position.

But Japan is not satisfied with its competitive advantage. Most Japanese automobile executives feel that further automation is an absolute necessity for two reasons. First, Japan has a relative shortage of workers and, as their standard of living and education improve, they will become less willing to work on assembly lines. Second, as car buyers become more sophisticated and the market more competitive, manufacturers will have to respond with even more variations that, in turn, will require even more sophisticated forms of robotization.

The traditional (and pervasive) mentality of American industrial society has been to focus on volume production and heavy mass consumption of goods. By contrast, Japan now focusses mainly on the information society, encouraging intellectual creativity rather than materialistic consumption. Japan's long-stated national goal is to become "the information utility of the planet" by 1995 at the latest. It intends to set up a Global Information Utility (GIU) that we all will be able to tap into.

Japan has set four minimum requirements for the GIU:
- There would be several Global Information Switching Centers (GISCs) throughout the world, each of which would be connected to scores of sub-Global Information Utilities (sub-GIUs) equipped with a number of large-capacity computers capable of on-line, real-time processing of the information;
- GISCs would be connected by satellites for user access to sub-GIUs throughout the world;
- Fees for GIU services would be low enough for citizens in any country to be able to use the services daily; and
- The basic computer language for GIUs would be an internationally standardized one, but individuals would be able to communicate in their own languages by using an automatic translation system.

To meet this ambitious goal, Japan is reshaping its telecommunications industry. Three bills relating to the telecommunications business became law in 1984. In a very real sense, 1984 was "year one" of Japan's Information Age, in which the restructured communications industry will ultimately make possible — in the words of the Japanese government — "the full development of information as the basic commodity of the new era" and "the transformation of information into great endless wealth." This kind of language isn't even part of the North American vocabulary! The global implications of these developments are stupendous. By the year 2000, it is likely that Japan will have the world's leading information economy.

Microchip Leadership

The most advanced microchips are technology drivers, and the country that makes them will be the undisputed leader in computers. This is the conventional wisdom of the global chip competitors, who agree that Japan leads in chip technology. By 1985, for example, it controlled about 92% of the world's 256K-chip market and nearly 70% of the total Dynamic Random Access Memory (DRAM) market. One of the main reasons for this competitive strength is cost: the production of a square inch of silicon (the raw material for chips) costs only $18 in Japan, versus $28 in America.

In the entire semiconductor business, Japan became the world leader in 1986. In that same year, the U.S. Department of Defense conducted a study of semi-conductor technology worldwide to determine the U.S. position. In 25 areas of semi-conductor design and production technology surveyed by the Defense Department task force, the U.S. was leading Japan in only five categories and was maintaining its position in only one area. Nowhere did the U.S. position appear to be improving against Japan. Since then, the U.S. has lost its lead position in micro-processor technology and in custom/semi-custom logic/design.

In 1985, Japanese executives were asked why they were continuing to make large capital investments in semiconductor plants and equipment when sales were slumping and prices falling. They explained that it was market share, not short-term profits, that determined their investments. Japan thereby achieved world superiority in these fast-evolving fields, and virtually every semiconductor company in Japan is still expanding. They are adding product lines, pushing research on future technologies, and formulating plans to further strengthen their position in microchip memories while gaining larger shares of other chip markets. In fact, the national goal of world leadership in computers led to a major effort to upgrade Japanese "very large scale integrated" (VLSI) circuit technology, starting in 1976, and this project will perhaps be Japan's most successful national industrial effort.

In the race to commercialize the new super-conductors that could revolutionalize the electronics, energy and transportation industries, Japanese companies are moving aggressively to develop materials and find ways to use them in products. By contrast, most U.S. companies are doing only basic research, or waiting for government research grants, or just monitoring the field. Both the U.S. Office of Technology Assessment and the Council on Superconductivity for American Competitiveness have concluded that Japan is already ahead in this race. Although major uses of the new materials are at least a decade away, super-conductors will probably be used to make computers operate at blazing speeds. Many Japanese firms are already working on high-speed computer chips (a pursuit abandoned by American companies), which, if perfected, would quickly put Japan well out in front in the computer field.

Software Development

Japan's greatest weakness in the field of computers has been software. But strong efforts are being made to overcome this and, in the process, to build a strong competitive edge for Japan's computer industry. The heart of this push is the 5-year national Sigma project to improve software quality and productivity by developing techniques that range from reusing parts of previous programs to fully automating the production of software. The aim is to do what no other nation has so far done: achieve absolute compatibility, so that any Japanese software can run on any Japanese computer. Programmers are able to use any of 10,000 software development workstations linked together in a national network, in addition to which many Japanese companies have extensive software-improvement programs of their own.

Leadership in software is particularly important because of its cost-cutting and strategic applications for users in all sectors of the economy. The trend is towards inexpensive, standardized software packages rather than expensive custom programs. Heavy Japanese R&D investment in this area will improve the country's software position. The world leader in application software productivity is Toshiba's "Software WorkBench" factory, which specializes in process control programs for industry. About 2000 programmers write, code and debug programs at workstations, all working in one large room so that program parts can be reused. An average of about two-thirds of the programming code comes from previous programs. This heavy reuse helps each programmer generate some 2000 lines of code per month — several times better than productivity rates in the United States — and contributes to the software's higher quality. Toshiba claims error rates of about 0.3-bugs per 1000 lines of code, which is 10-times better than typical U.S. rates. The company offers a 10-year warranty — any bug found within 10-years is fixed free of charge.

By contrast, U.S. software efforts are largely unco-ordinated. One research co-operative (the Micro-Electronics and Computer Technology Corporation) has been set up by a group of computer companies in Texas to work on software engineering, but its projects are not at the operating-systems level. The U.S. Defense Department's ADA software program (aimed at improving software quality, productivity and reusability for military systems) is closer to what the Japanese are doing. However, its scope is limited to co-ordinating military software activity. And it is taking a long time not only to get ADA tools into the marketplace but to overcome the rivalries that have dampened past American compatibility efforts. Other software engineering programs are being conducted by the EEC's joint technology program, ESPRIT, and by the West German government, which is also sponsoring an ADA project. The Japanese Sigma project is simply better organized than any other national effort; it involves co-operation between hardware and software developers, the government and computer users, all working to a long-term plan.

I believe that the "Confucian" mindset will, in the long run, prove itself to be better suited than that of Westerners to software development. This is borne out by a recent development in San Francisco, where the China Professional Resources Consortium is bringing programmers from China to meet the programming needs of American companies. This project is a startling admission of

the United States' lack of capability in advanced programming. The programmers typically will be hired for 18-months to write software for everything
from mainframes to PCs. Contract programmers in America are paid about $50
an hour, while those in China earn just $33 a month. Eventually, the company
will send programming work to China for completion.

Drive for Biotechnology Leadership

Biotechnology, as mentioned earlier, is one of Japan's major priorities for the
1990s. Most Japanese biotech researchers have zeroed in on healthcare — the
profitable worldwide market in vitamins, vaccines, antibiotics and genetically
engineered cell products. Much of this research hinges on immunology which is
at the core of a variety of new products being developed by Hayashibra. This
company began conducting clinical trials using alpha and gamma-interferon, as
well as cancer-attacking proteins produced by the immune system, in 1985.
Specific areas of research include cell fusion and recombinant DNA technology,
diagnostics, and therapies based on monoclonal antibodies.

Japan's rapid strides in biotechnology are all the more remarkable when one
considers that the country wasn't even in the race until about 1980, when the
Ministry of International Trade and Industry tagged the field as a priority.
Today there are almost 200 biotechnology companies in Japan. One of the
biggest attention-getters is an ambitious consortium announced in 1985: the
Protein Engineering Research Institute, where the goal is to develop methods of
producing customized versions of enzymes, antibodies and hormones by combining computer technology with traditional biochemical processing methods.
Preliminary research using these methods is highly promising. For example, just
a third-of-an-ounce of pure Hepatitis-B antigen (the viral protein that harms the
immune system) could provide enough vaccine to meet the entire Japanese market and, if the protein called Tumor-Necrosis Factor lives up to its early
promise, only 11-kg (25-lbs) of it will suffice to treat every cancer patient in the
entire world! These and other developments have made biotechnology a magic
word in Japan; large companies such as Mitsubishi now devote 40% of their
R&D budgets to biotechnology.

In comparison with these efforts, many of the most promising American
biotechnology firms are small and have no profitable businesses to sustain them.
In Japan's government-sponsored corporate world, a manager is free to take a
long-term approach, investing for years without showing any results. American
companies constantly have to worry about short-term results and stockholders'
expectations. Furthermore, in an attempt to neutralize America's advantage in
high technology by gaining access to its scientific breakthroughs, Japanese companies have set up bioscience laboratories in the United States, and Japanese
money now sponsors bioscience research at such noted American centers as
Harvard University. Many large Japanese corporations are now providing
investment capital for hard-pressed American start-up biotech firms in exchange

for access to scientific secrets. This trend was strengthened by the stock market crash of October 1987, in which American biotechnology stocks suffered huge losses.

Aerospace Thrust

Quietly but surely, Japan is also becoming a world leader in aerospace technology. In 1992, on a brand-new launch pad at the Tanegashima Space Center, a 41-meter (137-foot) high rocket weighing 234-tonnes (258-tons), with two solid rocket boosters attached to it will be prepared for lift-off. This will be the maiden launch of the H-2, Japan's heavy lifter. A milestone in the nation's space program, the H-2 will be a totally autonomous Japanese launch using indigenous technology. It will probably enable Japan to enter the commercial launch market, providing a competitor for Europe's Ariane-4, which made its first flight in early 1988. Before the turn of the century, the H-2 will be carrying a small Japanese-manned shuttle craft into orbit; the culmination of a single-minded, low-profile but enormously successful space program that began in 1961 with the launch of a small satellite into low Earth orbit. Japan already has about 40 satellites in orbit.

A Japanese polar-orbiting platform could also be installed in space as part of the International Space Station project being spearheaded by the United States. But Japan's program does not end there — the country plans to develop further versions of the H-2 to make it more compatible with NASA's space shuttle and Ariane-5. The intention is to offer commercial NASA-type space launch services and also enable the implementation of space station support missions.

Japan is not working alone in its space race. Like the U.S., West Germany is working on an advanced space-plane for the 21st-Century, and its studies have brought it into line with Japanese thinking, leading to co-operative efforts between the two countries. The vehicle could start flying as soon as 2005, keeping Japan at the leading edge of global aerospace technology.

Model of Technological Progress

Japan's huge success in global markets provides an instructive model for both developing and industrialized nations. The reasons for Japan's success are evident in the thoroughness, efficiency and resourcefulness that pervade Japanese society. They believe that their products can always be better, their work can always be done more efficiently and their methods, however successful, can always be improved. Japan's tireless approach to detail, and its constant search for improvements, distinguishes it from its competitors even more than the quality of its products and the cleverness of its processes. In Japan, technology is not an end in itself but a tool, helping to implement simple and efficient approaches to doing things better. The indefatigable desire to improve quality is dramatized by the pervasive slogan: "Do not inspect quality — create it and then build it into the product and the process from the start."

Education is also a national obsession in Japan, reinforced by detailed personnel and employment strategies in both industry and government. Japan's population is perhaps the most technologically educated and literate in the world. Not only is the average level of student achievement very high by international standards — especially in science, math, music and art — but 90% of all students graduate from high school. With only half the population of the U.S., Japan has more undergraduates in electronic engineering. Vocational training and adult education also aid national industrial policy. Economically, tax laws strongly favor saving and discourage borrowing, allowing the accumulation of capital needed to build strong industries.

National industrial planning is clearly the major factor in Japan's technological success, which was predicated on the ability to build a unified vision of Japan's future industrial structure that would best meet the changing conditions of the international marketplace. Through a co-ordinated effort that has enabled Japan to move steadily up the technology ladder, "Visions of the Future" white papers were created to gain a national consensus on issues ranging from Fifth Generation computers to biotechnology.

There are some 330 forums for vision-making (called deliberative councils) including the Industrial Structure Council and the Industrial Technology Council, with representatives from trade associations, government, academia, mass media, labor, and consumer and public-interest groups. These bodies constantly discuss which industries and technologies are most important for the country's economic growth (and should therefore be targeted for special favors) and which are becoming noncompetitive (and should be phased out).

The consensus that emerges from the vision-making process is then published and distributed throughout the country to serve as a basis for corporate strategic planning. In 1986, for example, Japan's Science and Technology Agency sought to consolidate the country's research supremacy with a new "Human Frontier Science Program" (HFSP) to promote both basic research and international co-operation in R&D. The program will focus on three areas: the biology of regulatory processes in organisms (such as the aging process), the development of new materials, and brain research.

Research in the latter area, as discussed in the next chapter, is a new frontier of growing importance and yet Japan is the only country which has so far decided to make it a specific priority. Indeed, Japan plans to develop a "neural computer" — which operates like the human brain — and other devices that can communicate directly (via the nervous system) with the body. As part of its HFSP effort, Japan has created a forum of corporations, universities and government-affiliated institutions to find practical applications for brain science technologies.

With these visionary approaches, in less than 40-years Japan has emerged from technological and economic obscurity to lead the world in almost every field of technology and scientific research. This technological supremacy, in economic partnership with its East Asian neighbors, will make Japan the economic superpower of the next long-wave cycle in global affairs.

G-Force T-7
Pushing Back High-Tech Frontiers

"Once the human mind is stretched by a new idea,
it can never shrink back to its original dimension."
— *Oliver Wendell Holmes*

Human inquisitiveness is the major G-Force of all innovation, and today we are witnessing a revolution in scientific exploration that is pushing back the frontiers of knowledge and understanding as never before. This investigative boom is moving towards an understanding of the deep reaches of both outer-space (the solar system and beyond) and inner-space (the human organism, brain/mind and consciousness). Indeed, many scientists believe the human brain/mind is a mirror image of the universe itself. Thus, as humans forge a keener awareness of their own inner functioning, they are likely to find a more peaceful and harmonic future within the grand cosmic scheme of things.

Brain/Mind Research
Writing in 1979, Gordon Rattray Taylor, then the Chief Science Advisor to BBC Television said:

> One might say that the brain mirrors the environment. Since the wiring and the thresholds are specified by the kind of world that exists, then there must be some kind of homology (matching) between the two. It is a homology of transition probabilities. Similarly the brain mirrors the internal world. It is the brain's task to try to reconcile the macrocosm with the microcosm. Prediction is one of the essential attributes of the brain, and the laws which govern future events are mirrored in the brain as well as the events themselves. The brain then constantly monitors the discrepancies between its own predictions and what is actually happening.

Other brain scientists have reached similar conclusions:

- "A holographic brain observes a holographic universe"
  - Karl Pribram, Neuroscientist, Stanford University, U.S.

- "An explicate order unfolds from an implicate order"
  - David Bohm, Physicist, University of London, U.K.

- "You and the world are embedded within each other."
  - Gerald M. Edelman, Director, Neurosciences Institute, Rockefeller University, U.S.

Both Pribram and Bohm have proposed theories that, in tandem, appear to account for all transcendental experience, paranormal (unusual) events and even "normal" perceptual oddities. For Edelman, the way we interact with the universe and learn to perceive it both creates the functional anatomy of the brain and gives order to the world. The implications for every aspect of life, as well as for science itself, are so profound that we cannot ignore the work that has been going on in this field, which began during World War II.

In 1977, Karl Pribram correctly predicted that soft sciences such as brain research would become the core of hard science by about 1990, just as cognitive psychology, once considered soft, took precedence over behaviorism. He also predicted the emergence of holism — a shift towards universal laws encompassing all of science. In the past two decades, there has indeed been a scientific explosion in the study of the mind — and three Nobel Prizes have been awarded for this work which is based on theories of symbolic computation and parallel processing by the brain/mind.

As we enter the 1990s, this thinking comes to the fore in the hard sciences of computer technology. Pribram's theory has gained increasing support and has not been seriously challenged. An impressive body of research in many laboratories has demonstrated that the brain's structures see, hear, taste, smell and touch by sophisticated mathematical processes. Information in the brain is distributed as a hologram. The brain apparently has a "parallel processing" capability with connections formed by paths traversed by light, in addition to its more limited digital or linear (computer-like) connections.

A 1986 book called *Parallel Distributed Processing*, by David Rumelhart and James McClelland, developed a new theory of cognition called connectionism, which assumes that the mind is a very large network of very simple elementary units. Mental processes are interactions between these units. The term parallel refers to the assumption that units excite and inhibit each other throughout the network simultaneously — in parallel operation rather than in a sequence of operations. The term distributed refers to the assumption that knowledge consists of the connections between pairs of units distributed throughout the network, rather than being stored in localized structures.

Modern research into computer systems is based on this concept of parallel distributed processing. The human brain weighs only 1.4-kg (3-lbs), but a computer with the same number of "bits" would be 100-stories tall and cover the entire state of Texas. In attempts to replicate the brain's super-computing efficiency, international efforts are underway to develop "neural" computers modeled on the brain itself. The U.S. Defense Advanced Research Projects Agency is advocating an 8-year program to create a neural network — the precursor of neural computers — which would replicate human thought processes and lead to artificial intelligence systems that would fuse streams of data in simultaneous high-speed processing. The European Economic Community has also embarked on a research project known as BRAIN (basic research in adaptive intelligence and neurocomputing). Japan, as usual, is leading the pack, with at least 15 firms already doing research to develop, by the year 2000, a completely new neural model that "will be better than anything then existing." Toshiba is developing on "educable" neural network in which learning and use are performed in a hologram which, like the human brain, continues to learn and adapt. New holograms are overwritten on the old ones which, as in human memory, fade away into long-term memory for later recall.

Brain research itself has been a major strategic activity of the two superpowers since the mid-1970s. Psychic abilities are being researched and developed in government-sponsored research programs in both the United States and the Soviet Union. Yet most people have been led to believe that psychic abilities and experiences simply do not exist, or at least are beyond their understanding. The public has essentially been misinformed. The governments of the United States and the U.S.S.R have quietly spent millions of dollars in a long-term, careful and successful effort to develop ever more proficient and potentially useful psychic abilities. The seriousness of this activity is demonstrated by the following excerpt from a 1981 U.S. Congress report of the Committee on Science and Technology:

> Recent experiments in remote viewing and other studies in parapsychology suggest that there is an "interconnectedness" of the human mind with other minds and with matter. ...Experiments on mind-mind interconnectedness have yielded some encouraging results. ... The implication of these experiments is that the human mind may be able to obtain information independent of geography and time.

The most advanced brain research in America is now carried out at the Beckman Institute for Advanced Science and Technology at the University of Illinois, whose primary mission is to probe the human mind and the nature of intelligence. Understanding how humans reason will allow us to reap enormous advances in medicine, psychology, education, computer science, engineering and nearly every other field of human endeavor. As Albert Einstein said, "Boundaries are only a state of mind." Ongoing research in this microcosmic area (the brain) can literally transform the macrocosm.

Nanotechnology

The ability to arrange atoms lies at the foundation of technology. As outlined by Eric Drexler of the Massachusetts Institute of Technology's Nanotechnology Study Group, molecular technology — or nanotechnology — can manipulate individual atoms and molecules with control and precision. Today's electronic microcircuits have parts measured in micrometres (millionths of a metre), but molecules are measured in nanometres (billionths of a metre). Tomorrow's biochemists will be able to use protein molecules as motors, bearings and moving parts to produce micromachines. Nanotechnology will move beyond science's current reliance on proteins, producing structures more complex than simple fiber strands. The next generation of nanomachines or "assemblers" will be able to bond atoms together in virtually any stable structural design. Electronic nanocomputers will "likely be thousands of times faster than electronic microcomputers — perhaps hundreds of thousands of times faster," says Drexler.

The potential effects of this technology are astounding. Nanomachines will replicate themselves by the ton, then reconstitute themselves (re-organize their molecules) on a pre-programmed basis, forming themselves into other products, such as computers, solar panels and rocket engines. They will also form themselves into disassemblers, which will be able to break down rock to supply raw material. Assemblers will be able to make virtually anything from common materials without any human labor whatsoever; they will radically transform technology, and hence the economy. As Drexler concludes, they will be "engines of abundance." Replicating assemblers will make solar power cheap enough to eliminate the need for fossil fuels, and enable the removal of atmospheric carbon dioxide to halt the "greenhouse" effect of rising global temperatures.

Molecular technology will also provide "engines of healing." Cell repair machines (which will be available by 2050 or so) will be comparable in size to bacteria and viruses, traveling through human tissue as white blood cells do today, and entering cells as viruses do. According to Drexler, we could build "planet-mending machines" to correct environmental damage. Cleaning machines could remove poisons such as dioxin by simply rearranging their atoms.

The Biotechnology Revolution

Biotechnology is a multidisciplinary field in which biological, physical and chemical sciences are integrated in various processes to produce goods. After microelectronics, biotechnology is the second great scientific and technological revolution of the late 20th-Century.

What gives biotechnology its revolutionary character is its range of applications. By applying biological techniques to industrial processes, biotechnology is creating new products, enhancing the productivity of traditional industries and helping to protect the environment. Many countries are investing in biotechnology. Some are using it to develop new industries such as bioelectronics, others to modernize traditional industries such as agriculture, food processing, fisheries and forestry. Biotechnology opportunities fall into six areas:

- The control of problems in raw-material-processing (such as pollution created by cellulose-processing);
- The modification of raw materials (such as the production of better wood pulp);
- The improvement of existing products (such as advanced pharmaceuticals);
- The production of new products (such as new proteins and bio-cosmetics);
- The management of waste residues (through such means as recycling); and
- The optimization of processing operations (such as interfaces with computers and robotics).

Now that technology has replaced essentially all human labor in Western agribusiness, farming output is about to get a shot in the arm from the biotechnology revolution. A whole new industry is forming on the basis of biotechnology in agriculture — 450 companies worldwide are developing animal-care products based on such techniques of molecular biology as gene splicing. Present research is focussing on several areas:

- Inexpensive diagnostics to spot diseases potentially dangerous to humans and animals;
- Genetically engineered vaccines that are safe and effective;
- Growth hormones (genetically engineered proteins to dramatically increase milk yield, reduce fat in meat and bring poultry to market faster);
- Fertility hormones and embryo-manipulation techniques that will lead to more births of higher-quality livestock.

One company is already marketing some two dozen types of diagnostics. Some livestock and poultry diseases are very costly to the agricultural economy; the beef industry alone, for example, is estimated to lose $50-billion a year worldwide through diseases that new techniques will cure. Other techniques will allow global milk production to double. In China, for example, dairy cows typically produce only about 270-litres (600-pounds) of milk per year — half as much as Holsteins in the West today. This is before allowing for biotech advances that will soon increase milk yield by up to 20% of present levels in Western countries.

Agriculture is also being revolutionized by plant genetics. Scientists at the U.S. National Institute of Genetic Medical Science, the Oak Ridge National Laboratory and the University of California have recently determined the atomic structure of the Earth's most common protein, a feat experts say may eventually help them increase food production and design new drugs. The protein, known as *RuBisCo*, is present in all green plants and transforms carbon dioxide into sugar to initiate photosynthesis, the process that makes plants grow. The world's plants produce 1.0-tonnes (1.1-tons) of *RuBisCo* each second, or 34-million tonnes (35-million tons) per year, and American scientists have already altered this protein's structure to make photosynthetic bacteria double their uptake of carbon dioxide, which makes plants grow more quickly.

A recent University of California study predicts that genetic improvements to the world's 28 most important crops will "allow higher yield, increased nutritional value, resistance to pests and disease, growth in adverse weather conditions, and reduced need for fertilizers" before the turn of the century.

This could help us move away from the pollution caused by expensive synthetic nitrogen fertilizers. Biological nitrogen fixation is a valuable method of using certain microbes' bacteria, or blue-green algae to make nitrogens available to a growing plant. The microbe absorbs nitrogen from the air and converts it into compounds that can be used by plants, satisfying the plants' need for nitrogen at low cost to the farmer and without polluting the environment. The most famous of the nitrogen fixing bacteria are those of the genus *Rhizobium*. These bacteria penetrate and live inside the roots of legumes (members of the pea and bean family). They form swellings or nodules on the roots; the plant obtains its nitrogen through the bacteria. Other bacteria, which work in a similar way, live freely in soil. Nitrogen fixation by this process could amount to 87-million tonnes (90-million tons) per year worldwide, compared to the 48-million tonnes (50-million tons) per year of fertilizer manufactured industrially today. Soil scientists believe this natural method will satisfy about 40% of the global need for nitrogen.

In the forestry and pulp and paper industries, researchers are examining: biological fungicides that could protect stored wood chips; methods of controlling pitch and slime in pulp and paper machinery; and ways to decrease the amount of waste fiber that leaves the mill. And geneticists are already cloning trees that will grow faster (and in nontraditional and difficult environments) in order to solve the world deforestation problem. Indeed, the newest frontiers of biotechnology are based on cloning, monoclonal antibodies and gene splicing. In 1988, genetic technologies were developed by Cangene, a Toronto high-tech company, to identify a single molecule and then reproduce it 1-million times or more — from "microcosm" to "macrocosm." This technology, which cost only $6-million to develop, can create pharmaceuticals and plants for less than 1-cent apiece.

Creating New Materials

The new age of "man-made" materials, which is the next step in the continuum from Stone Age to Bronze Age to Iron Age, is based on the creation of composite materials fused from such common elements as clay and sand together with synthetic materials such as plastic. Instead of taking raw materials and forming them into products, science can now identify the products needed and then "compose" them, atom by atom, from whatever materials are required.

Fine ceramics, which are harder and smoother than steel, are increasingly used in car and airplane engines and bodies. The telecommunications industry is being transformed by microchips made from gallium arsenide, ceramics, and fiber-optic cables made from glass as thin as a human hair — only two of which are needed to handle all trans-Atlantic telephone calls. Healthcare is being transformed by biomaterials (such as artificial tissues, skin, joints, arteries and organs) made from plastics, ceramics, glass, silicon, rubber, carbon, polymers and composite alloys. One new substance, chitin, is a raw material taken from crab shells, shrimps, krills or mushrooms to make artificial body parts. Scientists have also found that chitin, of which there is an estimated supply in nature of 97-billion tonnes (100-billion tons), can eliminate cholesterol from the body and enhance immunity to cancer. Other new composite materials are transforming the construction of houses, buildings and transportation infrastructures.

The Super-Conductivity Sensation

The intriguing phenomenon of super-conductivity, the physical state in which electric current flows without energy loss, is vividly apparent when a battery is attached to a wire of super-conductive material and then disconnected. In a process more like magic than science, the wire continues to conduct the current, even after the power source has been switched off. Moreover, as much as a year later, the electric current is still in the wire.

The new science of super-conductivity is forcing us to rethink all the ways in which we use electricity. It will revolutionize electronics and transportation, allowing computers to operate at blazing speeds and levitated trains to travel at the speed of sound, all at vastly reduced rates of energy–consumption. Super-conductivity can also transform the aerospace industry. For example, an orbiting satellite could potentially receive power directly from the Earth's magnetic field and then generate its own magnetic field, of sufficient strength to enable it to propel itself by opposition or attraction to the Earth — in perpetual motion in the cosmos.

Exploring Outer-Space

In 1957, the Soviet Union startled the world by placing the first satellite, Sputnik I, into orbit around the Earth. In 1969, the United States put a man on the Moon. Since then, we have seen the United States develop its space-shuttle technology and the U.S.S.R. put a space station into orbit. Now, the Soviet Union is launching its own fleet of various-sized space shuttles and the United States has embarked on a project to complete a large, permanent, manned space station by 1996.

Besides exploring planets for minerals and manufacturing various biotech and other products in space, humanity is also trying to make contact with other civilizations, which undoubtedly exist in the Solar System and beyond. One of the best prospects for this is Pioneer 10, a space probe now tens of billions of kilometres from the sun and carrying a plaque indicating, among other things, its origin and bearing images of a man and a woman. It will be the first Earth-craft to leave the Solar System and travel into the galaxy. Before the middle of the 21st-Century, it could be intercepted by space-faring explorers from this and other galaxies who may be able to decipher the message on the plaque and thereby make contact with us and share their own high-tech expertise.

In the view of Thomas Paine at NASA, "the inner solar system is the future home of mankind and in the 21st-Century we expect to see permanent settlements on the Moon and on Mars." Already, some 350 companies are lining up to go into space. They are realizing that space is not just a place where unusual products might be made in a rare environment of zero-gravity vacuum and extreme temperatures. General Motors, for example, is considering orbital experiments to learn about combustion, pollution-control devices and new materials. The 3M Company is pursuing space research to come up with new films, coatings and electronic materials. Weightlessness may allow the creation of purer drugs and the development of fundamentally new elixirs. Tests have already been done to produce substances in quantities 700 times as large (with purity five times as great) as is possible on Earth. Flawless glass, super-strong metal alloys and tough plastics are also potential space products.

This is only the tip of the iceberg of experiments in space. With every shuttle flight, something of scientific or commercial interest is studied and learned. By 2010, space industries could annually produce $65-billion worth of products and services for the 6th-Wave Outer-Space sector of the global economy, improving our lives.

President John F. Kennedy of the United States foresaw that the problems of the Earth would be solved from outer space. But he was only half right: they will be solved by pushing back the frontiers of both inner- and outer-space. Exploring these final frontiers of our humanity, we are likely to find solutions to most problems: from human disease to planetary pollution, from fear of each other to fear of our common future in the Universe. Once we reach the early decades of the 21st-Century, the frailty of our evolution on planet Earth will start to be perceived as a purely temporary stepping-stone to a cosmic future — one we will learn to understand and manage with our minds as we move out into the Universe and the galaxies in the centuries beyond.

G-Force T-8
Creating an Info-Rich World

"Knowledge ...is a rich storehouse."
— *Bacon*

The sole purpose of all our technological innovation is to satisfy our needs and aspirations. We do this constantly, in three interconnected ways:

- Through the direct application of new science and technology in such fields as agriculture, healthcare and education and in the creation of various products and services;
- Through the drive for productivity and efficiency (to eliminate work and create leisure); and
- Through the creation of sufficient real wealth to facilitate these achievements for a growing population by means of an ever-expanding economy.

The first two of these phenomena have already been discussed. The remaining technological G-Force is the unfailing ability of human ideas to generate wealth. Information is the predominant common denominator of 4th-Wave innovation.

Information science transcends the previous division of scientific fields to find application in every area of human endeavor. And information is a completely new type of commodity: it is invisible and yet is so abundant that it fills the entire universe. Indeed, the sum total of information constitutes a complete mirror-image picture of the entire universe as it is unfolding before us: the old 1st-, 2nd-, and 3rd-Wave material world; and the new 4th-, 5th-, and 6th-Wave information world. The future is a reverse "projected image" of the past. It is through information that the future world reflects it own past, evolving across the 6-Wave continuum of socio-economic development: from "Earth ... work ... service ..." to "information ... leisure ... outer-space ....".

And because information-based technologies will be the creators of true value in the future global economy, humanity stands at the threshold of an unprecedented age of wealth. The affluence of the 4th-, 5th-, and 6th-Wave continuum will be as increasingly widespread as was the decreasing poverty of the first three waves to date. Such an info-rich reinvented world is now within our grasp.

169

Substituting Information for Mass

As we leave the material world behind, the 4th-Wave Information Revolution magically substitutes information for mass. As Paul Hawken articulated in his brilliant book *The Next Economy,* in every product or service there is a relationship between the amount of "mass" (raw material) and the "information" (know-how) the product or service contains. For example, an ingot of lead has a high ratio of mass to information, while a personal computer has a high ratio of information to mass. Using more nonrenewable natural resources ultimately makes goods more expensive and hence less available. To maintain or enhance our standard of living we need to use fewer nonrenewable resources to produce a greater number of better-quality goods and services. This is what we are starting to do by producing high-tech products, from telephones to houses.

Innovative products are effective tools of socio-economic development, because they have a high information content (that is, value). For example, the U.S. Library of Congress is mostly "mass" — all its books could be stored in a more usable form on a single computer compact disk (with minimal mass and maximal information). The substitution of information for mass is achieved by raising the demand for information, which (because information is a factor of production) decreases the cost of goods and of the information itself. As a consequence, the traditional 1st-Wave natural resource and 2nd-Wave manufacturing sectors of the economy (which generated mass) are declining, while the information economy booms. Whereas a new mass economy is booming in the Third World, it has a higher information content than its Western predecessor.

In one sense, the information economy is nothing new, because we have always substituted information for mass. Information has constantly raised people's standard of living and eliminated the drudgery of labor as we have modernized the old waves of the economy. This has been achieved by creating new waves of innovative technology — in the form of software and/or hardware and in the form of information/knowledge and expertise — and applying them to different economic processes in ways that increase efficiency and productivity. By constantly producing "more with less," we have created new real wealth.

In Western countries, a century ago, we had a so-called agricultural economy, in which three-quarters of the population worked on the land, 7-days a week, at least 12-hours a day, simply in order to subsist. Today, the agricultural sector employs only 3% of the work force but is still North America's largest earner of export income. This increased economic output was achieved very simply: Western society applied information in the form of technology hardware (machines, combines, tractors) and software (fertilizers, husbandry techniques, breeding, new crop strains), to the agri-production process. This allowed farmers to "do more with less" — to substitute cheap technology for expensive labor. In the process, they enhanced their wealth, freed themselves from back-breaking labor on the land and created some leisure time. Today's North American grain farmer (with help from only his wife) can plant and harvest 500-hectares (2-square-miles) of wheat by working (driving tractors and combines) only three or four months a year. As agriculture became less labor-intensive, labor pools were created to exploit other natural resources in forestry, fisheries and mining. In these 1st-Wave primary industries, the entire process of substituting information for mass repeated itself. Today, these sectors also provide only 4% of the jobs in Western countries.

With the Industrial Revolution, the same thing happened. Wealth was created by substituting information (in the form of machines, steam power and coal technologies) for labor — using brains instead of brawn. Henry Ford's automobile production line, for example, totally transformed the economics of manufacturing. New technology enabled Ford to produce a simple black automobile in record time at record low cost. As a result, in 1914, he was able to offer a wage of $5 a day compared to the $3.50 standard daily wage in the automobile industry. By using superior technology, Ford brought a new product to market (which otherwise would not have been brought to market), and thereby not only increased his own profit but was able to pay people more. Henry Ford's superior "information" about "mass" production-line technology was worth at least $1.50 per-day per-worker to him in increased wealth (i.e., what he was able to pay his workers over-and-above his non-automated competitors). This wealth-creating formula is typical of technological breakthroughs.

The financial services industry has successfully substituted information for mass. For example, between 1972 and 1984, the British banking system increased its staff by 35% but was able to handle 130% more transactions, due to the implementation of computerized accounting and check clearing systems. Checks are now cleared directly from one computer to another in Western financial systems and the mass of paperwork is simply handed over in sacks along with a computer tape.

Global Transition to 4th-Wave Information Economy

Technology is not only a factor of production (like labor and capital), it has become increasingly information-intensive. Indeed, a model originated by American economist Robert Solow in 1957 and further developed by Eward Denison shows that half the increase in U.S. economic growth rates in the 20th-Century can be accounted for by growth in the technology factor. In other words, improved productivity is the only source of real incremental wealth. The other half of the economic growth came from increases in labor and capital input (which only stem from the prior creation of real wealth) and population growth. Today's robots and flexible manufacturing systems are extremely information-intensive. By 1987, robotization had reduced the blue-collar sector to only 14% of the work force in North America, where it is no longer possible to operate a productive factory, mine, fishery or farm without good technology and superior management information. This has not been achieved without social disruption in the form of unemployment and labor disputes. Yet these are not caused by the technological substitution, but by poor planning for its implementation. With proper planning, as Japan has shown since 1978, massive substitution of information for mass can occur while full employment is maintained with little disruption.

Technological substitution is taking place in every major world economy. The poorest economies now have the same work force distribution as Western countries had about a century ago. But with today's technology, they will modernize within 25-to-50-years. Changing technology has improved economic development over the past 20-years and, even in the poorest countries, has enabled 7% of the labor force to move from farming to industry. In the middle-income developing countries, employment in the 3rd-Wave service sector has also surged. Industrial restructuring and the emerging post-industrial information-based society are a worldwide phenomena.

What is Information?

In this new economy, information is the primary commodity, the common denominator and primary product of all activity in each of the 6-waves of the economy. Information is as valuable as gold. But, unlike gold, information is a renewable, inexhaustible resource. As a key factor of production, it is second only to human resources. When manipulated electronically, information is:

- Abundant (the universe is full of it);
- Inexhaustible (it cannot be used up; you can sell it, but you still possess it);
- Self-reproducing (it creates new knowledge);
- Cheap (increasingly inexpensive to produce — or reproduce);
- Flexible (adaptable to many applications);
- Instantaneous (it eliminates time constraints; it is constantly switched on);
- Mobile (it eliminates distance; you can send it anywhere and access it anywhere);
- Non-hierarchical (it transforms organizational structures into networks);
- Opportunity-creating (you can do new things with it).

Information is virtually the mirror-image of all previous commodities. Indeed, as Marshall McLuhan observed in 1964, when it is made electronic, information transforms all processes and relationships (from centralization to decentralization; from mass-production to customized production; from logical connections to intuitive linkages). Thus in the Information Age, we don't travel to work to produce things. Rather, the work (in the form of information) travels to us the instant we switch on our home computers. Information and knowledge, and information-intensive technologies, give us the power to do what we have never done before.

Information is power. The old adage "knowledge is power" has at last become literally true. "What one knows" rather than "what one owns" is becoming the new base for political, social and economic power. All this power stems from applied information in the form of technology. Information is thus the primary resource. Raw material resources are placing fewer limits on the production of goods as our growing knowledge improves our ability to substitute newly invented materials for scarce ones and to tap hidden supplies for recycling. Automation permits less effort (in working hours or machine energy) to produce more economic output. As a result, the value of economic commodities is tied more to their information-intensive usefulness and less to their material-intensive substance. For example, a book is generally valued more for the quality of its contents than for the quality of its paper or its binding, clothes for their current styling, cars for their high-tech features.

Knowledge-oriented enterprises have thus become the core activity of Western society, reflecting the fact that knowledge (information organized for a particular purpose) and its communication are now absorbing the human time, energy and financial value formerly invested in mass production and transportation systems. The education and information industries will be the twin pillars of the Information Society. Japan's Yoneji Masuda discerns that human values change along with knowledge; as material values are superseded by new time and information values, greater importance will be attached to the development of new abilities and the improvement of human life. The new emphasis is on the consumption of information and knowledge, rather than the consumption of commodities. Indeed, in a real-time environment, it is information (not time) that is money and money can be created nonstop, 24-hours-a-day, 365-days-a-year. All successful companies and countries are constantly undergoing the 4-STEP process of innovation and the resultant creation of increased wealth and leisure time. We must understand that this is what worldwide economic development is all about. Only as the total global work force continues to gain in experience, productivity and leisure will it boost its salaries, wages and benefits — as well as business profits.

High Mass Knowledge Creation

In the information society, "the knowledge frontier" determines the potential market. Increased possibilities for problem-solving and the development of opportunities in the global society are now the primary factors in the expansion of this information market. The most advanced stage of the Information Society will be what Masuda calls "the high mass knowledge creation society," in which computerization will make it possible for each person to create knowledge and go on to self-fulfillment (see Fig. 14).

The same will apply to politicians and nation states as they move away from protectionism towards global co-operation for economic development. The transcendant business of the future is "the opportunity development industry," which will open up personal, corporate and institutional possibilities for the entire planet. In these times of major change and massive world problems, it is opportunity development that provides the greatest chance for contribution to economic and political progress, as well as human spiritual growth.

Since information knows no boundaries, the entire world is getting caught up in the process of information gathering, with each country developing its own army of information workers. In the main, poor countries are poor because they have been exploited and are unable to get wide access to education and good ideas in the form of science and technology. The gap between rich and poor is really an "information rich-poor gap." This gap will be gradually eliminated through the universal spread of the global 4th-Wave Information Economy during the next long-wave cycle, from 1990 to 2050, making all 10-billion of us info-rich.

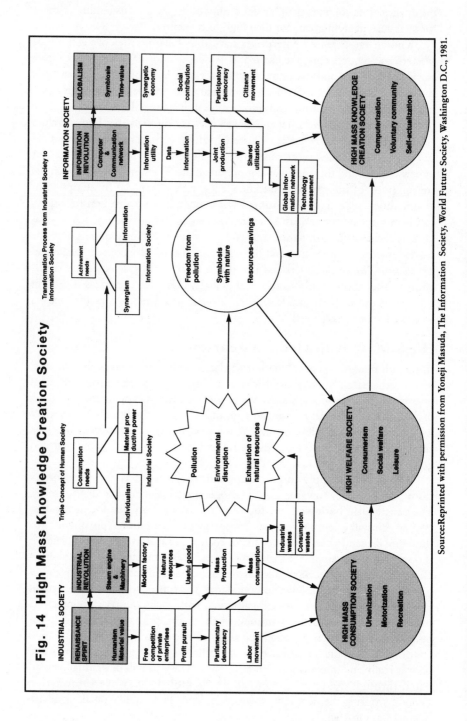

Fig. 14 High Mass Knowledge Creation Society

Source:Reprinted with permission from Yoneji Masuda, The Information Society, World Future Society, Washington D.C., 1981.

Section "E"

G-Forces of
Economic Modernization

Overview:
Redistributing Planetary Riches

"Settle the economics question and you settle all other questions."
— *William Morris*

All 5-billion of us have the amazing potential to "get rich." The direction and strength of the global economy is not as uncertain as we are led to believe. It is simply transforming itself very quickly, albeit with disturbing wrenches, into an economy of super-abundance. As a result of the compounding G-Forces of social motivation and accelerating technological innovation, the global economy is going through the biggest upheaval and restructuring in history.

New planetary riches are about to be created. These riches also will be redistributed worldwide as a result of two simultaneous mega-shifts in economic activity (and resultant economic and political power): from Atlantic countries to Pacific countries and from the developed countries of the North to the developing countries of the South. In parallel with this upheaval, the Western financial system is undergoing a collapse that is part of a regular 57-year cycle. The next economic boom, driven primarily by electronic technologies, will stem from the growth and application of the new commodity of information, which will be the creator of global wealth in the 21st-Century. In the new 6-wave global economy, energy and natural resource problems will gradually disappear as a result of low-energy-intensive industrialization, energy conservation, the discovery of new sources of energy and raw materials, the magic of recycling — and improved management of the planet's environment. At the same time, the old concepts of Capitalism and Communism are disappearing, as is global competition. Instead, the economic G-Forces point to the creation of a Planetary Information Economy (PIE) which, through the new information technology infrastructure, will redistribute its riches for the gain of all humankind.

Atlantic "Sunset", Pacific "Sunrise"

The world's economic center of gravity shifted from the Atlantic to the Pacific in the mid-1980s. This shift can be measured in a number of ways, such as the volume of trade conducted across the two great oceans, the flow of international financial transactions, or the relative changes in economic strength (as a percentage of the total global economy) of Japan, the United States and Western Europe. It also is clear that the major center of world finance, which moved from London to New York around the time of World War II, has recently moved to Tokyo. At the end of 1988, the market value of all stocks traded on the Tokyo Stock Exchange was more than 50% higher than the value of stocks traded in New York and five times the value of stocks traded in London — which only 50 years ago had the largest stock exchange in the world. This phenomenon of an Atlantic "sunset" leading to a Pacific "sunrise" stems mainly from Japan's rise to global technological leadership.

Although the United States is a Pacific nation and will be a major player in the new "Pacific Age," Japan's supremacy will lead to a shift in global economic — and political — supremacy to Southeast Asia. This will leave Western Europe to form its own economic union (by 1992, it has been agreed) and to look to Eastern Europe and the Soviet Union for its economic future. All economies will continue to grow over the long term, though at differing rates, but the economies of the Third World will grow the fastest (albeit from low starting points) to generate an increasing share of global wealth.

Manufacturing Shift from "North" to "South"

This Third World economic growth is already starting to occur due to the second major economic G-Force: the shift of the center of global manufacturing from the North to the South. (The terminology of North and South is a convenient shorthand to differentiate the developed from the developing world. With the exception of Australia, New Zealand and the Republic of South Africa, the developed countries are spread around the northernmost part of the globe; apart from the three exceptions, all the developing countries — collectively called the South or the Third World — are located to the south of the developed countries.)

Planetary production is being located close to the new mass market (the Third World), which contains 80% of the world's population. In varying degrees this "production" already encompasses almost everything from basic infrastructure needs (construction, railroads, highways, airports) to transportation (trains, automobiles, airplanes) and consumer products (fridges, stoves, TV sets, radios) as the South gradually stops buying from the North those things it can more economically produce for itself. Moreover, the South can take on many of the functions of the North's service sector, such as data processing.

As this shift in economic activity continues, the poor countries will develop their economies and become much more affluent, and most will eventually catch up to the Western countries — in terms of Gross National Product (GNP) per capita — during the latter part of the 21st-Century. The Third World's take-off in economic growth will be reinforced by the removal of its foreign debt burden, which will probably be wiped out as a result of the imminent disintegration of Western economies and the subsequent reconstruction of global economic affairs.

Long-Wave Economic Restructuring:
From "Mini-Depression" ...

At the same time as the Atlantic-to-Pacific and North-to-South shifts are occurring, the world financial system is disintegrating, just as it has done every 57-years in conjunction with the long-term cycles of technological revolution. The current world financial system was finally formulated in 1944, 15-years after the 1929 stock market crash, with the creation of the International Monetary Fund (IMF), the International Bank for Reconstruction and Development (IBRD or World Bank) and General Agreement on Tariffs and Trade (GATT). It started to fall apart in the early-1960s with the culmination of North America and Western Europe's 2nd-Wave manufacturing supremacy and the signs of maturity in their 3rd-Wave services economy. The first concrete signs of disintegration were a series of recessions, which began in 1962, the removal of the U.S. dollar from the gold standard in 1971 (because the fixed-rate system could no longer function) and the dramatic raising of oil prices by the OPEC cartel in 1973 and 1979.

Since then we have been living on borrowed time and on increasing mountains of borrowed money, awaiting the necessary cleansing of the system of excessive debt and waiting for new technologies to replace old ones. The problem has been compounded by unsustainable levels of military spending (especially since 1980) and a failure to address the global debt crisis (which first came to a head in 1982). At the same time, society's basic needs (such as the need to repair decaying highways and bridges, and the needs of the homeless) have been neglected, as has the need to adequately fund essential new growth areas like the space program.

Although Japan and Southeast Asia represent the strongest-growing parts of the global economy, and Western Europe continues to make a solid if unspectacular contribution, the United States is still the largest contributor to absolute global GNP. But because it has been both neglecting its own technological modernization and has failed to exercise the necessary geo-strategic action leadership to restructure the global financial system, the United States is dragging the entire system down and is largely responsible for the coming debacle — just as Britain was when the system last started to fall apart in the late-1920s.

Global economic systems have clearly stagnated. Latin America and Africa have been in depression for most of the 1980s. Western 2nd-Wave industrial sectors are overbuilt and have grown beyond their long-term equilibrium size of needed productive capacity, which, despite some restructuring, is still well in excess of market opportunities, creating overproduction and large amounts of corporate and consumer debt. This overexpansion will end very soon in what I call a "Mini-Depression."

The excess productive capacity of old sectors such as textiles and steel, whose equipment is physically worn out and financially depreciated, will finally make way for the new era of rebuilding and further replacement by new sectors such as computers and electronics. Decreased economic returns during this period will make it difficult if not impossible to repay debt, forcing thousands of individuals, farmers and businesses, as well as several nations, to default. Hundreds of U.S. and some foreign banks and savings institutions, which have been failing in record numbers, will collapse. Unemployment will climb to record levels, particularly in the already struggling sectors and regions, potentially leading to social unrest in many cities of North America, Western Europe and the Third World.

... To "Super-Boom"

There is, however, much room for optimism. Some of the dead wood was pruned from the Western economy by the so-called "Great Recession" of 1981-83. Bailouts and printed money allowed much of it to survive, but it will be gone soon — replaced by the shining success stories of the future global economy that are already evident. We have been building the base of the next economic boom for some time, creating "silicon valleys" of future prosperity in the West, and building and modernizing the economies of Southeast Asia and China. Above all, the economic impact of the new technological G-Forces will take us into the first boom phase of the next global long-wave cycle. Major technological G-Forces are already ushering in a new set of industries and new wealth. The microelectronic revolution, the space industry, biotechnology and genetic engineering, new materials and the promise of fusion energy are the new engines of the next phases of global economic development.

The "Mini-Depression" itself will also be less severe than we might fear, because, notwithstanding the remaining deadwood, there is significant entrepreneurial activity in the global economy. This was the case in the United States and Germany in the 1870s and 1880s, and again in America from the late-1930s into the 1940s. Such an entrepreneurial environment exists during every spurt of innovation between long-waves, but not all nations seem to take advantage of it. Although there is a strong burst of entrepreneurialism again in the U.S., the nations taking greatest advantage of the new technologies today are Japan and other countries in Southeast Asia. We can reasonably expect that, by the mid-1990s, the Pacific Rim countries (including North America) will drive the economy of the entire world into a "Super-Boom" that should extend well into the 21st-Century.

Information As Wealth Creator

This wealth will come as a result of the underlying G-Force shift, worldwide in scope but particularly strong in Japan and the West, to a 4th-Wave Information

Economy. The major contributors to the world economy are simply becoming much less intensive users of human, natural resource, energy and service inputs. World demand for resources, vis-à-vis economic output, is shrinking, and as the need for raw materials drops, their prices decline. A recent study by the IMF calculates the worldwide price decline at 1.25% a year (compounded) on average since 1900. In other words, the cost of industrial raw material input needed for a constant level of output is now only 20% of what it was in 1900. Even in the Third World, where huge demands on resources will be felt if the needs of growing populations are to be met, we will use production processes that are much less resource-intensive than those that historically have been used in the West.

The leading national economies of the future will be information/knowledge/high-tech-intensive (4th-Wave), leading to the eventual creation of a leisure infrastructure (5th-Wave) and the economic development of outer-space (6th-Wave). The common element of this mega-shift is the abundant raw material of information. And the integrated electronic information system of computers and global telecommunications networks is the vehicle by which wealth is both created, distributed and redistributed worldwide.

Beyond Capitalism and Communism

All these planetary economic phenomena, occurring simultaneously, are changing economic theory itself. Management expert Peter Drucker has pointed out that the first generation of economists, the mercantilists, believed that wealth was purchasing power. Another theory at the time stated that land created wealth. Yet another group of theories held that wealth was created by human labor. About a century ago, economic theory split in two. Mainstream economists gave up the search for any theory of the creation of wealth, became purely analytical, and made the fatal mistake of no longer relating economics to human behavior. Instead, they believed economics was a discipline that governed the market behavior of capital and commodities. Conversely, Karl Marx developed the labor theory of value, which defined the creators of wealth as human beings and their physical labor. Capitalism and communism were born.

Such simplistic theories no longer work. Future economic theory must do what today's economists fail to do: rather than incorporating human physical labor (which is constantly being replaced by technology), economic theory must incorporate human intellectual labor (knowledge work, from which all ideas flow), technology (which stems from those ideas to find application in the economy) and the information thereby generated.

As well, instead of steadfastly assuming that the individual nation state can control its own economic destiny, future economic theory must integrate the realms of domestic and global economies. The issue is not whether the United States and other Western countries will adjust to global interdependence. The global economy is the new reality. Though countries cling jealously to absolute nominal sovereignty, building military forces they cannot afford, real economic and military sovereignty has long been substantially eroded. Despite the persistent periodic efforts of Western governments to play King Canute, to try to preserve their favorable positions by refusing to restructure the global financial system, they cannot escape the reality of the global economic long-wave megacycle that is inexorably taking the world in new directions — towards what I call the 6-Wave "Planetary Information Economy."

The Planetary Information Economy ("PIE")

The new Planetary Information Economy (or "PIE") has three major hallmarks:
- It is built on relationships (between people and their ideas, information and related technology, and the economy, that is, the first three elements of the 4-STEP process of social development);
- It is dynamic (modernizing and integrating all six waves of national economies and integrating them into the global economy); and
- It will be politically non-military (instead focussing human and technological efforts on 6-Wave economic modernization and environmental restoration).

Information economics therefore must concern itself primarily with all facets of global welfare. The goal of society must not simply be the possession of more things, but the capacity to enlarge ourselves through the sharing of information and knowledge so that we all prosper by global socio-economic development. This will create an abundant life for all people and countries in harmony with the global economy and the planet's environment. Each person will be able to maximize his or her satisfaction only in collaboration with all other persons, in the self-sustaining stewardship of the "PIE" for future generations. Suitable relationships between people and technology, and between different kinds of technology and sustainable economic growth, still need to be developed. We can no longer treat people and technology as "residuals" from a steady-state economic growth model, because history shows that growth is not steady but rather fluctuates dramatically, moving between equilibrium and disequilibrium over a 57-year cycle. Thus, any viable theory of planetary information economics must have three other elements:
- Global efficiency — the generation of long-term global wealth from globalized information;
- Global equity — the distribution of long-term global wealth by information systems; and
- Global sustainability — the continuation and renewal of long-term global wealth through continous research and innovation.

As the next long-wave begins, moreover, it is also clear that the accumulation of human knowledge (and the rate at which the stock of knowledge is being increased) is one of the most important dynamics of modern economics. Yet information and knowledge do not appear as explicit entries in conventional business or nation state income and expenditure accounts because (with a few notably innovative corporate exceptions) these accounts are framed primarily in terms of production of goods and services, not knowledge accumulation; nor is information recognized explicitly as an economic product or an asset. The same applies to human resources. In short, current economic theory omits the two most important and dynamic elements of future growth.

At the center of the "PIE" are people — all 5-billion of us. We gather and process data and information from our environment, modify it based on our values and beliefs, and convert it into ideas and knowledge. This process of scientific exploration and R&D (research and development) results in the evolution of technological applications. Again driven by the G-Forces of social motivation, therefore, this human creative process is the hub of the Planetary Information Economy — and the wealth it will create.

Thus, although real increases in wealth come from productivity improvements (that is, from information and technological innovation) economic growth comes from productivity and population growth (from meeting the increasing needs for products and services of an expanding market). In poor 1st-Wave societies, people are an asset only insofar as they provide agricultural labor. Otherwise, the inability of the economy to meet needs other than food means that people are, in the overall sense, a liability. But the increasing ability of the new technologies to help us meet social needs and educate the global populace will transform the population into its own greatest asset. The "PIE" should stabilize in about the year 2050 at 10-billion people, with a gross world product of $300-trillion, and a per-capita income worldwide of $30,000 (in 1988 dollars). The end of the 21st-Century will likely see worldwide abolition of poverty.

The Geo-Politics of Prosperity

To achieve this global prosperity and optimize global social development, two crucial and urgent political acts must be carried out. First, recent efforts to eliminate economically wasteful military spending and to restore the planet's environment through new or modified industrial processes must be speeded up. This can easily be achieved by rechanneling only $3-billion per week (less than 2% of global GNP) out of the $1.2-trillion the world spends annually on military activities.

"Trillions" and "billions" of dollars roll off the tongue easily, but all those zeros prevent us from visualizing exactly how much money is involved. $1.2-trillion breaks down to $23-billion per week; $150-billion is about $3-billion per week. If that small amount could be diverted away from military spending and into the civilian economy, much more socio-economic progress could be achieved. Experts have calculated that this would, by the year 2000 alone, entirely eliminate Third World debt and solve such major problems as deforestation, topsoil loss and lack of self-sufficient energy use. Alternatively, every week for one year we could channel $3-billion away from defense contractors to one of the world's 50 major urban areas to replace shantytowns with new homes, provide running water, build schools and hospitals, solve garbage disposal problems, pave roads and build transit systems. The benefits of such investments to employment and income creation would be phenomenal. In addition, those investments would bring peace to the world — indirectly through refocussed economic efforts, and, as I shall discuss, directly through eventual global disarmament.

Secondly, the essential process of global economic modernization will happen only slowly unless there is major political reform of the world financial infrastructure. As the industrially developed countries face the essential transition to post-industrialism, they tend to be characterized by what I call the "industrial nostalgia" of Reaganomics, which has trapped the Third World in depression for most of the 1980s. Industrial nostalgia is evident in attempts to maintain political and institutional frameworks like the IMF and the World Bank when they are no longer suited to manage the global economy. Indeed, these institutions are the direct cause of most of today's global financial mess because they steadfastly refuse to change. They are, of course, controlled by the United States (and its allies) through its influence and voting rights. During the Reagan era, American economic philosophies ("trickle down"), policies ("supply side") and actions (maintaining the status quo) have been based on the U.S.'s erroneous and arrogant belief that only it can continue to lead and dominate world economic affairs.

Present institutions must be globalized. Without question, it must clearly be understood that the Western transformation to post-industrialism and the economic take-off of the Third World cannot take place within the world's prevailing fragmented financial institutional framework. Only full globalization of the financial infrastructure will open the door to economic well-being for future society at large. To resist economic globalization, as the world is doing today, is to flirt with a chaotic institutional framework whose result will be economic stagnation worldwide. A geo-strategic financial governance system for the world economy is now an absolute necessity. As the "Mini-Depression" strikes and as the Planetary Information Economy continues to evolve, the enlightened self-interest of even the most ardent state-centered nationalists will inevitably lead to a globalization of world economic affairs. Due to the social, technological and economic G-Forces at work, political integration and governance of the global economy is essential. Only in this way will the Third World economies take off and lead us into the next phase of global prosperity.

Whichever course is adopted, the economic G-Forces will ultimately bring the biggest upheaval ever in global affairs, redistributing planetary riches, and dramatically changing the global economic (and political) ranking of nations.

G-Force E-1
Atlantic "Sunset", Pacific "Sunrise"

"Consumed with a sense of destiny, Eastasia plunges on— unrelenting."
— *Roy Hofheinz, Eastasia Edge*

Almost unnoticed, the center of gravity of the global economy shifted from the Atlantic Ocean to the Pacific Ocean. This occurred in 1986, when, for the first time in modern history, the volume of trade across the Pacific exceeded that across the Atlantic. Since then, the Pacific trading nations have continued to storm ahead. Concurrently, the center of world finance has also shifted, from London to New York to — by 1987 — Tokyo. In April 1987, for the first time ever, the market value of all companies traded on the Tokyo Stock Exchange exceeded that of companies traded on the New York Stock Exchange. One year after the stock market crash of October 1987, the Tokyo exchange was 50% larger than New York's and more than five times the size of London's. The largest company in the world today is not Exxon or IBM; it is Nippon Electric of Japan, which is five times as large as either of them. According to *Business Week* magazine, 310 of the top 1000 companies in the world are Japanese, and those 310 account for 48% of the total market value of the top 1000. The list of ten largest banks in the world was once made up entirely of British banks, then of American banks; today all ten are Japanese. In 1986, the per capita income of the Japanese exceeded that of Americans for the first time. Today the Japanese are the new rich, and they are getting richer.

This distinct and dramatic G-Force shift in geo-strategic economic power is not yet acknowledged by Americans. Conversely, the Japanese are reluctant to accept the leadership responsibilities of economic power — due partly to their modest Confucian ethic — and partly to the humbling experience of World War II. But the Atlantic "sunset" and Pacific "sunrise" are the new geo-strategic reality of planetary economic affairs. And China and other countries of East Asia are part of this Japanese-led dynamic reality.

Booming Pacific Trade

As recently as 1970, there was nearly twice as much trans-Atlantic as trans-

Pacific trade. By 1984, however, the combined exports and imports between North America and Asia were worth $181-billion, close to the $197-billion trade between North America and Europe, Africa and the Middle East. In 1986, trade across the Pacific surpassed that across the Atlantic and by 1988 was 20% greater.

In the two decades before 1986, Asia's contribution to all world exports more than doubled to 19%. Asian countries have simply taken advantage of America's appetite for foreign goods. The high Pacific growth rate is due to the continued strength of the Japanese economy and the rapid progress of Pacific Rim economies — China, Taiwan, Hong Kong, South Korea and the six-member (Indonesia, Malaysia, Philippines, Singapore, Thailand and Brunei) Association of Southeast Asian Nations (ASEAN) plus Australasia. Between 1970 and 1984, Japan's exports to the United States rose by 40% to $60-billion and Southeast Asia increased its exports even faster. In 1984 alone, 19% of the worldwide growth of exports came from Japan, and a further 14% came from Southeast Asia, up from 10% and 8% respectively in 1976. In 1984, Japan overtook West Germany to become the world's largest exporter of manufactured goods. In every year from 1979 to 1984, Southeast Asia contributed more than did Western Europe to the overall increase in world trade. In 1976, for example, half of the annual increase in world imports comprised goods shipped to Western Europe. By 1984, that amount had dropped to only 13%.

These trends have continued in recent years and are a solid reflection of the total economic performance of the Pacific nations. By the year 2000, the combined GNP of East Asia will be 75% that of North America. And trans-Pacific trade will be 30% greater than trans-Atlantic trade.

This growth of East Asia has been spurred by the Japanese relocation of manufacturing into low-cost countries in the region. From 1981 to 1987, Japan invested more than $100-billion in ASEAN countries. What we are seeing is a replay of U.S. corporate investment in Western Europe in the 1950s and 1960s. In the Philippines alone, for example, there are almost 200 Japanese companies with investments in electronics, chemicals, textiles and transport. Almost all Sanyo's TV sets are made in Singapore. Toyotas are now assembled in Indonesia. Every nut, bolt or widget made by a Japanese-owned and Japanese-managed firm in Malaysia becomes a Malaysian export once it is loaded on a ship bound for Japan. Every Sony television tube or Sharp microwave oven exported from Thailand boosts that country's balance of payments. All Japanese money invested in acquiring land, erecting buildings and hiring labor in the Philippines becomes foreign exchange for that country to allot to domestic importers.

Such investment is the only way to build the global economy. Though Japanese assets abroad have topped $1-trillion, less than 10% of this is currently direct investment in foreign subsidiaries, and most of it has been placed in joint ventures in the developing countries. What the East Asian countries are now accomplishing as a result of this investment is precisely what we need to see in other developing countries. This phenomenon is worth nurturing and the Japanese investment flood-gates have scarcely opened.

Japan-China Collaboration

Japan, looking ahead, has targeted China as a major source of business. While political sensitivities stemming from Japan's wartime occupation of China are still to be overcome, in the next 20-years China will become as important a market to Japan as the United States is today. China has enormous labor pools and domestic markets and an extraordinary potential to expand and develop. Japanese exports to China rose by nearly 50% from 1983 to 1984, and doubled again in 1985 to reach $12-billion. This made China the largest overseas market for Japanese products such as television sets (30% of Japan's output), the second-biggest market for its automobile industry and the buyer of 20% of its steel exports. While China itself has now become the world's largest TV manufacturer, it uses Japanese technology and know-how and consumes virtually all its production of TV sets domestically. Japan is now China's biggest trading partner, and China is Japan's fourth biggest. As North America and Western Europe continue to wane, Japan and China will be the centerpieces of an amazingly powerful Pacific economy in the 21st-Century, just as the United States and Western Europe were in the Atlantic era.

By 1997, Japanese investment in China is expected to increase tenfold from the 1986 level. By the end of 1988, Japanese firms had entered into several hundred joint ventures in China, and Japan now leads the United States and West Germany in Chinese ventures. Yamaichi alone has a roster of 40 to 50 projects and is seeking Chinese counterparts for joint ventures on technology transfers of all kinds. In 1985, Japanese banks lent China $2-billion over ten years at rates below market interest levels. Since then, Japan has lent China $10-billion more and (in 1988) agreed to make another $15-billion available in the 1990s. The Bank of Tokyo reckons China will need to borrow $5-billion a year in the next few years and thinks Japanese banks will be prepared to lend to what they still see as a very good credit risk and excellent partner, the Tian'anmen incident notwithstanding.

Japan: The New Global Banker

The Bank for International Settlements reports that by late-1985, the international assets of all Japanese banks totaled $640-billion, compared with $580-billion for all American banks. Japanese bankers and money managers are building massive beachheads in the world's financial centers. For example, well over 100 Japanese banks and other financial firms now operate in Switzerland; included are 29 banks, 22 insurance companies and 52 securities firms. The same pattern is repeated in every major finance center around the world.

Japan's financial power has emerged so fast that the Western financial community and policy-makers are only now beginning to grasp its economic and

political implications. It is clear that Japan's 3rd-Wave financial sector growth —
at least in the short run — will come at the cost of the U.S., Canada and the
Western European countries, just as its 2nd-Wave industry and commerce grew
at their expense. A case in point is Japan's invasion of Britain. Japanese banks
began lending to British city governments in 1983. In just three years, 44% of
that business was in Japanese hands. Japanese banks now account for more than
40% of all the overseas lending coming out of London and 23% of all the
domestic lending done in Britain. Similar trends are evident in the U.S. banking
market.

Just as Japan dominates the world banking league, it could wrestle control
of the International Monetary Fund (IMF) and World Bank away from the
United States. Washington has long held veto power over decisions of the IMF
and the World Bank because it has been their biggest funder (it provides nearly a
fifth of the finances in each case). When the World Bank was formed in 1944,
the United States held more than 40% of its voting power. By 1960 this had fall-
en to about 30%; by 1975, it was down to about 23%. In 1975, Japan had only
4% of the votes, but it is now providing much more funding and is therefore
entitled to a much bigger vote than it has had. Unless Washington increases its
funding, Japan could ultimately hold the controlling votes. Japan has so far
declined to exercise its full voting rights at the World Bank, but by 1995 it will
possibly have the same share as the United States — about 11.5%.

The political power that goes with financial power is evident in other ways.
In the past two decades, Japan has gradually built economic and political influence in many developing countries through massive aid and investments. A
combination of recent trade surpluses and the traditionally huge savings of
Japanese people has enabled Japan to build a massive pool of capital that is just
beginning to spread around the globe. Recognizing the need to get the global
economy moving again, Japanese banks are also helping Third World countries
solve their debt problems. Partly as a tax-cutting exercise, the banks have set up
and funded a Cayman Islands company to buy at a discount their own doubtful
loans (Japan has lent about $50-billion) to developing countries. In 1987, Japan
announced another scheme to recycle an extra $30-billion to developing coun-
tries in the form of new untied official aid and private sector donations. Because
all these funds are provided on an untied basis, the recipient developing countries may use the money to buy goods and services from any country around
the world, not necessarily from Japan. The sum total of such Japanese economic
assistance, which had already reached $11.2-billion in 1985 (in comparison with
only $9.4-billion from the United States), established Japan for the first time as
number one in foreign aid. In addition to these massive increases in funding,
Japan has enriched its aid by an expanded range of capital grants, loan interest
rates, and expanded technological co-operation.

Another plan to help developing countries achieve greater economic independence is called the New Asian Industries Development Plan and Japan aims
to speed up the program by two years by doubling medium-term aid to devel-

oping countries. According to Japan's Ministry of International Trade and Industry (MITI), such a concerted effort — by both the public and private sectors of both the North and the South — is necessary before the world can achieve true prosperity. Although it does not directly tie trade to aid, Japan thus aims to foster economic exports from developing countries by nurturing local industries. In addition, Japanese trade policy is to encourage Japanese businesses — particularly manufacturing ones — to locate factories in valued export destinations.

In 1982, Japan overtook France as the world's fourth largest direct overseas investor. It then overtook West Germany in 1985, Saudi Arabia in 1986 and the United States in 1987 to become the world's leading foreign investor. From 1981 to the end of 1987, Japan's net overseas assets had climbed from only $11-billion to more than $240-billion. This figure actually downplays the magnitude of the international flows of money. From 1982 to 1987 Japan's gross assets climbed from $228-billion to more than $1-trillion. Nomura Research Institute reckons that Japan's net overseas assets will rise to more than $720-billion by 1995, three times the 1987 figure. The rapid rise in Japan's foreign stakes and the assured prospect of further high growth are certain to result in increasing dominance of Japanese products and financial influence worldwide.

U.S.-Japan Crossroads

Japanese foreign investment in the United States is now as pervasive as American investment was in Western Europe in the 1950s and 1960s, when the U.S. was accused of buying up Europe. Total direct investment by foreigners in U.S. factories, warehouses, mines, oil wells, land and other enterprises (not including portfolio investments) has grown since 1977 by a staggering 600% to reach $150-billion by 1987 — and about 80% of it is Japanese. The number of Japanese-owned manufacturing companies in the U.S. has increased from 32 in 1981 to about 900 by 1988. In automobile manufacturing, for example, Toyota alone now has six vehicle plants at various stages of construction or production that could make 2.1-million cars a year — more than a quarter of total U.S. auto output.

Other Asian countries are investing in the United States; an estimated 35% of this investment is concentrated in California. For example, three of California's ten biggest banks are now Japanese-owned, and some Taiwanese, South Korean, Philippine and Hong Kong financial institutions have also set up major branches there. Japanese financial institutions have started muscling in on U.S. investment houses. Sumitomo Bank has bought a 12.5% stake in Goldman Sachs, and Nippon Life Insurance has a significant interest in Shearson Lehman. Another notable feature of Asian investment in the U.S. has been the scramble for real estate, again led by the Japanese.

Having outpaced the United States in technological innovation, economic growth, trade and investment, Japan is now the world's second largest economy in terms of absolute GNP and is awash in the financial resources necessary to play the locomotive role in global economic growth. As a result, in 1987, the U.S. and Japan reached a historic crossroads: the emergence of Japan as the world's mega-creditor was the mirror image of America's transformation into the biggest national debtor in world history. Reagan's supply-side "miracle" was built on foreign goods, investment and printed money. By the end of 1988, America's net debtor position was $533-billion and climbing. All projections from multilateral institutions such as the IMF and the OECD suggest that these trends are now so deeply entrenched that they can only be reversed by far-reaching global economic policy changes or by a global recession. On present policies, by 1991, foreign loans and investments in the U.S. will exceed American loans and investments abroad by about $1-trillion.

This turnaround in the relative financial positions of the two largest capitalist countries is a profound development with considerable geo-political implications. The U.S.'s insatiable and unsustainable appetite has also produced columns of red ink in its trade accounts. No other major country has ever produced such a string of current account deficits in excess of 2.5% of its GNP. Having peaked at 3.3% of GNP in 1986, this deficit ratio has since fallen a little, but the IMF reckons that it will remain at 2.5% or above in the early-1990s, while Japan's surpluses could be a similar proportion of its GNP.

As a result of these shifts, another crossroad has been reached. The average per-capita income of the Japanese is now higher than that of the Americans: $20,000 a year, compared with $18,000. As recently as 1965, Japan's average was only one-quarter of America's, and in 1953 it was only $188— one of the lowest in the world. It is noteworthy that Britain's per-capita income was second-best in the world in the 1920s, but today it barely scrapes into the top twenty.

America is in danger of following the same route. By the early-1990s, the U.S. will need a $60-billion trade surplus just to meet the interest on its debt, which otherwise will go on rising inexorably. To achieve the necessary surplus, the U.S. will have to do the exact opposite of what it did in the 1980s — it will have to hold down domestic consumption and produce more exports. The necessary shift of resources into export- and import-competing products could amount to 4% or 5% of GNP — about two-thirds of the total defense budget for the country. These adjustments, which will be a far larger adjustment than was needed to meet the oil shocks of the 1970s, seem unlikely under present political realities. This will lead to a further relative decline in America's — and further advance in Japan's — global economic position in the 1990s and beyond.

Although it is largely unassimilated information to North Americans right now, future historians will mark the late-1980s as the time when Japan surpassed the United States to become the world's dominant economic power. While America's absolute GNP may remain larger than Japan's well into the 1990s, Japan will be the major economic and political force in East Asia and the world. This vast area is undergoing accelerated socio-economic growth that will not reach its peak until well into the 21st-Century, by which time it will have played a major role in reinventing the world.

190

G-Force E-2
Industrializing the Third World

*"The mission of a manufacturer is to overcome poverty; to relieve society as
a whole from the misery of poverty and bring it wealth."*
— Konosuke Matsushita
Chairman, Matsushita Electric

The world is redeciding who is going to make what. Coincident with the shift in
economic gravity from the Atlantic to the Pacific, a second major economic
G-Force is the shift in manufacturing activity from the developed countries (the
North) to the Third World (the South). There are two reasons for this. First,
most of the North has virtually satisfied its material needs, its marketplace is
almost saturated, and its population has virtually stabilized so that little market
expansion is taking place. In contrast, the population of the developing countries is still growing by about 90-million per year, and by the year 2050, 90% of
the world's 10-billion people will live in the Third World. Virtually all of the
material needs of this vast marketplace are still to be met. Yet this marketplace
also serves as its own low-cost labor pool and has most of the resources needed
for product manufacturing. As a result of these global dynamics, since 1970 we
have seen a rapid unfolding of the planetary production site, with production
activity shifting to the Third World. The economics of production have
changed: the Northern countries are no longer able to manufacture many things
for the rest of the world on a competitive basis. We are living on a giant ball, and
it simply does not make economic sense to extract resources and/or fabricate
them into products on the rich side of the planet for shipment to poor populations living on the other side. Whenever feasible, such economic activities will
increasingly take place as close as possible to the mass of the people, who will
produce what they need for themselves. This applies across the 1st- and 2nd-
Wave sectors of the global economy, from agriculture to forestry to mining to
energy to manufacturing. Thus, instead of providing resources and manufactured goods, the West will increasingly supply technology, information, knowledge and expertise to the Third World. If we manage ourselves properly, we
should all get rich in the process.

Fig. 15 Global Economic Imbalance

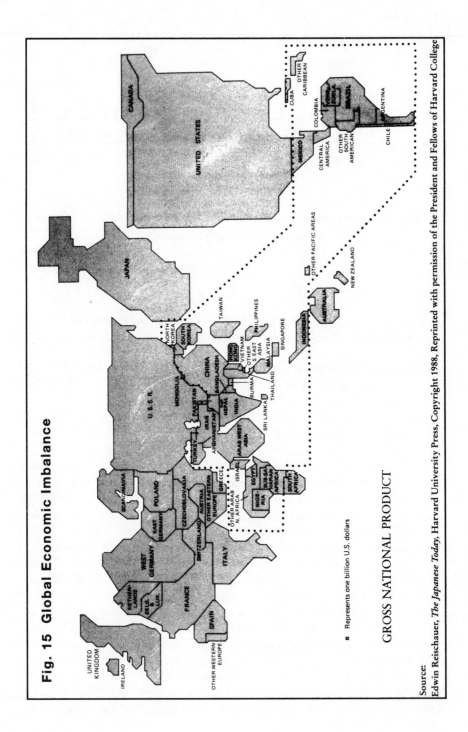

■ Represents one billion U.S. dollars

GROSS NATIONAL PRODUCT

Source:
Edwin Reischauer, *The Japanese Today*, Harvard University Press, Copyright 1988, Reprinted with permission of the President and Fellows of Harvard College

Fig. 16

Developing Economies Growing Fastest

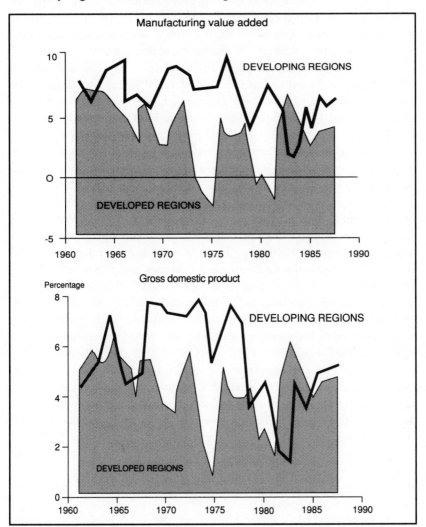

Source: UNIDO (1985, 1986, 1987 and 1988).

Global Industrialization

Today, the vast majority of world GNP is contributed by the Northern nations (see Fig. 15), in almost a reverse picture of the distribution of world population (Fig. 7) shown earlier. The resultant economic and population imbalance is globally destabilizing.

As the shift of manufacturing and technology to the South occurs, however, the Third World nations will ultimately become developed. Instead of being poor, they will become rich — just as the richest part of the North has done — by meeting the vast unmet needs of their large populations. Since 1960 the developing countries have been expanding their economies at a much faster rate than have the developed countries (Fig. 16) and are already challenging the stodgier Northerners, not just in textiles and steel but also in cars, electronics and a clutch of other industries. The challenge is bound to grow.

We must remember that industrialization began only 200-years ago. In 1780, Britain was the only industrializing country. Fifty years later, England was joined by France and Holland, but the rest of Europe was still very poor. In 1800, for example, the average German family spent 73% of its budget on food and 21% on shelter; only 6% remained for clothing and other needs. This is very similar to conditions throughout today's developing economies. Yet, by 1880, Germany became an industrialized country. The United States was also industrialized by 1880. As we enter the 1990s, we can see the potential for a much greater and faster international spread of economic modernization.

In all but four of the years since 1950, according to the United Nations Industrial Development Organization (UNIDO), the developing countries as a whole have achieved a higher growth rate of manufacturing value added (MVA) than the developed countries. Many older industries have moved to the South, the latest technology often being imported from the North. Textiles, clothing and electronic components started the migration in the late-1960s. More recently, some firms in the mature capital-intensive industries, such as automobiles, steel, ship-building and petrochemicals, have also moved — accompanied by a flow of credit and capital.

Developing countries have provided an increasing supply of numerous finished goods and services to the developed countries. These movements are part of the ongoing long-term process of relocation, adaptation and adjustment that is normal in global industrialization. To view this process from a short-run perspective or as the South's "causing" the deindustrialization of the North is a dangerous mistake. As discussed later, the answer is not to arrest the process but rather to resume sustained post-industrial growth in the North, thus spurring the 4-STEP process of change globally by helping the Third World industrialize faster.

In 1975 UNIDO adopted the "Lima target," whereby the developing countries should attain at least a 25% share of world manufacturing output by the year 2000. To meet the target, the developing countries must outperform the developed countries on average by 3.5% a year in GNP and 4.5% in manufacturing value added (MVA). They had outperformed the developed countries since 1967, and the differential in their respective MVA growth rates was actually 5.5% in favor of the developing countries by 1975. The Lima target thus seemed achievable. However, once the stagflation of the 1970s and the "Great Recession" of the early-1980s descended upon the world economies, Third World debt snowballed and the MVA growth differential narrowed and even became negative. The Lima target seems to have slipped out of reach — at least temporarily.

The underlying principle of the Lima target is that the South's growth in GNP is related to the North's. Growth in the North leads to an increase in the demand for goods and services produced in the South. In turn, Northern demand creates income in the South, pushing up the South's GNP growth. Thus, to achieve the Lima target means that the North must grow by about 3.5% and the South by about 7%.

However, if the North's growth rate in GNP were to fall to or below 2.5%, then the growth rate of the North's demand for Southern goods and services would fall to zero or even become negative. This would defeat the South's efforts to finance its imports from the North of products needed for industrialization. Reduced import demand from the South would further lower growth in the North. This is now happening. In 1987, for example, the GNP of developing countries (excluding China) grew by only 2.1%, down from 3.2% in 1986. Western countries grew 2.7% in 1987 (more than the Third World!), about the same as in 1986. Only China, which continued to be the world's fastest-growing economy in 1987 with 9.6% growth, exceeded the 7% Lima target for developing countries.

The Lima Target will again become realistic once the global financial system is pruned of debt and restructured for a healthy take-off based on the new generation of technologies. This is because total annual economic growth is a combination of three factors: the absolute annual increase in the size of population; the real annual increase in productivity; and the rate of change in the labor force, measured as the total number of annual hours worked by the total labor force. In the North, the total number of hours worked is declining by about 0.5% per year while population is increasing at slightly less than 1% a year, for a net gain in the size of the economy of about 0.5% per year. Therefore, productivity in the North must increase by about 3.0% every year (which should be attainable, given access to new technologies and information) if the overall 3.5% target is to be met; or by about 2.0% to guarantee the safe overall level of 2.5% net growth for the North. In the South, population is still increasing by almost 2% a year, and total hours worked are increasing by about the same amount for a net gain of about 4% per year. Therefore, productivity increases achieved in the South also need to be in the order of 3% each year. This should be achieved easily (bearing in mind the relative backwardness of Third World production methods) through increased education and access to more modern technology.

The Lima targets will also be met through the ongoing redistribution of global production efficiency. Many parts of the South have emerged as efficient locations for the production of an increasing number of product lines, particularly in Southeast Asia. Further changes in North-South comparative advantage will, in all likelihood, continue in the decades ahead. Even greater participation by the South in manufacturing will enhance global production efficiency. In short, such global industrial redeployment, implicit in the Lima Declaration and Plan of Action, is necessary for a more efficient co-operative management of the global economy.

In contradistinction to this essential global transfer of productive efficiency to the South, however, the thrust of Reaganomics was that wealth had to be generated in a "reindustrialized" North so that it could then "trickle down" to the South. Very clearly, this has not happened and will not happen. In fact, mathematically, the *reverse* must happen. The Northern countries will become better off only as a result of a "trickle up" of economic activity from the South. The global economy can grow only if we stimulate economic development in an "industrialized" South.

Neither is it useful to advocate that the developing countries model themselves on island miracles like Singapore or Hong Kong. Singapore and Hong Kong became what they are primarily because of their Chinese entrepreneurs, their positions along the routes of world capital and world transportation, and because of their strategic location near Japan and China. Their performance could be duplicated scarcely anywhere in today's world. A different approach is required in large, heavily populated countries if the sheer size of their populations is not to cause total collapse and chaos. Their economies must be built from the ground up; not by trickles of capital from abroad but by major investment in education and industry.

Multinational Role Model

The Bata Shoe Company is an example of how a company can build Third World economies from the ground up. Bata set up shop in Canada after World War II with the mission of becoming "the shoemaker to the world." If Bata had set up plants all the way across Canada to produce shoes to export to the rest of the world, the company today would probably be bankrupt, because it would not have been able to compete with the low production costs that exist in the South. Instead, Bata realized, four decades ago, that it had to set up plants in local markets. The company now has about 100 plants all over the world and has captured 30% to 40% of the world's shoe market.

Bata has become successful by going to the local marketplace, working within the local environment (using local resources, local technology, local people), building a factory, building a school, building housing, building a hospital and establishing the local economic infrastructure. Bata realized it could not otherwise make shoes and put them on the market (which it does now at about $1 per pair for its local employees) in the Third World. The company's profits are re-invested in yet more Third World plants to make yet more shoes for the ever-expanding global population.

This is the exact opposite of what the exploiting colonists did by expropriating Third World capital back to London, Paris, Amsterdam or Madrid. In the long run, that approach did not work because it failed to build up those developing economies. The old empires lost political control over the countries they colonized in part because they failed to create economic development and the people demanded control over their own affairs. Unlike Bata, the Northern empires failed to see that the real economic potential in the world is in the South: in meeting human needs (whether for shoes or anything else) and in turning massive problems into opportunities for mutual prosperity. Following the Bata example, many multinational corporations are now playing a vital role in developing the new global economy. Much of the technology, management, talent and private capital needed to solve the world's economic problems are clearly in the hands of multinationals. They have the capacity to custom tailor these resources to the economic requirements of a given country or individual development project. They have a special capacity to transfer information and know-how to others in the most effective ways — a learn-by-doing, on-the-job process.

This North-South transfer of economic activity, using the Lima target model, will bring as much relative economic benefit to the North as it will to the South. The multinational corporation is an agent of change. An even partially successful multinational must be on or near some leading edge of innovation to prosper. Through their economic activities, the best multinationals are spreading the blueprint for a new economy over the entire world. By focussing on the vast unmet needs of the South, an increasing number of such corporations are able to generate economic growth for themselves, for the South and for the entire world. Redistributing manufacturing to the South and focussing on the production of information and know-how in the North, which is then transferred to the South for hard economic production, will create a vibrant world marketplace.

What Nations Must Do

In stunning contrast to global enterprise, national governments are presently inadequate to the task of dealing with the planet's economic necessities. The mixture of benign and arrogant neglect of what needs to be done is astounding.

The nations of the North and the South must blend their expertise and work towards the attainable Lima objective. They must forge agreements on the vexing but essential reforms of global trade and of monetary and financial structures and institutions. Structural adjustment is central to exploiting changing opportunities. In the South, we must seek out and promote those industries that best use local resources of human capital and raw materials, and which generate sufficient export earnings to finance necessary imports. In the North, we must create retraining programs to smooth the transition from the older industries. We must realize that all countries are customers of each other; that they must all continue to grow and prosper so that they can continue to be customers. And we must educate the citizens of the world, so that these needs become part of the political will of all nations.

The global challenge of adapting new technology and of industrial restructuring can only be met in an expansionary global context. If the challenge is met, the South can also expect to enjoy rapid growth in the modern electrical machinery sector, including semiconductors and computers, where it already accounts for 9.4% of global production. Many of the South's new entrepreneurs will increasingly be found in this sector. Such expansion and restructuring will create opportunities for the Third World to play its full role in the long-term post-industrialization of the world.

As this occurs, the Third World and China will continue to take on global manufacturing, together accounting for about 60% of global output by 2050. Japan, the United States and other Western countries will continue to deindustrialize and become advanced post-industrial economies.

The collective challenge is to meet the needs of the growing world population. This represents the largest economic opportunity ever offered to humankind. In meeting the challenge, the whole world — not just the South — will gain in prosperity in the 21st-Century.

G-Force E-3

Reinventing the Global Financial System

"The path of progress has not followed a straight ascending line, but a spiral with rhythms of progress and retrogression, of evolution and dissolution."
— *Goethe*

The money machine is about to stop working. Camouflaged by Reaganomics — what U.S. President George Bush once called "voodoo" economic policies — the Western economic system is stressed by "debt fatigue" and is disintegrating, just as it has done about every 57-years in parallel with the technological G-Force revolutions of the last two centuries. We are living on borrowed time — and increasing mountains of borrowed money — awaiting the necessary cleansing of the system.

The 57-year Long-Wave Economic "Mega-Cycle"

Economic disintegration is not a new phenomenon. It is a G-Force of Western economic history. The Soviet economist Nikolai Kondratieff described a long-wave cycle of about 60-years in general economic activity. The Kondratieff Wave (or long-wave, as it has come to be known) is characterized by an upward and a subsequent downward trend, each lasting 25 to 30 years. This long-wave phenomenon was further studied by economist Joseph Schumpeter in conjunction with other well-known shorter-term economic cycles, which we call business cycles. He astutely postulated that if such economic cycles of various durations were occurring, then they were all happening at the same time, compounding each other's effects. Schumpeter aggregated all the known short and intermediate economic cycles with Kondratieff's long-wave cycle. This identified an undulating long-wave "Mega-Cycle" of about 57-years' duration (shown as a thick wiggly line in Fig. 17).

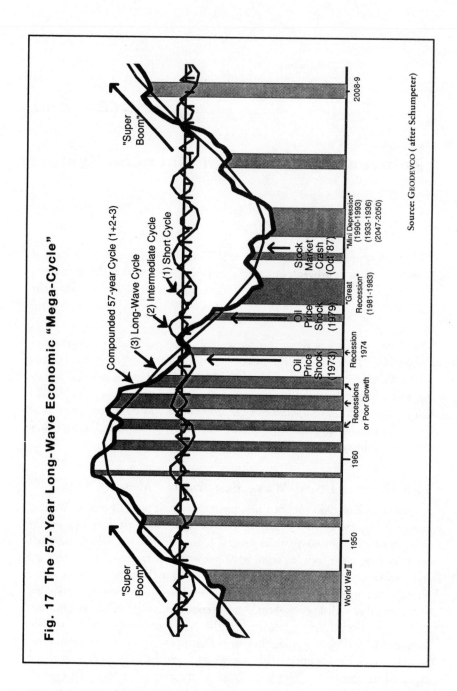

Fig. 17 The 57-Year Long-Wave Economic "Mega-Cycle"

Source: GEODEVCO (after Schumpeter)

The economic slowdowns or recessions that have occurred in North America (and usually throughout the West, in varying degrees) during the current long-wave cycle are superimposed on this chart. It cannot be coincidence that all these recessions — without exception — parallel the compound 57-year cycle identified by Schumpeter. Notice from the figure that only two economic slowdowns occurred during the 26-year upswing following the Great Depression. During the recent 31-year downswing, however, there were 9 recessions of various lengths and degrees of severity (as measured by changes in GNP). In other words, economic experience validates the long-wave cycle theory. Usually, but not always, the serious recessions came immediately after the year in which the short, intermediate and long cycles all fell in concert (for instance, 1961, 1970, 1980 and 1989). When all the cycles fall together, every 9.5-years, Schumpeter's 57-year compound cycle (the thick wiggly line) falls below the normal (smooth) line of Kondratieff's long-wave cycle, marking a decline in total GNP.

GNP declines most severely when the "Mega-Cycle" is at its lowest ebb. This economic phenomenon has been called a Depression. In reality, the "trough" in the "Mega-Cycle" is marked by two very severe recessions — what I call "Mini-Depressions." The first "Mini-Depression" of the current long-wave cycle was in 1981-83 and was dubbed the "Great Recession" by economists because it was the deepest recession since the 1930s.

The "Mini-Depression" (1990-1993)

The second "Mini-Depression" is due to occur from 1990 to the end of 1993, give or take one year. Because it will occur at the very bottom of the long-wave "Mega-Cycle," this "Mini-Depression" will be more severe in depth and duration than that of 1981-83. We are perched on the edge of randomness and chaos. The industrial economies could easily collapse no matter what scenario plays itself out. The world is so tightly interlocked that vulnerabilities have risen to unprecedented levels. Those who still insist, even after the 1987 stock market crash, that we are merely passing through a long-needed "correction" are suffering from economic illiteracy. Caught up in rising expectations, fueled by greed, they blindly ignore all the economic and noneconomic signals that are flooding in from all parts of the planet. On the economic front alone, the sequential warning signals have been rampant during recent years: floating currencies, energy cartels, inflation, unemployment, debt, disinflation (declining rates of inflation), deficits, bankruptcies, leveraged buyouts and junk bonds (high-risk, high-interest-bearing borrowing instruments). Present global economic cross-currents make it indisputable: we have entered the bottom of another long-wave. Like the stock market crashes of 1873 and 1929, the 1987 crash was the final signal that excesses of spending and money-inflated growth could not lead to any creation of real wealth.

As in the late-1920s and early-1930s, the world is awash in bad debt, but this time worse than ever before. Third World countries alone owe more than $1.3-trillion — almost 50% more than in 1982. This debt is growing much faster than the world economy; every day it becomes harder to service. According to the World Bank, "no country involved in rescheduling its debt since 1982 has significantly reduced its debt ratios." The crisis has been in remission at best. Inevitably, many countries will experience serious repayment problems and some will declare a total debt moratorium. In 1989, the new president of Venezuela cancelled all payments on the country's foreign debt and called on creditors to forgive all African debt and halve the value of all Latin American debt. Another $2.7-trillion in bad debt is owed by the U.S. government. American farmers, consumers and business people together owe yet another $1-trillion in bad debt. The U.S. savings and loan industry is insolvent to the tune of about $150-billion. And this is just a fraction of the problem.

All this bad debt must be cleared away before the world economy can grow again. During the last recession, in 1981-83, the necessary cleansing of debt from the global economy was prevented by countervailing U.S. monetary policy. The Third World, which anyway has been experiencing Depression conditions since 1980, is in a mess today primarily because of America's failure to find the political will to deal with the debt issue, which has been recklessly neglected and mismanaged.

To make matters worse, the United States has printed reams of money and indiscriminately flooded the world with excess cash liquidity. This attempted self-protection of the American economic status quo has achieved nothing except to make the debt mountain harder to service. Instead of carrying out real budget adjustments at home, the United States has been carrying its own deficits through the simple device of international borrowing. In other words, rather than becoming more productive to create real wealth, the U.S. has been — and still is — living off the rest of the world. This has hidden the coming "Mini-Depression" from American citizens who will be stunned by the reversal in their economic progress. During the recent period of "prosperity," incomes have increased but purchasing power has declined. For example, the average real income of American families in 1987 was no higher than in 1973. "Prosperity" has been built on debt. The "richest" economy in the world has inexorably become the world's largest net debtor. America is living beyond its means.

Any correction in U.S. monetary policy (for instance, printing less money) or fiscal policy (raising taxes) — while necessary — would now come too late for America (and the Western economy) to prevent the "Mini-Depression." The United States has not balanced a budget since 1960. The last opportunity to redress the situation was presented in the 1983-84 time frame but blissfully ignored by then U.S. president Reagan. His 1980 election promise of a balanced budget now seems hopelessly irrelevant. The Reagan presidency incurred more public debt than all previous American presidencies combined. If President Bush does not correct this profligacy, America's debt will exceed that of all other countries combined by the mid-1990s. It took America a decade to get into that hole. The "Mini-Depression" will make it deeper. Even though a real economic recovery should start worldwide in about 1993 (assuming Third World debt is dealt with), it will take at least a corresponding 10-years for America to get out of its hole. In the modern world, no nation can afford to lose 20-years of economic progress in the race for the future. Through extreme levels of deficit spending Reagan has driven the American economy into the ground.

Even if the U.S. spending stops, at least the Western part of the global economy is going to come crashing down with that of America. A debt/deflation scenario is already being played out in the North American farm, oil and commodities markets and in 1990 will spread beyond the stock markets to commercial and residential real estate and to the corporate and government sectors. With real incomes stagnant, borrowers are less able to service their mounting debts, and business and bank failures will increase. Prices will soften as the rising real debt burden further depresses demand, forcing additional liquidations. In such a debt/deflation spiral, more defaults and liquidations will again reduce income and wealth, forcing further cutbacks in demand and further price cuts — and further debt defaults.

The bad debts are now so huge ($5-trillion worldwide) that the write-down can no longer be managed smoothly, at least not within existing world financial institutional arrangements. A panic "meltdown" is likely — accompanied by beggar-thy-neighbor reactions of protectionism, debt repudiation, political turmoil and international economic disintegration. No amount of Third World debt rescheduling schemes (such as the Baker or Brady plans,put forward by the two most recent U.S.secretaries of the treasury) or fiddling with existing international mechanisms can now prevent the disintegration of the Western economic system into the largest debt/deflation collapse that the world has ever seen.

The spreading economic collapse will hurt every nation. Much of the Third World, already in a Depression since 1980 (due to debt austerity and deflating commodity prices) and faced with protectionism and aid cutbacks, will be unable to afford food imports for its hungry populations or to repay its massive foreign debts. Between 1980 and 1987, for example, GNP per capita declined each year by 3% in Venezuela, by more than 2% in Argentina and by nearly 2% in Mexico. Across Latin America, average real incomes have fallen by an average of about 2% every year throughout the 1980s, that is a compound drop of more than 17% in only 7-years. Loan payments on foreign debt are increasingly resented. (Witness the Venezuelan riots in early-1989.) The resulting loan defaults could topple the entire international financial system, deepening the crisis and perhaps also overturning many political regimes (as almost occurred in Mexico in late-1988).

With the American economy in disarray, it is likely that the Soviet Union will make distinct political moves in the Middle East and other vulnerable areas to take advantage of U.S. weakness. America will be unable to do much, and its inaction during this period is likely to further alienate Western Europeans, who consequently could disengage from NATO, adopting an independent military and parochial economic posture ("fortress Europe") which, in turn, could further encourage the Soviets to make new incursions (trade, not tanks) into Eurasia.

Under President Bush, the U.S. could become more nationalistic and politically conservative during the disintegration of its economy. The military-industrial establishment, however, will further lose its political influence during the crisis, as the government struggles to manage budget cutbacks and prevent hyperinflation. Reform movements under the Democrat-dominated Congress (1989-92) eventually could lead to a type of social democracy (and a new style of Democratic president in 1992) and increased government involvement in the economy. The booming Pacific Rim countries will, as in 1981-83, go into recession as the world economy disintegrates, but will not slip into "Mini-Depression." Japan will clearly emerge as the world's economic leader and will exercise a geo-political leadership role in the eventual restructuring of the world economy.

Restructuring the Global Economic System

After the imminent economic collapse — it seems nothing will be done before — the early-1990s will necessarily see the global economic system reconstructed to take advantage of the 4th-Wave phenomena of post-industrialism and global economic interdependence. The current international monetary system was designed to operate in the handwritten ledger-keeping age of the Western 2nd-Wave industrial economy. It cannot be expected to cope with microelectronic 4th-Wave post-industrial global activities. Today, information about all countries' diplomatic, fiscal and monetary policies is instantly flashed onto 200,000 video screens in the world's foreign currency trading rooms. Not only are international transactions now conducted at electronic speed but a whole new series of nations and multinational corporate players has entered the world money game. And increasingly they are playing the game with data and information, not raw materials and widgets. The new international financial system is a technological system. The problem is that we insist on thinking that all we have to do is tinker with the existing policy mechanisms and restructure existing monetary institutions such as the IMF and the World Bank.

Global interdependence is also being ignored. As Michael Blumenthal, a former secretary of the U.S. Treasury and now chairman and CEO of Unisys Corporation, points out, "In most countries monetary policy still reflects the illusion that the pursuit of an independent national policy remains an effective and appropriate means of setting interest rates, controlling inflation and influencing the overall level of economic growth." The notion that monetary policy can be effectively managed nationally is obsolete. Sovereign rights no longer provide enough power to make such decisions durable. Nor can the value of a national currency be more than superficially protected by intervention in foreign exchange markets by so-called central banks — of which there are now more than 160.

Each country has its own banking system, supervised and controlled by that country's central bank (for instance, the U.S. Federal Reserve System, the Bank of Canada, the Bank of England), which provides money to the country's banking system. At the global level, there is no parallel to the central bank. This is the glaring weakness of the world financial system. It is like a baseball game played without rules or umpires.

The International Bank for Reconstruction and Development (IBRD), set up to "reconstruct" Europe after World War II, is known as the World Bank, but in no way is it a global central bank; it acts mostly as a foreign aid agency. The closest thing to a global central bank is the International Monetary Fund, which was created by the Western countries in response to the economic chaos of the Great Depression. The charter of the IMF provides it with seven objectives:

1) to promote international co-operation (in reality, the only co-operation is among the "Group of 7" rich countries who control the system to their own ends);

2) to facilitate the balanced growth of international trade (we have the worst trade imbalances in history);

3) to promote exchange stability (almost all national currencies — all 160 of them — float up and down like corks on an ocean);

4) to foster a multilateral system of payments (half of world trade is now done by barter because traders don't trust the system);

5) to make natural resources available to members (resources are controlled by cartels);

6) to seek reduction of the duration and magnitude of payment imbalances (we have the worse imbalances in history); and

7) (added in 1969 when things began to crumble) to manage international liquidity to avoid economic stagnation and deflation as well as excess demand and inflation in the world (clearly a joke in today's world).

The IMF has utterly failed to meet its mandates, especially the last one. The global financial system is under such serious stress and strain that such a weak-kneed organization, controlled as it is by the interests of the financially ailing United States, cannot possibly begin to cope with the post-industrial global economy now enveloping us.

Periodic attempts to strengthen the system have failed. These began with the creation of Special Drawing Rights (SDRs) in 1969, in an attempt to create a global currency. But SDRs, a mixture of the world's major currencies, account for such a small percentage of international reserves that this mechanism has failed simply because the United States insists on trying to control the international financial system with the value and quantity of *its* currency, which it prints at will. The U.S. dollar itself, however, was unhooked from gold in 1971 — an arbitrary, overnight measure by a desperate U.S. president Nixon — and any pretense of international currency stability has since vanished. Monetary conference after monetary conference has failed to come up with solutions.

The oil shock of 1973 (OPEC tripled oil prices) prompted the first so-called "economic summit" of Western government leaders on the initiative of France and West Germany. The 1975 meeting favored intervention to maintain "orderly markets" in foreign exchange. In 1982, these leaders ordered a "study" of exchange-rate intervention, essentially admitting that during ten years their summit meetings had achieved nothing and that they did not understand the new global economy.

At the World Bank meeting in Toronto, in 1982, Mexico announced that it was unable to service the debt it had built up in the 1970s. This "debt shock" occurred in the midst of the greatest recession in 50-years. Although the U.S. reluctantly admitted, three months later, that another global monetary conference (like the one that saw the IMF created) was needed, such a meeting has never been held. In 1983, the summit leaders ordered a second study of the international monetary system, and in 1986 they promised co-operation and ordered yet another study of what needed to be done.

World Bank/IMF and summit meetings are now all talk and no action. They have become annual media jamborees where political leaders, while trying to groom their political images on prime-time news, are able to communicate only their dithering incompetence to govern. These meetings should be the natural venue for far-reaching co-operation agreements and international monetary reform. Instead, this annual babble (of positions worked out in advance) has failed even to achieve currency stability. Unless our global and domestic leadership can deal with global bad debt, which now stands at more than $5-trillion, and restructure the world financial system, the "Mini-Depression" could quickly turn into the biggest and most traumatic "Mega-Depression" in human history. Unless they act soon, the Western nations will become the stagehands and actors rather than the directors of the rapidly unfolding play of the global economic future. Japan in particular must don its new mantle of leadership and insist on a reform of the system.

Repeated appeals for a fundamental reform of the international monetary system, comparable to that accomplished in 1944 when the IMF and World Bank were created, continue to fall on deaf ears. The majority of today's financial policy-makers fail to comprehend the global economic future into which they are supposed to be leading us, and instead try, in vain, to sustain the old 2nd-Wave system.

As a result of this astounding lack of leadership, the world is following a path similar to that taken in the 1930s. Both the Great Depression and the world war that followed can be traced to world leaders' ineptitude, demogoguery and lack of courage in political decision-making about the need to restructure the world economy. The IMF, which was founded as a statement against the economic orthodoxy that created the turmoil of the 1930s, now represents a new orthodoxy that has perpetuated the turmoil of the 1980s. Its supporters cannot bear the thought of the IMF undergoing change, let alone disappearing. Instead, they talk valiantly of finding new ways to restructure debt and fund it in a global environment where money knows no boundaries and has no regulatory structure to control it.

Such fumbling in the dark misses the point. We need a transformational breakthrough in our collective thinking: a recognition of the new nature of money. In a world where money (or, rather, "information *about* money") constantly flows around the world at electronic speed, we need a new geo-strategic management system to control both money *and* information (which are equally intangible). This new institution must also act in the interest of *all* the players of the new global money game.

The seeds of the present crisis — and its solution — lie not in temporary, cyclical factors but in fundamental long-wave adjustments and socio-economic restructuring worldwide. In parallel, the solution lies not in the mythical magic of the marketplace of Western economies, but in collective global action; not in delaying tactics to preserve national power and the status quo, but in the willingness to share power and let go of the past. Above all, we cannot afford to remain inactive. There is nothing pre-ordained about present structures. They were created by human imagination, they can be changed or replaced by human imagination.

In short, we desperately need some common sense. With America as massive debtor and Japan as massive creditor, a truly international economic superstructure must be devised, with reduced American and Western European leadership and increasing leadership for Japan and all the other countries of the world. If the U.S. continues to resist change, then Japan must exercise initiative to call together the world's major countries, including representatives of all developing countries, to create a consensus about the need for such a transnational geo-strategic superstructure for the global financial system. Though the transition requires more political will than now exists, a new infrastructure presents a less traumatic transition to a new economic order than would the total collapse of what exists today.

Proposed New Infrastructure

The next long-wave "Mega-Cycle" must be managed or it will manage us, and we will miss the enormous opportunities for economic development now presented to us by new technologies.

A new blend of global fiscal and monetary mechanisms would include a Global Central Bank (or, if absolutely necessary, a modified IMF) that would take charge of the geo-strategic management and regulation of the world financial system, including:

- a single world currency standard for international transactions (or even a modified SDR); and

• a Global Equalization Tax — an international system of taxation (perhaps levied as a value-added tax on each country's GNP) that in one fell swoop would replace the present contentious system of IMF funding quotas, replace complex trade barriers and replace all forms of foreign aid and overseas development assistance organizations, including the World Bank.

The Global Central Bank should include all nations as its members (socialist bloc as well as developing countries), and its management and control should be genuinely global. It would be empowered to put as much proportional pressure on deficit countries to adjust their balance of payments (such as the United States today) as on surplus countries (such as Japan today) so that the present asymmetry of treatment is removed. The Global Central Bank would act as the lender of last resort to the world system, refinancing short-term debt and providing safety nets against unforeseen liquidity crises. It would play a decisive role in recycling financial surpluses — in collaboration with the private capital market — in the post-industrial economy that will generate the new wealth whereby surpluses would be achieved. The Global Central Bank would regulate the international banking system (through its national members) and global money supply, global interest rates and national currency values. It would not only monitor market and capital-flow developments but would have the authority to set minimum capital requirements for all major financial institutions involved in global transactions (large banks, security houses, perhaps even insurance companies) and to institute universal accounting and recording standards.

The only way to relieve world liquidity pressures is to restore to major currencies their roles in paying the bills around the world. In the last economic boom of the 1950s and 1960s, the U.S. dollar essentially became the world currency, finally replacing gold in 1971. The U.S. dollar is being asked to do too much. Unless the Japanese yen, the British pound, the Swiss franc and the Deutschemark can take up the burden, the economic recovery coming from the 4th-Wave technologies will die of monetary thirst.

In Western Europe, the European Currency Unit (ECU) is already turning into a genuine currency and will ultimately replace national moneys, of which it now is a mixture. In early-1988, West Germany in fact proposed that the EEC consider the creation of a European Central Bank and a single currency (to supplant all existing Western European currencies by 1992). This will probably happen now that total EEC integration is planned for 1992. The Western European banks have had a multilateral clearing mechanism for ECU payments since in 1984, and the ECU is the world's fourth largest circulating currency after the dollar, the pound and the yen. In the last few years we have also seen different steps to "internationalize" the yen by making it more attractive for settling international trade transactions and the like.

These moves are really a step towards three relatively stable international currencies: the U.S. dollar, the Japanese yen and the European ECU. These currencies, however, can only be a prelude to the evolution of a single global currency, which must be introduced soon. Such a world currency unit, which would be issued by the Global Central Bank (and which I will call a "Global"), would stabilize the international system and stop speculation against the other national currencies.

The Global should also be backed by a "basket" of real world economic resources. These resources should be gold plus all of the natural mineral and energy resources used in 1st- and 2nd-Wave economies, and would extend to the 4th-Wave commodity of information. As well, because nearly all primary commodities, such as oil, wheat and copper, are currently traded in dollars, and even though their real value will continue to decline in the deflationary transition to a post-industrial economy no matter how they are priced, this adjustment would be cushioned by pricing them in Globals, which, of course, would be backed by all those primary commodities themselves.

Each domestic currency, instead of floating against the dollar, would then be pegged against the Global, but allowed to trade within a certain narrow band of rates against the new standard. The Global would also be the only international reserve currency, and all present-day national reserve currencies such as dollars, pounds and yen (and SDRs), would be phased out. The increased supply of Globals would subsequently be limited by the real increase (that is, after inflation) in world economic output and exports so as not to generate inflationary pressures. The Global would be distributed based on each country's balance-of-payments needs, adjusted for any foreign aid they still might receive.

As part of the transition to this global currency, the U.S. dollar should simultaneously be devalued by about 40%, to about 100-yen per dollar. This would effectively devalue by about 40% (from end-of-1989 levels) the debt of all developing countries, which are now held in dollars. Alternatively, all of these debts could be converted to Globals while taking into account a reduced value for the dollar. All the debt would be refinanced in Global bonds issued by the Global Central Bank: that is, they would be wiped off the books of the debtors (and their present bankers). This proposal is similar to ones made in 1988 by James Robinson, chairman and CEO of American Express, and in 1989 by Carlos Perez, president of Venezuela and leader of the group of largest Latin American debtors, known as the Group of Eight.

The Global Equalization Tax (GET) would be similar in effect to the present system of federal/provincial equalization payments in Canada (a redistributive tax designed to encourage investment and economic development in depressed areas for the benefit of all Canadians). There is no reason why such a taxation system cannot be created worldwide. However, unlike what didn't occur in Canada, it must be phased in with a geo-strategic 6-Wave economic development policy for the developing countries.

The GET would also eliminate the need for foreign aid. The present resource transfers from rich to poor nations are totally voluntary, completely dependent on the fluctuating political will of the rich nations. Attempts by the United Nations, the Pearson Commission and the Brandt Commission to foster greater discipline in this field through a proposed 0.7%-of-GNP target for official foreign aid have failed miserably to date. As well, most assistance flows through bilateral channels rather than multilateral institutions. As such, it is greatly influenced by bilateral political relationships and corruption. Also, the international framework for resource transfers has excluded the socialist bloc, which until recently has provided little direct assistance.

Even if adequately funded, the bulk of current aid does not work. First, the aid relationship has negative connotations because it perpetuates the dependence of the Third World on the developed nations, instead of encouraging a relationship of partnership. In addition, aid is often used to acquire arms, to persecute racial and ethnic minorities and to cover deficits caused by inefficiency or corruption in order to enable regimes to stay in power. Notable examples are Nyerere's Tanzania, the Marcoses' Philippines and General Zia's Pakistan. In short, voluntary foreign aid fails to create prosperity because it is not geo-strategically managed to develop human capital, the real source of wealth creation.

What is needed is an institutional framework involving specific multilateral commitments by all nations. We should not shy away from new techniques of global economic development, even though they may at first seem revolutionary. The compulsory Global Equalization Tax — on the GNPs of *all* nations, rich or poor, each according to their own situations (perhaps modified to reflect GNP per capita and purchasing power) — would eliminate all these less-than-effective forms of foreign aid. International resource mobilization could then become fully funded and automatic, and would be accepted not just as an international obligation but as a responsibility towards the development of the entire global marketplace to its fullest potential. International taxation can be introduced through a variety of devices, such as a progressive income tax on all nations, with a minimum exemption, perhaps based on their GNP; indirect taxes on consumption of nonrenewable resources by all nations; a taxation on armament and defense spending worldwide; a charge for polluting the environment; and royalties on the use of the global common property of, for example, the development of new frontiers in information and technology transfer, ocean-bed mining and outer-space development.

Through this generation of revenue from the resources of the economy, at about 2% (not 0.7%) of GNP, the Global Central Bank would be able to finance itself as well as reallocate and redistribute these resources in the best interest of developing the global economy. Sooner or later debt has to be paid — or taxed away. A Global Equalization Tax is the only way to rebalance the global economy and restore a stimulating environment for us all. Thereafter, national or corporate comparative advantage will stem only from improvements in efficiency and productivity — in the broadest sense of international resource allocation — in a true globally competitive environment, which, nevertheless, is working to a co-operative, common agenda.

This global model is not new. Something quite similar was sketched in the early-1980s by Mahbub ul Haq, when he was director of planning for the World Bank. Let us hope that this global reconstruction occurs faster and more peacefully than it did last time. Before 1995, such a geo-strategic economic management system *must* be in place. By then, the "Mini-Depression" will have run its course, having swept away all the excessive borrowing of the 1980s, setting the scene for a breakthrough to the economic "Super-Boom" that will inexorably follow — just as it has done every 57-years in recent centuries. A new system is essential if the next "Mega-Cycle" is to be effectively managed and global prosperity is to be obtained.

G-Force E-4
Building the Planetary Information Economy (PIE)

"Information is wealth."
— *Francis Bacon*

The shining success stories of the future global economy are already evident. We have been building the base of the next economic boom for some time. "Silicon valleys" of future prosperity, modernized regional economies, and technological G-Forces are taking us into the "Super-Boom" phase of the next global long-wave cycle. In particular, wealth-creating information is the new engine of the next phases of economic development worldwide. We are building a Planetary Information Economy ("PIE") and it is a "growing PIE." The nations taking greatest advantage of this phenomenon are Japan and the other countries of Southeast Asia. By the mid-1990s, we can reasonably expect all the Pacific Rim countries (including North America) to drive the economy of the entire world into a super-economic growth path (a "Super-Boom") that should extend well into the 21st-Century. In turn, this will dramatically change the global economic rankings of nations.

Micro-Model of "PIE"

The best model of the micro workings of the pie comes from Japan. The way that Japan analyzes its 4th-Wave information economy is reproduced in Fig. 18. Information activities have a great influence both on the 4th-Wave information industries (through the commercialization of information) and on the non-information industries, as well as on households and government institutions.

213

Fig. 18

Micro-Model of Planetary Information Economy (PIE)

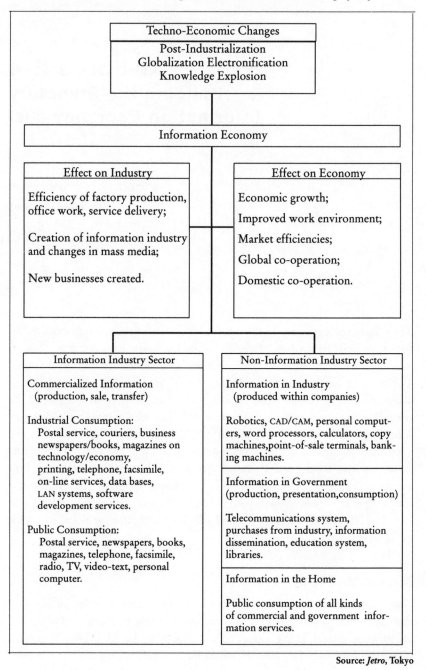

Source: *Jetro*, Tokyo

Fig. 19

Information-Related Industries

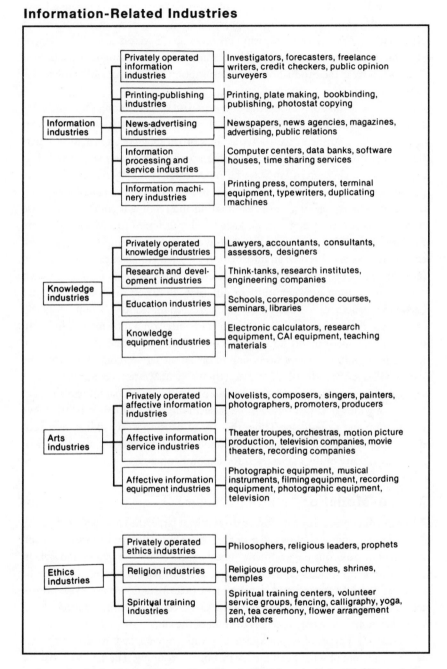

Source: Reprinted with permission from Yoneji Masuda, *The Information Society* (World Future Society, Washington, D.C., 1981)

In addition, information helps modernize the other five waves of the 6-wave economy. For example, it is not possible in the West today to operate a farm, forest, fishery, mine, oil well or factory without the latest in computerized information. Similarly, the tourism and outer-space sectors are totally dependent on information (see Fig. 19). The common element throughout the economy, therefore, is the production and consumption of information — the major activity of the PIE.

Because information, knowledge and expertise will be among the most valuable commodities in the future global marketplace, 4th-Wave Western economies have strong export potential in a broad range of information activities. Very often, however, these valuable commodities are overlooked. For example, in every Western 1st-Wave farming, forestry, fishing, mining and energy sector, there is a wealth of technology and experience. Information on such processes as breeding, cultivation, exploration and refining is embedded in these sectors. It needs to be dug out, packaged and transferred to a world desperate for knowledge and expertise. The 2nd-Wave manufacturing sector of these economies will also become an information supplier. Companies such as Boeing (aircraft) and Otis (elevators) already use electronic systems to pass product design information between units in different countries; these companies are becoming manufacturing databases, which are also linked to subcontractors and customers. As markets globalize, so do these electronic information links. In terms of information and knowledge content and work actually performed, futuristic manufacturers are becoming information-service conglomerates. The same applies to the 3rd-, 4th-, 5th- and 6th-Waves of Western economies.

Countries and companies that remain plugged in to global information can keep pace with world markets and the accelerating global diffusion of 4th-Wave information and technology. Those that try to develop solely indigenous, protected approaches will find themselves unplugged from the global techno-economic prosperity of the Planetary Information Economy.

Macro-Model of "PIE"

In macro-dimension, for a nation or the world at large, the PIE is depicted in Fig. 20. At its center are people — all 5-billion of us. We gather and process data and information from our environment, modify it based on our values and beliefs, and convert it into ideas and knowledge. The subsequent process of scientific exploration and research and development (R&D) results in the evolution of technological applications. Driven by the G-Forces of social motivation, therefore, this human creative process is the hub of the PIE.

As the G-Forces of technological innovation are applied, we create the five waves or sectors of what I call the Earth-bound economy. The 1st-Wave natural resource sector is that of agriculture and primary resource extraction based on the use of land and raw materials. The 2nd-Wave sector is that of manufacturing

Fig. 20

Macro-Model of Planetary Information Economy (PIE)

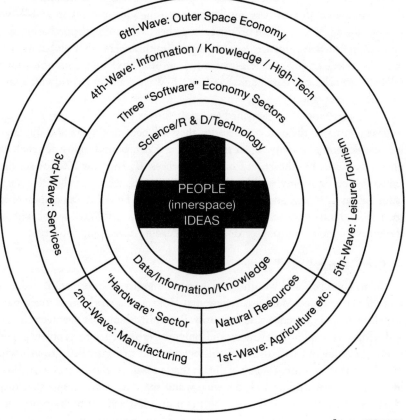

Source: GEODEVCO

and processing based on "hardware" to make raw materials into products. Then come the three components of the "software" economy: the 3rd-Wave service sector, the 4th-Wave sector of information, knowledge and high technology, and the fast-emerging 5th-Wave leisure and tourism sector. These five waves encircling the core of people form the Earthly portion of the PIE. In any country (and in the world at large), as a new wave is built to predominance, the previous waves shrink (as in the 6-Wave bar chart, Fig. 2), even though the total PIE is still growing. Right now, the 4th-Wave is assuming the greatest role in creating wealth in Western economies.

Surrounding the entire Earth-bound five-wave economy is the 6th-Wave Outer-Space economy, which we started to build with the first satellite launch. Space developments will not only build the 6th-Wave sector in its own right;

like information, they will also have huge spin-off effects for the further modernization and growth of the Earth-bound economy. For example, proliferating 6th-Wave satellite technology links with the 4th-Wave information sector to provide essential communications to help in 1st-Wave agriculture and mining ("weather watch" for farmers and "remote sensing" for miners), in 2nd-Wave manufacturing (to link global producers together to co-ordinate purchasing and output), in 3rd-Wave finance, education and healthcare (24-hour global money markets, tele-learning and tele-medicine), in 4th-Wave telecommunications (global networks and data banks) and in 5th-Wave tourism (worldwide hotel and airline reservations).

As space stations are launched and staffed over long periods (probably up to several years) in the next two decades, they will become centers of technological and economic activity, again transforming Earth-bound industries such as pharmaceuticals, healthcare and material sciences. By the year 2020 or so, the Outer-Space Economy will be the fastest-growing sector of the Planetary Information Economy and, in Western countries, will be as large an employer as the 4th- and 5th-Wave sectors are today. By then, the 4th-Wave sector will be the largest economic output sector in today's leading developing countries.

A Growing "PIE"

The new, abundant and wealth-generating commodity of information makes a mockery of any neo-Malthusian view that looks at the world as a "fixed pie" with limited and nonrenewable resources. Pessimists think that new technology and additional capital investment will only exacerbate current problems. The Club of Rome and its adherents still believe that uncontrolled growth will rapidly exhaust resources. They maintain that we will eventually run into absolute limits on such things as food, energy and space for waste disposal. Other pessimists have concluded that we must consume less and cut back on production if we are to live with limited resources and stop environmental damage.

This linear worldview is the product of minds that are fixated on old technological processes. Studying the G-Forces of change that are building the PIE shows us that it is possible to create a "growing pie." In this new expanding economy many situations are reversed: the more information one produces, the more one can produce because knowledge begets more knowledge. Because all real wealth stems from information (used to achieve efficiency) and from meeting the needs of a growing population, we can thus generate exponential growth in wealth. Rather than reducing production and economic growth, we must do exactly the opposite. It is now necessary to increase economic (that is knowledge) production as fast as possible (a process that is environmentally sound) in order to restore and protect the environment (with that improved knowledge and wealth). If pessimists remain bogged down in their 2nd-Wave "smokestack" thinking, their call for decreased economic activity will, ironically, only allow the environment to decay further.

Instead, it is possible to conceive of the world's population living in afflu-ence and a restored environment. Even in developing countries, electronic and other, clean, high-tech production systems will ultimately permit rapid develop-ment of the 4th-, 5th- and 6th-Waves of their economies. By 2010, for example, China's present 1st-Wave dominated economy will likely become an equal mix of all six waves under its current modernization program. According to its own long-term plans, by 2020 China will have most of its people working in the 4th- and 5th-Waves and its own space station will be in orbit. The country likely will be the world's leading producer of computer software and one of the world's leading tourist resorts. Its aim is for everyone in China to "get rich." These pos-sibilities are not as difficult to realize as they might first appear. As I shall dis-cuss, China has implemented far-sighted economic strategies and is well ahead of targets as it enters the 1990s.

The Geo-Politics of Prosperity

In theory, then, the prospects for the global economy are outstanding. Advanced technologies and the new wealth-creating commodity of information should allow us to build a prosperous global economy. To achieve this global prosperity, however, and to ensure that global social development is optimized, the world needs two crucial political acts of geo-strategic leadership. First, pre-sent financial institutions must be globalized, along the lines I have discussed. Second, global prosperity over the next 60-years depends on the extent to which political decisions focus on three policy options:

- **Industrial Nostalgia** (still being attempted by North America and Western Europe);
- **Western Post-Industrialization** (dramatically led by Japan); and
- **Third World Economic Take-Off** (led by China and Southeast Asia, the latter fostered by Japan).

Fig. 21 illustrates how these three policy options will either enhance or retard the potential "Super-Boom" of the next long-wave cycle.

Western Industrial Nostalgia is currently acting as a drag on the entire glob-al system. To the extent that it predominates into the 1990s, it will stretch the coming "Mini-Depression" into a "Mega-Depression" followed by only mod-est global economic growth during the next long-wave. Indeed, an over-pre-dominance of Industrial Nostalgia would stunt economic growth and would cause a total collapse in the global economy around 2010, a collapse so devastat-ing that major international wars would almost certainly ensue.

War would most likely occur because slow and uneven global economic growth has three major effects on social attitudes:

- It focusses attention on the growing inequities of economic distribution at home and abroad;
- It erodes the perceived legitimacy of individual states, which are expected to defend and advance the material well-being of their people; and

219

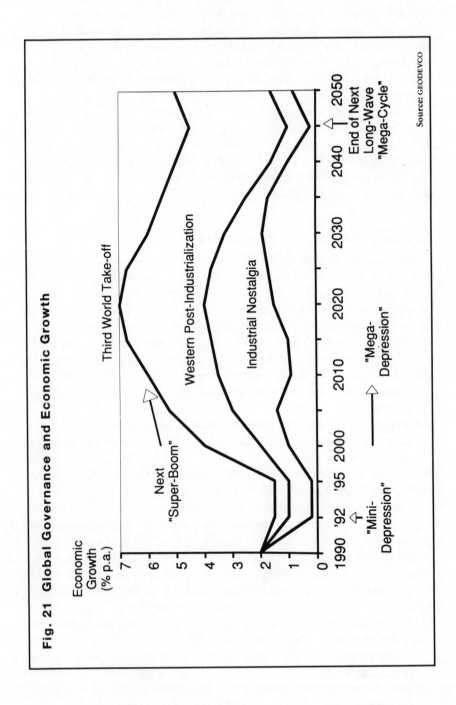

Fig. 21 Global Governance and Economic Growth

- It ultimately accelerates the questioning of material affluence as a value in its own right.

A stubborn and widening gap between rich and poor creates a sense of alienation in society. This tends to persuade the middle and professional classes that their own interest lies with political change, in common cause with the poorer segments. Political change takes precedence over political stability and governments are finally replaced (as in the Philippines) or their legitimacy is seriously challenged (as in Mexico and Burma). These political changes occur because people need a sense of economic security, which in turn depends on the belief that there is sound management of economic affairs and that benefits are accruing across society.

This belief is lacking in the world today. As Ravi Batra has documented in *The Great Depression of 1990*, there are limits to the levels of disparity that any society can tolerate without coming apart at the seams. Extremely rapid growth in one country or group of countries (or in one area or sector of a country) with increasingly unequal distribution elsewhere in the society is the combination most likely to undermine traditional values. Any extreme rich-poor gap impedes the construction of a new consensus that pushes forward the global economy. The greatest obstacle to the achievement of global social resilience, which must be based on an inclusive sense of shared values, is the drifting apart of the rich and the poor. People become frustrated at the inability of the global economy to deliver general prosperity and are increasingly aware of inequality; this fuels the anger that is behind so much of the turmoil in the world today. Industrial nostalgia exacerbates the situation by trying to preserve the status quo.

Much stronger economic growth will occur if the developed countries more aggressively switch their emphasis to post-industrialization. As Japan has demonstrated on a go-it-alone basis since 1978, this would bring another upsurge of the long-wave economic cycle across the West. However, this strategy would concentrate growth in the West, and whatever global growth occurred would be diminished by the continued nonparticipation of the Third World. This trickle-down approach will not work. If it prevails in the U.S. and Western Europe, social unrest and wars could spread across the economically stagnant Third World.

In contrast to the trickle-down approach, a rising tide would lift all boats — as Japan has again shown us in Southeast Asia. The strongest economic growth worldwide, and for the developed countries themselves, will occur only if post-industrialization in the West is accompanied by top-priority attempts to generate economic activity in the developing countries. As Third World economies take off, they will rocket the global economy into economic prosperity through to at least the middle of the 21st-Century. But the Western transformation to post-industrialism and the economic take-off of the Third World cannot take place within today's fragmented financial institutional framework. Only full globalization of the financial infrastructure will open the door to society's economic well-being.

New Global Economic Rankings

In company with the economic G-Forces already discussed, the expanding PIE will bring about a dramatic change in the global economic (and political) ranking of nations. All other things being equal (access to knowledge and technology, ability to apply it innovatively and productively to create wealth, and domestic economic policies that equalize people's purchasing powers regardless of where they live), the size of a nation's economy (its GNP) would be precisely in proportion to the size of its population. In theory, we would all enjoy an equal standard of living. This is simple mathematics, not socialist utopianism. But, of course, other things are never equal: in today's world, average per-capita incomes range from less than $200 a year in the least-developed countries to $20,000 a year in the most-developed.

I do not forecast that this rich-poor gap will close by the year 2050, but it will shrink remarkably. This assumes that the world's economic leadership will pursue the only logical course and reconstitute the global financial system by no later than 1995, and that policy-making will then be designed to foster the Third World Take-Off scenario outlined earlier for the global economy. Of course, nations will not be able to gain absolutely equal access to knowledge or technology, nor will they innovate equally or be equally productive. Rather, countries such as Japan will be more innovative than others. Consequently, the average annual rates of economic growth of various economies will differ, as shown in the following table.

Table 5
Forecast Average Rates of Economic Growth (GNP)

Economies	(% p.a., by decade) 1987-2050					
	1987 to 2000	2000 to 2010	2010 to 2020	2020 to 2030	2030 to 2040	2040 to 2050
U.S.A.	2.0%	3.0%	3.5%	3.5%	3.0%	2.0%
EEC	1.5	2.5	2.5	2.0	2.0	2.0
Other West	2.0	2.5	2.5	2.0	2.0	2.0
Japan	4.0	5.0	5.0	4.5	4.0	2.0
U.S.S.R.	5.0	4.0	5.0	4.0	3.5	2.0
COMECON	3.0	2.5	2.5	2.0	2.0	2.0
China	7.0	7.0	7.0	8.0	8.5	5.0
Third World (ex. China)	5.0	7.0	7.0	7.0	8.0	5.0
World Averages	3.7%	4.7%	5.1%	5.3%	6.0%	4.0%

source: GEODEVCO

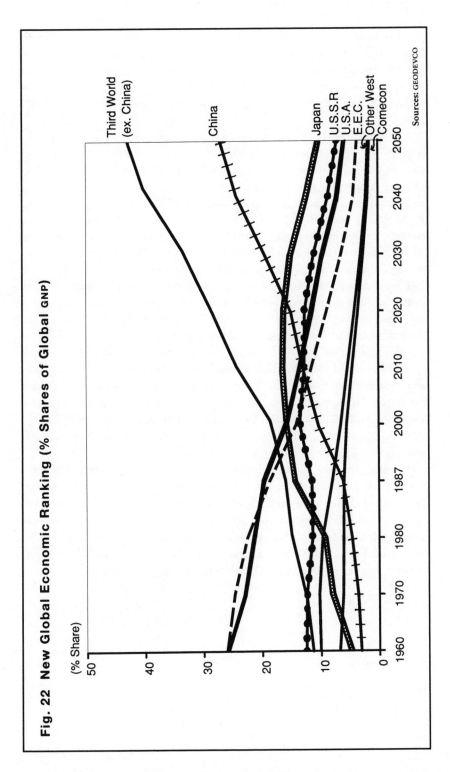

Fig. 22 New Global Economic Ranking (% Shares of Global GNP)

Sources: GEODEVCO

The resultant projected average growth rates for the world economy at large are conservative in comparison to both existing national rates and the growth rates achieved during the last long-wave cycle. Under ideal — Third World take-off — circumstances, the global economy could grow as much as 5.3%, 6.8% and 6.8% in each of the three decades between the years 2000 and 2030.

The result of these growth rates will be a new global economic ranking (Fig.22). While the United States still had the largest economy (as a share of GNP) in 1987, after the year 2000 Japan will surge ahead (it is already ahead in GNP per capita). But even Japan's economic supremacy will not last because it lacks a sufficiently large population base. By 2030, China (including Hong Kong, Macao and Taiwan) will have become the world's largest economy, a position it will retain beyond mid-century. Next to China, the rest of the Third World will grow fastest, and, by 2050, the total Third World (including China) will account for about 70% of total world GNP (compared with about 22% in 1987) — that is, much closer to its by then 90% share of world population (75% in 1987). Other major countries will nestle together at the bottom of the global economic ranking (Japan will contribute 10%, the U.S.S.R. 7%, the U.S. 6%), more in relation to their share of world population by that time.

Average annual per-capita incomes (in constant 1988 dollars) will climb around the world by 2050. That of the United States will be about $56,000, almost identical to those of the Soviet Union and China, which will both have caught up. Japan, today already leading in average income levels, will have surged to $148,000 per person. Incomes across Western and Eastern Europe (EEC and COMECON) and the rest of the West (Canada, Australia, New Zealand) will be in the $32,000-$37,000 range.

Average incomes in the Third World (excluding China) will still trail the world's at $22,000. However, this figure is higher than those prevailing in even Japan or the United States today, and it could be even higher if these GNP forecasts turn out to be too conservative. As it is, this represents remarkable progress. If these forecasts hold up, world GNP will reach $325-trillion by 2050. With world population then standing at 10-billion, average global per-capita incomes will exceed $30,000 (in 1988 dollars). We will all be rich.

G-Force E-5
Eliminating Global Energy Shortages

"Sumtotally, the physical constituent of energy cannot decrease; it is never used up but simply converted to another form of energy."
— *R. Buckminster Fuller*

The misconception that the world is running out of energy needs a decent but final burial. World economic development to date has been extremely energy-intensive. Since the mid-1970s, however, a new G-Force has emerged: the world has become more energy-efficient and, in 1987, used less energy than in 1973, the time of the first oil-price shock. The post-industrial, information-based economy is not energy-intensive. Moreover, even developing countries will use modern production methods such as robots in their 4-STEP development process instead of old-fashioned machines, saving yet more energy. These global developments, coupled with alternative and abundant energy supplies (wind, solar, photovoltaic) and the discovery of fusion power and applied super-conductivity, will solve the global energy problem forever.

Expanding Energy Resource Base

In face of the sharp increases in the price of conventional oil in the 1970s, countries around the world were forced to expand their energy resource base — other energy sources were suddenly more economical. Even though oil prices have declined, they remain high compared with pre-1973 rates. We thus continue to experience a rapid worldwide expansion of natural gas and coal production, and the emergence of many new types of renewable resources such as biomass (municipal, industrial and agricultural waste converted to energy).

This expansion of the energy resource base has been accompanied by a tremendous expansion of both energy research and technological development. This R&D has been applied to virtually every known type of existing and new energy resource, to transportation systems and to general energy use. Consequently, in the case of oil, there has been steady progress in the exploration for and development of oil and gas in ever deeper ocean waters using offshore drilling platforms. For example, aerospace technologies are part of a massive electro-hydraulic control system for Norway's first deep-water oil production installation. It will increase North Sea oil production by 125-million barrels that otherwise could not be recovered. The coal industry has developed new methods of finding coal, and new coal-mining and burning methods are constantly and significantly reducing the environmental effects of coal use, even in the Third World.

Nor is the fossil fuel resource base being exhausted. Estimates of recoverable conventional oil are published annually, and current figures indicate recoverable reserves sufficient to last at least 30-years at the present annual rate of oil consumption (see Fig. 23). Although 30-years is not a long time, these figures tell us only how much conventional oil has been precisely located through intensive drilling in specific locations and how much can be extracted at present prices and with present technology. The figures do not tell us how much oil can be extracted in the future from the same fields if prices and technology change. Nor do they take into account undiscovered oil fields. This is significant because, with recently introduced technologies, two-thirds of the world's oil in undrilled oil fields is now recoverable. Nor do the figures tell us anything about the potential for other types of oil (such as tar sands), which exist in very large quantities. Also, since nearly three-quarters of the Earth's surface is covered by oceans, probably the bulk of the world's sedimentary oil reserves have still to be discovered.

World Going "Off Oil"

In any event, energy substitution is steadily reducing the oil-intensity of world economic activity. In 1986, the seventh consecutive year of declining oil-intensity, the world was using 24% less oil per unit of economic output than in 1979. A range of other energy sources has helped reduce oil dependence. Chief among these are coal, natural gas, renewable sources of energy, and nuclear power. In the past 15-years, oil's share of world energy use has fallen from 41% to 31% and continues to decline. By the year 2000, oil will have been largely eliminated as a fuel for power plants and many industries. Instead, natural gas will continue to play a much more central role in the world economy, and the use of coal, renewable energy sources and even nuclear power will also have expanded.

As the use of oil declines, the OPEC cartel weakens as a political force. When the "Mini-Depression" occurs, oil prices will hover around $10 per barrel (in 1988 dollars). This price trough will bring with it a further reorganization of the petroleum industry, uniting governments and companies in actions to limit the damage of price declines and the contracting petroleum age. Although OPEC is now an ineffective cartel, in the late-1990s, something like a GOPEC (a global organization of petroleum exporting countries) might well be formed. This will not be a cartel but rather a global energy management structure to regulate oil supply and demand in the interests of an orderly market.

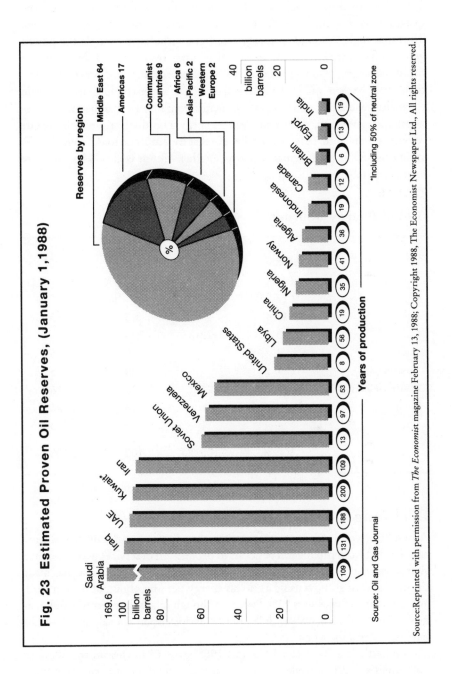

Fig. 23 Estimated Proven Oil Reserves, (January 1, 1988)

Source: Oil and Gas Journal

Other fossil fuels such as coal, lignite and peat are also available in large quantities worldwide, and the estimates for these resources are rising every year. The same applies to nonfuel energy resources, including hydro-electric power, geo-thermal energy, the wide variety of biomass resources and the variety of ocean resources, including sea currents, wave energy and tidal power. In addition, some systems still in the R&D stage, such as super-conductivity, magnetic electricity generation, static electricity, energy from magma chambers and volcanoes, and, above all, solar and fusion energy, could all prove to be major resources. In fact, some forecasters believe that by 2050, due to economical substitutions and environmental concerns, neither oil nor coal will be used any longer (see Table 6).

Table 6

Global Energy Sources

	1985	2000	2050	2100
Coal	27 %	24 %	- %	- %
Gas	18	25	15	5
Oil	33	22	-	-
Fission	4	7	10	5
Fusion	-	-	28	45
Hydro-electric	18	21	32	16
Solar	-	-	13	26
Wind	-	1	2	3
	100 %	100 %	100 %	100 %

Sources: *International Energy Agency*; forecast for 2050 and 2100 by GEODEVCO.

Declining Consumption

Around the world, conservation concerns, the advent of post-industrial society and the shift from production of goods to production of services have brought a shift to less energy-intensive industries in the West (see Table 7). Japan has made the biggest savings, now using 31% less energy per unit of output than in 1973, and the United States uses 23% less, even though in absolute terms it still guzzles twice as much energy per dollar of GNP as does Japan. Canada and Australia have performed the worst.

Nevertheless, between 1973 and 1985, growth in GNP in the Western economies was 2.4%, while the average annual growth in energy consumption was only 0.1%, compared to pre-1973 growth of 5.2% annually. This decline is due to the ongoing adoption of energy-saving technologies. In the United States, for example, the official fuel efficiency ratings for automobiles (miles

Table 7
Declining Energy Intensity in the West

	1973	1979	1985	Change 1973-85
	(megajoules per 1980 dollar of GNP)			(percent)
Japan	18.9	16.7	13.1	-31 %
U.S.A.	35.6	32.9	27.5	-23
U.K.	19.8	18.0	15.8	-20
Italy	18.5	17.1	14.9	-19
W. Germany	17.1	16.2	14.0	-18
Netherlands	19.8	18.9	16.2	-18
Australia	21.6	23.0	20.3	- 6
Canada	38.3	38.8	36.0	- 6
			Weighted Average	-25 %

Source: *International Energy Agency*, Energy Conservation in IEA Countries (Paris: OECD, 1987)

traveled per gallon of gasoline) improved by 28.5% between 1967 and 1985. The eventual adoption of new energy-saving technologies, such as cars that can achieve 90-miles to the gallon, and superinsulated houses, would mean that world economic growth could be sustained at the current rate through the year 2020 without any increase in energy consumption.

Clearly, the movement away from energy-intensive, heavy-industry-dominated economic systems is driven by major social, technological and economic G-Forces. Although economic progress causes an increase in the purchase of energy-consuming automobiles, appliances and industrial equipment, the latest generation of virtually all energy-using technologies is more energy-efficient.

As well, existing equipment is eventually replaced by new energy-efficient technologies. New automotive technologies raise fuel economy. New gas furnaces use 28% less fuel than traditional ones, and fluorescent socket-type light bulbs use up to three-quarters less electricity than conventional ones. The world's most advanced steel plant (near Shanghai, China) is more than 25% more efficient (using Japanese technology) than the world's average.

Even so, the world has barely tapped the conservation potential of energy-efficient technologies. According to a study by the World Resources Institute, any energy-efficient technologies already in existence could reduce per-capita energy use in industrial countries by 50% while economic growth continues. Developing countries could reach the standard of living enjoyed in the mid-1970s by Western Europe with only a modest 30% increase in per-capita energy consumption. In other words, because of the deindustrialization of the West and the shift of manufacturing activity to the Third World (where less energy-intensive processes will increasingly be used), we will also see a parallel reduction in energy consumption in the Third World. At the same time, global population could roughly double, living standards in developing countries could be improved far beyond satisfying basic needs, and economic growth in the industrialized countries could continue, all with an increase in the level of global energy use in 2020 of only 9% above the 1980 level.

Future Third World Energy Needs

Of course, energy consumption in Third World countries will grow at about 3% a year as their economies take off, increasing their share of global energy consumption from the current 32% to 66% by 2020. Although more energy will be used, Third World manufacturing has so far focussed largely upon light engineering and assembly, which is not energy-intensive. If the 2nd-Wave sector continues to modernize in this way, more energy will be freed for household use. Today, for example, the Third World has just 120-watts of electricity per person, compared with 2900-watts per person in the United States. Although Third World nations now use six times as much electric power as they did 20-years ago, some 2-billion people in developing countries, mostly in rural areas, still have no electricity at all.

Many developing countries have invested heavily in alternative energy sources. Brazil, for example, has invested extensively in alcohol fuels and energy-saving techniques, and South Korea has been building nuclear reactors. Some developing countries might even be able to skip the bulk of heavy industrialization altogether and, like Singapore, move rapidly towards post-industrial modes of economic development. Although those Third World countries that still rely on oil imports now have diverse economic prospects, the oil they have to buy will become less and less expensive. Also, because they are using more efficient production systems than were enjoyed by their Western predecessors, most of these countries are unlikely to experience significant increases in energy consumption. And, like the West, they are going "off oil" anyway.

Hydro-power is the predominant and most rapidly growing energy source in most Third World countries, supplying 41% of electricity. Many developing countries have excellent hydro-power potential. Whereas by 1985 North America and Europe had already developed 60% and 40% of their hydro-power potential respectively, Asia had harnessed only 10%, Latin America 9% and Africa 6%. In 1980, the World Energy Conference predicted that global hydro-electric output would quadruple by 2020. Developing this energy source, of course, costs money. Lending for Third World electrification now approaches $50-billion each year and the World Bank projects that developing countries will invest $60-billion in electric power each year, just to keep up with demand.

This high-investment problem is being largely overcome in some countries. In China, 76,000 small hydro-power plants supply 9500-megawatts of power, and the plan is to more than double this capacity in the next 13-years. Such systems are particularly important in rural areas that electricity has not yet reached. These Chinese plants are the foundation of what the World Bank calls "the most massive rural electrification effort ever attempted in the developing world." About 40% of China's rural townships and one-third of its counties now get most of their power from small hydro-dams.

Future Energy Options

The overall scale of the global nuclear structure is impressive. At the end of 1987, the world had more than 400 nuclear power plants in operation, generating about 16% of the world's electricity, ranging from 65% in France to 16% in the United States. Approximately 130 reactors are being built around the world and the International Energy Agency projects that there will be 65% more nuclear power available by the turn of the century.

Nevertheless, some countries are closing down their nuclear facilities. U.S. nuclear capacity will probably peak early in the 1990s, and then slowly decline as aging plants are closed down. Their replacement is unlikely until the waste disposal problem is resolved. And Sweden recently announced plans to dismantle all of its 12 nuclear power stations, starting in 1995, in favor of natural gas production and hydro-electric and wind power.

Yet, existing nuclear fission (atom splitting) technology cannot be abandoned easily without excessive economic risks. It therefore must continue to play a significant role during at least the next 50-years because the development of safe fusion (atom joining) technology as a replacement seems at least that far away. The first generation of fusion reactors will use a mixture of two isotopes of hydrogen as fuel. The first, deuterium, which is extracted from sea water, is in virtually inexhaustible supply. The deuterium in one gallon (four litres) of sea water could produce as much energy as 120-litres (30 gallons) of gasoline. The second type, tritium, is also plentiful, coming from salt mines. These fuels have high energy content, their production is environmentally safe and no dangerous ashes are produced by fusion. Moreover, runaway reactions such as the one at Chernobyl are impossible.

The largest experimental fusion reactor, designed to trap hot plasma inside a donut-shaped container, is being designed in Munich by a team of 40 physicists and engineers from the EEC, the U.S.S.R., the U.S. and Japan. In the interim, in what could possibly be the most important technological breakthrough of the century, U.S., Soviet, Hungarian, Italian and British scientists separately claim to have achieved a fusion reaction in a glass jar at room temperature. Both methods have produced fusion reactions for brief fractions of a second. Domestic use is still decades away. The first application of fusion technology may, however, be developed as a hybrid fission/fusion system fairly soon.

Super-conductivity is the latest scientific breakthrough that most experts believe could lead to incredible savings in energy: trains that virtually fly across the country on a cushion of magnetism; efficient electric cars; powerful yet smaller computer and particle accelerators; safer reactors operating on nuclear fusion rather than fission; and a host of other rewards still undreamt of. Researchers around the world have created materials that become super-conductors of electricity. In the conventional transmission of electricity, as much as 20% of the energy sent through hydro lines is lost in the form of heat. If super-conducting cable were used, not a single kilowatt-second of energy would be lost, and billions of dollars would be saved. Furthermore, an entire city's electrical energy needs could be supplied through a handful of underground cables. This new technology could also transform nulear energy. According to the director of the Plasma Physics Laboratory at Princeton University, super-conducting magnets could produce more intense fields at less expense and thus could "make fusion power possible and practical."

In transportation, cars could possibly run on tiny electric motors that draw current from super-conducting storage devices. At Ford, a study group is already re-thinking the feasibility of the electric car. As well, high-speed trains traveling on cushions of electro-magnetism could become commonplace. The new materials promise electro-magnets far more powerful and economical than those in use today. And it is the electro-magnet that lifts and propels levitated superfast trains in Japan, West Germany and Britain. As long ago as 1979, a prototype fitted with super-conducting electro-magnets reached 530-km/h (321-mph) on a test track in Japan. That beats any conventional rival, including Japan's celebrated Bullet train, which reaches 250-km/h (149-mph) and the French version, which provides the world's fastest regularly scheduled rail service at speeds of up to 310-km/h (186-mph).

The 21st-Century will also see the onset of the "solar age." The Earth intercepts a solar energy beam of immense power (1200-trillion kilowatts) and, although more than a third is reflected back by cloud cover and a fifth is absorbed by the atmosphere, 46% of it is available for our use. Solar radiation available on the ground is estimated to be at least 1000-times more than we would ever need. Thus, if only 2% of the land mass were used to capture solar energy, and if only 10% of the energy were converted into heat and power, energy use could increase 500% and we would not need to worry about shortages.

There are now three primary technologies available for capturing this solar electricity:

- Photovoltaic cells, which are made of silicon and directly convert sunlight to electricity;
- Solarthermal power stations, which capture the Sun's heat and use it to produce steam that spins a turbine and a generator; and
- Solar ponds, which are large expanses of salt water that are carefully controlled so that the captured heat is kept at the bottom and then siphoned off to generate electricity.

All three approaches are at similar stages of development, several experimental systems are already operating and more advanced and larger systems are being designed and built. These technologies work best, of course, in desert or Mediterranean climates with clear air and intense sunshine. This makes solar energy of particular advantage to developing countries. By the turn of the century, large solar receiving plants will be economically viable and successfully commercialized. By 2010, worldwide solar pond generating capacity is predicted to reach 3500-megawatts of power; the other solar-thermal technologies will provide 10,000-megawatts.

Solar energy can also be captured in outer-space and radiated to the Earth. The Soviet Union plans to build huge satellites that will convert sunlight into electricity for cities and industries on Earth, feeding electricity into the normal power grid. The Soviets will deploy the first phase of this project, called Star Electricity, early in the 1990s. The Moscow Institute of Avionics is building a test satellite that would unfold in space to create a huge reflector with a working area of about 110 square metres (1200 square feet). The institute has said that full-scale reflectors could be in routine use by the year 2000.

Another simple concept that is technologically feasible today and economically beneficial beyond dispute, but not yet politically attainable, is the potential link-up of all the world's national electricity grids into one planetary hydro network. This idea was conceived by Buckminster Fuller. He pointed out that we live on a revolving sphere, half of which is asleep while the other is awake, and most of the world's land mass is a contiguous entity, coming into close proximity at the Bering Strait, a narrow channel of ocean between Alaska and Siberia.

Linking the Soviet and U.S. electricity grids across the Bering Strait would create a 24-hour system that would effectively double the operating capacity of the world's hydro-power. A nation experiencing peak demand could then "borrow" electricity from a country in a different time zone that had low demand. All that is needed is a few kilometres of ultra-high-voltage (or super-conductive) wire to connect the intercontinental grids. Hydro grids in more than 50 countries are today connected with neighboring nations, albeit in the same time zone. A Soviet-U.S. connection would cost less than 1% of the two nations' combined annual military budgets. As geo-political differences disappear over the coming decades, the economic attraction of such a scheme could be overwhelming.

Very clearly, there is not now, never has been, and never will be, a permanent energy shortage in the world. The world can run out of oil and it won't matter because other and cleaner sources of energy are abundant, and conservation and energy-efficiency are increasing constantly. Finally, let it be remembered that — as any physicist will confirm — energy does not get "used up" when it is "consumed." Rather, energy is simply converted into another form of energy or into matter which contains energy. Energy never disappears. It simply takes on a different form. All we have to do is learn how to tap that form. By the early decades of the 21st-Century, major breakthroughs in super-conductivity and aerospace technologies will bring virtually free solar power to the furthest reaches of the planet — in abundance.

G-Force E-6
Ensuring Resource Self-Sufficiency

"Pollution is nothing but resources we're not harvesting. We don't lack
resources — just imagination about resources."
— R. Buckminster Fuller

The geo-strategic mind of Buckminster Fuller makes us realize that, as with energy, there is no materials shortage on our planet and all pollution and waste are simply unharnessed materials. Economic development of the Western world has been achieved at the expense of intense global resource exploitation, but the entire world is learning that this depletion cannot continue. Rather, we can become a less resource-intensive planet by recycling many materials over and over again. As well, however, science and technology are developing brand-new alternative materials that can be substituted for many traditional resource-intensive raw materials. In addition, the 4th-Wave Information Revolution is based on the Earth's most abundant and readily available resource, silicon, which comes from sand. Thus, even though there are vast unmet needs among the world's growing population — which normally would consume extraordinarily large volumes of the planet's resources — science and technology coupled with resource recycling are creating a G-Force that will avoid such exploitation. With the substitution of new materials for old and the further improvement in recycling, the world can achieve resource self-sufficiency within 20-years — and maintain it forever.

Declining Resource-Intensity

Some important raw materials such as iron, bauxite (for aluminum) and uranium are in essentially unlimited supply and others will last for several decades (see Table 8). Their availability will be extended as new supplies are discovered. Prospects are also good that supplies of another 30 elements can be made relatively secure if sufficient R&D is undertaken.

At the same time, however, fewer and fewer raw materials are being used in industrial processes. A measure of the declining importance of metal, for example, is the change in the ratio between the consumption of metal and the GNP of

Table 8

Global Mineral Resources (1988)

	Known Resources ('000 tonnes)	Lifespan (years)
Bauxite	20,300,000	200
Cobalt	3,000	116
Copper	505,000	65
Iron Ore	108,000,000	410
Lead	165,000	48
Platinum	37	176
Tin	10,000	40
Uranium	4,300	500
Zinc	240,000	41

Western countries. Since 1973, there has been a 30% drop in the nickel used per unit of GNP, a 20% drop for copper and a 40% drop for tin. We are at the end of the 2nd-Wave "metal-bashing" age in the West, and the rate of raw material consumption in many industries has fallen. The automobile may provide the best example. The average 1988 car weighed almost a third less than in 1978. Not only has the absolute metal composition declined but plastics have been substituted for metals. The reduction in metal demand is therefore not occurring because of slow economic growth but because of rapid post-industrialisation. The world is simply using fewer raw materials, and this is a major G-Force of change.

The economic argument of diminishing returns as applied to resources ignores the long-term trends of the 4-STEP process. It overlooks increases in knowledge, improvements in production techniques, and discoveries of new resources or substitute resources, recycling and other socio-technical changes. Doomsday forecasts thus predict resource exhaustion. This thesis will not stand up to even cursory scrutiny. If a resource is becoming scarce, its value will increase. Over the course of recorded history, however, the price of natural resources has constantly declined. This is true in both rich and poor countries, and no matter whether you compare material prices with incomes, purchasing power, the consumer price index or GNP. We constantly produce more with less. Moreover, we constantly substitute cheaper materials. Even though natural resources are cheap and abundant, science is allowing us to concoct substitute materials that are both cheaper and more suitable to our purposes.

The demand for lighter, energy-efficient materials began after the oil shocks of the 1970s. Overlapping the metals, chemical and electronic industries, the "new materials" industry develops nontraditional materials through the precise control of the molecular structure of their raw components (such as plastics, ceramics and rare minerals) to create new combinations, which are often 1000 times stronger than the original materials. For example, glass is brittle and pure polyester is not very tough. But their glass fiber composite is 500 times stronger than either glass or polyester alone. Various polymer modifications also give better acid or wear resistance to many materials. A polymer-modified mortar is replacing concrete, and "high-fiber" composite is replacing aluminum and plastics. A new wall coating called Infitex that can insulate a building from the outside is applied as a foam spray. The impact-resistant surface resembles stucco. Another new construction product is a pollution-free briquette made from waste wheat in Canada.

One of the most promising areas in new materials lies in the design of plastic- and carbon-based composite products, which could be used in car engines and car bodies and as a lightweight material in the aerospace industry. Much research in this area is being carried out by major American, Western European and Japanese companies. The potential industrial applications are very broad, and once machining, shaping and durability aspects are refined, such new materials will extensively replace metal in consumer products of all kinds. As well, electricity-conducting plastics will ultimately replace metallic conductors; these plastics are already used in some Japanese-made cameras.

Superstrong ceramics, once used almost exclusively by the military for such applications as bullet-proof vests and impact-resistant helicopter seats, are now finding their way into such diverse commercial products as integrated circuit packages, cutting tools, and protective tiles for the space shuttle. These structural ceramics offer better resistance to heat, wear and corrosion than do metals. Both U.S. and Japanese automakers are hoping to use such ceramics to build lightweight, heat-tolerant gas turbine and diesel engines that will be more durable than conventional metal engines and as much as 50% more fuel-efficient. The first ceramic diesels could be on the highways in the early-1990s, and eventually available for the mass production of almost any product.

Garbage In, Resources Out

Resource recycling offers the world the opportunity to recover resources for repeat use, to trim waste disposal needs and related costs and to simultaneously combat global environmental problems. Until recently, it has been economically more advantageous to dispose of waste materials than to recycle them. Now we are finding that the recycling of paper, metals and glass, as well as plastics and organic wastes, would significantly lessen the demand for raw materials and energy worldwide.

Making paper from discards instead of from virgin timber not only saves valuable forests but also reduces the manufacturing energy use by as much as

74% and requires 60% less water. Paper waste represents millions of hectares of forests. If it were recycled, exactly half the paper used in the world today would meet almost three quarters of paper demand and would preserve 8-million hectares (20-million acres) of forest per year. For example, the print run of one Sunday edition of the *New York Times* consumes 75,000 trees. Large quantities of paper are also used to package food. Indeed, the U.S. Department of Agriculture says that Americans spent more for food packaging in 1986 ($28-billion) than farmers received in income. Across the industrial countries, packaging contributes about a third of the weight and half of the volume of all household waste. Now, however, there is a large and growing demand for waste paper. Paper products use about 35% of the world's annual commercial wood harvest, a share that will probably grow to about 50% in an information-intensive society. To avoid potential shortages and higher prices, about 200 of the approximately 600 paper mills in the U.S. already use waste paper exclusively, and another 300 use it for up to 30% of their needs. Japan and the Netherlands lead in waste-paper recovery and use. In 1980, Japan collected and recycled 47% of the paper used in the country, and the Netherlands, which has been a leader in paper recycling for decades, recovered 44% of its paper. The world in total is now recycling more than 25% of its paper, up from 20% in 1965; this percentage could reach 40% by the year 2000.

Throwing away an aluminum beverage can wastes as much energy as pouring out that can half-filled with gasoline. Thus the most active advocates of aluminum recycling are the aluminum manufacturers: they use 95% less energy to recycle the metal than to smelt it from bauxite ore. Consequently, such companies as Reynolds and Alcoa promote recycling and support recycling legislation. More than half of the 300-billion aluminum beverage cans Alcoa produced since 1981 have been reclaimed. According to the Worldwatch Institute, on average a recycled aluminum can is back on a supermarket shelf within six weeks. Despite these successes, the world is still far from achieving the technical potential for aluminum recycling, either of scrap or finished products. Scrap is produced in the smelting, cutting and fabrication of aluminum products. Italy produces half its aluminum from scrap, while West Germany and the United States produce only one-third of theirs from recycled aluminum. There is also a large world market for recycled aluminum, and international trade of scrap aluminum now represents 7% of world aluminum production.

The world's steel industry now meets half of its iron requirements by using scrap (including steel mill scrap). Consumer scrap recovery accounts for about one-third of the iron and steel recycled. Many other metals are also alloyed with iron to increase its strength and rust-resistance. The sorting and reprocessing of these alloys has become a sophisticated recycling business. An automobile, for example, contains not only iron and steel but also copper wire and zinc handles. Scrap recycling processes are now so efficient that virtually all the zinc in recycled automobiles can be recovered.

Disused batteries and worn-out electrical appliances often contain such rare metals as manganese, mercury, galium and even gold. The amalgam method is proving a successful way of extracting such metals from wastes. The original process, developed 50-years ago in Germany, did not find wide commercial application because it generated further unwanted wastes. But a new process developed by the Japanese ingeniously uses the mercury extracted from waste batteries as a medium for refining the other extracted metals. The mercury is recycled, and harmless wastes are simply disposed of by water. The Japanese system boasts a purifying capability of 99.99%. The system can be applied to the processing of low-grade ore and the refining of metals, as well as the treatment of industrial waste in general.

The U.S. throws away more garbage than any nation in the world. Residents of New York City collectively discard 24,000-tons of materials each day. After being compacted, a year's worth of this waste would cover five city blocks to a height of 60-stories, burying most of Manhattan's skyscrapers. The average daily per-capita garbage disposal problem is 20% worse in Greater Los Angeles. But Tokyo citizens create 40% less garbage than do Los Angeles residents. Wherever it is produced, this garbage contains valuable metals, reusable glass containers, recyclable paper and plastic. Any North American city the size of Chicago disposes of more aluminum than is produced by a small bauxite mine, more copper than a medium copper mine and more paper than a good-sized timber stand. In many ways, such a city is a "mine." The question is how to extract its resources most effectively and how to get the maximum value from the collected materials.

It is not easy to convince time- and convenience-oriented consumers to separate recyclable materials from their garbage. However, impressive results are being achieved. At least fifteen American states have passed legislation that either promotes or requires recycling of residential garbage. More than 500 communities now offer curbside collection of glass, paper, metal and other materials. The State of Oregon recycles more than 20% of its waste, and all towns in Oregan with 4000 or more people must offer curbside collection of recyclables. New Jersey, which now recycles more than 15% of its garbage, passed a law in 1987 requiring towns to set up additional recycling programs for autumn leaves and at least three "marketable waste materials" of their choice. New York State and Philadelphia recently set goals to reduce their garbage by 50% by 1997, partly through recycling programs. The province of Ontario, Canada, in 1989 set a goal to recycle 50% of its garbage by 2000. These programs are spurred by steeply rising dumping fees at landfill sites. It now costs so much for disposal that the revenue recovered from recyclables is a bonus. The system of requiring cash deposits on soft-drink and other containers as a consumer incentive is also paying off handsomely. New York City is the largest market in the United States for this kind of recyclable; within two years of implementing the deposit law, it realized savings of $50-million in clean-up expenditures, $19-million on solid waste disposal and up to $100-million on energy.

Converting Wastes to Energy

Waste, as Buckminster Fuller told us, is simply another form of energy. Some 400 waste-to-energy plants now operate in Brazil, Japan, the Soviet Union, the U.S. and various nations in Western Europe, which has about half the total. Since 1960, the number of incinerators in Japan has tripled and their overall capacity has grown twentyfold. Japan's recycling efforts go back a long way but began in earnest in the mid-1960s. They were reinforced by the energy shocks of the 1970s because Japan was a highly energy-intensive and resource-intensive economy, and is essentially dependent on international sources. Now, about a fifth of Japan's municipal waste is recycled, and efforts to increase that amount continue. Waste materials are collected in surprisingly diverse ways, which shows that systems can be made to work in any number of circumstances so long as the collected waste can be sold for a reasonable price.

In Machida, "the garbage capital of Japan," a new recycling program and computerized processing converts 90% of the city's garbage into resources and energy. A growing number of U.S. cities are integrating recycling into their waste management plans. A 1986 survey by the U.S. Conference of Mayors found that 62 waste-to-energy plants were already in operation, 26 were under construction and 39 were in the advanced stages of planning. Such plants require no change in waste-collecting patterns and also have a guaranteed market for the energy they produce.

Biotechnology as well is solving garbage disposal problems. Certain bacteria eat sewage and can be used to help get rid of whatever waste is left after recycling. One European company supplies bacteria to an Italian manufacturer of sugar from beet, to Hungarian paper mills and to Mediterranean fruit canneries. Most of these are "aerobic" bacteria, which use the oxygen in air. Their cousins, the "anaeorobes," convert much more of the waste to methane gas, leaving behind less sludge. Other micro-organisms are being used to convert bagasse (waste from sugarcane) and other waste vegetation into protein supplements for animal feed and human consumption. In most sugar refineries, bagasse is burned — an inefficient way to get rid of it. As one of the predominant crops in tropical areas, sugarcane generates huge amounts of bagasse for such processes.

The Gas Research Institute, a utility-sponsored group searching for new sources of natural gas, has set up a huge waste digester at Walt Disney World in Florida that generates methane gas from a mixture of sewage and chopped water hyacinths. The waste flows into settling tanks to remove solid sludge, then into long channels in which the water hyacinths grow. Six days later, water clean enough to be discharged emerges at the other end. Meanwhile, the hyacinths are harvested, chopped, mixed with the sludge from the settling tanks, and the whole lot is fed into a digester to make methane. The residue can be used as cattle feed. Such plant-based sewage treatment systems are starting to be used elsewhere in the southern United States. A typical system can treat about 5-million gallons (19-million litres) of sewage each day and, unlike conventional treatment facilities that cost a fortune to operate, this one makes money.

As if all these measures were not enough to guarantee resource self-sufficiency, it must be remembered that we have "barely scratched the surface" of the Earth in tapping its resources. Since 1970, however, Soviet scientists have been drilling in the Arctic towards the center of the Earth. By 1984, the hole had reached a depth of almost 11-kilometres (7-miles), passing through copious deposits of iron, copper, zinc, titanium and nickel. In addition, the bottoms of the world's oceans contain numerous minerals in the form of nodules and other formations, which, if they become economically feasible to tap, again would add to the planet's resource base. The same is true of the polar regions.

Clearly, we have the opportunity to improve the material well-being of all the world's people, and to do so without great cost to the environment. Furthermore, it is unlikely that the world will run short of any element before 2050 and, should this occur, there is plenty of time to develop substitutes for any limited resources. Any future resource shortages will be at most only transient events and a stable world population will not be imperilled or impoverished by the lack of materials required for civilized life in the 21st-Century.

G-Force E-7
Restoring the Planet's Environment

"The chess board is the world, the pieces are the phenomena of the universe, the rules of the game are what we call the law of nature."
— *Thomas H. Huxley*

The Universe is indeed "unfolding as it should." Unfortunately, just as most of us have been deceived into believing that we are running out of energy and resources, some would also have us believe that we are irrevocably destroying the planet's environment. Again, this is a faulty assessment based on a misunderstanding of the physical nature of the universe. I do not wish to minimize the pressing environmental global trends that, in our mutual interest, we must reverse as quickly as we can. It is clear, however, that many of the notions concerning the state of the environment are unfounded. The planet does not need "saving." It has periodically been coming apart — only to be pasted together again — since the proverbial Garden of Eden. Fundamentally, the Earth is in orbit within a self-correcting stable-state environment — the solar system. Our responsibility is to help it self-correct, and I believe we have the ability to do so.

Integrity of Nature

Everywhere in Nature, there exists an integrity far more powerful than science has yet envisioned. This great integrity (or G-Force) of Nature demands of us something beyond mere intellectual genius or stop-gap measures to correct another temporary deterioration of the environment. The integrity, basic health and strength, and wholeness of Nature cannot be seen by those who are not themselves whole. The barrier to a harmonic global future is our purely mental and parochial thinking about a whole host of issues. We have the audacity to think that we have the power to destroy the planet's ecological system — but, except for an all-out nuclear conflagration, this is simply not so. The Earth's environment is remarkably stable, self-correcting, and able to overcome relative-

243

ly minor disturbances that are imposed on it by ignorant and still primitive humans.

Yet, there are growing concerns about the biosphere and the planet's ecological structure. There are worries about the depleting ozone shield; many say that the atmosphere is hopelessly polluted, that the global climate is permanently changing, that forests and vegetation are hopelessly degenerating, that oceans, lakes and rivers are polluted beyond recovery. I share some of these valid concerns about our one and only "life-support system" — but we had better take a fresh look. Granted, the planet's ecological balance is delicate, but many of its problems are more mythical than real. Any chaos in the conduct of our husbandry of the planet is simply due to our lack of long-term vision, long-term planning and adequate geo-strategic management processes.

We must also realize that as a species we are at a very early stage in our evolution. Our main problem is that we lack sufficient knowledge about the long-term ecological trends of an evolving planetary society. We have no experience on which to draw. In reality, while the problems are not slight, the present situation is but a microsecond in the long continuum of our (and our planet's) development. At this essentially primitive stage in our own intellectual development, therefore, most people do not yet appreciate that the Universe is, in fact, "unfolding as it should." We *should* be concerned. But we should *not* become pessimistic, for this very pessimism can produce the demise we fear most. Rather, we must calmly and realistically assess the situation. And we must realize that all solutions come from ideas and imagination; we must become more imaginative. We possess an unlimited richness of ideas and imagination that is virtually untapped. As we learn to develop our knowledge, we will continue to solve our problems, including those of the planet, and truly achieve the status of a mature global civilization.

This requires of us the same powerful integrity that Nature is showing us. What is more, this achievement is within our grasp — and relatively soon. For now, we must realize that we are merely suspended between old problems and new opportunities, that we are in transition between old and new social values, between old and new technologies, between economic retrogression and progress, between political polarization and co-operation in governing the planet. As we come to understand the current transition across the 4-STEP cycle of progress, we will realize what needs to be done to rebalance the environment.

Ecological Deficits

In reality, we have created *temporary* ecological deficits. Pollution of the natural environment is the problem most frequently cited as the most serious threat to the world's ecological balance. This pollution has many sources: spreading urbanization, increasing nuclear activities, more widespread use of chemicals, growing quantities of hazardous waste and degradation of the ozone layer. Earth, water, air: nothing, we are finding, is free of pollution. The next most serious threat is deforestation and desertification. It is said that if current rates of land degradation continue, close to one-third of the world's arable land could be destroyed within 20-years, and the area of unlogged productive tropical forest could be reduced by as much as a half.

Most of these ecological deficits (that is, system imbalances), such as loss of tree cover or top soil, often go unnoticed until they begin to affect our economic well-being. But we are learning that decisions to satisfy today's human needs and desires at the expense of tomorrow — letting our children pay for the damage — are the root cause of these deficits that are diminishing the resource base on which our economic productivity and future wealth depend. We are also learning that these resource deficits are relative short-term consequences of the rapidly fading 2nd-Wave Industrial Era. In the future, with proper attention, these deficits will disappear as quickly as they arose — within about 50-years, which is not a long time on the continuum of evolution, or of economic development.

This time frame could even be shortened, because a growing number of governments, businesses, institutions and individuals are fast realizing that the planet's system is out of balance in various ways. That increased numbers of people are concerned and doing something about these problems is an encouraging sign. The causes of most environmental imbalances are attributable to people (their increasing number and exploitive behavior), technology (lack of access to and misuse of it), money (its maldistribution and misapplication) and politics (lack of governance and political will). These causes are correctible through corresponding changes in social, technological, economic and political behavior — that is through the various G-Forces of the 4-STEP process. Therefore, the cure for environmental imbalances, and the prevention of still worse ones, will require better research, planning, education, training, organization and geo-strategic management. This will take time. It will also take time for the biosphere to respond; reforestation, restoration of degraded land, and post-industrialization are not instantaneous processes. However, many such corrective actions are now being taken to restore the planet's environment, and more are being planned.

Replanting the Forests

Forests have traditionally been "mined" instead of managed. A recent United Nations Environment Program assessment shows that the world is losing about 11-million hectares (27-million acres) of its tropical forest every year — an area the size of England. At the same time, the productivity of millions more hectares is being destroyed or seriously impaired because, as trees disappear, the land becomes poorer. Wood will continue to be required for many purposes, including construction and heating. And, as the world population doubles over the next four or five decades, the need for forest products and services will continue to increase. Nevertheless, despite these needs, we need long-term structural changes to increase the global price of timber products to better reflect their replacement cost (rather than their extraction cost) and to create incentives for conservation.

Fortunately, in 1987, many Third World nations and the big international aid agencies made a start with the $8-billion Tropical Forests Action Plan, which aims to achieve a balance between tree harvesting and planting by the year 2000. Other efforts are under way to co-ordinate the activities of 17 countries, representing 92% of world tropical timber exports (Brazil alone accounts for 31% of the world's rain forests), through the International Tropical Moist Forest Reserve System. The host nations will receive annual payments to act as "custodians" of reserve areas, to be monitored by annual inspection.

More trees will be planted in energy farms, and other reforestation endeavors are planned. Trees are being genetically improved, and in some countries, they are becoming more important as an alternative crop for farms. Numerous reforestation programs are taking place around the world. In Gujarat State in India, for example, the government distributes free seedlings (250-million in 1983), and tree farming has become the main source of income for many farmers. Nepal too has mounted a vigorous campaign to replant its denuded hillsides; tree nurseries and plantations have been established in more than 400 villages. In Malaysia, conversion to plantation crops such as rubber and palm oil has been a success. Local foresters say that other tropical countries will reduce the rate of deforestation because as economic development proceeds, land use stabilizes; and as levels of education rise, people in producer countries begin to care about conservation.

In North America, the forestry sector is often accused of recklessly mining its forests. This view is utterly misinformed. Some forest companies in Canada and the United States are failing to replant much of the land they clear of trees. But they are not representative of the timber industry at large, particularly so in the United States. Moreover, the U.S. Forest Service is probably the best in the world at forest management. This extremely professional organization, with a management capability as good as the leading edge business corporation of any industrial sector, operates on the basis of a 50-year plan for the stewardship of the forest resource and ecosystem under its authority. The harvesting of trees is carefully planned several years in advance, wildlife and ecosystems are preserved, and trees are replanted within weeks of felling. The agency is also a pioneer in research, both to develop new strains of trees and to find more efficient ways of using timber in final products. The agency is also very active in transferring its know-how to the developing countries.

The world's most ambitious and successful reforestation program is taking place now in China, where official goals call for extending forest cover, which was 8% of the country's territory in 1949 and 12% in 1988, to 20% by the year 2000. Forest cover has already reached 20% or more in 75 cities and more than 200 counties. China's long-run target is to restore trees to one-third of the country. Forest management policy now emphasizes replanting rather than felling, and in some areas, lumberjacks have been reassigned to planting trees. China also regards old trees as "living historical relics." Computers keep track of trees that are more than 100-years old (30,000 of them in Beijing alone), in order to preserve them. In 1986, a local government agency in Beijing was fined the equivalent of $25,000 for felling two ancient trees.

The original Great Wall of China was constructed to protect Beijing and southern China from military invasions. Today, China is building Great Green Walls to ward off invasion by sandstorms and encroaching deserts. This Great Green Wall project is a massive shelter belt stretching across northern China. One portion of it is 3000-kilometres (1800-miles) long. Even the streets of Beijing have benefited. The dust storms that used to plague the capital in spring and winter have been successfully subdued by shelter forests on the northern outskirts of the city and beyond.

In 1981, China adopted a resolution encouraging each citizen over the age of 11 (except the old, sick and disabled) to plant three to five trees each year, or to do the equivalent amount of labor in other reforestation work. More than 200-million people have been involved in the campaign annually in recent years. In 1988, 7-billion trees were planted in rural and urban areas, mainly by young-sters. In one major project, 3-million young people have been planting trees and grass along the middle and lower reaches of the Huang He (Yellow) River. This effort is part of a seven-year program, started in 1984, to control soil erosion. Every year the river carries 1.6-billion tons of ochre-colored silt to its lower reaches from higher areas that suffer serious soil erosion; hence the river's name. During the program's first phase, completed in 1986, more than 6-million hectares (14-million acres) of barren land were planted. Phase Two of the plan (1986-90) calls for the greening of another 6-million hectares of desolate land.

Chinese agronomists estimate that this project already produces an annual net benefit of $630-million to the economy. And the climate and the environment have also been improved. Consequently, crop yield has increased by one-fifth, mainly because of a 30% decrease in wind speed — trees used as wind-breaks have helped reduce evaporation so that soil moisture has quadru-pled. Planting of trees for shelter and planting of grass has also boosted stock breeding in China: one region increased its animal herds by three-quarters between 1980 and 1986. More animals also means more manure for the crops: grain output also rose by three-quarters between 1982 and 1985 solely because of the trees and the manure. As well, projects to expand irrigation in previously dry areas by 184,000 hectares (455,000 acres) now bring local supplies of drink-ing water to half a million people for the first time.

Restoring Climatic Balance

As China and other countries demonstrate, not only can soil erosion problems be halted but deserts can be pushed back, forests can be replanted, agricultural output can be expanded and the climate improved. Such reforestation programs can help reverse today's global climatic problems. The accumulation of higher levels of carbon dioxide in the atmosphere, which could cause a gradual warming of the Earth, stems mostly from the combustion of fossil fuels and deforestation (trees consume carbon dioxide to produce oxygen). Today, more carbon is being released into the atmosphere than trees, plants and oceans are removing. If this continues, the average global temperature could rise between one and three degrees Celsius.

Some climatologists believe that global warming would dry up the land and cause sea levels to rise due to melting ice caps and expansion of the volume of sea water as it heats up. This linear thinking is flawed. Other geo-strategic climatologists argue that the warming would increase the humidity of the atmosphere, and evaporating moisture from the warmer oceans would add to this humidity, which would then condense and fall as rain. This rain would fall on lands that might have been made drier by the initial warming process and would cool the land and the atmosphere. As well, the extra clouds (from the humidity) would reflect the Sun's radiation and counteract the warming. All this would restore the climatic balance.

In any event, the present warming trend falls within normal climatic cycles. The big heat waves seem to correspond with economic cycles. Climatic changes may in fact be the primary cause of economic booms and busts. The biggest heat waves of the last century were in the 1880s, 1910s, 1930s, 1950s and 1980s — coinciding with major recessions. These regular intervals would also confirm the theory of many climatologists that atmospheric phenomena recur cyclically as a result of factors such as lunar phases, sun spots, the direction of stratospheric winds, and periodic oscillations in the Earth's rotation. Indeed, there may be no link at all between the average temperature of the planet and the percentage of carbon dioxide in the atmosphere. A 1988 study by the U.S. National Oceanic and Atmospheric Administration shows that the U.S. climate has varied little. Since 1895, the average U.S. temperature has fluctuated between 11°C (52°F) and 12°C (54°F), with no statistically sigificant long-term trend either up or down in any of the 48 contiguous American states. The same was true of annual rainfall, which ranged from about 84-centimetres (33-inches) to 92-centimetres (36-inches) yearly over the entire 92-year period. Nature clearly has an extraordinary capacity to maintain its equilibrium.

Clearly, the integrity of the planet is much too powerful to acquiesce to even major destructive industrial processes. On the other hand, the planet is likely to respond favorably to environmentally sound projects. For example, a number of groundwater research projects are under way in the Sahalian zone bordering the Sahara Desert. One project aims to tap into enormous basins of underground water stretching from Senegal to Ethiopia. The water, trapped 1000-metres (2700-feet) deep during the last Ice Age, was discovered in the 1970s during oil explorations. The water will be used to irrigate a continent-wide green belt of fast-growing trees and shrubs to stop desert encroachment. Research shows that, in about 30-years, air circulation patterns will change as a result, reducing the threat of desertification and increasing the rainfall. Reforestation will restore oxygen to the atmosphere and restore the climate, enabling the green belt to push back the desert rather than vice versa.

Most atmospheric pollution has been generated by the industrial societies. In 1985, for example, 26% of global carbon dioxide emissions came from the United States, 21% from the Soviet Union and 17% from Western Europe. A further 11% was generated by China (currently a heavy coal burner) and 20% by the rest of the Third World. However, a number of new and largely unheralded technologies promise to allow electric power plants and industries to burn more coal while reducing air pollution. These "clean coal" technologies will help reduce emissions of sulphur dioxide (which causes acid rain) by 99% and carbon dioxide (which contributes to the greenhouse effect) by 14%. In 1984, the first plant using these technologies went into operation at Barstow, California; as well as being less polluting, it also boosts power output by more than 50%.

Moreover, the global economy is becoming much less energy-intensive and switching from oil to natural gas (which is one-third less polluting than oil) and other clean-burning fuels such as nuclear and hydro-electric power. Japan, a rapidly post-industrializing economy, accounted for only 5% of global carbon dioxide emissions in 1985. Carbon emissions are thus being reduced as the world de-industrializes. Between 1973 and 1980, worldwide carbon emissions increased by only 1.1% per year, compared with 4% per year in the pre-1973 decade. Carbon emissions have decreased every year since 1980. Thus, although 2nd-Wave industrial technology was powerful enough to at least marginally disturb the natural renewing cycles of Nature, we are now starting to reverse that process and protect the biosphere.

Managing Pollutants

Some oceanographic institutes believe that the world's oceans are in serious trouble from toxic pollution. But a four-year study conducted by the Regional Seas Program of the United Nations Environmental Program (UNEP), aided by seven international bodies and nearly 100 scientists from 36 countries, concluded in 1982 that "the world's oceans are able to assimilate the toxic substances in most areas, and remain relatively stable," and that the level of most toxic substances has decreased in many coastal areas. The study team concluded that the ocean is not in jeopardy for the foreseeable future. UNEP even advocated that the ocean be used as a dumping ground for certain pollutants!

The oceans occupy about 70% of the Earth's surface. It is much more difficult for the smaller land mass to absorb hazardous wastes. As industry has expanded, thousands of chemical substances have been produced and marketed and the numbers increase every year. Industrial waste is a major hazard to the environment, but strategies that minimize waste generation now offer cost-effective approaches to this problem. With the technologies and methods now available, industrial waste can be cut by at least one–third within 10-years, according to the Worldwatch Institute.

Of course, in most cases current methods of managing industrial waste still reflect the "out of sight, out of mind" mentality of the 1950s and 1960s. It is estimated that two-thirds of the hazardous waste produced in the United States is disposed of in injection wells, pits, ponds and lagoons, and landfills; another one-fifth gets discharged to sewers or directly into rivers and streams. Only a small fraction is recycled, destroyed, detoxified, or otherwise rendered harmless, despite numerous examples that point out the feasibility and cost-effectiveness of such programs (see Table 9). The 3M Company probably has the longest-standing commitment to waste reduction of any major world corporation. Through its Pollution Prevention Pays program, launched in 1975, the company hopes to halve its generation of wastes.

Little is known about the long-term environmental consequences of toxic wastes. Radioactive waste is a particular problem because it must be solidified or contained within an impermeable material to prevent leakage into the environment. Such an impermeable material has now been developed through the chemistry of geopolymerization; it is a synthetic rock of phenomenal strength, heat stability, freeze-thaw resistance and long-term durability. It will start to be used in the 1990s to entomb toxic waste dumps and entire nuclear generating stations, as well as for routine stabilization of radioactive and toxic wastes.

It has been recognized that agriculture's dependence on toxic chemicals is unhealthy, and more ecologically sound, economically sustainable pest control methods are being developed. Perhaps no country has worked harder and accomplished more in nonchemical methods of pest control than China. Natural insect enemies keep crop pests in check on some 5-million hectares (12-million acres) of farmland in Guangdong Province, where a wasp that lives on the eggs of moth pests is controlling sugarcane stemborers at one-third the cost of chemical controls. In Jiangsu Province, cotton growers have implemented an integrated pest management (IPM) strategy that includes planting sorghum between cotton plants to attract the pests' natural enemies, changing tillage practices, and applying chemicals at lower effective doses than before. Pesticide use has dropped 90%, pest control costs have decreased 84% and cotton yields have increased significantly.

In 1976, about a third of Brazil's soya bean growers adopted IPM, reducing insecticide use by almost 90% within 7-years. Cotton farmers in Texas using IPM have net returns per hectare averaging almost $300 higher than other cotton farmers. Apple growers in New York State and almond growers in California had profit increases of $500 and $750 per hectare respectively over farmers not using IPM techniques. But despite these examples, IPM's potential has barely been tapped worldwide.

Table 9

Industrial Waste Reduction (Successful Examples)

Company	Products	Strategy and Effect
Astra (Sweden)	Pharmaceuticals	Improved in-plant recycling (and substitution of water for solvents) cut toxic wastes by half.
Borden Chemical (U.S.A.)	Resins; adhesives	Altered rinsing (and other operating procedures) cut organic chemicals in waste water by 93%.
Cleo Wrap	Gift wrap, paper	Substitution of water-based (for solvent-based) ink virtually eliminated hazardous waste.
Duphar (Netherlands)	Pesticides	New manufacturing process cut toxic waste per unit (of one chemical produced) from 20-kg to 1-kg.
Du Pont (Colombia)	Pesticides	New equipment (to recover chemical used in making a fungicide) also cut waste discharges by 95%.
Du Pont (U.S.A.)	Paints, finishes	New solvent recovery unit (eliminated disposal of solvent wastes).
3M (U.S.A.)	Varied	Company-wide, 12-year pollution prevention effort has halved waste generation.
Pioneer Metal Finishing (U.S.A.)	Electroplated metal	New treatment system design cut water use by 96% and sludge production by 20%.

Source: Worldwatch Institute, based on various sources.

Biotechnology is having a similar effect. Either alone or as part of an IPM design, biological methods can provide long-lasting solutions to pest control problems. Typically, a beneficial organism is introduced into a pest-plagued area and becomes a permanent part of the ecosystem. The pest and the introduced natural enemy reach a population balance that keeps pest damage below the economic threshold. The use of fungi, bacteria and other disease-causing agents as "bio-herbicides" shows perhaps the greatest promise for supplanting chemicals in weed control, according to the Worldwatch Institute. Several U.S. companies have developed herbicides that apparently pose little risk and that either break down rapidly in the environment or will not escape into groundwater. To developing countries, IPM and biological control promise to reduce poisoning and deaths from toxic pesticides while creating more sustainable crop production systems.

Environmental Management

The only lasting solution to environmental problems, of course, is to reduce the emissions of pollutants in the first place and to manage the environment. In 1799 Napoleon Bonaparte pointed out that "under a good administration, the Nile gains on the desert; under a bad one, the desert gains on the Nile." The environment has simply gone through a period of bad administration, which is now being corrected. During the past decade, the number of environment ministries or departments in governments has grown from less than 10 worldwide to one in almost every country of the world.

To assist in better geo-strategic management of the planet's environment, UNEP has set up the Global Environment Monitoring System to synthesize data from a range of observation sites to produce a total, constantly changing picture of world pollution. Experts use the data to produce pollution control strategies. As management becomes focussed in this way, extensive information is available to forecast environmental trends and, hence, to assist in the planning and management of our only "life-support system." We are finally realizing that, in Theodore Roosevelt's words, "To waste, to destroy our natural resources, to skin and exhaust the land instead of using it so as to increase its usefulness, will result in undermining in the days of our children the very prosperity which we ought by right to hand down to them amplified and developed."

Although good administration costs money, restoring the environmental balance also generates wealth because pollution controls save money in the long run. According to UNEP estimates, the industrialized countries now lose up to 5% of their GNP annually through pollution damage. In the U.S. alone, pollution damage to pastures and cropland claims $150 per hectare, and the health cost and reduced work efficiency caused by air pollution cost $48 per capita. These losses are preventable in the West. Japan, long accused of neglecting its environmental responsibilities, in 1989 launched a three-pronged strategy of massive donations for environmental programs, development of preservation technology and Japanese leadership in global forums. Tokyo announced a 21% increase in global preservation program spending for 1989 and will place the highest priority on preservation projects when it distributes foreign aid to developing countries.

The U.N. has also calculated that industrializing developing countries can control pollution with an expenditure of as little as 0.5% of GNP. Over the long term, therefore, global GNP can be increased by as much as 4.5% per year over current levels simply by better ecological management of the planet. Even the usually pessimistic Worldwatch Institute has estimated (in its *1988 State of the World* report) that with only $150-billion per year we can restore the environment and put the Third World on the path to sustainable economic growth. That sum is a mere 1.25% of global GNP.

One of the most advanced environmental management systems in the world has been established in Switzerland. Since the inception of tough laws to clean up the ecosystem in 1957, more than $17-billion has been spent by various levels of government and the private sector has kicked in another $5-billion in waste pre-treatment and other facilities. Today, 84% of all waste water goes through purification stations. The leftover sludge is used to fertilize fields. Factories must deliver hazardous wastes to licensed operators for safe disposal. Modern incinerators safely burn all materials, including dioxin. Farmers are not allowed to discharge animal wastes onto frozen ground, thereby keeping ammonia out of waterways where it would kill fish. High-phosphate detergents were also outlawed, and rivers and lakes are re-oxygenating so well that oxygen levels are no longer being measured. The Swiss have achieved this environmental miracle through a high degree of co-operation and the political will to pass legislation (and apply available technology) at all levels of government.

Globally, the new emphasis on environmental management is highlighted by the Global Ozone Agreement, which was signed in 1987 and reinforced in 1988. For about 40-years, 2nd-Wave industry has released chlorofluorocarbon (CFC) gases into the atmosphere. (These compounds are used, for example, in airconditioners and in aerosol products.) As CFCs reach the upper atmosphere, the sun's radiation releases their chlorine atoms, which then destroy the ozone that protects the Earth from the Sun's damaging radiation. Increased CFC levels thus contribute to the greenhouse effect. Data collected since 1978 indicates that a total ozone loss of about 5% occurred during the decade to 1987.

Fortunately, substitute materials can be developed for almost all present major uses of ozone-depleting CFC. Some alternatives already exist, and manufacturers say they will be able to replace CFCs for some uses almost immediately. Other substitutions will take only five to 10 years. The U.S., Canada, Sweden and Norway banned CFC use in aerosols in the late-1970s, but it was not until 1987 that 46 nations came together to sign the Global Ozone Agreement. Under this pact, the release of harmful chemicals into the atmosphere will be frozen at 1986 levels. By 1999, agreed-upon production cuts will reduce atmospheric releases by half. Thus, while the CFCs now in the upper atmosphere will continue destroying ozone for a few decades to come, the deterioration will be gradually slowed down and eventually stopped, whereupon the ozone will then be re-established by the planet's natural oxygen-generation activities.

We are witnessing the emergence of a new environmental ethic, which places the planet — not human beings — at the center of our thinking. While its "vital signs" have not been good, planet Earth is analogous to our own living organism. It is merely in a state of shock and needs to be treated much as we would treat a human who is in shock. Humans can suffer two types of shock: mental and physical.

In the case of mental shock, the immediate medical prescription is a tranquilizer or mood-elevator (depending on the state of mind) plus counseling to restore a balanced mental perspective. Indeed, medical treatment of physical disorders may be ineffective until mental stability is restored. Mental stability cannot be said to exist in a global society that has been misappropriating resources to the tune of more than $1.5-million per minute on armaments or chopping down trees at the rate of 50-hectares per minute.

This exploitive attitude stems from our urge to dominate, which comes from misplaced fear and insecurity. Consequently, and paradoxically, the urge to dominate Nature destroys the environment, which reduces the strength of the planet's (and our own) life-support system. Whatever our worth, we cannot continue to think that we are the masters of Nature, or of the Universe. We need to reverse our entire thought process. On the one hand, we must realize that we are but a minute particle in the global ecology. On the other hand, we are the only creatures with the intellectual capacity to create technologies and master them, and that in itself should be reason enough to make us more humble and responsible. We need to abandon our human-centered thinking and instead adopt planet-centered thinking; to realize that the human brain is destined to create, not to destroy. Only then can mental shock be overcome and physical healing begin.

When the human body has suffered physical shock, it can be brought back into chemical balance with antibiotics and simple remedies such as fluids and salt. In the case of poisoning, blood pressure drops and circulation slows. Similarly, the arteries (which are the lifeline of the human system) can paradoxically become clogged with the richness of life (cholesterol, for instance).

Human "pollution" problems have their counterparts at the planetary level. Air and water pollution and deforestation are the result of both the wealth and the poverty of socio-economic development. To achieve wellness, the planetary system, like the human system, needs appropriate levels of diet and nutrition (that is, money and technology). This applies to both the overwhelmed and the undernourished parts of the system.

The vital signs of Earth are plain for all to see and understand. The diagnosis: we need better planning and management of our resources, new priorities for the use of these resources, and a more equitable 4-STEP distribution of them between the overwhelmed and the undernourished parts of global society. Socially, we must satisfy basic psychological drives. Technologically, we must create an information-rich environment. Economically, we must redistribute these planetary riches. Politically, we must restructure geo-political power to govern the environmental system. The life of Earth is in our hands — and in the integrity with which we humans behave and perceive ourselves in the Universal scheme of things.

G-Force E-8
Reinventing Capitalism and Communism

*"It doesn't matter whether the cat is black or white
so long as it catches the mice."*
— Deng Xiao-Ping

The black and white checkerboard pattern of global economies is fading to gray. The world entered the 1950s with two apparently firmly entrenched economic systems. In the global post-industrial age, however, absolute forms of both capitalism and communism lose their relevance, and neither will work satisfactorily. The last global economy — the 2nd-Wave manufacturing one that ended about 1970 — was marked by competition. The Western capitalist system was based on and still predominantly operates on the premise of competition. And the communist system competed (and still competes) with the capitalist system for strength. Company fought company and country fought country for a greater share of the global economic pie. Today, of course, the world has no pure form of either capitalism or communism because, in an interdependent Planetary Information Economy (PIE), this simplistic dichotomy does not work. Neither private capitalistic competition nor public communist co-operation is flexible enough for a real-time global economy. Rather, the emerging model is a hybrid form of socialistic entrepreneurialism (or entrepreneurial socialism) that will optimize the 4-STEP goal of global social development. This G-Force is reinventing economic ideology.

Capitalism stemmed from the exploitive colonial system of the Industrial Age, in which workers and other resources, at home and abroad, were hostage to the captains of industry. Colonialism of any kind cannot work in an integrated and interdependent global village of 5-billion (soon to be 10-billion) humans whose aspirations have changed. Capitalism must continue to become more socially responsible to all the human "shareholders" of the planet. Only by meeting all human needs — not those of the capitalists alone — will capitalism retain any viability and preserve for itself any meaningful role in the future of human affairs. Enlightened corporate leaders have already recognized this. Their governments are also increasingly socialistic. In the United States, for example, many socialist programs such as welfare and food stamps are so firmly in place that not even the right-wing Reagan administration was able to remove them. Indeed, in the 1980s, that administration bailed out the failing Chrysler Corporation and virtually nationalized Continental Illinois Bank — intervention that smacked of state control.

The communist system arose largely in opposition to capitalist colonization — which will have vanished from the Earth by 2010, if not sooner. Oppressive and exploitive right-wing regimes are simply not viable in the modern 4th-Wave global society. Conversely, ultra-left dictatorial communist regimes, which attempt to control economic resources, will retard, not further, the cause of their people. In order to modernize and to meet the needs and aspirations of its people, a society must release its creativity and entrepreneurial initiative.

Neither capitalism nor communism is suited to the challenge of the post-industrial Planetary Information Economy. The Industrial Age fostered competition for scarce resources and shifted the critical factor of production from labor to machines. In the post-industrial age the critical factor shifts again: to knowledge or brain-power and co-operation in the sharing of information in order to maximize wealth and social welfare.

Co-operation Replacing Competition

Nationally and corporately we are seeing the last gasps of competition, which is increasingly found to be self-defeating. Although economic trading partnerships are still being forged — and global free trade is ultimately essential — many of these agreements are a defensive (that is, competitive) posture against other nations and are doomed to fail. For example, Canadian and U.S. attempts to implement free trade in the 1990s will impede both countries' global trade opportunities, especially with their fellow Pacific Rim countries that, currently at least, view the deal as protectionist.

Protectionism of any stripe creates a closed economy that breeds internal mediocrity, ultimately undermining a nation's ability to offer international-level technologies to the global marketplace and leaving that country vulnerable to more advanced foreign technologies. The Planetary Information Economy is an open system. No country or group of countries (not even the EEC or a combined "Ameri-Canada") can be an island unto itself and expect to succeed in the much larger global environment. Although the EEC, COMECON and other trading blocs are a natural evolution of co-operativeness, they perpetuate competition in another guise and can only be an interim stage (I hope a short one) in creating a transplanetary economic framework that will co-operate on a free trade basis by, say, 2010 at the latest. The economic "Super-Boom" which will last from the late-1990s through to 2025 or so, should create the relaxed, non-protectionist environment wherein this tranformation can take place.

Co-operation is also sweeping across the corporate sector. Long known for their adherence to the principles of private competition and "survival of the fittest," Western companies now are forging co-operative alliances. To avoid being bought out by competitors, companies (paradoxically) may merge defensively with other competitors. The more enlightened companies, of course, are realizing that open co-operation brings greater rewards — and continued entrepreneurial independence. Research and development, for example, has become so complex and costly that many forward-looking companies are turning to a new approach that stresses co-operation over competition. Computer and microelectronic companies have found that they can no longer afford to independently research the areas that will keep them at the leading edge of technological change. In 1982, following Japanese examples, a number of high-tech business leaders in the U.S. pooled their research resources and formed the Micro-Electronics and Computer Technology Corporation. U.S. Steel (now USX) and Bethlehem Steel have conducted joint research on thin sheet steel casting, as have Honeywell and Bellcore (Bell Communications Research) on telecommunications services.

Foreign companies are also beginning to collaborate — as in Bellcore's venture with a German firm to develop high-speed fiber-optics devices that will quicken Bellcore's lab-to-market delivery. Now that the Japanese are going into the aircraft business, Boeing prefers to work with them rather than against them. Many Japanese companies are entering such co-operative joint ventures to overcome the competitive protectionism that would prevent them from entering the U.S. and other markets. The GM-Toyota joint venture, for example, allows them to share capital and risk and to link U.S. product innovation with low-cost Japanese production technology. Such ventures represent the first major examples of a distinct shift from competition to co-operation.

These G-Force moves to co-operation are not restricted to individual companies; they are also occurring on an industry-by-industry basis. The automobile industry is making the most dramatic strides towards co-operation. Eventually the developments will lead to a single global automobile infrastructure. Joint ventures are proliferating. Three Japanese companies (Suzuki, Isuzu and Toyota) now manufacture small cars for GM, and Toyota is discussing a joint venture with GM in Australia. Ford recently bought Aston Martin in the U.K. and is now collaborating with Volkswagen in Brazil and Argentina to jointly operate a $4-billion company called Autolantia. A new Australian light truck comes with a Dodge body and Chrysler engine, and is assembled in Taiwan. And the list goes on.

The globalization of the automobile industry is reaching into the communist bloc countries. Plaxtons, the largest manufacturer of buses in the U.K., is teaming up with the world's largest bus maker, Ikarus of Hungary, to produce a line of buses for Britain. Daihatsu of Japan is negotiating a joint operation in Poland. Fiat long ago set up a plant in the U.S.S.R., and both Volkswagan and

American Motors have joint-ventures with state-owned enterprises in China. These and other ventures demonstrate how easy it is to cross the boundaries between socialist planning and capitalist markets.

Similar joint ventures are evolving in the electronics, telecommunications, transportation and service industries. For example, Toshiba, General Electric and Siemens of West Germany have created a shared library of components for customized computer chips, and Toshiba is also building a jointly owned factory in Japan with Motorola of the United States.

The railways and the trucking industry have long competed for customers. Recently, however, Union Pacific Railroad and 11 U.S. regional trucking lines agreed to etablish a rail-truck network that combines the economies of rail with the flexibility of trucks. The otherwise fiercely competitive international and domestic airlines are also starting to pool their marketing and distribution efforts. Eastern and Continental, TWA and Japan Airlines, Delta and Japan Airlines, Pan Am and American, New York Air and Continental are all pairing up. Some airlines are going further: TWA and Northwest Orient are sharing their electronic reservations systems, as are Pan Am and American.

In the major professional services sector, full-blown mergers have occurred. In advertising, Young and Rubicam recently reached across the Pacific to join forces with the Japanese advertising firm Dentsu. In accounting, Coopers and Lybrand merged with Matsumoto and Yamada in the largest international merger of its kind. Many other companies in those professions have since taken their cue from these 1983 international joint ventures.

Central Planning & Free Markets

Many ultra-capitalist economists, business leaders and politicians are still out of step with this global shift from competition to co-operation. They insist that the only contribution a business corporation can make to the public interest (that is, to global society) is to meet demand at a profit. They believe that "the business of business is business," and that only with this philosophy can the business corporation optimize returns on the resources it manages. This tenet is clearly out of touch with modern-day reality. Public interest, of course, is a concept which shifts with the mood of society. Today's mood *favors* the global public interest. In the Planetary Information Economy, there must be an explicit recognition that corporate behavior responds to socio-political as well as pure market forces.

Corporations are, whether they like it or not, more and more social as well as economic institutions. Only by meeting social needs can a business prosper in the marketplace and thereby foster economic growth. The leading-edge multinational corporations have learned this during the past two decades. Inter-company ties and affiliations open up access to global markets and transfer technology and management skills. Some of these ties are already starting to provide for specialization among countries on a sectoral (product line or component) basis, so that worldwide productivity will be enhanced and greater output gained from relatively lower resource inputs.

Global economic progress also demands much more co-operation between the private and public sectors of nation states. As the ventures with China and the Soviet Union are starting to show, multinational corporations can work well with nation state governments, no matter what their political stripe. As well, the nation states are learning that the new geo-strategic corporation is not out to exploit their country as did the majority of multinational corporations in the 1950s and 1960s or as colonizing nation states did before them. The economic G-Forces are bringing the world together in the time of its greatest need — and its greatest opportunity.

The public and private sectors have collaborated before in such circumstances. One of the best co-operative efforts between the private and public sectors was the Marshall Plan, which, after World War II, allocated to Western Europe $80-billion (in current purchasing power) of U.S. public funds to rebuild itself. U.S. business corporations played a major role in transferring technology and management techniques to Europe and in training their European counterparts in the U.S., thereby restoring the Western European economy to prosperity that, in turn, fostered a flourishing world economy. Similarly, the first Moon landing was rendered possible by NASA which in turn depended upon thousands of large, medium and small American firms that were specifically contracted or subcontracted for this purpose. The economic R&D spin-off (about 30,000 new industrial and consumer products) is widely recognized as one of the major engines of economic growth and technological innovation since the 1960s.

Similar collaborative ventures today could turn many world problems into opportunities. Jack Behrman of the University of North Carolina has proposed a NASA- or NATO-like contractual relationship in which a single prime contractor would be selected from among several bidding companies — probably large multinational corporations, expert in a particular sector (such as housing) that needs to be developed in a given developing country. A new government-business co-operation would result, reducing the still prevalent adversarial orientation and moving the world towards less destructive nationalistic policies on industrialization and trade.

Such long-term commitments to socio-economic goals by the private sector of course requires long-range planning and development in collaboration with governments. Unfortunately, planning in the public and private sectors in capitalist countries is generally fragmented. This fritters away the national effort and renders it more costly. Government planning must be co-ordinated with private sector planning to make it a national effort. It must also be decentralized to the local level for effective implementation either by the state-owned enterprise or in collaboration with the private entrepreneurs and companies.

International firms, as pointed out by André van Dam, former strategic planner for Corn Products International, would derive significant benefit from an interrelationship between internal company planning and local government planning policies, which inevitably impinge on the firm. Conversely, no government — capitalist or communist — can abstract itself from the business plans of the corporate enterprise sector. It is to their mutual advantage, says van Dam, to know each other's plans and intentions. Government and industry should thus become "partners in progress."

Such teamwork implies that common interest must override private (conflicting) interests. This rules out Adam Smith's "invisible hand" (the marketplace), which anyway has failed, in this period of global transition, to distribute rewards and penalties, abundances and scarcities in a reasonably equitable manner between the different stakeholders in the post-industrial society.

Since Adam Smith wrote his *Wealth of Nations* in 1776, many scholars have been concerned with the evolution and future of capitalism. In a famous 1975 article in the *Harvard Business Review*, George Lodge identified an ideological transition under way in the United States. He defined the traditional U.S. ideology in terms of the five "Lockean pillars": individualism, property rights, free and competitive markets, limited government, and specialization of skills. Some 1800 readers of the *Harvard Business Review* whom Lodge surveyed believed that the 1975-85 decade would see the U.S. move towards a new communitarian ideology and depart significantly from each of Locke's pillars. While 62% of the surveyed readers believed that the traditional ideology was dominant in 1975, 73% anticipated that the communitarian ideology would dominate by 1985. In 1988, a U.S. panel of 40 business scholars and practitioners in long-range planning and futures research found that the ideology of free enterprise had in fact declined, as measured by Locke's five pillars. The panel also conducted a forecasting study to anticipate the future of U.S. free enterprise by the year 2000 and found that a continued decrease in all five pillars was likely to occur.

In my view, we are witnessing, as illustrated by the Western stock market crash of 1987, a massive disintegration of the Western financial system. The coming "Mini-Depression" (which, if poorly handled, might turn into a "Mega-Depression") could be bad enough to bring about the end of capitalism itself. We may thus witness the end of the political era in which Reagan and Thatcher worshipped markets as the best way to run national and international economies.

But markets are too unpredictable and disruptive to be the only tool of economic management. They can be extremely efficient at allocating resources under the rules of a larger plan but, left unregulated, they are manipulated by speculators and can be a huge disaster. Reagan and Thatcher have said that the secret was to reduce the role of government, to encourage the competition of private wealth, and to let markets choose the winners. To support this belief, they created an artificial boom (1983-89) that was primarily based on printed money and funds borrowed from abroad. In reality, of course, the "boom" has created masses of poor, homeless and unemployed — and a global debt mountain of unprecedented size. The specter of the destructiveness of this "capitalism gone mad" now haunts the world's economy. Corruption and leveraged buyouts of companies with high levels of "junk bond" borrowings are rampant in the financial markets. In its quest for limitless profits, capitalism has defiled human relationships by turning them into money relationships, corrupting business people and politicians in the West and Japan.

Capitalism of this sort has little appeal left for the human spirit in search of new meaning. On the contrary, to invoke loyalty to capitalism because of the prosperity it brought in the past — or can make now overnight — is regarded by the vast majority of Western intellectuals as not just materialistic but corrupt, and certainly not suitable for the post-industrial future. In the U.S. there is a developing trend toward a broad socialist (if not anti-capitalist) movement, elaborating a liberal democratic alternative within American politics. George Bush's sneers at "liberals" in the 1988 U.S. election confirmed the movement's growing momentum.

For this liberal trend to reach fruition, there would have to be a totally socialist vision and movement — one that treats the four key factors of human activity (kinship, community, economics and politics) as equally important, entwined and mutually defining. As Jesse Jackson and others have started to show, the United States is now at a point in its history that can spawn a coalition of organizations currently fighting around issues of class, race, power within society, and imperialism. Economic hardship and continued relative decline in America's global stature will bring these groups together in the 1990s.

While such an orientation will differ fundamentally from equally obsolete Leninism and Marxism, it would be well suited to the evolving socialist dynamic in many Western countries. Even in the United States, where Reagan in 1980 was determined to reduce the size of government by transfering workers from the public to the private sector, the ongoing growth of the welfare state has continued to provide growing segments of permanent public employment. Government activities in the Western countries will continue and grow because they provide the necessary security for a workable economic model, which its adherents will still call capitalism.

In the United States, many socialist programs are in place. Canada and Sweden, two of the world's richest economies, are highly socialistic, practicing much government intervention. Britain — Margaret Thatcher notwithstanding — is a social welfare state economy. After the Western economy collapses, I believe it will take only a few years before socialist (or socialist in all but name) governments are firmly entrenched in both Britain and the United States. Because of certain internal population dynamics, the United States is rapidly becoming a socialist country anyway. George Bush, with his "kinder, gentler nation" concept, could well be the last Republican president in American history — unless he reinvents capitalism and fosters an entrepreneurial but highly socialistic economy.

"Socialistic Entrepreneurial" Models

In recent years, many corporations have made attempts to adopt an ethic of social responsibility. To my knowledge, the best is being made by Magna International, the world's largest auto parts manufacturer. Magna's organization is based on a recognition of the need to create a long-term, entrepreneurial, employee-participative, community-oriented environment. These corporate aspirations are articulated in a "Corporate Constitution," which stipulates, among other things, that 10% of pre-tax profits are to be allocated to employee shareholders, 2% to charitable, cultural, educational and political institutions "to support the basic fabric of society," and 6% to encourage long-term entrepreneurialism within the company.

The brightest examples of national economic performance in the capitalist world are Japan and West Germany. It is very important to note, however, that both countries are economically centrist. Germany is liberal-democratic and focusses on efficiency. Japan is also liberal-democratic and focusses on the co-operative creation of wealth. Both focus geo-strategically on the opportunities for change created in the global marketplace. The old capitalist dinosaurs of the U.S., the U.K. and Canada do not. Indeed, like Japan, most of the dynamic political economies of Southeast Asia have developed a rare degree of central economic planning, with intense co-operation between government and industry. It is a unique mixture, combining free market competition with corporate-state consensus planning — and it works.

This model is successful because Asians embrace consensus and compromise as a natural way of life and of making progress for the economic benefit of all, backed up by the traditional Asian values of hard work, frugality and efficiency. Japan set about the task of becoming *ichi ban* (number one) with a degree of collective commitment and forward planning that leaves the other developed countries looking distinctly pedestrian.

We are in a crisis period of change for both capitalism and communism. Elements of capitalism and communism do have a future, but not one that most people would expect. Neither will entirely disappear as a model, but neither serves its original purpose any longer. Therefore, new economic frameworks must be implemented and ideologies modified. A logical extension of the emerging "mixed" global economy would be deliberate encouragement and guidance of investment by the individual nation state — the key to long-term economic planning that now exists in forward-thinking communist countries such as China and Hungary, and in modern capitalist countries such as Japan. Indeed, as already illustrated, the distinction between what are called the private and public sectors is becoming blurred in modern capitalist and communist economies.

In their pure forms, both are unsuited to post-industrialism. The French government's NORA Report, published in 1978 after a year-long study ordered by then president Giscard d'Estaing, became a best-seller in France and one of the world's most quoted official verdicts on the political implications of computer technology. In a conclusion that is still anathema to political establishments, the report said: "In a post-industrial economy both capitalism and communism lose their meaning," because in a 4th-Wave information society, wealth is created with a minimum of both capital and labor and because "all citizens can receive immediate and wide information [that is, wealth] from multiple sources." The report said that both the liberal and Marxist approaches will be "rendered questionable" by the end of the 2nd-Wave production-based society.

Alvin Toffler has long argued that Western governments have reached a state of "almost total paralysis" because of political systems that were fashioned before the telephone, let alone the computer network. Now, the telephone and the computer are being integrated into a worldwide telecommunications infrastructure that changes policy-making forever. Computerized information technology exerts a novel force that enables systems to simultaneously operate on a centralized and a decentralized basis.

Communism thus still favors central planning and "social" values of security, public welfare and equity, but it also is learning to embrace local market mechanisms to create an innovative environment for these goals to be achieved. Capitalism leaves the planning to the corporate sector and favors "entrepreneurial" values of market freedom and innovation. Communism is recognizing the drawbacks of its dictatorial inefficiency and bureaucratic structures. Capitalism is recognizing the social costs of competition and hierarchical structures. Both are recognizing that they must transform themselves as the new technology takes us to an information economy. Information is at once a social leveler (it is socialistic) and also an instigator of innovation (it is entrepreneurial). Both communism and capitalism are dissolving into a new hybrid form of political economy: socialistic entrepreneurialism.

Reinventing Communism

The key to the future of both capitalism and communism lies in China's 1980s initiatives in opening up its economic system to the outside world. This new direction, including the establishment of an ambitious national goal of quadrupling economic output between 1980 and 2000, elicited enthusiasm from the Chinese people and unleashed their pent-up energy and innovation. Magnificent results have been achieved since 1978. China is now outpacing every other national economy and will easily achieve the modernization goals it has set into the 21st-Century.

Like China's Deng Xiao-Ping, in 1985 Mikhail Gorbachev went beyond the routine 5-year state planning system to implement a 15-year target of doubling Soviet economic output by the year 2000. By then Gorbachev wants the U.S.S.R. to be "standing on the threshold of the Information Age." I have no doubt that he will achieve this goal by opening up the system, both internally and to the outside world, adopting many aspects of the Chinese model initiated by Deng.

Since 1978, China has been building what Deng calls "socialism with Chinese characteristics," articulating a new interpretation of traditional socialism. Socialism is now evaluated according to the level of productive forces, moving beyond the old Marxist practice of ignoring these forces. China admits that state ownership and centralization had been overemphasized by an "ultra-leftist" ideology that "fettered the forces of production." Of course, China still believes the socialist system is superior to capitalism. However, its leaders say that socialism need not be confined to public ownership. China thus intends to avoid "the unwarranted early replacement of the market economy" with a product economy (that is, an absolute communist economy in which products are not marketed but are allocated by the state).

Under Chinese socialism, then, different types of ownership may co-exist and a large amount of private and other nonpublic ownership is being encouraged. For example, there are now 70,000 privately operated businesses in the city of Shanghai alone. The idea that remaining state-owned enterprises must be controlled by the state has given way to the idea that "there may be an appropriate separation between proprietary rights and management power" in these enterprises, which can issue shares and become relatively independent commodity producers. By late-1988, the priority for major state-owned businesses was to shift to a joint-stock system with shares offered to the public and workers, thereby separating the government from the enterprise. Managers now report to a board of directors, not to the Communist Party, and firms can go bankrupt.

As well, reports *Beijing Review*, China is moving away from the "outmoded theory that market forces are opposed to planning," and is creating a mixed economy which "integrates the marketplace with central planning." By setting the market against socialist planning, traditional Marxism excluded market mechanisms and maintained that a highly centralized and highly unified management system was the only way for a socialist planned economy to operate. For China, the development of a "socialist commodity economy" demands market mechanisms and economic regulation by "the law of value" (supply, demand and prices). Its mixed economy will be regulated in two ways: (1) centralized/decentralized planning based on market mechanisms and (2) market regulation under the guidance of planning. This is what China calls a "sound socialist market system," and it has far-reaching significance for the development not only of China's brand of socialism but for international communist ideology in general.

China has also instituted an "open door" economic system involving international competition, as opposed to "the old closed economy" where progress was blocked by poor technology and shortage of capital, causing China to lag far behind other developing countries. China is now open to both socialist and capitalist countries, and is striving to expand international co-operation. Between 1979 and 1987, more than $65-billion was committed for investment in China by foreigners: 80% of it has come from overseas Chinese, particularly from Hong Kong. Of this, $19-billion has so far been invested in a mixture of more than 10,000 wholly foreign-owned and joint ventures, of which 39% are already operating. China believes that it has formulated a new Theory of Socialist Economics: "By studying the commodity economy and assimilating what is useful of Western economics, Marxist economic theories may develop not in isolation but in the vigorous atmosphere of the open door policy."

Of course, many people are skeptical of the claim that communism can reform to the reality of the post-industrial Planetary Information Economy because it was created to suit the social and political system of the 2nd-Wave Industrial Age. Typical of that age, therefore, communism became an institutionalized system of highly regimented, disciplined and bureaucratized nonparticipation. Consequently — outside of what seems to be happening in present-day China, Hungary and the Soviet Union — skeptics believe that communism will fail to transform itself from an industrial past to a post-industrialized future. After Japan, however, China is clearly the most "futuristic" country in the world in terms of understanding the post-industrial Planetary Information Economy. It is modernizing all six waves of its economy, and almost every senior- and middle-level bureaucrat and planner at the state and provincial levels of government has read — and thoroughly understands the implication of — books such as Toffler's The Third Wave. It is also very clear that Gorbachev understands the implications of the Information Age and is determined to institute major reforms so that the U.S.S.R. is not left behind.

Neither those who are overly hopeful or those who are downright skeptical about Gorbachev's chances of achieving reform understand what is happening in the Soviet Union or China. Westerners who expect great results from Soviet or Chinese reforms believe that communist ideology is being abandoned, that these countries have "seen the error of their ways" and are embracing capitalism. Those who feel that communist ideology has not been abandoned conclude that no serious reform is therefore possible. Both conclusions are fundamentally naive. The new thinking in both China and the Soviet Union is not a basic departure from socialism; the reforms are occurring within the framework of socialism, particularly Lenin's conception of its humanist essence.

The Soviet and Chinese reformers believe that central planning can best manage socio-economic development because it broadly improves well-being while avoiding cyclical economic crises such as unemployment, uneven development and excessive debt — that is, it is essential to stable management of the 4-STEP long-wave cycle and the current transition to a 4th-Wave global information economy. All that is needed is to open up the system to the world, decentralize the planning and incorporate market mechanisms to encourage rigorous achievement of central goals.

Thus, whereas capitalists think you must choose between a market or a planned economy, modern communists think you must give the market a role within the plan. The plan is not abandoned, it is reinforced. Central planning has long been decentralized in China to permit localized economic decision-making whereby provincial leaders and factory managers can exercise their own initiative. Following Deng's formal edict that China should "seek truth from facts," Marxist ideological dogma is thrown into question on the basis that no single economic truth exists.

Following Gorbachev's elevation to absolute power as President of the Soviet Union in late-1988, the Kremlin called for similar radical experiments with market economics and a "new concept of socialism" (based on ideas to be borrowed from the rest of the world) and a move away from state control of the economy. Gorbachev has proposed a gradual transition to a system of long-term (25-to-50-year) leasing of land to "individual farmers and outside entrepreneurs ... for personal benefit and profit." He has also extended this idea to the leasing of factories to their managers, as China is doing with its contract responsibility system.

In many respects, the mood in the communist world is reminiscent of that within capitalist states during the Great Depression: there is a sense that a fatal flaw exists in the system. I suggest that the same mood is growing again in the West and that this will coalesce as the "Mini-Depression" strikes home. People the world over have a deep inner feeling that there is something seriously wrong with the world economy and with the systems that have been used to try to govern it. Aspirations are not being met.

The two major communist societies have recognized the need to reform and get themselves in league with the new international future. Much the same can be said of Japan and perhaps some other mixed economies of Southeast Asia. No such future-oriented mindset is yet evident in the governments of North America and Western Europe, except perhaps among certain segments of West Germany, Greece and France.

We must therefore conclude that China and the Soviet Union, along with Japan, are providing the future direction for world political and economic affairs. In order to modernize its economy and achieve political reunification with Hong Kong, Macao and Taiwan, China has adopted "socialism with Chinese characteristics." By "seeking truth from facts" about the advantages of both communism and capitalism in pursuing economic development goals, China is drawing up a practical strategy for "socialist and capitalist co-existence" in a unified China.

This concept of "one country, two systems" is unique in the world, but it gives us a glimpse of an emerging global reinvention of and accommodation between capitalism and communism. As such, China's economic reform process is leading the natural evolution of global economic thought. Gorbachev has embraced the same spirit, saying that "the paths of socialism and capitalism will inevitably intersect and interact within the limits of one and the same human civilization."

Paraphasing Deng, I believe that black and white cats working together will catch more mice than if they work separately. Co-operation and joint-ventures, between private and/or public partners are emerging worldwide. Capitalism is disintegrating, or, at least becoming more socialist, and China is leading the Soviet Union in rewriting Marx. Probably as early as 2020, I have little doubt that the Chinese model, if it is maintained with full and unswerving vigor, will be the widely-accepted economic model of the new increasingly-socialist global economy, finally evolving into a hybrid of socialistic entrepreneurialism.

G-Force E-9
Converting Military Waste to Earthly Eco-Development

"Every gun that is made, every warship launched, every rocket fired ... [is] a theft from those who hunger and are not fed — those who are cold and not clothed. This world ... is spending the sweat of its laborers, the genius of its scientists, the houses of its children."
— Dwight D. Eisenhower

One of the major reasons for the unsustainability of the present world economic system is that it is being bled to death by megalomaniacal spending on weapons — more than $1-trillion per year is being wasted on building and maintaining machines to destroy machines. Now, the United States, with its nightmarish Strategic Defense Initiative (SDI or Star Wars), is threatening to destroy the budding 6th-Wave Outer-Space economy also. The Soviets are competing to do the same. The world simply can no longer afford nuclear or any other kinds of weapons. Military spending competes with and impedes productive economic growth, and the Soviet Union and the U.S. have been destroying each other's economies through a military competition neither can afford. If the global economy is to be unshackled from depressing conditions (which are themselves often worse than war conditions), we must find ways of switching away from military (dis)investment towards peaceful eco-development. By rechanneling investment into genuinely constructive works that will allow us to meet our social aspirations, we can create a new G-Force for peaceful economic progress that will reinvent the world.

Economic Disinvestment

Weapons are the most unproductive form of economic investment. Once a missile is loaded into its silo, it produces no return whatsoever on investment, its material cannot be recycled, it creates no further jobs. As a rule of thumb, for every 1% of GNP devoted to military spending, overall economic growth is reduced by 0.5%. Thus, if the United States were able to eliminate the 7% of GNP it now spends on defense, the economy would grow by an extra 3.5% — more than twice as fast as normal. For the Soviet Union, which spends 14% of its GNP on military affairs, the economic benefits would be even more significant.

On a global level, this economic trade-off is dramatic. For example, the budget of the U.S. Air Force alone is larger than the education budget for 1.3-billion children in Africa, Latin America, and Asia. The Soviet Union in one year spends more on military defense than the governments of all the Third World countries spend for education and healthcare for their 4-billion people. The industrialized countries on average spend 5.4% of their GNP for military purposes and only 0.3% for foreign aid. It costs $600,000 a day to operate one aircraft carrier, yet every day in Africa 15,000 children (who could all be fed for under $30,000 a day, according to UNICEF) die of hunger or hunger-related causes.

Yet there is a myth in America that war and the preparation for war are good for the economy. This stems from the country's experience in World War II: the U.S. gained economically, being insulated from war damage while its major rivals in world trade were destroyed. America captured global markets and was able to reorient world production, trade and finance around itself. In reality, the peacetime trade-offs of American investment in military versus civilian resources are enlightening. Just 7% of U.S. military outlays from 1981 to 1986, for example, amounted to $100-billion, a sum that, in 1987, would have totally rehabilitated the U.S. steel industry and made it the most efficient in the world. The navy's F-18 fighter program is costing $34-billion, an amount that could upgrade America's machine tool stock to the same level as Japan's. The cost overruns to 1981 on the Trident and F-16 programs were $33-billion, enough to have rehabilitated 20% of the bridges in the United States. The cost overrun (again to 1981) of $13-billion on the U.S. army's heavy tank program could have maintained the water supplies for 150 American cities for another 20-years. And so on. Similar comparison could be made for Soviet and European military waste.

In addition to this military disinvestment, the superpowers now are spending massive amounts to put weapons into outer-space. But instead, as President John F. Kennedy envisioned, many of the problems of Earth must be solved or turned into massive opportunities through the economic potential of space. For this reason, there is a fast-growing movement to stop the placing of weapons in space. Thousands of scientists and engineers across the United States and in other countries have refused to work on research projects associated with the Star Wars initiative. They are campaigning to have all research funding and resources for outer-space weaponry redirected to develop space for economic purposes — that is, to use the 6th-Wave Outer-Space economy for the further development of the five waves of the Earth's economy.

The leading organization in this campaign is the Washington-based

Institute for Security and Cooperation in Outer Space (ISCOS). Formed by Dr. Carol S. Rosin, formerly the highest-paid woman executive in the U.S. aerospace industry, ISCOS supports international co-operative military, commercial, industrial and other ventures in space that are of a nonweapons nature. In what may sound like a contradiction in terms, ISCOS proposes that the military continue to support the development of space without the development of space weapons by developing military surveillance of weapons on Earth through satellite systems, or perhaps by helping build space stations or mining the Moon or asteroids and by building co-operative technologies that can be applied to human and environmental needs on Earth.

ISCOS thus approaches the entire concept of outer-space and arms control quite differently than do peace groups. Working with the military and the private sector to view space as a strategic and economically viable resource, ISCOS envisions solid alternatives to SDI. It emphasizes the economic benefits of weaponless space and the industrial, civilian, military, scientific and other applications for solutions to world problems, and an end to the superpower arms race at the same time.

Military expertise and resources thus can be used for economic purposes in space, just as they can on Earth. Genuine security can be provided not through weapons, which in fact do not create a secure world but make the world more insecure, but by building co-operative space ventures to enhance disarmament verification, superpower understanding and economic development. Such co-operation would not be new. Most people are unaware that the United States and the Soviet Union have signed more than 1000 agreements with more than 100 nations (including each other) for co-operative space activities, covering such areas as tele-conferencing, life sciences, biomedical experiments, and search and rescue. There have been extensive exchanges of space research information: countries launch each other's satellites, experiments and people; and the two superpowers have agreed to collaborate on a joint mission to Mars.

Space for Eco-Development

The outer-space economy itself will generate great wealth. Annual revenues from space industrialization, which were only $1-billion in 1977, will reach about $80-billion in 2010, according to a NASA study. Proven or potential space applications, of benefit to the world in general and developing countries in particular, range from space manufacture and space medicine to navigation systems for ships and airplanes, emergency communication systems for maritime search and rescue operations, and telecommunications and direct broadcasting.

Missiles create budget deficits, but satellites are generators of economic wealth. Satellite communications are already fully operational through international networks and through growing national networks connecting important urban centers. They also hold high promise for integrated rural development, providing distant–learning systems, promoting cultural awareness and a sense of responsibility among citizens, and encouraging self-reliant agricultural development of rural communities and the monitoring of their local environment. A satellite broadcast educational communications experiment, which covered 2400 villages throughout India, was a resounding success that increased knowledge in areas such as health and hygiene, with previously illiterate children gaining significantly more than those already literate.

The considerable list of economic opportunities that co-operative military/industry space enterprises could pursue include office automation, automatic distribution, automation of process industries and parts manufacturing, electronic controls for road traffic and railroads, aviation support equipment, communication equipment, electronic self-instruction devices, electronic libraries, electronic medical diagnostics and remote learning.

As well, the enterprises of the military airframe industry are specialists in lightweight, high-strength design and fabrication. They have demonstrated considerable ability to use lightweight alloys for the fabrication of aircraft and other flying structures that require great strength. The same technology can be applied to civilian products, such as prefabricated houses, railroad cars, monorail transportation systems, electric road vehicles, and hydrofoil and surface-effect boats. With 2-billion houses to be built and extensive urban transportation systems to be constructed in the world by 2050, a "conversion" of these types of technologies and support resources would have tremendous economic impact.

While industrialized countries would expect somewhat different economic benefits of space than the developing countries would, there are many common areas of interest. Benefits expected for the next 20-years can be divided into three categories:

- Third World: agriculture, housing, telecommunications, healthcare, education.
- Western countries: tourism, new products, electronic mail, electronic networks.
- Global society: abundant energy, rapid transportation, disaster prevention and control, environmental clean-up, material processing, resource survey, new materials development, disarmament.

Military "Conversion"

To divert military funding to socio-economic uses will not be easy. For example, some 30-million people are now trained to kill each other (if military cooks, clerks and drivers are counted as part of the machinery of war). In reality, these millions of otherwise productive human resources do nothing for the economy. Indeed, the civilian population has to provide for their every need while they stare each other down across barbed-wire borders or gaze into radar screens. The historical functioning of the military industry complex indicates that, to be nationally and globally significant, a "conversion" from military to civilian activities will require a serious transnational political and economic movement towards that goal.

274

Trusted leaders must proclaim conversion to civilian work as a viable — not to mention noble — national objective. This has begun to happen in China during the last decade. The organization for such an effort has to be persuasive, encompassing military industry organizations, unions and professional societies, as well as activity at the state and community levels. Only if concrete economic opportunities are identified can institutional and occupational conversion be carried out with confidence and with reasonable expectation of success.

Even then — and even if a majority of American and Soviet citizens rejected the war economy in favor of these economic ideologies as a way of life — the power of the government and private institutions of the military economy would still have to be overcome before a conversion to a civilian economy could occur. Although the U.S. Congress declared in 1958 that "military activities in space should be devoted to peaceful purposes for the benefit of all mankind," every U.S. president since then has opposed legislation promoting plans for economic conversion of military activities to civilian use. They have taken their cue from Defense Department officials who regard such concepts as a blueprint for diminishing their power, not one for resolving world problems. Because of such military pressures, governments of nations with heavily militarized economies have resisted efforts to set up conversion programs.

In the end, conversion will depend on the public and its political power. Once a sufficient part of the population refuses to yield to the self-interested coercion of the military complex and the local communities within which it resides, alternative public policies will be achievable. The defeat of the supersonic transport jet program in 1972 was just such a case in point. An environmental issue (jet noise) gripped the imagination of enough people to cause them and the majority of the U.S. Congress to reject the economic claims and pressures of managers and trade union officers in the aerospace industries who mounted an all-out campaign for the airplane. It is possible that the upcoming "Mini-Depression," partly a result of the drain of the war economy and related debt, will eventually evoke a similar political challenge to the war economy directorate. Indeed, the recent disarmament agreements already point in this direction.

Money is motivating disarmament. It also could motivate defense contractors (and their employes) who are presently attracted by huge defense projects. Commercial applications in the civilian marketplace can yield even more attractive economic returns to the defense sector and its workers. In 1985, for example, 40 American companies threw their support behind five new University Centers for the Commercial Development of Space, with each company making an initial annual budget commitment of about $1-million, which was matched by NASA. These research centers are exploring projects such as: the low-gravity manufacture of metals and alloys, ceramics, glass and plastics; the growth of crystals with unique properties that can be used to build optical computers; the production of magnetic super-conductive alloys that cannot be made on Earth;

the development of sensors and data analysis systems for observing the Earth from orbit; and the manufacture of crystals that can be used to determine the structure of biological molecules.

More and more Americans are beginning to doubt the conventional wisdom that the military is the best source of jobs and prosperity and that U.S. economic resources and resilience are unlimited. The severe decline in America's industrial base and economic power may yet provide the impetus for establishing a national framework to convert to a non-military economy like Japan's. Indeed, in a contrary approach, Japan is investing 1-trillion yen ($6.2-billion) in its Human Frontier Science Program, which focusses on biotechnology. Japan has invited other countries to participate. In announcing the plan, then prime minister Nakasone pointedly compared the project to the negative, militarizing effect of Star Wars.

A similar mood is growing throughout the world, reinforced by the realization that even a small reallocation of spending will achieve miracles. For example, it has been estimated that the cost of all the farm equipment needed to increase food production and approach self-sufficiency by 1995 in low-income countries now experiencing food shortages would be only 0.5% of a single year's world military spending. The Worldwatch Institute estimated in 1988 (see Table 10) that an economic rechanneling of only $150-billion a year would, by the year 2000, eliminate all Third World debt, completely solve major problems such as deforestation, topsoil loss and lack of self-sufficiency in energy use, and finance population management programs.

Table 10
Investment for Sustainable Economic Development

	($ billions — rough estimates)					
	1990	1992	1994	1996	1998	2000
Protecting top soil	4	14	24	24	24	24
Reforestation	2	4	6	6	7	7
Population control	13	22	28	31	32	33
Energy efficiency	5	15	25	35	45	55
Renewable energy	2	8	12	18	24	30
Payoff debts	20	40	50	30	10	-
Total	46	103	145	144	142	149

Source: Worldwatch Institute (1988).

The world has a simple choice: either we can continue to overindulge in an expensive arms race with characteristic vigor, or we can take deliberate steps toward a more sustainable international economic order. But we cannot do both! As of late 1987, the world got an arms reduction accord. In the 1990s, we must achieve a full peace accord. By the year 2000, we will have learned that we must invest in people and their productive economic ideas; that research must be directed towards solving global problems and creating new opportunities.

Section "P"

G-Forces of
Political Reformation

Overview:
Restructuring Political Power

*"Political power means capacity to regulate national life through national
representatives. If national life becomes so perfect as to become self-
regulated, no representation becomes necessary. In the ideal State,
there is no political power because there is no State."*
— *Mahatma Gandhi*

Newspaper headlines are full of it. Around the globe, government infrastructures at all levels are being overwhelmed by the G-Forces of social motivation,
technological innovation, economic modernization and all-pervasive information. Because we live at a time of historical change, the existing nation-state system looks powerful, but in truth it is increasingly dysfunctional in both of its
essential roles, which are to evolve into a mature, consensual coalition of global
governance and to devolve into participatory local governance. As metaphor,
the "global village" thus provides a bi-focal set of lenses through which national
political systems must re-vision and re-invent themselves, globally and locally.
Politics in the 21st-Century will be the art and science of the governance of the
possible. To qualify as leaders, our politicians must simply and plainly make the
global system governable and learn how to govern it in a participatory way so
that it solves problems, maximizes opportunities, and satisfies social aspirations.
If our political systems remain nationalistic and nonparticipatory, however,
global social development will be thwarted and we risk chaos. Only if we ensure
that our national governance evolves into global participatory systems and
devolves into local participatory systems will global aspirations best be achieved.

6-Wave Dynamic of Political Participation

The reformation of our political systems is the essential fourth stage of the
4-STEP process of global social development. As shown in Fig. 24, social, technological and economic G-Forces are driving the world towards political reform
and participatory globalism. Participatory globalism is itself an ongoing

G-Force across the six waves of social development. Unfortunately, we are now trapped in outmoded concepts of governance, which are nationalistic, nonparticipatory and stifled in bureaucracy — a natural outgrowth of the 2nd- and 3rd-Wave milieu. But our political infrastructure does not have to stay this way. Political reform has occurred repeatedly as societies have developed. Conversely, when political reform has not occurred, social development has been impaired.

Politics and governance first appeared in the 1st-Wave agricultural society. In feudalist society, power shifted from tribal chiefs to lords of the manor, dukedoms and kingdoms. Politics was essentially local, because people did not travel far and communications traveled slowly. This led to local electorate registration and what we still call political representation. As transportation and communications improved, power spread to the national level, though society was governed by a small elite, and often by a single dictator.

The transition to the 2nd-Wave manufacturing society, with its innovations in transportation and communications and its continued economic modernization, resulted in further political reform. The mass-production-factory model became pervasive, resulting in the institutionalization of mass education, central banking and national governments with mechanistic bureaucracies. The division of labor and poor working conditions led to the formation of labor unions and the manufacturing emphasis created a labor- and commodity-dominated economy. National political parties gained strenth even while the political process — one of so-called majority rule — was still controlled by the elite, and particularly the economic elite. In a process of slow and continuous transformation, however, all elites and aristocracies inevitably decline. In the first stages of decline, they maintain power by making bargains and concessions that deceive the people into thinking a policy of reform is under way. Sooner or later, real concessions must occur, or the disillusioned people revolt.

Politics and governance changed again after World War II, with the transition to the 3rd-Wave service economy. But while the rhetoric switched to that of "public service" in the West and "to serve the people" in China, national political systems and leaders have failed to adapt to the changing milieu. Most political systems have become uncoupled from their local constituency and from the new global setting of national affairs. The growth of multinational corporations was matched by that of international labor unions, but this globalization tended to isolate local members who became nonparticipatory and, hence, unrepresented. The United Nations was formed with good intentions, but it is controlled by a nationalistic elite detached from global reality. National bureaucracies became more entrenched and still exhibit a "batch-processing" working style. The television age brought politics into our living rooms, placing our leaders under close scrutiny — and leaving us disturbed (though entertained) by what we saw. Increasingly in the West we committed the ultimate suicide of disenfranchisement by tending to elect actors, not doers. The politician who cannot act on TV is not electable.

Fig. 24

G-Forces of Political Participation

Factors of Political Reform	1st-Wave Agricultural Society	2nd-Wave Manufacturing Society	3rd-Wave Services Society	4th-Wave Information Society	5th-Wave Leisure Society	6th-Wave Outer-Space Society
Social G-Forces of Motivation	Serfdom Basic needs Illiterate Rural tribes	Secure job Material goods Literate Urbanized	Meaningful job Health/social services Diverse needs/interests	Stimulating job Information needs Decentralized "Technopolis"	Leisure ethic Pursuit of knowledge "Global Village"	Freedom Search for other intelligence Global consciousness
Technological G-Forces of Innovation	Hand tools Farms Horse travel Word-of-mouth communication	Machines Factories Rail, ship, auto Radio	Computers Offices Jet, auto Telephone TV/Media	Real-time networks Remote locales Satellites, PCs Segmented media	Global information utility Voice-activated uni-language Global media	Space Infra-structure Instantaneous inter-planetary communication
Economic G-Forces of Modernization	Laborers Family farm Village economy Communes Barter trade	Divn. of labor Corporation Commodity economy Colony/trade Central bank	Service workers Multinationals Service economy Nation state Cartels/blocs IMF/IBRD/GATT	Info. workers Conglomerates Info. economy Interdependence Global Central Bank, etc.	Freelancers Multi-domestics Leisure economy Global economy Global taxation system	Planet workers Global co-operatives Global free trade "PIE"
Reformed Political Institutional Systems	Slave labor School house Lords of manor/kingdoms Revolutionary government Local govt. Elite/dictators	Unions Mass education Mechanistic bureaucracy Political parties Constitutional government Elite/majority rule	Intl. unions Higher education Computeristic bureaucracy Geo-politics Nation state/UN Majority rule/referenda	Intl. division of labor Individual learning Real-time bureaucracy Multi-parties/blocs Electronic issues voting	Techno-slaves Globalized learning Geo-strategic action Global leadership Global governance Real-time partocracy	Android labor Bio-computer/brain inter-connection Geo-planetary leadership Planetary governance Planetary partocracy

Source: GEODEVCO

With the emergence of the 4th-Wave information society, the dynamics of politics are changing dramatically. The real-time global village environment not only demands that political leaders look the part; they must also prove that they know what on earth is going on, and that they are taking effective action. With the knowledge explosion, constituents are as informed as their representatives. Indeed, with such a diversity of social needs and aspirations, representation of the many by the few is no longer workable. 4th-Wave politics and governance must keep up with the 4-STEP process of global change, which will fortunately provide us with the chance to redemocratize government. As the 5th-Wave emerges, a democratic system of real-time "partocracy" (participatory democracy) will devolve in national political affairs and global government will evolve along with it.

Globalization of Governance

The 4-STEP process of social, technological and economic G-Forces is also redistributing geo-political power among nations. Traditionally, the modern world has been dominated by a succession of single economic, and more recently by two military, superpowers. There are signs that military power is being overwhelmed by economic power and that economic power is about to be significantly redistributed among several nations or groups of nations, thus creating a multipolar economic, and hence political, world.

In the evolving multi-polar world, the prospects for peace and participatory global governance are much brighter. In such a world there would no longer be such thing as a superpower and no veto power. That forces the creation of various global frameworks through which a consensus can be forged.

A mature civilization will be achieved only when we evolve to a true system of global governance for the single global tribe. Skeptics will dismiss this as a dream, but I think not. Never have we had as great a capacity, intellectually and materially, to shape our destiny. Never have our motivations and aspirations for unity been so overwhelming. Never have the opportunities been greater.

It is also imperative that we begin establishing full public participation in the political process. Leaders must recognize that the new nature of power is its ability to emancipate human creativity. The nation state system stifles creativity — our greatest resource. Within nation states it is increasingly essential that planning and decision-making authority be delegated downwards, closer to the people who are most affected. Real leadership must articulate a global vision of what is possible and what needs to be done, and then empower people to do it well. To grasp the new opportunities within our reach, leadership must mobilize and tap the latent energies and creative capacities of the world's people and our new information-based resources.

Only in these ways, globally and locally, can the people really be served. In the end, it is men and women, the teeming populations of the planet, with their innate and still largely untapped capacity for comprehension, creativity and vision, who will be responsible for achieving global social development. The future is clearly one of our own making; it is one of people–power, global and local. To survive in such a world, state-centered governments must become people-centered, encouraging the transfer of individual loyalties towards regional, then global and, eventually, universal purposes.

Humanity then will be able to govern itself — and its world — in a geo-strategic and opportunistic way. Politics will truly become of/for/by the people. By 2050, the socio-economic development of planet Earth will be close to complete, and the Universe will be unfolding as it should.

G-Force P-1

Disarming the Planet

"People in the long run are going to do more to promote peace than are governments. Indeed, people want peace so much that one of these days governments had better get out of their way and let them have it."
— *Dwight D. Eisenhower*

The world has almost finished "growing up" (that is, completing its natural process of political maturation) and, as Dr. Helen Caldicott says, we are about to "take the toys away from the boys." The weapons of war are fast becoming obsolete. Nuclear bombs, for example, are already too clumsy to use. While we now have the ability to destroy ourselves in perpetuity, surely we will not be so stupid as to try. Any country that launches one "first strike" nuclear warhead guarantees that it will itself be wiped out by retaliatory launches. A famous Chinese military strategy admonishes that if defeat is inevitable, you should run away or you will be killed. It is time for us to "run away" from nuclear weapons. The world can simply no longer afford to build them, except at a horribly negative cost; they are the world's most unproductive economic investment. Even the superpower leaders have realized that this idiocy must stop. After all, the weapons belong to the people: we paid for them, and now we want rid of them.

Overcoming the Social Causes of War

In the past, nations have usually gone to war to acquire land or resources. As information becomes the primary but abundant and shared resource, however, squabbles over resources (even Mid-East oil) will fade. Territorial possession also becomes meaningless (except for stateless groups, such as the Palestinians) because national boundaries will be obsolete in the electronic global village.

War has also been caused by miscommunication and misinformation which has often led to antagonistic differences. Nations and groups still tend to believe

285

in incorrect or incomplete stereotypes of each other, which causes an exaggerated, mutual fear. This has contributed, for example, to an escalation of the cold war. Each side believes itself threatened by the other and is driven to accumulate more weapons than the other to feel secure. We are now realizing that this has not created security at all, but has rather made the global village considerably less secure.

In the age of global communications and growing international travel, it also becomes less possible for a country to promote internal cohesion by creating fear of an external enemy. Reagan practiced this when he characterized the Soviets as the "evil empire" in order to rationalize a boost in military spending. The Soviets likewise fight capitalist imperialism as an "evil" force. An increasingly intelligent global population sees through such fabrication and its accompanying Orwellian doublespeak, such as Reagan's attempt to label a nuclear missile a Peace-Keeper.

Such false pride is an extension of the biological drive to ensure individual and group survival by mastering the environment, including one's neighbors. More dangerous is moral pride, whereby we create dogmatic values about right and wrong, good and evil, and freedom. There is a striking difference between Soviet and American concepts of freedom: for Americans, individual freedom is a "God-given" right; for the Soviet Union, freedom is a conditional privilege granted by society. Because moral pride leads one group to view another with different values as being morally evil, Reagan's characterization of the Soviet Union as the evil empire and Soviet characterization of capitalism in the same vein are understandable.

Yet it is increasingly clear that nuclear weapons cannot resolve social frustration. In short, war as a social institution is obsolete. Moreover, from a psychological standpoint, the power of the military as an institution rests ultimately on the consensus of the population that the military is preferable to the social anarchy bound to ensue in its absence. This consensus, in turn, rests on a sense of community, and now we are creating a global community. World nations and their peoples are steadily becoming more interdependent — that is, they must increasingly seek to enhance each other's social welfare, not the advanced state of war technology.

Technological Obsolescence of War

Wars have always been fought by the latest technology available. A new weapon, once invented, is impossible to "disinvent". But it can become obsolete. Nuclear weapons are becoming a worthless tool of cold war foreign policy — their only realistic use today — because in the new information "hot war" of fighting for global public opinion, political leaders become heroes by getting rid of weapons. The "mutually assured destruction" (MAD) of their use is making these weapons obsolete.

For the first time in history, then, the latest technology of war is being eliminated because it no longer has practical or political use. Attempts to render nuclear arms obsolete by developing the next generation of aerospace technology (Star Wars) to create some magic umbrella that will effectively defend against warheads launched by our neighbors are also misdirected. Nuclear warheads can no longer be used in the global village, so it is extremely unlikely that they will ever be launched. Star Wars is as obsolete as the weapons it is intended to negate — and hence a complete waste of money.

Bankrupting the Economy

War is clearly related to economics, and money has become a powerful motivator to disarm the planet. Despite how military competition has promoted accelerated scientific discovery and contributed to technological innovation, defense spending ultimately destroys the economic well-being of a nation — and of the world. In the extreme, political rebellion and insurrection are quite possible when citizens feel they are receiving less than their entitlement. To improve their economic situation, groups turn to aggression and political violence (Iran, the Philippines, Burma, South Korea, South Africa). The economic benefits of military spending are minuscule compared with its debilitating costs through increased inflation, the huge sacrifice of consumption and the direction of R&D away from the civilian economy. Without global economic growth, now seriously jeopardized by military spending, there is no hope for achieving the common prosperity that will constitute the basis of real global security.

Weaponry is now so expensive that disarmament will probably happen much faster than most people think. America cannot afford it; through the 1980s the country has wrecked its economic future by trying to afford it. The defense-dominated federal budget has been driven into deficit and the consumption this has stimulated has created a persistent trade deficit. The coming "Mini-Depression" will help to stop U.S. military spending in its tracks; this is a crucial step to restoring a balanced budget.

The Soviet Union, too, cannot afford its military spending and doesn't want it. Economics is therefore the driving force behind U.S.-U.S.S.R. disarmament. When Gorbachev first met U.S. Secretary of State George Shultz, he mentioned that the superpowers ought to be discussing global trends that affected them both. Shultz got the message and, for his Spring 1987 conference with Gorbachev, took along charts, graphs and projections comparing the economic growth rates of Japan, China, the United States and the Soviet Union to the year 2010. These economic rankings showed the superpowers in economic decline against Japan and China — and by the end of that year, the world had a treaty to get rid of short-range nuclear missiles. At the end of 1988, Gorbachev announced a reduction of Soviet armed forces personnel by about 10% over two years. In 1989 there were mutual initiatives to reduce numbers of conventional weapons. By 1995 we will probably have a superpower peace accord to eliminate all nuclear weapons by the year 2000 and conventional weapons by 2010.

We are realizing the economic benefits of investing not in weapons but in people and their productive ideas. This is the only rational basis for attaining common global security. More than 140 countries attended the 1987 U.N. conference on the relationship between disarmament and economic development. Though the U.S. conspicuously boycotted the conference in the belief that the problems of disarmament are separate from those of development, educated thinking and political priorities make it inevitable that disarmament and development be recognized as related, interdependent issues. Development through disarmament is integral to the concept of world peace and security. Only disarmament can free the pool of funds needed for the essential economic development of the Third World and at the same time rid the developed countries from the detrimental burden of military expenditure. This is what geo-strategic thinking is all about. Military spending and Star Wars extravaganzas have no appeal for a world public that eagerly awaits the solutions to its more immediate economic problems.

Redefining National Security

Politically, governments cannot boost arms expenditures and yet deal effectively with the global forces of change. The term "national security" can no longer be used to justify national armies, new weapons systems and armaments. Military protagonists can no longer brush economists aside with banal justifications such as "what do dollars matter when national survival is at stake?" A bankrupt nation has no power and has lost all global influence.

The real threats to the security of nations — threats with which military forces cannot cope — are global. The world is faced with the absurd technological incongruity of high-tech fighter planes soaring above fields plowed by oxen and watered by hand. The two superpowers have the ability to survey virtually every square metre of each other's territory by satellite, yet the world's scientists have barely begun to survey the complex ecosystems and eliminate back-breaking peasant farming. Each year, the world spends several times as much on research to increase the destructiveness of weapons as in attempts to raise the productivity of agriculture. Indeed, the value of trade in international arms exceeds that of most other goods, even grain. Technology (from the root word technologos) means "craft, guided by wisdom." It cannot be used to foster what Stanford University social scientist Willis Harman calls "non-peace," that is, fear, distrust and hostility. Instead, we must use it to create a world commonwealth in which war has no legitimacy whatsoever. That's security.

Countries other than the superpowers are also beginning to redefine their national security and are emphasizing economic progress over military prowess. As recently as 1982, China was spending 14% of GNP (as much as the U.S.S.R.) for military purposes, then one of the highest levels in the world, and had 4-million soldiers. In 1985, it began to systematically reduce its military expenditures, and in just two years the level had fallen to 6.5% of GNP (about the same as

America); further substantial reductions are planned by 1992. In 1985, China began investing large sums to retrain 1-million soldiers for their return to civilian life and to convert military manufacturing plants to civilian production, such as the building of much-needed washing machines, refrigerators and televisions. By 1988, China's military force had been reduced by 30%. (It is worth noting that China lowered its military outlays unilaterally, despite its 3000-kilometre (1800-mile) border with the Soviet Union.)

If political and military ideology continues to give way to economic pragmatism worldwide, conflicts and insecurities will dissolve. For both the United States and the Soviet Union, maintaining a leadership position will increasingly depend on reducing military expenditures to strengthen their faltering economies. The 1987 Nuclear Arms Reduction Agreement has set the stage for demilitarizing the world economy, a process that will feed on itself because the improved living standards it brings will encourage a further reduction of wasteful military spending.

The disarmament process must also extend to the Third World. The preoccupation with East-West relations has dangerously diminished global understanding of the Third World socio-political nexus in which most conflicts now arise. About 20-million civilian and military war and war-related deaths occurred in about 100 conflicts in the Third World between 1945 and 1989. A factor that is not yet sufficiently recognized is the enormous human economic cost that these conflicts have imposed on the countries involved and on the world economy at large. Arms imports alone are reckoned to account for a quarter of the accumulated $1.3-trillion debt of developing countries. For a country struggling to be recognized and respected in a system so far determined by military power, the acquisition of weapons has been seen as a way to nation-building, prestige and potency. Nevertheless, many developing countries are starting to realize that national security cannot be purchased on the arms market except at enormous cost to their economies.

Information to Destroy Weapons

In the global village, information suddenly brings social, technological, economic and political functions together in an intense heightening of human awareness and responsibility. Every group in every nation is now politically "involved" with every other, thanks to the electronic media and real-time information networks.

The field of battle has shifted to mental image-making. In McLuhan's words, "ink and photo are supplanting soldiery and tanks" and the cold war has become a new electric battle ("hot war") of information and of images that goes far deeper and is more obsessional than the old "hot wars" of gunpower and industrial hardware. In the old hot wars we used weapons to knock off the enemy one-by-one. Today, we use photograph, film and television to simultaneously immerse an entire population in new, persuasive imagery. This breaks down cultural, tribal and class barriers because "the enemy" is perceived as being as good and as clever as we are. Gradually, the world is coming together — being "retribalized" — in common cause.

McLuhan also observed that "weaponry makes more vivid the fact of the unity of the human family." In other words, the very inclusiveness of information as a weapon — and *about* weapons — becomes a daily reminder of our oneness. Nuclear weapons were thus necessary to teach humanity how their destructiveness could cause us to commit mass suicide. That lesson learned, weaponry becomes a "self-liquidating fact."

The tribal community provides security for all members of a tribe but, at the onset of the 4th-Wave Information Age, we are becoming a single *global* tribe, where our *global* security depends on all of us working together. At this point, all power is delegated to the mass civilian population of the global tribe. The instinct to survive is the strongest psychological drive we possess, and, faced with the imminent prospect of extinction, we are today being transformed by the realization that, to save ourselves and those we love, we must also help and love others who have been totally alien to us.

The instinct for global survival is overcoming the primitive instinct of national tribalism. And the superpowers are not exempt: they are like Siamese twins — they either must live and work together, respecting their differences, or they will die together within an hour or two. We must drop our ancient need for a tribal enemy. We do not need to fulfill our egos; we need only to fulfill our common destiny on the planet.

People-Power

We don't need any more military heroics; we need heroes of peace. We are the ones who give legitimacy to social institutions, no matter how powerful those institutions seem to be. We also have the power to withdraw that legitimacy. War is no longer a heroic and legitimate pursuit; it has become the obscene decimation of civilian populations and the destruction of resources we need for global economic progress.

In the global village, the common enemy is our own out-of-date mindset. New mindsets realize that power that must be constantly struggled for and aggressively backed by military prowess (as every dictator ultimately discovers) is not power at all. Rather, it is coercive brute force. The macho military machine presents a heroic image of war to cover up its own deep-rooted sense of impotence. Star Wars creates a dangerous illusion of American omnipotence, representing an escape from an inability to formulate a rational approach to the challenge of the nuclear age. In contrast, real power in the modern world derives from internal strength and confidence, which endow the bearer with the capacity and legitimacy to act on the basis of natural and proven merits.

People have drawn on such inner strength to eliminate weapons before, with astonishing swiftness. In the 16th-Century, Japanese swordsmiths learned how to make guns to which the Samurai warriors became heavily addicted. Battles were fought with such great loss of life that the leading Samurai felt that guns were ruining their honorable profession. The sword was reinstated as the only military weapon, and guns were relegated to ceremonial purposes; the supremacy of the less lethal sword was maintained for another 250-years. The motivation to give up advanced weaponry was the political power of an ideology to restore a traditional way of life.

As physicist Freeman Dyson has observed, if we could at least abolish Star Wars and nuclear weapons — even for 50-years — that would give us time to apply new technologies to the urgent problems of the world and create a level of social well-being in which the need for all weapons would be superfluous to our way of life. As with the Samurai, we must appeal to the soldiers' professional pride. Once the military learns that it can do something much more valuable in creating global opportunities with the techniques at its disposal, instead of putting useless missiles in silos, maybe even its pride will soar to a new height.

Military officials in Washington and Moscow already use the awesome power of information to prevent mass destruction. They have improved their communications links so that they can keep in touch with each other during even the worst crisis. Since 1987, Nuclear Risk Reduction Centers have been operating around the clock in Moscow and Washington to prevent conflict resulting from "accident, misinterpretation or miscalculation." The centers are linked electronically and each side transmits to the other documents, diagrams, charts and maps. In effect, both sides are now so afraid of killing each other accidentally that the weapons have become subservient to the power of information. Accurate information is the very antithesis of armed uncertainty. Now all that matters is "information *about* weapons." Information is eliminating weaponry, and the legitimacy to wage war is evaporating. Disarming is the only honorable course remaining.

As Jonathan Schell wrote in his outstanding book *The Fate of the Earth*, knowledge, not weaponry, is the ultimate deterrent. All weapons were born *out* of knowledge, and they will be destroyed *by* knowledge. The increasing public knowledge that weapons threaten the survival of our species and that their cost is severely retarding our economic progress is already disarming the planet. As Schell argued — and as the superpowers now recognize — we must also realize that nuclear disarmament cannot leave conventional weapons in place. Any form of national defense will only perpetuate obsolete concepts of national sovereignty, and therefore the freedom to re-arm. Anyway, the nuclear powers would hardly disarm if superiority in conventional arms was retained by others.

It is one of the urgent tasks of global politics and leadership to create a genuine atmosphere of global security, to manage change in an anticipatory, proactive way that follows a meaningful agenda. We must create a global disarmament governance system for all weaponry and for military science. Politicians should concentrate on improvements in "livingry," not weaponry, and on making our world more predictable and controllable. Real security will come from a feeling that our children will be able to have the kind of life we feel should be possible — that they will indeed inherit the Earth. That will be the true mark of global maturity, of a move from national political immaturity and "un-civilization" towards one of mature planetary civilization.

G-Force P-2

"Amexicana": Traumatic Rebirth
of America

"We're living on borrowed time and
increasing amounts of borrowed money."
— *Paul Volcker*

The rise and fall of great powers is a G-Force of history. Today, the nation which reached for the stars and made "one giant leap for mankind" is faltering badly and in danger of burning out rather dramatically. Sadly, unbeknownst to the majority of Americans, just like Britain before it the United States has a waning economy and suffers from a social, cultural and political malaise that runs very deep. America was "shot" with the 1963 assassination of John F. Kennedy and, governed by various degrees of incompetence ever since, has not yet overcome the trauma. The American dream has become a nightmare punctuated by disaster after disaster at home and abroad. In trying to make the dream a reality, America has borrowed so heavily against the future that it is virtually bankrupt and the dream is now in danger of slipping beyond reach forever. The U.S. became a debtor nation in 1985, thus entering a period of relative decline as a global power. The good news is that the nation can be revived and prosper again, but it probably will be as a "socialistic entrepreneurial" society, joining forces with Canada and Mexico, to play a new global role in the 21st-Century.

Loss of Global Direction

Only a generation ago, American power was able to move the world. The 1950s were "the American Decade": U.S. intervention restored the Shah of Iran to his throne in 1953; the CIA inspired the overthrow of a leftist government in Guatemala in 1954; American diplomatic pressure prevented the humiliation of President Nasser of Egypt by British, French and Israeli forces in 1956; and, in

1958, 8000 U.S. marines and army troops landed in Lebanon and averted a Syrian takeover. How the world has changed.

Ever since Kennedy's brief, shining 1961 inaugural promise of a new global role for America, national disgrace has been written into U.S. history books. A disastrous war in Vietnam displaced one president from office. The Watergate scandal drove another to resign under threat of impeachment. The Islamic revolution deposed the Shah and held Americans hostage for more than a year while Washington stood by powerless and another president left office. In Lebanon, fighting factions backed by Syria forced the pullout of U.S. marines from Beirut, and America seems unable to restore peace — at least on its own terms — in nearby Central America. The Third World debt crisis and its own unprecedented budget deficits have left Washington transfixed, caught in the headlights of the onrushing global future.

Yet America would have the rest of the world believe that most of its problems are the fault of the Soviet evil empire or "unfair" Japanese trading and competitive practices. The real problem is America's almost reckless economic abandon in the 1980s, its increasingly inferior technology and production efficiency, its ignorance about the new global economics and its lack of a geo-strategic vision. Reagan put America on a stepped-up "war-time" economy but failed to realize that wars are, if still possible, no longer practical. Today's power stems from shifts of currency by computer, from information and from the manufacture of products superior in quality that people everywhere are willing to buy.

Above all, America has no realistic vision of its global role. Overwhelmed by the G-Forces of change, it has made the same fatal mistakes as previous powers. Nation-state politics inevitably fail to dominate global economics, which will always dwarf even the largest state. Political states progressively become more enmeshed in an interdependent world economy. For a time, the leading state (once Britain, then America) can stabilize the system, keep the markets open, recycle capital and serve as the innovator of world industrial progress. This economic leadership role self-defeats, however, because the leading state becomes overburdened and a negative trade balance ensues. At that point, the leading power becomes a burden on the global economy. Having lost its technological leadership, the U.S. has lost its economic prowess.

Today, the nation is living (and defending commitments) far beyond its means. After World War II, the American "empire" expanded too far. By 1970, as political scientist Ronald Steel has pointed out, the U.S. "had more than 1-million soldiers in 30 countries, was a member of four regional defense alliances and an active participant in a fifth, had mutual defense treaties with 42 nations, was a member of 53 international organizations, and was furnishing military or economic aid to nearly 100 nations. America now maintains more than 3000 domestic and international military bases when even the military itself says it doesn't need more than 300.

Whereas its global commitments have steadily increased, America's share of world manufacturing and of world GNP has steadily declined. The decline is felt not only in older manufacturing sectors such as textiles, iron and steel, ship-building and basic chemicals but also in robotics, aerospace technology, auto-mobiles, machine tools and computers. Except for aerospace, America is now a close second in almost all areas of R &D and a distinct second in technological application. The resulting uncompetitiveness of U.S. industrial sectors has pro-duced staggering trade deficits.

All of this has happened before to other great powers that have almost always declined — and hastened their fall — by shifting expenditure from civil-ian progress to the military and by trying to maintain their national prowess. Spain, the Netherlands, France and Britain did exactly that. Now, as historian Paul Kennedy points out, it is the United States' turn. When they started losing their economic competitiveness, the debate in these nations was about how to restore it — how to make themselves as strong and productive as they were two and three decades before.

These same arguments have echoed across the United States since 1980. As well, there has been a characteristic right-wing patriotic response, which main-tains that the country is not really declining but rather it just has to get back to old standards and reassert those virtues that made it great in the first place. But without a vision for its global future and unwilling to set its house in order with increased taxation, America has been able to pay its way in the world only by importing ever larger amounts of foreign capital and by printing dollars. This has transformed it from the world's largest creditor to the world's largest debtor nation in the space of a few years.

The United States' living standards are destined to plummet in the short term. Real weekly earnings for most workers in 1988 were no higher than they were in the early-1960s. Real median family income in 1988 was no higher than in 1973, despite a sharp increase in the number of two-career families. To try to cushion declining incomes and maintain living standards, Americans have both eaten into their savings and saved less. Net private savings (net income saved by households and private companies) has declined from 8.1% of GNP in the 1970s to 6.1% of GNP in the 1980s. Consequently, net national savings (net private sav-ings minus the public sector's dissaving) has declined from 7.1% of GNP in the 1970s to 3.4% in the 1980s. During the recession of 1981-83 and during the eco-nomic slowdown of 1986, net national savings dipped below 2% of GNP. During the 1980s the U.S. investment rate has been the second lowest in the industrialized world (just above Britain's), and 22% of that investment was financed by foreigners. Meanwhile, the rate of growth in the real net output per worker throughout the 1980s has averaged only 0.4% per year, which is abso-lutely the lowest in the Western world. In other words, Americans are no longer productive enough to provide themselves with the standard of living they are accustomed to.

If productivity growth proceeds at its current meager rate (and does not decline further) the average American worker in the year 2020 will be producing only 14% more real goods and services than in 1986 — about one-third of the potential. America's real standard of living will have hardly budged over a span of 60-years! The 1980s therefore stand to be looked back on as the turning point when America took the British route to second-class economic status. During Britain's 75-year decline, productivity growth rates were only 0.5% below those of its industrial competitors. Because America's corresponding gap is more than three times as large, its decline is proceeding far more swiftly and, at present rates, will not take even the 60-years extrapolated above. Martin Feldstein, formerly an economic adviser to the Reagan Administration, has estimated that the economic adjustment required to get back on track might mean a 50% cut in the annual rate of increase of real American incomes throughout the 1990s, that is, a cut from its trend growth of 2% per year to nearer 1%.

When the U.S. finally ends its dependence on foreign capital, either because of shifts in its economic policies or by force of the global marketplace, the nation will be faced with extreme austerity. The longer the delay in policy changes or the longer the dependence on foreign capital persists, the more extreme the adjustment. Americans with the most vulnerable incomes — two-income families, minority workers, young adults laboring under two-tier contracts and service employees who receive no benefits — will suffer the most serious losses.

What most Americans and their politicians don't yet fully realize or accept is that the country is no longer a strong and dominant creditor nation like it was in the 1950s and 1960s, that America has turned into a debtor nation and that when others control the money you dance to their tune. Lester Thurow of the Massachusetts Institute of Technology has calculated that since foreign borrowing finances the trade deficit which represents about 4% of GNP, this effectively allows Americans to consume 4% more than they produce. When the ongoing foreign lending stops, Americans will lose 4% of their comsumption, plus they will have to pay about 1% from GNP as interest on all foreign debt accumulated to date. Consequently, a 3% GNP growth would become a 2% GNP decline — and that means recession.

Famed Wall Street guru Henry Kaufman has observed that, more than any other measure, a budget shows more about a nation's economic morality, its willingness to accept discipline, its capacity to respond to changing financial and economic conditions and what adjustments it will tolerate. The U.S. political system has balanced only one budget since 1960, and the Reagan Administration borrowed more money in only eight years than all previous American presidents combined!

President Bush's Challenge

Inheriting the biggest economic mess in history, the result of what he called "voodoo economics," George Bush can be the start of America's revival. His main challenge is to convince Americans that prosperity is not inscribed in the U.S. Constitution. It must be worked for in collaboration with other nations.

An economy that will be spending 40-cents of every dollar of new wealth earned abroad to pay interest on money already borrowed and spent is fundamentally unsustainable. Unless decisive corrective action is taken during the Bush Administration, the United States will experience what Reagan's budget director David Stockman has postulated: profound economic trauma leading to a social and political upheaval of potentially historic proportions. Bush's priority is to extricate America from growing foreign debt and place it on the road to 21st-Century prosperity. Before that challenge can be met, Americans must be prepared for a perceptible fall in real after-tax income combined with a similar decline, or at least a total freeze, in government spending — for both social programs and defense — until at least 1995.

Domestically, Bush must also address America's deep social malaise. The country's many pockets of severe poverty are seedbeds of much of today's crime and potential social unrest. The unchecked growth in the use of narcotics is destroying future generations of American workers and is also a major source of crime. *Time* magazine reports that, as a result of the cowboy-like freedom to bear arms, more Americans are killed on U.S. soil by guns every year than were killed in Vietnam during that entire war. These and other cancers are eating deep into the body and soul of America. Strong leadership is required to eradicate them. A "kinder, gentler" approach is necessary but not sufficient; urgent and serious surgery is required if the country is to be saved and its spirit restored.

Meeting such challenges is difficult at the best of times. Indeed, under conditions of relative prosperity, Reagan shirked these responsibilities and made the problems worse. The coming "Mini-Depression" (1990-93) will sharply reduce tax revenues and increase demands on social programs, thereby increasing the budget deficit. It will also strengthen sentiments to protect dying 2nd-Wave industrial companies. But the challenge can no longer be postponed; America must be transformed from a consumption-driven 2nd-Wave economy to an investment-driven 4th-Wave economy.

Simultaneously, the President must exercise global leadership and lose no time in forging international agreements to restore order to the global economic system. We are in the midst of the second great transition of global economic power in this century. From 1920 to 1940, the U.S. failed to recognize the strength it had inherited from Britain and the responsibility that went with it. The world lurched from one financial crisis to another, and then to war. From 1970 to 1990, the world has again been lurching from one economic crisis to another. This time, the U.S. has been defiantly trying to retain economic power that it has in reality already lost to Japan.

Yet for historical and strategic reasons, the Japanese are reluctant to assume the leadership responsibility they know is now theirs, thus perpetuating in the world the myth of American power. Reagan used the wrong global approach, blaming Japan (and West Germany) for problems of America's own making, pushing them to adopt inflationary economic policies counter to their own interests. Bush must understand the Japanese better; he must think long-term and act through co-operation, not through short-term confrontation. In the world economy, Japan is now on an equal footing with the United States, and American policies must reflect this equality of responsibility. Tremendous leadership will be required to reduce U.S. trade barriers, not to protect declining 2nd-Wave industries. America now is in desperate need of a George Bush who will do what needs to be done.

Part of the new American vision must include a plan to immediately eliminate Third World debt. Following the Venezuelan debt riots of early-1989, there are strong signs that this global crisis is finally going to be addressed at long last. America's economic stake in the Third World is significant, accounting for 40% of U.S. trade. If Third World countries can resume strong economic growth (which requires full elimination of their debt), they could account for as much as 50% of all U.S. trade by the year 2000. President Bush must be a global centrist leader with a vision of America's new shared role in world affairs. If not, the decline of the nation's economic and geo-political stature will be devastatingly swift.

Post-Bush Strategic Agenda

If Bush does what needs to be done, he could be re-elected in 1992. More likely, however, is that he will be a one-term President, driven from office on the heels of the "Mini-Depression" for which he will wrongly be blamed. Whatever the 1992 election brings, during the medium-term (from 1993 to about 2008) the United States must focus on economic investment in R&D and productivity improvement. Should it not do so, it will pay a severe price in the long-term. In addition to lower labor productivity, lower real wages and reduced global political influence, this price will reflect the utter lack of preparation for the aging of the country's population and for America's second-rank position in an entirely different world economic league.

True vision requires the forging of a farsighted yet realistic connection between the present and the future. America, like Britain before it, seems largely oblivious to the G-Forces of change going on around it and is in danger of bungling its future. Unlike Japan, China and now Russia, America has no long-term plan, no goal, no strategy for its global future. The U.S. government must reperceive the nation's international role and articulate a vision to guide the country to play a prominent part on the global stage of the 21st-Century. Without such a geo-strategic plan, America will follow Britain further down the international league table of world superpowers.

America must begin to understand that the global economic development process is not one of borrowing but one of saving and investing in people and technology to create purchasing power. That is the real magic of the new global marketplace. And 85% of that global marketplace in the year 2000 will be in the developing countries. Japan is geo-strategically exploiting this future marketplace through its multinational trading and investment conglomerates. China, with a fifth of the future global market, is doing the same within its own borders. The Soviet Union is geo-strategically forging impressive trade and technology transfer links with scores of developing countries. These future economic superpowers understand that their own long-term prosperity and growth depend on going global and developing the new mass market of the Third World. America, in contrast, has turned inward on itself in the vain belief that this would protect and maintain its artificially high debt-based standard of living. This myopic defensive stance was doomed to fail.

The politics of contemporary U.S. capitalism must be refocussed. The elusive American dream can still be realized if future Presidents balance their budgets and genuinely lead the nation — beyond the next election — into the 21st-Century. In parallel, U.S. corporations must set 20-year R&D budgets and downplay the quarterly shareholder reports so that they can concentrate on long-term technological innovation and productivity. Investors must stop throwing money onto stock market casino tables and instead select a long-term yielding portfolio of future-oriented companies that will lead America into tomorrow's global economy. Education reform must be an ongoing priority, reinventing the learning process to restore values, goals and discipline for the 21st-Century, so that America can become an "empire of the mind." The distant global horizon is bathed in golden sunshine, but only geo-strategic planning will decide whether for America it is a sunset or a sunrise.

America has repeatedly seen sunrises. As analyzed by Harvey Wasserman, the author of *America Born and Reborn*, since the American Revolution the U.S. has been through five major cyclic transformations (see Fig. 25). Each begins with a burst of energy — usually sparked by a Democrat assuming office — which carries into an awakening. Then America usually finds itself engaged in a war, followed by a conservative reaction, which brings the cycle to a close with an aftermath of emotional and economic instability (such as we experience today). Each cycle ends with a severe economic downturn that then leads to a burst of new activity — the "storm before the rainbow," to use Wasserman's words.

In his book *The Cycles of American History*, Arthur Schlesinger identifies a similar model that alternates between public purpose and private interest, between idealistic reform and restrained democracy. Schlesinger also believes we are now witnessing the burnout of the most recent conservative ascendance and the age of Reagan/Bush will soon fade into memory. Shortly after 1990 (by the 1992 election), "there should be a sharp change in the national mood and direction." The people who were young in the Kennedy years will come to full political power. This phase will continue into the first decade of the 21st-Century, when, picking up on Wasserman's model, America is most likely to awaken to its new Pacific and global potential.

Fig. 25 U.S. Cycles of Rebirth

Cycle Term	Phase 1 Burst of Energy	Phase 2 The Awakening	Phase 3 War	Phase 4 Reaction	Phase 5 Aftermath	Final Event
1776-1819	Glorious Revolution	Great Awakening	American Revolution	Federalist Era	Jeffersonian Era	Crash of 1819
1820-1896	Andrew Jackson	Trascendental Revolt	Civil War	K.K.K. "Great Barbeque"	Gilded Age	Crash of 1893
1897-1930	Election of 1896	Socialist Bohemian Revolt	World War I	Red Scare	Roaring Twenties	Crash of 1929
1931-1960	F.D.R. New Deal	Rebellious Thirties	World War II	McCarthy Cold War	Fat Fifties	Recession of 1957
1961-1975	J.F.K. New Frontier	Psychedelic Sixties	Vietnam War	Nixon Plan	"Me" Era	1973 Oil Crisis/ Recession
1976-1992	Jimmy Carter's New Spirit	Equal Rights	Iran: Loss of Middle East	Moralist New Right	Reagan/Bush Feel Good	Depression of 1990-93
1993-	Jacksonian Globalism	Pacific Awakening	?	?	?	?

Source: Adapted from Harvey Wasserman

Americans have become increasingly concerned with new issues (humanism, feminism, racial equality and ecology) in the last couple of decades. Today there is a growing interest in Oriental philosophy and a search for new answers that the "Pacific Century" promises. The public purpose of the 1992-2000 period could well be a coalescing of the "rainbow" momentum that Jesse Jackson has been building and that Kennedy gave us a glimpse of in 1961-63. If this cycle repeats, the initial burst of energy will coalesce around a strong leader and a progressive platform with socialist overtones. When the new leader takes power, a whole new surge of optimism and hope will take over, with expectations peaking dramatically as we approach the turn of the century.

As we enter the 1990s, the baby boom generation is recognizing that, with Reagan having ridden off into the sunset, the era of the Wild West frontier is over, that Americans can create a *new* frontier only if they learn to accept the existence of other values from the global environment that can enrich them. America has always been a rich source of ideas and alternative lifestyles and philosophies, and this openness is the country's main hope. Such values as equality and ecology can be the next generation's ticket to continued, if adjusted, affluence and life purpose.

Trends Towards Socialism

This new frontier is also changing the underlying politics of America, with demographic shifts and mediocre economic growth changing the socio-political consensus. The United States of the booming 1950s and 1960s managed to avoid overt "class" distinctions but today about a third of blacks, Hispanics and visible minorities live below the poverty line. Given the lower birthrates of whites and the still high rates of blacks and Hispanics, and given the changing composition of the flow of Hispanic and Asian immigrants into the United States, the mix of American society is now changing dramatically. By the year 2000, Hispanics, blacks and Asians will account for 30% of the U.S. population and by 2010, California will have a non-white majority. These rapidly growing blocks of voters do not generally share the individualistic frontier mentality of the Reagan generation, because they were exploited by it. Their political preference is clearly left of center — 90% of blacks vote Democrat and all upper-level black politicians are Democrats. Sometime early in the 21st-Century, Hispanics (most of whom are also left of center) will outnumber blacks, and the 1992, 1996 and 2000 elections could launch a few dozen new blacks and Hispanics into Congress, which is already solidly Democrat-controlled.

The earnings gap between American rich and poor is also significantly larger than in any other advanced industrial society, and yet state expenditures on social services claim a lower share of GNP than in all comparable countries except Japan. Average real family incomes for black and Hispanic families fell by 11% between 1973 and 1988, twice the national average. Minorities will also be hit disproportionately by the elimination of lower- and middle-management jobs that are likely to be squeezed out by 4th-Wave computer information systems. As well, lots of high-paying jobs in manufacturing are giving way to millions of relatively poor-paying jobs in services — at least in the short-term. Consequently, a government that cuts back on social expenditure in the 1990s — as America may be forced to do — runs a clear risk of provoking a political backlash. Nowhere is this better recognized than in the Bush Administration, which to its credit is trying to recruit blacks to the Republican Party.

These are just a few of many signs indicating that the United States is fast approaching the time when it could become a distinctly socialist country. The American left could come back with a vengeance. Third World, non-Caucasian characteristics in this capitalist, Caucasian nation are everywhere starkly visible across the continent, particularly in large cities. New York's Central Park is a perfect picture of the extreme dichotomy of American society. Condominiums cost more than $2-million and bejewelled, fur-coated white ladies pamper silky-haired dogs as they walk them along Central Park South. Yet right beside them are the homeless — white as well as black — who are everywhere. Across all of urban America, almost all the "servant" jobs (garbage collectors, taxi drivers, waiters, maids, porters) are performed by non-white Americans.

Undeniably, powerful new political leadership has emerged on the American left, headed by Jesse Jackson. He has twice been a strong Democrat candidate for president and has registered millions of first-time voters for his party. With voter turnout down to an all-time low of 50% in 1988, it is blacks, minorities and women who are most likely to kick life back into the American dream in 1992 and beyond. Theirs is in many ways a different dream. As Jackson pointed out in his 1988 campaign: "We don't want welfare, we want fair share; we don't want charity, we want parity." It seems inevitable that his followers will get it, perhaps after 1992, and a Jackson (or Andrew Young) federal government would certainly be more interventionist in economic affairs, gradually becoming more socialist with a socialistic entrepreneurial economy emerging by 2000.

As we have seen, the 4th-Wave entrepreneurs and knowledge workers tend to be more socialistic than the corporate executives or capitalists who preceded them. This again portends a socialist future in America, which is home to most of this new genre of the Western socio-political scene. At the same time, the predominance of these intellectual entrepreneurs and professionals bodes well for the nation's revitalization and global strength. Small, new companies created most of the 20-million new jobs in the 1980s. The continuing immigration into U.S. society reflects the opportunities America offers, and it contributes to the nation's renewal. These new Americans bring — in addition to cheap pools of labor — entrepreneurial and intellectual skill: 36 of the 114 Nobel prizes awarded to Americans between 1945 and 1984 in science and medicine went to immigrants.

These builders of the new economy have a different worldview. They see the new frontier as one of global co-operation. This larger purpose will gradually replace the old individualistic values in American corporations, governments and education, paving the way for a new America that really will be able to "stand tall" in the global affairs of the 21st-Century. It holds the promise of the Kennedy vision of an America able to tackle Third World problems and forge a global alliance with Japan, Europe, the Soviet Union — and America's closest neighbors.

"Amexicana"

America is bordered by two essentially socialistic or mixed economies — Canada and Mexico — each with its own problems and opportunities.

Economically, Canada accounts for 10% of the combined U.S.A./Canada marketplace, more than 70% of Canadian trade is with America, and America's major trading partner is Canada. Despite this degree of economic security, Canada's federal budget deficit is proportionately much worse than America's. The country has also been largely dependent on American technology. And while Canada does not share America's growing social problems to anything near the same degree, the country is socio-economically balkanized and faces some major political traumas.

By dogmatically pursuing its French-only language laws, for example, albeit to protect its francophone culture, the province of Québec is in danger of isolating itself from the North American and global marketplace. Even Québec's growing entrepreneurial class recognizes — if its politicians do not — that the global *lingua franca* is English. The future success of this class may allow Québec to overcome its fear of cultural assimilation, but the language issue will likely remain an emotional one that continues to politically divide Canada. It is virtually impossible for a federal political party to come to power without the support of the Québec electorate. And, because of its fear of cultural assimilation, Québec always supports the federal party — and party leader — most sympathetic to its cause, and frequently holds that party — and the rest of the country — hostage to its demands. This political blackmail will not be possible in the long-term future for the francophone population in Canada is steadily decreasing, but for now it weakens federal democracy, balkanizes the country, saps its social energy and weakens economic progress. If the next generation of Québécois can reach a higher level of political maturity and overcome its fear of assimilation, the province — and Canada — will be free to achieve its greater potential. For this to happen, Québec must be "re-Canadianized" within the larger North American and global context.

Isolated from the rest of Canada by Québec, the Atlantic Provinces are socially (through family ties) and economically (through trade and tourism) closer to the New England states. This proximity, however, has not yet made these provinces affluent. Thanks to the conditioning of Canadian federal government aid over several decades, these provinces are trapped in a social welfare mentality (unemployment in Newfoundland is perenially around 15%, even in the best of times) that now expects federal aid as a birthright. The provinces have failed to diversify out of, or to modernize, a distinctly stagnant 1st-Wave fishing industry and are economically underdeveloped. Their best prospect is to further develop the tourism sector, drawing on the huge New England and New York markets. Again, however, this will further distance these provinces from the rest of Canada and reinforce north-south ties with the United States.

Similarly, Canada's prairie provinces have strong north-south links with the American Midwest, and like the Midwest, they have not yet sufficiently diversified out of their globally noncompetitive, predominantly grain-growing economy. Like Texas, Alberta has also counted too much on an oil bonanza that will probably never return. Nevertheless, these provinces are reasonably self-sufficient and record steady if unspectacular economic progress even in the worst of times. They are gradually realizing that they are no longer the "bread basket" of the world and are instead developing new industries that hold good potential for the future. Alberta also will become a leading center of tourism for jet-setting Japanese and the rapidly growing urban populations of the American northwest that will be drawn to the breathtaking scenery in the Rocky Mountains.

Psychologically isolated from the rest of Canada by those mountains, the Pacific province of British Columbia is starting to capitalize much more on the economic vibrancy of the Pacific Rim. But such progress is still being negated by a social malaise of labor strife and a prevailing 1st-Wave forest-industry mentality that is causing the province to fall further behind the post-industrial world. In comparison with the neighboring American states of Washington and Oregon, for example, British Columbia is clearly not keeping pace, either in developing its high-tech or its Pacific potentials. Even so, Vancouver is strategically located and ought to be able to play a full part in the booming American northwest and Pacific Rim economies during the next half-century.

The remaining 50% of Canada's economy is accounted for by the central province of Ontario. As economically strong, as vibrant, as innovative and as high-tech as California, Ontario is the center of economic gravity in Canada and the undoubted epicenter of Canada's future post-industrial efforts. Toronto, the baby boom capital of Canada, is the nation's corporate headquarters and the center of finance, media and information. The province is the country's leader in high technology and a major North American tourism mecca. Though far from the Pacific Rim, Ontario has a growing trade with Southeast Asia and other parts of the developing world, and its overall prospects are spectacular.

Canada's prosperity essentially rests on its ability to export modern technology, expertise and information. The country that developed the telephone is now reinventing the telephone and is a world leader in integrated services digital network (ISDN) technology. Canada is also a leader in satellite technology and a major participant in the NASA space shuttle and space station programs. Nevertheless, the country has been very dependent on imported technology through its largely "U.S. branch plant" economy and must at least double its R&D efforts if it is to stay internationally competitive in other fields.

Geo-politically, Canada enjoys an excellent reputation for its political impartiality and sensitivity, and its distinctly un-American image, particularly in the Third World. Indeed, Canada can play a major role by helping the United States restore its global image. As well, Canada's increasingly multicultural population provides the country with a unique edge in its ability to conduct business around the world. Unfortunately, since the retirement of prime minister Pierre Trudeau in early 1984, Canada has declined to play the activist international political role of which it is capable and which, by tradition, the world expects it to play. The world is crying out for innovative political leadership, and countries such as Canada should be initiating bold measures to address the festering Third World debt issue, to revitalize the U.N., the IMF and the World Bank and so on.

Yet Canada's global ability is in danger of being impaired by the recently increased focus on U.S. trade and close political pandering to the United States. The hasty 1988 U.S.-Canada free trade agreement provoked legitimate fears in Canada about loss of its economic and hence political sovereignty. Admittedly, this planned economic integration of North America by the year 2000 is essential to Canada's long-term prosperity. Without such economic integration, a country with only 27 million people — as highly educated as they are — will become an international economic backwater. With it, Canada can gradually become a full sovereign member of a North American common market, modeled on the EEC, with political integration also probably inevitable some time in the twenty-first century.

However, this is being achieved at the expense of expanding ties in the Third World. In the long run, such ties will be much more economically and politically fruitful for Canada than will those with the United States, which, currently at least, is in economic and political decline. With the free trade agreement signed, it is now vitally important for Canada to focus its efforts on the reform of the international financial and political frameworks, without which the free trade agreement will be for naught. Furthermore, as long as it maintains its political independence — indeed, if it is to do so at all — Canada must be independently active in geo-political affairs.

Mexico, the U.S.A.'s third-largest trading partner after Canada and Japan, is more afraid than Canada of potential U.S. economic and political domination — and justifiably so. However, the Mexican economy is mired in $110-billion of foreign debt — mostly owed to the United States — and economic integration with the U.S. marketplace is essential if Mexico is to get itself back on the road to prosperity.

Because of the debt, Mexico is one of the world's most unstable countries and possibly unstoppable forces are pushing it towards political revolution. A continued isolationism and superior moralism will not solve the country's growing problems of international insecurity and domestic instability. Mexico needs a more mature and realistic assessment of domestic needs in the context of international affairs. Like Canada, it must no longer vacillate in its intent to attract capital investment but must develop a coherent, broadly based set of measures that will achieve long-term growth. By failing to do so, the ruling PRI party has been losing its grip on the middle class in the big cities and industrialized areas, and it only narrowly won the 1988 election by what appears to have been massive fraud.

The economic challenge is daunting but not impossible to meet. The country must create the largest number of jobs in its history at a time when, burdened in debt, economic growth is increasingly difficult. Nearly 15-million young Mexicans will enter the job market by the year 2000, leaving the economy with the task of creating 1-million jobs each year. Unless the U.S. writes off all Mexico's debt, the consequences are staggering. Those who do not find jobs will have three choices: go to the United States, take to the streets, or revolt. These young people are urban, schooled to some extent and, thanks to crossborder TV, share much of the modern American mindset. Their expectations, which dwarf those of their parents, will be easier to meet if the debt is dealt with.

In the 15-years prior to the 1982 debt crisis, Mexico's GNP grew by an average of 6.7% each year. In the seven years since then, GNP has annually fallen an average of 2.3%. Restoring growth will restore a measure of stability. Even then, Mexico must overcome one of the most unequal income distributions in the world — the primary cause of revolution anywhere. The poorest 20% of Mexicans receive only 2.9% of the nation's total income, and this group has suffered a real decline in its standard of living every year since 1979. The richest 10% of Mexicans take home 40.6% of the national income and, seeking safety, bank most of their capital abroad. This situation is clearly not sustainable and will have to be rationalized.

The archaic Mexican political system cannot survive a true liberalization of the economy, which necessarily implies an open political arena. Since 1920, every sitting president has named his successor. (Following the 1988 election fiasco, this probably will never be allowed to happen again.) The reason most Mexicans have so far accepted such an undemocratic system is that they fear a new one might bring violent conflict. This is the same irrational fear that maintained Marcos in the Philippines. But an oligarchic one-party system can no longer cope with the urbanized, modern, burgeoning society of 90-million people. As in the Philippines under Marcos, the monopolistic presidency and one-party system will likely be overthrown at the 1994 Mexican election unless it brings in drastic political reform.

Politics in Mexico is ruled by unions, and their corrupt mafioso-style bosses have propped up presidents for their own gains. An encouraging sign is that

President Salinas in 1989 arrested the head of the oil union and 36 other union leaders, charging them with corruption, stockpiling weapons, and state conspiracy. Further impetus for political reform could occur if opposition parties win a majority in the midterm legislative elections slated for 1991. This would give the leftist opposition power over the nation's budget and enable it to pass legislation banning any further payments on Mexico's foreign debt — one of the opposition's avowed election platform policies. If the U.S. does not write-off that debt before 1991, it may well have an unfriendly "leftist" state on its borders.

Astoundingly, even after the 1988 election, American policy-makers persist in believing that political instability and violence cannot come to Mexico. They are often so incapable of thinking beyond the materialist categories of exchange rates and oil prices that they fail to see the reality of Mexico's growing crisis. To prevent Mexico's economic and political system from collapse, the U.S. must cancel the debt and increasingly integrate Mexico into the "Amexicana" economy of America, Mexico and Canada. This integration will speed up if Mexico opens up to imports and foreign investment and, like Canada, signs a free trade deal with Washington.

America, Mexico and Canada thus need each other: the U.S. needs Mexico's resources, its young workers and its underdeveloped markets; Mexico needs its U.S. debt to be written off and to acquire U.S.-Canadian investment and technology; and tiny Canada needs huge markets for its resources and technology. While the U.S. population of 250-million is growing by only 0.7%-per-year (as is Canada's 27-million), Mexico's population of 90-million is undeveloped (per capita income is only $1,850) and growing at 2.4%-per-year.

The integration of an "Amexicana" common market will surely be a drawn-out, delicate process, but the creation of a single 367-million-strong marketplace (560-million by 2050) will ultimately prove irresistible. With Mexico and Canada then in close economic union with the U.S., their semi-socialist economies will inevitably further influence American policy to lean the same way. This, coupled with the increasingly "Third World" makeup of "Amexicana" (blacks, Hispanics, Asians), should enable the union to forge further economic links in Latin America and Asia and across the Third World.

If it is to participate in the Pacific Century, America must restructure its socio-economic policies so as to rebalance income distribution, rebalance its budgets, invest more in advanced civilian technologies and transfer them to the Third World — whose debt it must play a role in writing off. An increasingly socialist country, the U.S.A. can then be reborn and prosper if it develops a geo-strategic vision for its global role in the 21st-Century, forges an "Amexicana" alliance with Mexico and Canada, and focuses on global economic development.

G-Force P-3

Perestroika: Gorbachev's Global "Check-Mate"

"Gentlemen, this man (Gorbachev) has a nice smile, but he has iron teeth."
— *Andrei Gromyko*

The new mood in Moscow, where change has become a value in itself, is a surprise to all. The United States is perplexed at what to do with Mr. Gorbachev, the likes of whom the modern world has never seen. As it is, since the mid-1960s, U.S. leaders frequently have been geo-strategically naive and shortsighted; Mikhail Gorbachev (who rose to the Soviet Politburo in 1981) is geo-strategically acute and farsighted. Soviet leaders are chess players and Mikhail Gorbachev is the grand master. Though I would dearly love to take Gorbachev and his reforms at face value, I believe — at least for now — that his *perestroika* (restructuring) is part of a grand strategy designed to invigorate the economy so that Soviet foreign policy can resume its expansionist goal of global dominance. The *glasnost* (openness) is a clever smokescreen to disguise the ongoing gambit and ultimate "check-mate!"

The essential characteristic of a radical reformer in an ultra-conservative setting is the ability to hide ultimate purpose behind immediate rhetoric. By playing to the global audience and its aspiration for peace, justice, and a saner world, Gorbachev is geo-strategically employing ambiguity, concealment and deception concerning the Soviet Union's global designs. His pronouncements on the state of the Soviet economy's failings are part of the lie. When the Soviet Communist Party issued its ideological blueprint for the 21st-Century in late-1985 (six months after Gorbachev's rise to General Secretary), it reiterated that capitalism was "historically doomed" and reconfirmed the mandate of the Soviet constitution that communism is to be spread throughout the world. They

309

have no doubt that communism — no matter how reformed — will win the race with capitalism and, with the West mired in "Mini-Depression" in the early-1990s, Gorbachev will enjoy increasing economic wherewithall to forge Soviet geo-political aspirations to the fullest degree, and virtually unhindered. This chapter will explore how this will be accomplished at home, and how the expansionist G-Force of Soviet history will reinvent global politics as Gorbachev continues to take the world by storm.

Gorbachev: Entrenched as World's Top CEO

Although he did not occupy the position of General Secretary of the Communist Party until 1985, Gorbachev has effectively been running the Soviet Union since Yuri Andropov came to high office in 1981, and he is taking the country by storm. He has totally restructured the Politburo, revamped the military and named himself President. The world has perhaps never before seen a political leader like him. He has marched onto the world stage as chief executive officer (CEO) of what is effectively the largest corporation in the world — a corporation in desperate need of invigoration; a "turn around" operation of immense proportions. Undaunted — indeed, excited by the challenge — Gorbachev has taken control of the Soviet Union and is geo-strategically managing its direction.

After assuming almost absolute power in June 1985, he literally tore up the draft of the five-year plan for 1986-90, calling it "too modest" in its goals and too short term in nature. The new plan aims for at least 5% annual GNP growth and calls for the economy to double within 15-years, to be accomplished by a profound 4-STEP restructuring of the Soviet Union. Like China a decade before it, the Soviet Union is ripe for reforms, which should see it move ahead in leaps and bounds to (in Gorbachev's words) "stand on the threshold of the Information Age" by the year 2000. Gorbachev is young enough — and firmly entrenched enough — to see it all through.

Courting Social Aspirations with *Glasnost*

Before Stalin, the Soviet Union was an agrarian 1st-Wave society. Today it is a 2nd-Wave complex urban network. As this progress has occurred, the urban dimension has in some ways become ruralized by the mentality and behavior of its formerly peasant makeup. This parochialism has been reinforced by their leaders' isolation from the outside world and a suffocating bureaucracy, resulting in a widespread social malaise of disenfranchised and demotivated citizens. Beginning with Andropov, and to an even greater extent under Gorbachev, the Soviet leadership has increasingly recognized the general malaise of Soviet society and searched for ways not only to overcome it but (like China) to try to transform popular frustration into an engine of economic growth. While most sovietologists still see the Soviet state in the context of centralized, totalitarian power, the Kremlin now knows (as Lenin taught) that politics must respond to the currents of the 4-STEP process of change.

This is the real purpose of *glasnost,* which is designed to court the popular sentiments of a dramatically changing society. Soviet society is being restructured by the same urbanized "baby boom" phenomenon that the West is experiencing. This highly educated, stabilizing work force — 42-million of whom the Soviets claim are "knowledge workers" — is concerned about lifestyle and living standards. They represent a consumer and producer market of huge potential that can, under the dynamic leadership that Gorbachev now provides, build an advanced and prosperous nation. *Glasnost* is thus designed to release the nationalist mood in hopes of turning creative energies towards technological, economic and political goals. However, its implementation is carefully calculated and controlled, symbolically relaxing bans on activity at the political and religious margins of society. *Glasnost* will not grant independence but is aimed at building a truly confederate Soviet Union.

The country has about 100 ethnic groups, each with its own history, language, culture and religion, which defines its identity and shapes its aspirations. Primary among these groups are the Ukrainians, Baltic peoples and Muslims. Linguistic and cultural affinities make the Ukrainians the easiest to "Russify," but nationalist feelings run high and the Ukrainian Catholic Church is a prevalent force for identity. The Baltic peoples — Lithuanians, Latvians and Estonians — have a strong national consciousness, a strong orientation towards Western Europe and are well educated and socially modernized. However, the recent emergence of "nationalist fronts" and declarations of political "independence" are all carefully orchestrated by Gorbachev in the hope that political freedoms (within certain limits) will spur these economies to further modernize and hence contribute to the overall modernization of the Soviet bloc at large — of which they will remain a part.

Soviet society is being transformed also by significant demographic changes. Population data are incomplete but the 1979 census revealed that about 10% of Soviet people were Muslim and 52% were from the Russian republics. However, back in 1970, of the population under the age of 10, Russians accounted for only 47% and Muslims 18%. Other published data shows that the Russian republic population increased by only 5.6% between 1979 and 1987, while that of Tadzhikistan's Muslim population, for example, grew by 26.5%. These diverse growth rates are due to the fact that, as revealed in a 1985 survey, Russians have only 1.9 children per family (below replacement level) while the Tadzhiks have 6.3 children. As a result of these trends, probably less than 44% of the total Soviet population is now Russian and 18% is Muslim. Among today's under-10-year-old group the Muslim share may now be 36% versus only 30% for Russians, with other groups comprising the remainder. By the year 2000 or so, the U.S.S.R. could be a Muslim-based society.

Islam is not, however, the problem to Moscow that Western observers would have us believe or that Muslim disturbances within the U.S.S.R. and elsewhere might imply. Islam is a geo-strategic opportunity to Moscow and *glas-*

nost will try to ensure it. Though Islam is in contradiction with atheistic Marxism — and, since Marxism tends to have its own theocracy, the clash between the two systems can be severe — many Third World countries have found Marxism attractive as a way to assert national identity against Western colonialism. The Soviet Union thus gains sympathy as the standard bearer against imperialism. At the same time, Marxism is adapting to the style of the more advanced theocratic societies — indeed it must if such countries as Poland are to progress economically as Gorbachev has announced — which are already beginning to be run on more open and pluralistic (*glasnost*) lines.

It thus will be possible for religious groups to re-emerge in this more open Marxist environment, and Islam will be accommodated within communist society just as Catholicism has been in Poland. Gorbachev — whose mother is a devout Christian — is introducing legislation to broaden religious rights, and in Poland the Communist leadership has concluded a diplomatic *concordat* with the Vatican. East Germany has also loosened its stance towards the strongly nationalist Evangelical Protestant Church. Whereas the late Iranian spiritual leader, the Ayatollah Khomeini, once condemned the Soviet Union for its atheist ideology, in 1989 — prompted by the uproar over Salman Rushdie's novel about Islam, *The Satanic Verses* — he said Iran did not need relations with the West and instead urged strong ties with Moscow to help fight the "devilish" West. Upon Khomeini's death, newly-elected Iranian president Hashemi Rafsanjani signed major economic deals with Moscow. As Islam finds accommodation with *glasnost*-Marxism, Gorbachev will be aided both at home and abroad. Other Islamic countries may also find it easier to feel at home in the Soviet fold.

Nevertheless, the newly found social freedoms and electoral reforms under *glasnost* do not augur a Western-style multiparty democracy but rather the emergence of a democratized one-party system. The 19th Party Congress in 1988 approved a wide-ranging package of political reforms designed to bring an end to the direct rule of the Party in day-to-day affairs by means of the 1989 election of a Parliament. In this election, non-Party voters had a choice of at least two candidates for every government position — and thus the freedom to vote out of office any Party functionary whose performance they deemed unsatisfactory, which is precisely what occurred on a widespread basis. Moreover, this new, elected parliament has the power to vote Gorbachev out of office. In essence, of course, continued parliamentary support gives him an electorate-based mandate to overcome bureaucratic stalling and restructure the economy.

Technological Advancement

In an overall sense, the Soviet Union is technologically on a par with the West. It is beyond dispute that Soviet researchers have blazed new trails — in mathematics, mechanics, physics, chemistry, biology, earth sciences, social sciences, metallurgy, engineering, physiology and medicine, and the Soviets probably lead the world in aerospace. The outlays on R&D in the U.S.S.R. amount to more than 3% of GNP (higher than the United States but less than Japan), and 3-million people are employed in the scientific community.

The major problem is poor diffusion of technology into the production sector, with an average six-year lab-to-market time in such fields as telecommunications, robotics and computerization. Gorbachev aims to reduce this lag to about 2-years. Soviet economists expect that would provide a staggering 8% annual increase in labor productivity — and therefore in GNP growth. Even half of that improvement would be a huge boost to the economy.

To achieve this goal, investment in the machinery industry is already drastically increasing and, as in North America, industry is being restructured through large industrial amalgamations to integrate science and production, to rationalize the division of labor and to firmly establish co-operative links between universities, research institutions and manufacturers. Gorbachev has also set in motion a widespread program to improve the quality of production and, more importantly, find some way to foster innovation and master the production of new high technologies: computers, computer-aided design, microprocessors, fiber-optics, ceramics, electronics, robots, lasers, optics and biotechnology. These are now the main thrust of technological diffusion throughout the Soviet economy. To further compensate for its technological lag, Moscow is importing foreign technologies from Western Europe and Japan.

For the long term, Gorbachev is promoting technological self-sufficiency. The Soviets' great intellectual and material resources can match those of Japan and the United States and, coupled with their persistence in attacking any problem, these should allow them to become self-sufficient in the latest technologies. Obviously, if they can match Western achievements in aerospace and military endeavors, they can do the same in other technologies.

The cornerstone of Gorbachev's technology program is a plan to "computerize" the entire economy. He says: "If we stop for one minute, we will fall behind by one mile." Clearly, the Soviets understand the significance of computers. As long ago as 1975, they mapped out how the whole country would be interconnected by a giant computer network in the 1990s. In 1970, computer-based automated control systems were operating in only seven industrial sectors of the Soviet economy, but by 1982 they were used in all industries. While still far behind the West, the production of microcomputers doubled between 1981 and 1983 and that of microprocessors increased fivefold. Even more extensive plans and rapid development are envisaged in the 1990s, and the Soviets believe that a centrally planned socialist economy will take much better advantage of modern computers than capitalist economies, in which economic activity is uncoordinated.

Hopeful Westerners say that the Communist Party's "grip on society" will be lost with the introduction of personal computers into the Soviet Union because the state would not then be able to control information. However, Soviet scientists maintain that, though the state currently restricts "business information," they foresee no problem with sharing general information. Thus, although it is recognized that computerization will cause some changes, just as tape cassettes and videotapes have done, Soviet society has to adapt to new technologies, "even if it means changing the legal structure" surrounding information. That is the view of Andrei Ershov, a Soviet expert on personal computers who designed the computer literacy program that was introduced into the Soviet Union's 60,000 high schools in 1985. To build computer literacy, more than a million personal computers will be in schools by 1992, and plans are well under way to retrain a vast army of teachers and organizers.

Post-Industrializing the Economy

The myth of a crumbling Soviet economy is understandably one of the most pervasive, for evidence of waste and inefficiency is everywhere. Even Gorbachev has questioned the validity of past economic growth statistics. The CIA estimates that, despite all the queues, shortages and shoddy goods, Soviet economic growth rates over recent decades have exceeded those of the Western economies. While still trailing the West's GNP per capita, the Soviet economy has out-performed the West.

Plans to double GNP between 1985 and 2000, while slow to show results, should be met by modernization efforts taking place in each economic sector. In 1st-Wave agriculture, land reclamation and irrigation mega-projects and imported technology are designed to make the country self-sufficient in grain production before 1995 — notwithstanding recent poor harvests — and reduce the 1985 total labor input from 30% of the work force in 1985 to less than 10% by the year 2000. In the 2nd-Wave industrial sector, a major expansion of capital investment, rapid technological innovation and entrepreneurial incentives are slowly gearing up to meet the Soviet baby boomers' pent-up demand for improved lifestyles. My forecast is for economic output to at least double between 1985 and 2000, exceeding Gorbachev's goal, making the U.S.S.R. an emerging 4th-Wave economy by about 2010. This will be aided by announced cuts in military personnel and a planned 19% reduction in the manufacture of arms and military hardware in favour of civilian production between 1989 and 1991.

This economic performance will be achieved primarily through improved productivity. Between 1985 and 1988, 90% of economic growth came from productivity improvements, and in some factory experiments labor productivity is 300% higher and unit costs some 50% lower than in 1985. Nor is there any lack of energy resources to fuel economic growth. About half of the world's natural gas lies beneath Soviet soil, enough to propel domestic industry (and provide for energy exports to the rest of Europe) for at least 200-years. As well, economic decision-making is being decentralized to enterprise managers (as China has done), with the staff of the central planning agencies being cut by 40%.

Anyone who doubts the prospect of Gorbachev's economic reforms succeeding has only to consider the evolution of China since Mao's death. Mao's successors took as their first priority economic modernization. This entailed such reforms as decentralization of decision-making, dismantling of the collective farm system and greater latitude for the "private" sector. Like China, Gorbachev also realized that better relations with the West were essential to the modernization program. The first set of economic changes are part of a long-term plan. Stage two in the 1990s will take Russia down the bolder path followed by China, East Germany and Hungary. The Soviet Union's adaptability and prospects should not be underrated. The outcome by 2000 will be the creation of an essentially post-industrial, entrepreneurial Soviet economy. As the Western economies suffer a "Mini-Depression," the Soviet Union will not only gain much relative economic power, it will also be free to divert yet more investment from the military and enjoy the increasing economic wherewithal to forge its geo-political aspirations to the fullest, virtually unhindered.

Geo-Strategic Foreign Policy

Politically, Gorbachev has brought an entirely new generation of geo-strategic thinkers into the Kremlin. He is now running Russia as a multinational corporation, acutely aware of the economic opportunities of the global marketplace. Gorbachev will maintain friendly relations with his main competitor, the United States, while aggressively pushing for major market share gains in Western Europe, the Middle East and Africa and in tomorrow's mass market of the Third World. The goal is to ensure that geo-strategic expansion can resume, picking up pace in the 1990s through trade and technology-transfer marketing — not through invasion with tanks.

Gorbachev re-iterates that "the foreign policy of a nation is inseparable from ... its socio-economic goals and requirements." The Soviets now use economic trade for geo-strategic political goals. Russia, of course, had always pursued Stalin's doctrine of "two world markets": the socialist and capitalist markets. Soviet leadership has repeatedly emphasized the Soviet policy to drastically increase trade among socialist countries and with the Third World while holding down trade levels with capitalist countries. Gorbachev's view is one of global interdependence, with little distinction between socialist and capitalist markets which are seen as a genuinely international phenomenon operating over and above the existing political systems.

Nevertheless, while Moscow has intensified industrial trade with the West, it often uses it as a political weapon to build a lobby within trade-starved Western European industry. This was recently manifested in the cases of Belgium and Italy. After an outbreak of swine fever in Belgium, Moscow cancelled all agricultural imports from that country. The ban stayed in effect for a few years, although the swine fever was soon eradicated. The Soviet move was punishment for Belgium's agreement to station U.S. cruise missiles on its soil. The Italian government was recently told that unless it agreed to step up high-technology exports to Russia, the Soviet Union would start cutting back its purchases of Italian goods. Needless to say, new trade deals were soon forged with Italy. It has also entered into a series of credit arrangements with West German, British, French and Swiss banks, increasingly denominated in the European Currency Unit rather than the dollar.

Gorbachev's ideal strategy is to create some sort of "invisible hand" or marketplace to guide the multilevel flow of goods and services among three major trading blocs. The "invisible hand" is already busily at work — it is Soviet expansionism through trade — and the Soviet Union is now working towards the creation of this three-part global economy. As Moscow's policy elite sees it, the West will provide the advanced technology, the U.S.S.R. and Eastern Europe will provide much of the middle-level technology; and the Third World will provide chiefly its labor and raw materials. Very clearly, this is a new geo-strategic view. The old school of thought was that Soviet rivalry with the United States would be better served by manipulating Third World resentments against the West.

The new globalist view in Moscow regards the problems of the developing countries as a useful lever for tilting the balance in favor of the Soviet Union. The growing gap between many developing countries and the West in the 1980s has created a sense of alienation and a Third World chauvinism, which presents unique opportunities to spread socialist ideology. Moscow is therefore aggressively pushing trade as a means of shepherding Third World states into the Soviet fold, and its planners project much increased trade with the Third World in the next 15-years. While this would be commendable if it builds Third World economies, Soviet goals have sinister political motives. This new thrust was enshrined as doctrine at the Communist Party Congress in February 1987 whereby the Soviet Union will particularly concentrate its foreign (trade) policy on the important, rapidly industrializing, quasi-capitalist Third World countries.

Long-standing Soviet policy towards India is explicitly put forward as the model. The U.S.S.R. has already put into service more than 60 industrial and other facilities in major branches of the Indian economy. Fifty more projects are either under construction, being designed or being negotiated. Today, for example, Soviet co-operation projects form the basis of India's state sector, producing about 8% of India's electricity, 36% of steel, 37% of aluminum, 77% of metallurgical capacity, 47% of energy-generating equipment, 43% of mining machinery and 42% of crude oil refining. While this foreign investment is to be welcomed, as Canada has discovered with U.S. investment, it impinges on national sovereignty. This is particularly the case, as with the Soviets, when that investment comes direct from a foreign state. Soviet-sponsored enterprises in other developing countries tend to follow a similar pattern.

Wakening to the reality of the coming "Pacific Century", the Soviet Union is also promoting the fact that it is a Pacific nation and wishes to play a role in maintaining peace in the Pacific. Succeeding in attracting Japanese money and technology into the eastern parts of the Soviet Union, it has offered nothing more than a dialogue over some disputed island territories claimed by Japan.

These overtures not only appease Japan but they also reassure China. Since breaking off relations with the Soviets in the 1960s, however, China has persistently raised three obstacles to a restoration of political relations: the presence of Soviet troops in Afghanistan, Cambodia (Kampuchea) and along the Chinese border. Since the withdrawal from Afghanistan was announced, Gorbachev has promised to reduce the troops on the Sino-Soviet border and to ensure that Vietnam pulls its troops out of Cambodia soon. With these obstacles now at least partially addressed, Gorbachev met with Chinese leaders in Beijing in 1989. By adopting *perestroika* at home, Moscow has theoretically matched China's economic "four modernizations." By promoting *glasnost*, and placing himself firmly at the helm of Soviet affairs, Gorbachev has positioned Moscow ahead of Beijing in achieving political reforms. While China will never again allow Soviet interference in its affairs, by placating China over the three obstacles and meeting with Deng Xiao-Ping, Gorbachev has effectively regained the position as the leading proponent of Communism in the world.

Soviet expansionism is also being furthered from outer-space. Soviet military space forces are both impressive and, in the opinion of General John Piotrowski, commander in chief of the North American Aerospace Defense Command and the U.S. Space Command, are "superior in significant respects" to those of the United States and its allies. He believes that, even based on current capabilities, the Soviets could try to dominate space rather than co-operating with other space-faring nations. More than 90% of the Soviet orbiting spacecraft have military or military-related missions. More than 85% are exclusively military systems, compared with about 65% for America. The Soviet space strategy is integrated with combined arms plans and military operations on Earth, and General Piotrowski says that the Soviets have a four-phase strategy to dominate space so as to control events on Earth.

The Soviet's space shuttle made its first flight in 1988. A whole fleet of mini-shuttles will follow. By 1992, the Kosmolyot space plane could become the first passenger shuttle, running to and from permanently manned space laboratories, manufacturing plants and military command posts. The Soviet lead in space was confirmed at a 1987 three-day conference in California of top officials from every major space program in the world. The U.S.S.R. could become the world's dominant military space power by the year 2000. In sheer numbers of launches per year, the Soviets edged past the U.S. as far back as 1967. In 1982, they sent up 101 space shots, in contrast to only 18 by the United States. More impressive, Soviet cosmonauts have logged some 15 man-years in space, against less than five for American astronauts. Soviet space stations will soon have permanent crews of up to 30 people, some of them plotting Soviet expansionism on Earth.

The U.S.S.R. thus reveals a keen understanding of the G-Forces of change and already Gorbachev has brought changes to his country that could never but partially be undone. By restructuring itself domestically through the 4-STEP process of change (from *glasnost* to *perestroika*), the Soviet Union will — if it chooses to do so — be able to pursue its global expansionism through strategic economic linkages worldwide in the 1990s. Relatively untouched by the "Mini-Depression" and the global debt crisis, the Soviet Bloc will become an economic superpower among equals — "Amexicana" (U.S./Canada/Mexico), "Eastasia" (Japan/China/Pacific) and "Third World" (all non-aligned countries) — by the early part of the 21st-Century. The debt-induced "Mini-Depression" could throw many Third World countries into the Soviet-aligned camp and politically entangle Western Europe and the Middle East in the Soviet economic cobweb (see later chapters). If this occurs, by the year 2050, the Soviet empire could outrank "Amexicana" by a considerable margin — and may even control the entire planet from outer space.

While he will not live to see it, that will complete Gorbachev's global "check-mate". I hope Mr. Gorbachev proves me wrong!

G-Force P-4
Soviet Unification of Europe

"I like Mr. Gorbachev. We can do business together."
— Margaret Thatcher

Money and security tie countries together; but so do kinship, familiarity and values. Geo-politically, these dynamics are reshaping the world, and nowhere is this better illustrated than in Europe. Caught between the superpowers in the middle of the East-West axis since the end of World War II, and separated by an eroding Iron Curtain, Eastern and Western Europe seem destined to forge a common future together. The strongest forces for a unified Europe are generated from Tokyo, Washington and Moscow, but they come to a sharp focus in the two Germanies — they will ultimately determine Europe's future. They are the two richest countries of East and West Europe, both technologically and economically; they are driven by a strong social motivation to unify; they are both strong enough to draw their respective neighbors into the process; and the security and economic interests of Moscow, Washington and Japan will be enhanced by a demilitarized and peaceful Europe. The catch is that both Eastern and Western Europe will increasingly need the Soviet Union for trade, energy and continued prosperity in the 21st-Century. Margaret Thatcher might like to do business with Russia, but her successors may have no choice.

Disarming Europe

Everything about post-war American policy towards Western Europe — the Marshall Plan to rebuild the continent after the war, the creation of NATO and backing for the creation of the EEC — testifies to the primacy of U.S.-U.S.S.R. relations. These relations are still primary in U.S. foreign policy, and will remain so in the near future, but America has growing concerns and interests elsewhere that will ultimately become more important.

Troubled by mounting budget deficits, Washington is now forced to find ways of cutting its military spending. America allocates $140-billion per year

319

(almost half of its annual defense budget) to NATO. In contrast, the U.S. contributes only about $25-billion to Pacific defense, and yet the Pacific (not the Atlantic) now represents its best economic future. Moreover, the Soviet Union is more of a Pacific power than an Atlantic power so that, in effect, the East-West axis has swiveled 180-degrees. This about-turn will ultimately force the U.S. to sharply reduce its NATO allocation. Hence the ready U.S. response to Gorbachev's European disarmament proposals.

Nothing pleases Moscow more. Soviet foreign policy is preoccupied with driving America out of Eurasia. Gorbachev is constantly trying to influence the anti-nuclear and anti-American feelings in Western Europe in a way that will shape its governments in the 1990s. Western Europe is politically vulnerable to the subtle application of Soviet military power on the continent, which poses significant problems that will become more challenging. One-third of West Germans live within 100-kilometres (60-miles) of the Soviet bloc, and the shortest distance from East Germany to the English Channel is only 640-kilometres (400-miles). The presence of NATO nuclear weapons has deterred the Soviet Union from putting Western European defenses to the test, despite Moscow's favorable balance of forces.

Many of NATO's weapons are now being removed, however, essentially "de-nuclearizing" Western and Central Europe. The next 10 to 15 years offer the U.S.S.R. a geo-strategic window of opportunity in Europe: its conventional military forces are at the height of their power after impressive retooling and investment during the 1970s, and therefore can easily be reduced as Gorbachev has proposed. It would still be very easy for a quick, conventional (non-nuclear) strike into Western Europe, which no alliance would be able to prevent. This ever-present danger will be exacerbated as the U.S. continues to pull troops, money and weapons out of Europe and may force Western Europe into the Soviet sphere of influence.

Economic Links

Economically, Gorbachev is also spreading money around to win friends and bolster this Soviet influence. He hands out enough contracts to keep many Western European order books filled for several years. Deals in 1987 and 1988 included more than $4-billion in new chemical plants and $1-billion each for steel and automotive projects.

The Soviet Union also agreed in 1984 to supply Western Europe with 40-billion cubic metres (30-billion cubic yards) of natural gas between then and 2004. By 1990, Soviet gas will already provide 20% of what EEC countries require and will meet 35% of needs in West Germany and France. The gas will be paid for with hard currency, technology, equipment and consumer goods. In 1989, following on the heels of Finland and Turkey, Greece agreed to a counter-trade deal with the Soviet Union for more than 2-billion cubic metres (1.5-billion cubic yards) of gas per year from 1992 to 2016. More than gas is coming

down the pipeline: all of Europe is becoming economically (and hence politically) dependent on the U.S.S.R. for its energy needs.

For Western Europe, a broader economic relationship with Eastern
European will become increasingly appealing. Formed as long ago as 1975, the
Conference on Security and Co-operation in Europe includes all countries of
Western and Eastern Europe (except Albania) and the U.S.S.R. Designed to
make Europe a more secure and humane place, it has become instead a vehicle
for trade and economic co-operation. Under its auspices, a meeting was held in
1987 between the EEC and COMECON (the Council for Mutual Economic
Assistance) "to establish official economic relations" between the two sides. In
1988, COMECON agreed to form into a totally integrated Eastern bloc common
market, with a collective division of labor until at least 2005, whereupon it hopes
to be economically integrated with the EEC. By the end of 1988, EEC-COMECON
trade relations were formalized, opening the way for deals between individual
members of both sides. The unofficial goal is to eliminate all trade barriers
between Eastern and Western Europe by 2005 at the latest.

The Western European agreement to transform the EEC into a single common market by the end of 1992 is a laudable and necessary step in the process of
global integration. By 1992, all remaining economic barriers within the 12-
nation bloc will be eliminated and all transborder customs procedures will be
streamlined if not phased out entirely. The economic benefits of a united 330-
million person marketplace are gradually overcoming the European
Community's natural divisions. Nine major languages are being overlaid by the
lingua franca of English. Economic disparities (from the wealthy West Germans
to the less-well-off Greeks) are being smoothed out somewhat by taxation
adjustments and full labor mobility — and the promise of common prosperity.
Within a couple of decades, all EEC citizens could carry a common passport.

Soon after 1992, the European Free Trade Association (EFTA) group of
Sweden, Norway, Finland, Iceland, Austria and Switzerland will probably join
the EEC, making it an even more powerful economic unit. This unity will create
a huge population marketplace as big as North America and Japan combined.
Strong as it is, however, the EEC (with or without the EFTA) poses no threat to
Japan or the United States, which are already technologically and economically
ahead of it by a significant margin. The EEC also has growing socio-economic
and political problems that could detract from its global competitiveness.

Social Malaise
While much of the continent is reasonably prosperous and, as always, full of
culture and charm, the European Community is vexed by how to socialize the
benefits of the single market. One problem is that about 20-million young
Western Europeans — on whom future prosperity depends — are unemployed.
In 1986, 63% of unemployed men in Belgium had been without a job for a year
or longer. The comparable rate was 46% in both France and Britain and 32% in

West Germany. Most Europeans now tend to accept this situation as inevitable, having created the good life for the majority and then an expensive welfare state to support everyone else. In Britain, unemployment benefits now cost a staggering $30-billion a year, more than the annual North Sea oil revenues, and the social welfare safety net has become a birthright. Indeed, the welfare state mentality has created an unemployment trap that sees welfare bring in almost as large a pay packet as does full-time work for the working class.

For Western Europe, this problem is exacerbated by political differences. The issue of Social Europe is the pet subject of EEC president Jacques Delors, a French socialist. His views are staunchly opposed by Margaret Thatcher, who maintains that economic gains should be left to "trickle down." As I have argued earlier, and as Thatcher and Reagan have both shown, "trickle down" does not work. It is therefore likely that Thatcher's opposition will be overwhelmed, particularly as the president of the EEC's Council of Ministers is also from socialist France.

Neither has Margaret Thatcher's "trickle down" been able to prevent Britain's further demise from a global political and economic power to a second-rate Western European nation with a sick economy and a pathetic social attitude to go with it. Any expatriate who returns or reads the British press is struck by the prevailing but isolated establishment, an immobile bureaucracy, a managerial class lacking entrepreneurial vitality, a disenchanted labor movement, a working class stifled by welfare and a middle class that apathetically watches the nation crumble.

With the collapse of the country's old industrial base, Thatcher has created a new feudal leisure lifestyle: a bizarre mixture of medieval society spotted with pockets of high-tech. The economic system is polarizing between the defunct industrial North (with its forced unemployed proletariat) and the post-industrial South (with its lethargic elite gentry). As James Bellini has concluded, Britain now confronts its last colony — itself. As a former Brit myself, it is saddening. Without a more comprehensive plan, the country's best possible future lies in the 5th-Wave: as a quaint tourist resort.

Technological Weakness

As a whole, Western Europe's global prospects are not much brighter. Now the "museum" of Western civilization — and in a four-way economic competition with Japan/East Asia, the United States and the U.S.S.R. — its chances for independent prosperity seem slim.

Except for West Germany, Western Europe has little unique or particularly superior technology to offer the world. Despite its achievements in aerospace, the EEC has fallen distinctly behind in all major 4th-Wave technological fields, including robotics, biotechnology, computers and aerospace. Most serious, perhaps, is its almost total dependence on imports of advanced semiconductors, those electronic microchips now found in everything from computers to talking teddy bears.

The EEC's $4.5-billion Eureka (joint high-tech) program launched in 1985 has not changed this situation. Eureka should not be over-exaggerated; the project is simply too slow and too late, and the financial commitment is not even sufficient to achieve the stated goal of keeping Western Europe in the critical high-tech race. Without technological leadership, economic prosperity will fall short of expectations.

Political Maturization

As well as providing for the unity of its markets, the EEC's unanimously ratified Single European Act provides for a significant streamlining of the political and administrative decision-making process. The act also covers fields of common concern (the state of the environment, for instance) and creates a permanent secretariat for co-operation on foreign policy.

These changes are Western Europe's major strength and reflect a marked shift in popular sentiment away from national sovereignty to a Pan-European loyalty. A comprehensive EEC-wide opinion poll in 1987 revealed that two out of three EEC citizens favor a "United States of Europe" within 20-years. Moreover, nearly 60% said they would also entrust such a European supranational authority with responsibility over economic policy, defense and foreign affairs. Different levels of political maturity (from Britain's centuries–old parliamentary democracy to Spain's recent escape from right-wing dictatorship) are being transcended by the West European Parliament and its EEC-wide popular elections. Western Europe is providing an excellent political model for the world.

However, as the 1989 EEC election showed, there is also a distinct political trend towards socialism in Western Europe. Various brands of socialism and communism already exist at the national level in Sweden, Norway, Finland, France, Spain, Portugal, Italy and Greece. Not even Thatcher can salvage Britain from an inevitable decline into the socialism and quasi-Marxism that is already overt in the governments of, among others, Liverpool and Glasgow. (Indeed, her extreme right-wing stubbornness is perhaps the final straw breaking Britain's back.) The head of the EEC is an avowed socialist. These elements all make West Europe vulnerable to a process of "Sovietization."

"Sovietization"

The geographic East-West split is an unnatural division for Europeans and something for which they cannot find much justification. With World War II fading into history, there is a growing Europeanness in Europe, particularly among the baby boomers. As pointed out by Willy Brandt, president of the Socialist International, the "Europeanization of Europe" is occurring on both sides of the "eroding" Iron Curtain, with dramatic exchanges of people and ideas "bringing about a new longing for unity."

The East-West barriers are eroding and, during recent years, Social

Democratic leaders besides Willy Brandt have been fanning out through the Eastern bloc signing agreements. In 1985, the West German Social Democratic Party (in opposition) concluded a pact with East Germany calling for the creation of a "Central European Zone," which would be free of chemical weapons. Shortly thereafter, the party signed an Environmental Agreement with Czechoslovakia, a "European Economic Co-operation Pact" with Hungary and a "Nuclear Weapon-Free Zone" agreement with East Germany.

The political reforms in Poland, Hungary and the Soviet Union's Baltic republics — which could soon lead to more democratic if not multiparty systems there — are also reducing Western European fears. Gorbachev is now the most popular political leader (according to opinion polls) in Europe, and even surpasses Thatcher in Britain. "Gorbymania" is all the rage in West Germany, which now is the technological, economic and political center of gravity of Europe.

Moscow is successfully exploiting the duality of German feelings. In 1980, 71% of West Germans considered the Soviet Union a threat to peace. In 1989, the figure was down to 11%. With growing ties between Bonn and East Berlin, Moscow seeks to transform Germany into a quasi-neutral member of NATO, thereby alarming and further fragmenting Western Europe. The aim is quite simply to bring West Germany into the Soviet sphere of influence. The U.S.S.R. would, of course, gain West German industrial expertise and valuable influence with the country's many friends in the Third World. Finally, and more importantly, a unified Germany will provide the Soviets with a nuclear-free buffer zone. In 1988, East German president Erich Honecker called for just such a nuclear-free zone.

Honecker's visit to West Germany in 1987 was a major initiative in the move to reunify Germany. Indicating that he favors tight bonds between the two states, he said the border "could no longer separate the two Germanies and the day that it links us together will come if the Germanies make further efforts." Still separated by a 1380-kilomitre (863-mile) border bristling with armed patrols and barbed wire, the two states have nevertheless settled into a wary but increasingly pragmatic relationship held together by more than 70 bilateral agreements governing everything from postal communications to sharing of electricity. West German chancellor Helmut Kohl also reiterated his country's insistence on seeking the reunification of Germany, saying Honecker's visit promoted East-West dialogue and "reinforced the nation's awareness of unity." Indeed, the goal of German reunification is enshrined in West Germany's constitution. Official U.S. policy also endorses reunification, in the hope that this will draw East Germany — and, with it, the Eastern bloc — into the Western fold. This is an increasingly naive hope. In reality, the reverse is occurring. The Soviets are successfully creating not just a neutralized West Germany, but a pliant, self-doubting and weak-willed one in the heart of NATO.

Gorbachev is swaying West German opinion through the massive cuts in Europe-based nuclear systems and the unilateral withdrawal of all its forces from East Germany. The reunified Germany will create a nation that will not only economically overwhelm the rest of Europe but will be politically neutral. This will hopelessly weaken NATO and, in effect, ultimately allow the Soviets to politically dominate the entire continent, perhaps without ever making another military move. Indeed, since the signing of the agreement to eliminate nuclear missiles in Europe, reunification will come relatively soon.

Before the disarmament agreement was signed, a working group of high-level Soviet officials was already weighing a new Soviet proposal for a "confederation" of the German states without foreign troops on their territories. The final proposal may turn out to be a modified version of one made in 1957 by East Germany for a "contractual joining together of the two sovereign German states" on the basis of a ban on the production and/or stationing of nuclear weapons in both German states; their withdrawal from NATO and the Warsaw Pact, respectively; mutually agreed-upon limitations on their national military forces; and the phased evacuation of all foreign forces.

As we have forecast since 1981, the Berlin Wall has been torn down dramatically. This will lead eventually to much freer access across the entire border between what, in name only, will be maintained as two German states. The reunification of Germany and, following it, the Sovietization of Europe is inevitable in the late-1990s.

The global public relations aspect of the reunification between two such strong countries from the communist and capitalist worlds would not be lost on the Third World — or on Moscow's other neighbors in the Middle East, who may then be more inclined to achieve an accommodation with Moscow.

America's turn to the Pacific, the Soviet removal of East European missiles and other weapons, the exhaustion of North Sea energy by the year 2000, and the increasingly socialization of its member states, will seal Western Europe's fate. In the early part of the 21st-Century we are likely to see the emergence of a "United *Soviet* States of Europe".

This huge political bloc will nevertheless contribute further to global multipolarity and, ultimately, global governance. Indeed, the European parliamentary system could significantly influence yet more political reforms inside the Soviet Union and create participatory democracy for the entire Eastern Bloc.

G-Force P-5
Ichi Ban: Japan's Global Role

*"In the past, the term Big Power was interpreted almost always to mean a
military power; that is rapidly changing. Instead, the term's meaning has
shifted and now refers to economic power."*
— *Koji Matsuno,*
President, Hitachi

Japan is reinventing the entire concept of global power. In less than two generations it created a demilitarized model of technological and economic supremacy.
From an average annual income of only $188 per person in 1953 (less than that
of Brazil or Malaysia), having been the World Bank's second-largest borrower
(after India) in 1963, and stunned by OPEC's oil-price shock of 1973, Japan has
turned the tables of history. It is now the richest country in the world, no matter
how you care to measure it, with a per-capita income of $20,000 and more inter-
national investments (in 1988) than any other country. With less than half the
population of either superpower, Japan's GNP exceeds that of the U.S.S.R. and
will surpass that of the U.S. before the end of the 1990s.

The major key to Japan's success is its long-term vision of where and how it
fits into the evolving global system. Galvanized by the reality of post-industrialism, which came into sharp focus in the 1970s, Japan set a simple goal: to
become *ichi ban* (number one) in global technology and to become the
"Information Utility of the Planet" by 1995. That goal is close to realization.

But the miracle does not stop there. Having fully understood the 4-STEP
process of development, and having created enormous wealth with its technological innovation and 4th-Wave information sector, Japan now has two subsequent goals to achieve. The first is to meet the new social aspirations of its own
people by using its stockpile of wealth to enhance their lifestyle. The second and
concurrent goal is to develop further as a political model of global leadership, to
play the lead role in building the global economy, and to use its political power
to develop in the 21st-Century what it calls a "global community consciousness" that will lead to worldwide economic progress. This Japanese reinvention
of geo-politics will be a major G-Force of the next half century.

Geo-Strategic Visioning

One key to understanding Japan as it concerns us here is the way the country gathers and retrieves information — on markets, technological advances and its competitors' marketing strategies. This knowledge of global trends is organized in two main streams: one describes the changing global marketplace, the other reports on other countries' product and service developments. With this geo-strategic intelligence, the economic world holds no unpleasant surprises for Japan. Indeed, Japan believes the future is something to be created, and it uses the information to plan its domestic and international future several years in advance. Moreover, it applies the information in a socially oriented way, to identify opportunities to meet human needs and aspirations.

Japan's long-range vision comes from a tradition of long-range social forecasting for policy formulation. Japanese sociologists argue that their country's main national characteristic is a "future orientation." Japan simply has a different time sense, which emerges as foresight, focussed intention and the geo-strategic management of change. Strategies for change are structured around public policy White Papers (or visions, as they are called) that are practical, orderly and programmatic. Because the Japanese see change as an intrinsic part of reality, they have an unsurpassed capacity for purposeful, dedicated and communal action that is conditioned to follow these technical public policy goals. The Japanese believe, for example, that the next phase of global economic development will be based on an organization of science for the 4th-Wave production of knowledge. As well, the Japanese ability to combine government economic intervention with dynamic private-sector business competition (a Socialistic Entrepreneurial economy) is a mark of their success, which flies in the face of assertions that central planning and market economics are contradictory.

In developing its domestic economy, therefore, Japan adopted a co-operative approach, with business and labor co-ordinating their activities within a national long-term plan. Japan does not believe in protecting dying industries, or in trying to maintain the industrial status quo, or in simplistic attempts to encourage existing industry to be more competitive. Economic growth stems from the recurring long-wave rise and fall of technologies (and the industries on which they rest), and Japan believes that protection for declining industries can only nip new industries in the bud. Japan holds the view that manufacturers in both Western Europe and the United States are losing their competitiveness to Japan and the Newly Industrialized Economies (NIEs) while the NIEs are also developing new information service industries that Western Europe and the U.S. are largely ignoring. In this new wave of economic growth, Japan believes it is economically irrational to erect trade barriers to protect old manufacturing industries in the belief that they form the critical industrial base. Rather, this preservation interferes with the development of the new national and world economies. Instead, says Japan, the West should be developing a new industrial base by challenging the frontiers of technology.

328

Japan adopted a new industrial strategy in 1978 with the passage of its Declining Industries Act. This act identified a number of industries (including steel, ship-building, automobiles, petro-chemicals and textiles) where Japan knew it would not be able to compete in the 1990s (at least not from a domestic manufacturing site) because these industries were too intensive in their use of raw materials, energy and human labor. Under the Act, capacity in these industries has been gradually wound down and the emphasis switched to phased-in post-industrial activities, especially in fields that are not material-, energy- or labor-intensive.

Japan's competitive advantage is already coming from these "infant" industries and high technologies. Infant industries are those which, although confronted by strong foreign competition and comparatively weak at the outset, are destined to develop a strong competitive advantage. As they gain experience and increase production, these industries will amass technology and develop a skilled labor pool. In addition, Japan believes that the developing countries is where the need to develop such industries is most pressing, and it aims to lead in their creation. When it comes to high-tech industries, comparative advantage depends on the amount invested in R&D and production experience. In such industries, says Japan, whoever pioneers production will have decisive influence on future patterns of world trade. In this regard, and also wishing to make a meaningful global economic contribution, the Japanese believe that all its R&D should be geared to developing science and technology that will serve the entire world. Japan will thus seek to become a locus for international research and will oversee the dispersal of the fruits of this research to other nations.

Addressing Social Aspirations

The current generation of young adults in Japan is more consumer oriented, better educated and more professional than their parents. Tokyo will soon boast not just the world's highest property values but the world's largest concentration of "knowledge workers," of valuable information, and of workers with productive skills. At the same time, according to Japanese forecasts, 24% of Japan's total population by 2030 (20% in America and 22% in Canada) will be over age 65. This means that a smaller proportion of the professional work force will have to support all the others. This will affect savings rates, labor practices, and demands for social security expenditures. Japan has recognized this twin problem and is already formulating policies to improve the lifestyle of all its citizens.

The 1987 White Paper on National Life recognized that Japan lags significantly behind Western nations in housing and other societal services. While some of this is due to such problems as the sometimes astronomic rise in land prices, Japan blames not only its small land base but its societal system, which has stressed production efficiency over everything else. Although Japan boasts the world's highest per-capita GNP, and income is distributed much more evenly there than in many Western countries, it has a low standard of road paving and sewage disposal, and has relatively fewer libraries, museums and public parks than other industrialized nations.

The ongoing appreciation in the value of the yen is now providing Japan an opportunity to improve these services. In a 1987 survey, 49% of Japanese stated that "life has reached a sufficient level in terms of material richness," and they wanted to achieve a lifestyle with enough leisure time to "nurture richness of the heart." This far outstrips the number of people who opted for more "richness of things" (34%). The number of people who aspire to psychological values over material and monetary values is increasing year by year in Japan. In an attempt to meet these aspirations, huge public capital spending projects are under way, and Japan plans to open its market fully to foreign goods so that its own people can work less.

As in other countries, Japan's economic success is leading to internal political reform. The Liberal Democratic Party (LDP) has been in power for more than 30-years. This absolute power has led to massive corruption, culminating in the resignation of two Prime Ministers in 1989. The Japanese electorate has become a passive spectator. Door-to-door canvassing at elections is illegal for fear that politically ignorant voters might be bribed. Instead, voters are bombarded by the din of loudspeakers from candidate vans criss-crossing their communities in endless succession. The Japanese elite believes that the ordinary citizen should have no more than a peripheral role in politics. This feudal holdover is the root cause of the elite's corruption. Clearly, if Japan is to become a modern participatory democracy, electoral reform and political conflict of interest guidelines are an urgent requirement, as the 4-STEP process dictates.

Techno-Economic Power

Can Japan preserve its richness and stay a non-military superpower? Japan is one of very few countries that has not been involved in a war of any kind in the past 40-years. By the year 2000, the children of affluence — people who do not know of the war — will form the vast majority of the population, and they will have a Pacific worldview. Under the slogan "build the nation with technology," Japan has greatly increased R&D expenditures ($62-billion in 1986, three times that of 1976).

Japan's economic success has not altered its vision of economic power without military power. The Japanese believe that nuclear weapons have rendered all-out warfare untenable and that they will not suffer for their modest level of military preparedness. Article 9 of Japan's Constitution, imposed after World War II, renounces aggression as a means of settling international disputes, prohibits the maintenance of any armed forces and limits defense spending to only 1% of GNP. Although this arrangement is now seen as impractical if Japan is to help America maintain Pacific peace, it is extremely unlikely that Japan will again become a military power. Whereas the Japanese Self-Defense Force was established in 1954, this was simply a matter of Japan asserting its right (under Article 51 of the U.N. Charter) to protect itself against armed attack. Accordingly, Japan's weapons are defensive only: no forces operate overseas, the air force has no long-range bombers and the navy has no combat ships larger than a destroyer. Japanese law also strictly forbids arms sales abroad, and the Japanese have renounced the use of nuclear arms. The recent increase in defense spending marginally beyond 1% of GNP was done to placate the U.S., which claims Japan should share more of the burden of global defense.

The new world view of Japan is that it can best play a techno-economic role in the world, and that world peace will be best enhanced by developing the economies of the Third World. As this view comes to predominance with the new generation of Japanese in the 1990s, it is unlikely that Japan will acquiesce to increased levels of military spending. Instead, it has agreed to complement U.S. military strategy, with the U.S. providing the offensive power, such as long-range bombers, and the Japanese the defensive force, such as mine-sweepers. The U.S. and Japan have also agreed on the strategic importance of protecting the key sea lanes of Southeast Asia and the three straits — Tsushima, Tsugaru and Soya — to the west and north of Japan. Thus, although Japan is the world's seventh-largest military power, and there is some concern that this military power could grow, it is highly unlikely that Japan will ever spend as much as 2% of GNP for defense. On the contrary, as the world continues to disarm, it may again fall below 1% of GNP.

Japan prefers to build on its successful economic model, which has demonstrated that civilian technological prowess is much more important than military technological prowess. It intends to concentrate more on maintaining its lead in sophisticated technologies such as electronics, computers, robotics, biotechnology and new materials. If current trends continue, by the year 2000 the U.S. military could be dependent upon Japan for component technology. Already, some Japanese corporations are refusing to sell powerful integrated circuits and the machinery to produce those chips to American rivals. With its civilian technological supremacy, Japan is therefore now depriving the United States of advanced military capability. To the extent that the U.S. becomes dependent on others for leading-edge technology, America is likely to lose further power — military as well as economic.

Japan also aims to have a leading 6th-Wave Outer-Space economy and to develop space for economic, not military, purposes. If the last 30-years are remembered as those in which the frontiers of space were dominated by the military interests of the U.S. and the Soviet Union, the next 30-years could well be recalled as those in which Japan (and other Asian countries) launched space stations for peace. The groundwork for this has been laid. In 1961, Japan became the world's third nation, and the first in Asia, to launch satellites. Since then, more than 30 have been launched, with applications ranging from communications and the monitoring of the Earth's resources to astronomy.

Japan's space program has concentrated on the development of launch vehicles and satellites, with the objective of making Japan independent of U.S. space technology. In 1995, Japan is likely to become the third nation with manned space flight when it launches its two-to-four-person shuttle capable of taking along more than a tonne of cargo. Japan is also developing its own 300-passenger hypersonic space plane, which will be ready to fly by 2005. The country's interest in the U.S. Star Wars program must also be viewed within the framework of Japanese hopes for a high-technology route to global security. The country is intent not to fall behind in science and technology, and Star Wars is the point of focus for high-tech breakthroughs. However, Japan is participating in SDI research only for its technological benefits. Moreover, Japan has decided it must have its own project, just as America has its SDI and Europe has its Eureka program. Thus, the Human Frontiers Program is the major emphasis for Japan.

Shaping Japan's Global Leadership Role

Japan's major security concern in the Pacific relates to what Zbigniew Brzezinski has called the "linch pin" states of South Korea and the Philippines. Peace in both is critical to the economic progress of Japan (and all of Southeast Asia). While both countries are major outposts of U.S. power, they are vulnerable to events that could alter their international allegiances. From the Soviet standpoint, a successful North Korean takeover of South Korea (at present remote, notwithstanding South Korea's political instability) would transform the strategic situation in the Far East. It would give the Soviet navy access to the East China Sea, driving the U.S. off the mainland, exposing all the principal islands of Japan to a military threat and outflanking China's industrial northeast. As well, if the Soviet Union extended its influence from Vietnam to the Philippine archipelago, Southeast Asia would be subject to a significant Soviet reach into Japan's principal maritime trading routes.

Japanese wealth is being used to diminish these risks. Japan's increasing foreign investment in Southeast Asia ($20-billion in 1986) and its rapidly expanding economic aid are strategic in enhancing the common security of the Pacific area. Given the strength of the Japanese economy, for example, it is not inconceivable that defense spending *plus* economic aid will soon reach 4% of GNP. Japan has other considerable resources, aside from capital, with which to play a security role in the Pacific. Japanese bureaucrats bring great skills (careful planning, long-term continuity, integrity and high job-performance standards) and Japanese trading companies have the capacity to put together major commercial international development projects.

The entire thrust of Japan's global investment policy is geo-strategic, focussing on the restructuring of the Japanese economy "so that it can make a more positive contribution to the world economy as a whole." In future, high technology will be the biggest component of the world's economy and trade, and Japan aims to reach the stage where it can positively contribute to "the world's store of technology and knowledge." At the same time, Japanese foreign investment is diversifying. In 1986, 22% of Japan's accumulated investment was in the United States, 24% was in Asia, a further 19% was in Latin America, and 4% was in Africa.

The Japanese have quickly realized that technological and economic co-operation among all nations is necessary to achieve peace and prosperity. To this end, a series of roundtable discussions called Japan in the Global Community were held in 1985-86 to consider Japan's global role and formulate ways in which it could contribute to a better world. Recent Japanese opinion polls show that the younger generation in particular feels an urgent need for Japan to become more international, to create a new image of international society as a global community and to foster what it calls "global community conscious-ness."

Rather than spending too much time on alleviating tedious trade frictions with other countries, Japan feels it is more important to focus on the interests of developing countries and the "abject poverty suffered by an estimated 1-billion people in the world." The country thus aims to define its global role in terms of using its economic strength for the "welfare of the world," and also contributing culturally and politically to the global community. Economically, it will make its contribution by continuing to supply high technology, commodities, capital and other management resources and providing open markets in Japan for Third World products. It will use its economic strength to promote international cultural exchanges and to provide sites for such activities. It will support political activities that safeguard international security and stability but, unlike the Soviets or Americans, it has no imperialist aspirations. To co-ordinate these efforts, it has set up the Global Industry and Culture Research Institute to create a balanced economic and cultural base in Japanese society, which will be appreciated by other countries.

Economic stability in Asia is linked to social and political stability, which Japan will try to maintain through its economic strength. Two specific areas of focus will be co-operation in energy development and the creation of information networks. Many energy resources lie untapped in the Pacific region, and an energy development system will be readied to meet expected demand. Japan will also establish information infrastructures such as computer networks, databases, regional communication, broadcasting and Earth resource satellites, and land receiving stations, with Japan acting as a broadcasting center throughout the area.

It is also the instigator of the Pacific Economic Co-operation Conference (PECC), an OECD-style policy body that brings together individuals from government, business and academia in Japan, China, South Korea, Thailand, the Alliance of Southeast Asian Nations, Australia, New Zealand, Canada and the United States. The U.S.S.R. has observer status along with Mexico, Chile, Colombia and Peru. With its members thus encircling the Pacific, the goal of

PECC is to maximize the vast potential of the Pacific Rim, "not simply for the benefit of the Pacific countries but to enhance the well-being and prosperity of human society as a whole."

Japan also plans to campaign for the developed countries to open their markets to exports from the developing world, to encourage direct investment and to promote economic and technological co-operation. It believes that if the West infringes upon the principle of free trade in pursuit of its own interests, attempts to protect outmoded 2nd-Wave industries that have irreversibly lost their international competitiveness, then a true solution to Third World problems will remain a distant dream. Indeed, it believes that this will result in further debt escalation and political instability. Measures to resolve the Third World debt problem will continue to be initiated by Japan and it has removed all tariff barriers from Third World exports to Japan.

Geo-politically, Japan also intends to make patient and steady efforts to turn the U.S. and the U.S.S.R. away from military rivalry and towards constructive economic ties. Japan believes that a strong military is not the only way in which a country can contribute to its own and the world's security. Rather, a stable economy is the essential element of security for a given nation or the region of which it is a part. Japan, which has never shared Washington's deep ideological antipathy to Moscow, believes that the East-West bipolar military confrontation is the very antithesis of the idea of global community.

What is most needed today, says Japan, are efforts to create a system in which all nations can benefit through interdependence without recourse to arms, and a common set of values that opposes armed conflict. Indeed, increased stability in interdependent relations allows governments, corporations and individuals to reach beyond national boundaries to establish multidimensional, multilevel networks. Such interdependence tends to undermine conflict between nations and reduces the effectiveness of military means in conflict resolution. At the popular level, Japan believes that a consensus is needed on the importance of peaceful coexistence.

In order to effectively cope with interdependence, Japan will cultivate "global community consciousness" and improved systems for international exchange that will reflect that consciousness. It thereby believes that it can pursue a course of long-term development together with all nations of the world and that, in time, a true global community can be a reality.

G-FORCE P-6

Modernizing China for Super-Stardom

*"So far as economic reforms are concerned, all we have to do now is speed
up their implementation. Political reforms will be more complicated."*
– Deng Xiao-Ping (1987)

After stumbling about for centuries, the Chinese giant has, since 1978, learned
not only to walk but — economically at least — has been racing ahead at
breathtaking speed and with focussed determination. Politically, however, the
tragic and brutal imposition of martial law in Beijing in 1989 shows that post-
revolutionary China is still ruled by a feudal mentality that does not understand
the meaning of political reform, either in and of itself or within the context of
the 4-STEP process of economic development. China has stumbled again and,
without political reform, the dazzling economic progress of the 1980s could be
for naught.

In post-Mao China, prosperity is a major aspiration, and the goal is to
increase per-capita income to the level of that in advanced countries by the
100th-Anniversary of the People's Republic, in 2049. After the Communist
authorities finally gained national political power in 1949, they set out to
improve China's technologically backward subsistence economy. But, because
of erratic and myopic economic policies, the economy made poor progress and,
particularly during the late-1960s and early-1970s, regressed badly and fell dramatically behind that of its Southeast Asian neighbors. However, following the
political rehabilitation of Deng Xiao-Ping in 1977, the economy took off like a
rocket. Deng announced the "Four Modernizations" program, whose goal is to
quadruple GNP between 1980 and the year 2000, requiring real GNP growth of
5% per year compounded.

These economic reforms have worked wonders. Since 1978, real GNP
growth has averaged about 8% (60% ahead of target), and the Chinese economy is consistently outperforming every national economy in the world. The
technological and economic modernization program follows the 4-STEP process

of social development and is extremely farsighted, with China forging its own path and, at the same time, re-inventing the world with its own distinctive brand of socialist reforms. China's grand strategy for its future modernization has been driven by its cultural heritage: dedication, hard work and an overriding desire to bring Hong Kong, Macao and Taiwan back into China. Now, it must overcome the political blunder of the Tian'anmen Square incident in 1989. A reunified and modernized China would be the next economic superpower after Japan, and China's efforts to achieve political reform will represent a major G-Force of the 21st-Century. Is this still possible?

Social Motivation

Before the Tian'anmen Square incident in Beijing, the mainland Chinese people have tended to be passive in nature, respecting the wishes of their elders to a degree that modern Westerners find astonishing. This behavioral respect for patriarchy was reinforced by Mao's repressive Cultural Revolution (1966-76) and by the collectivized poverty, widespread lack of education, and periodic purges by the autocratic one-party state.

Deng's economic reforms, albeit often frowned upon by his patriarchal peers, have led to the gradual emergence of a new civil society which finally gained confidence to reveal itself during the Tian'anmen demonstrations. These economic reforms are manifest in private family farming, widespread access to education, somewhat relaxed intellectual and cultural freedoms, extensive foreign travel and study, expanding domestic tourism, the flourishing of private enterprise, and the decentralization of decision-making throughout the state enterprise and political system. All have served to create large, informal, nation-wide networks of reform-minded people — networks essentially independent of Communist Party control. In addition, Deng himself has worked hard to formally remove the Party from the day-to-day affairs of the economy.

This new-found independence has led to new political aspirations in society. As a result, the majority of Chinese will no longer kow-tow to their elders or the Party and, as discussed later, political reform will become inevitable as new generations of Chinese come to power.

During China's recent phase of modernization, the mood of the people, from the most senior official to the lowest peasant, has been upbeat and positive. Their "can do" attitude was infectious and pervasive — and visible progress fed the optimism and captured the world's imagination. Their drive is a reflection of China's "this-worldliness." Their respect is for reason and reality and the concept that a person's value is only realized in relation to that of his fellows — a great consensus of collectivity in which the destiny of the individual is closely related to that of the society at large. This great strength of Chinese culture will continue to stand the country — and the world — in good stead if it continues to open up to the outside world.

The question facing China is how to create a modern culture, borrowing ideas from the West, and yet which is still Chinese. Chinese sociologist Zi

Zhong-Yun points out that the experience of Chinese learning as essential principle and Western learning as practical application has proven a failure; it must become Western learning as essential principle and Chinese learning as practical application. Western learning covers modern material civilization, modern methods of scientific management, including Marxism (which, of course, was also introduced from the West) and capitalism. This formula calls for the application of all foreign things in combination with specific Chinese conditions. Thus China is creating "Socialism with Chinese Characteristics," intending to reunify with capitalist Hong Kong, Macao and Taiwan under the rubric of "one country, two systems." Yet Chinese traditional culture can remain central while Western technology can be imported to develop economic power.

It has become fashionable — and I have done the same — to talk of China, Japan and other East Asian countries as Confucian societies. It is important to understand that Confucianism has changed over the past 2500-years, absorbing thought from international culture. Modern Chinese Confucianism still emphasizes education, hierarchical order in society — based on ethical, not religious, precepts — but it has become very forward looking. Although still espousing the paradoxical concept of "people's democratic dictatorship," China is struggling and experimenting with forms of pluralist democracy, which it calls political reform. The Chinese mind — and hence Chinese culture — has a unique ability not only to accept paradox but to combine differences and put them to a synergistic and constructive use. Thus, in achieving the goals of "one country, two systems," Deng Xiao-Ping proclaims that: "It doesn't matter whether the cat is black or white so long as it catches the mice." Though the introduction of Western technology and capital will invariably bring in more Western cultural influence, China is not afraid of Western technology. There is a wide-ranging awareness of the need to modernize the economy and an unhesitating fascination with Western innovations. In my experience, China and Japan are the most futuristic countries (techno-economically) in the world. China's plans are at least as far-reaching as Japan's, and its leading futurists and economic planners are, intellectually, about a decade ahead of those in North America and Western Europe. It was in central China, for example, where I was first challenged by the startling question, "What comes after the third wave?" (This led me to conceptualize the 6-Wave economy and to develop a preliminary model of the Planetary Information Economy (PIE), both of which now form part of China's economic planning.) In China, there are several thousand futurists in every sector of the economy, who are building scenarios of the country's long-term development, activity the likes of which does not exist even in Japan.

As well, thousands of young people are being sent to study in the West and are absorbing an understanding of the requirements of scientific and technological modernization and its management. At any one time, about 80,000 Chinese scholars and students are studying abroad, in Western market economies like Japan, the United States, Canada and West Germany, and in modern centrally planned economies like Hungary and East Germany. Every day, thousands more Chinese government officials, traders and technical experts scour the world for technology and knowledge. At the same time, thousands of Western, Third World and Eastern bloc scholars arrive daily in China to give lectures and seminars.

Coupled with the introduction of technical seminars from Western companies interested in doing business in China, this is bringing massive amounts of information into the country about modern approaches. China is like a giant sponge, soaking up information from around the world for use in its own way — and in the way most suitable to its modernization efforts. In the process, and coupled with major educational reforms, China is turning its 1.1-billion people from a liability into an economic asset of unprecedented global magnitude.

High-Tech Priorities

To meet the economic aspirations of its enormous population, China realizes that modernization depends on the very latest technologies and that as a nation it cannot forever depend on foreign technologies. In 1986, therefore, China published its first policy White Paper on science and technology development strategy. Referred to by officials as the White Book, it deals with the development of science and technology in China, policies and legislation, research and exploration, and the commercialization of technical achievements. The main chapter, "Development of High Technology," spells out China's plans in 10 priority high-tech fields: very large scale integrated circuits (VLSI) or super-chips, computers, computer software, telecommunications, biotechnology, new materials, aerospace, remote sensing, lasers, isotopes and radiation.

In a revised 1987 edition of the White Book, the priority was shifted slightly to a consolidated list of seven fields: biotechnology, energy technology, new materials, information, automation, space, and laser technology. In 1988, China announced a plan to speed the development of high technology and new technology industries to help the economic boom in their coastal areas, concentrating on those high-tech products with less investment and quick economic returns.

In computer technology, as of 1986, China had about 140 computer enterprises, with a total of 100,000 employees, including technicians, operators, systems analysts and software programmers. Chinese super-chip technology has reached a precision of 5-microns, 1000 products are at the international standard, and major plants are producing 3-inch-diameter circuits. By 1990, China will have 1-to-2- micron VLSI technology, and is already researching sub-micron technology. Chinese research institutes are spending large sums of money on futuristic projects, such as developing super-fast gallium arsenide chips, which are just starting to make inroads even in Western countries. More than 25 companies make silicon crystals for chips — triple the number of silicon suppliers in the United States. While China may need a decade to become cost efficient in chips, some companies are convinced that it can be competitive in other parts much sooner. Within five years, Xerox (China) plans to buy 70% of its components locally — everything but the key electronics elements — for its local production in China. In computer technology, an executive at Hewlett-Packard expects China to become as advanced as Taiwan or South Korea within five to ten years. Philips, of the Netherlands, has a joint-venture factory that will make 70-million chips a year, and Motorola (U.S.A.) is negotiating to co-produce VLSI chips in China in the early-1990s.

Striking achievements have also been made in ideogram (Chinese-character) processing; one laser system can process 60 characters per second, in seven to eight different typefaces, and high-speed information retrieval systems can process 1000 characters per second. So far, about 200,000 such systems have been installed, operating in both Chinese and English. To intensify its research ability, the country is planning to set up development centers for microelectronics, computers, program control switchboards and various electronic products such as computers that can "read" Chinese characters and understand the human voice.

Despite many software successes, China is lacking in advanced software, and projects are under way to develop industrial production software, system software, software packets and yet more advanced Chinese-character processing technology. China will soon have more than 100,000 software experts (versus only 10,000 in 1985). Its software technology has already reached the international level of the mid-1980s. By 1990, the output value of the software sector will comprise 25 to 33% of the whole computer industry.

China aims to become a world leader in software development. The Chinese way of thinking, which is quite different from that of the West, will aid in this drive. For example, the Western alphabet favors a chain of inferential thinking, the mark of left-brain logic and reason. Chinese writing, on the other hand, is pictorial and thereby invests each ideogram with both right-brain intuition and left-brain reason. Being whole-brained, the language is more suitable to advanced computer programming and the development of artificial intelligence.

For this and other reasons I believe that China will indeed become the world's leader in computer software development. A San Francisco company is already going to China, finding programmers and transferring them to the United States to work. Eventually, the company will try to send programming work to China for completion by Chinese programmers. When it comes to programming ability not even the Japanese can keep up with China. The giant firm Mitsui, seeking desktop-publishing software to package with its laser printers, found the Beijing Stone Group to be superior in both quality and price.

In biotechnology, although China stills lags behind the West, priority is assigned to the development of new biotech products that are urgently needed and that have high economic benefits, such as monoclonal antibodies, gene engineering vaccine, amino acid products, new enzyme preparations and single cell protein. Emphasis is also being placed on cultivating quality breeds of plants and animals by combining biotech and conventional breeding, through tissue culture and embryo transfer technology respectively. In particle physics, China has built its own electron-positron collider (which smashes atoms together at great speed to produce energy), allowing the country to create synchrontron radiation energy for wide application in computers, materials science, biotechnology, petrochemistry and aerospace.

In aerospace technology, China launched its first rudimentary satellite in 1970, and in 1984 an advanced telecommunications satellite was launched. The country has since launched more than 20 of its own satellites (which are used extensively for telecommunication and remote sensing activities). China has also become the third country, after the U.S. and the U.S.S.R., to launch recoverable satellites. During the slowdown of the U.S. space program between 1986 and 1988, China used its Long March 3 rocket to place two commercial satellites into geo-stationary orbit for American companies such as RCA. In addition, companies from 19 other countries have used China to launch satellites. China is also a partner in the Hong Kong-based AsiaSat consortium, which will launch a U.S.-built satellite on a Chinese rocket in 1990 to provide shared communications services to all of China and most of Asia.

With four launching bases already established, China is now talking openly about manned space flights, and trainee astronauts are already flying in space shuttle simulators. There are plans for a mini-shuttle; a space station feasibility study is complete; and an eight-booster version of the Long March rocket, which could place a small space station into orbit by 2005, is under development.

6-Wave Economic Modernization

Although its GNP is already the seventh-largest in the world, China is still a poor, 1st-Wave agrarian economy with annual GNP per capita ranging from $100 (for the poorest peasants) to $600 (for professionals) and averaging about $400 nationwide. Nevertheless, its average GNP is about 50% larger than India's. If recalculated in more realistic terms (that is, in terms of comparative purchasing power), it would be much higher because the cost of food is subsidized by the state and housing is provided virtually free. Living conditions are also much better than in most Third World countries. China's per-capita food availability of roughly 2600-calories per day is at least 10% above minimum nutritional requirements. Life expectancy is currently 70-years, which is ahead of about 20 developing nations that have a higher per-capita GNP.

China's economic potential, therefore, must not be underestimated. After all, Japan's per-capita GNP was only $188 in 1953, and China has made similarly remarkable progress since 1978. China's economy grew by a startling 7.5% in real terms in each year from 1978 to 1984. Growth in 1985 dramatically topped 19%, fell back to 7.4% in 1986, but reached 11% in 1987 and averaged 12% in

1988. While periodic inflation continues to occur, no other country has economically outmatched China since the reforms began in 1978. In 1988 *The Economist* magazine pointed out that if the growth rates of the world's main economies during the 1980s are maintained until 2030, China will then be the world's largest economy.

The Chinese have adopted a systems approach to development, and they see the economy and society (both domestically and internationally) as mutually interactive and dynamic. The resultant double-pronged approach is to develop the rural (agricultural) and coastal (Pacific Rim) economies first.

As a result of modernization efforts so far, workers in the 1st-Wave agricultural sector declined from 74% in 1978 to 61% in 1986. The reforms in agriculture have liberated the energies of 800-million Chinese in the countryside. In the eight years to 1986, rural incomes tripled (after inflation), and the stage is now set for their continued rapid annual growth. At the same time, 2nd-Wave manufacturing employment grew from 15% to 22%, and aggregate 2nd-Wave output places China among the world's top five producers in several industries: fifth in chemical fibers and metal cutting machine tools; fourth in steel and leather shoes; third in coal, sulfuric acid and nitrogen fertilizer; second in cement; and first in cotton cloth and television sets. China's 3rd-Wave service sector employment grew from 11% in 1978 to 17% in 1986, when about a quarter of its GNP came from this sector, almost as much as the 29% generated by agriculture. During the early part of the 21st-Century, China will become a modern 4th-Wave information-based society; the 5th-Wave tourism sector is already growing dramatically, with modern hotels springing up across the country.

Following a different economic development model than other Third World countries, however, modernization in China's agriculture sector has not been accompanied by a mass migration to the cities. Almost all developing countries have seen a mounting exodus of people from the countryside to a few metropolitan areas, resulting in sprawling slums, pollution, and an unbearable strain on utilities and services. China's development program focuses on generating rapid growth within the rural areas where the resources are. The nation is raising its economic performance "vertically" with minimum "horizontal" movement of people. Villagers are not rushing to urban centers. Instead, their villages are being urbanized with modern amenities and services and the development of local, small-scale enterprises. This rural modernization will be spurred further as technologies and wealth are spun off into the interior from the rapidly modernizing coastal regions.

The second prong of China's economic development strategy, to develop the coastal region, is driven by geo-political considerations. As mentioned earlier, an overwhelming driving force of the country is its own reunification: the reincorporation into China of Hong Kong (in 1997), Macao (1999) and ultimately Taiwan. (No agreement has yet been reached with Taiwan, but its old protector, the United States, recognizes that there is only one China, that

Taiwan is a province of China, and that the PRC government is the sole legitimate government.) To achieve reunification, based on Deng's concept of "black and white cats," China's economic model of "one country, two systems" seeks to accommodate the capitalist economies of these three territories.

To help demonstrate to the Chinese living in these territories the mainland's conviction to its new economic policies, China has strategically established a string of Special Economic Zones (SEZs) and "open cities" (a Gold Coast) along its entire Eastern coastline. As well as being designed to attract foreign investment and technology from the West, these cities are specifically located adjacent to the three territories in order to make the economic development process attractive to the overseas Chinese living there.

For example, in Fujian Province, Xiamen and other cities have been singled out for economic development. These are a demonstration to nearby Taiwan of China's ability to participate in international trade and to take advantage of technological advances. China-Taiwan trade (conducted unofficially via Hong Kong) grew by 60% in 1988 to $2.4-billion. China hopes that official trade with Taiwan may one day be conducted directly and to a greater extent by strong economic development in Fujian. Average per-capita income in the Province has more than doubled between 1979 and 1986, with total industrial and farm output set to quadruple during the decade to 1997. There are more than 140 enterprises with some $400-million of foreign investment in Fujian Province, most of it coming (via Hong Kong) from overseas Chinese in Taiwan.

Farther south, Guangdong Province borders on Hong Kong and Macao and so also has a key role in the "open door" and reunification policies. Three Special Economic Zones (SEZS) have been set up on the coast of the province. Between 1979 and 1986, the province signed 75,000 joint ventures and other agreements with overseas investors, attracting $12-billion, most of it from overseas Chinese in Hong Kong and Macao. One of these SEZs, Shenzhen, is a 300-square-kilometre (100-square-mile) area just across the Hong Kong border. Hong Kong, which is the seventeenth largest trading unit in the world, will return to the Chinese flag in 1997, when Britain's 99-year lease over the territory expires. Hong Kong is to be granted substantial autonomy, allowing it to keep its capitalist way of life for at least 50-years. To this end, the Shenzhen SEZ is fast becoming an economic middle ground, integrating more every day with the life of Hong Kong, so that the absorption of Hong Kong in 1997 will become relatively easy. The Zhuhai SEZ borders on Macao and is meeting with similar success.

Prior to the Tian'anmen incident of 1989, China thus made great strides in planning for the transfer of Hong Kong and Macao to Chinese sovereignty and in reducing tensions with the authorities in Taiwan. The sophistication with which the Chinese handled these thorny issues has been an important factor in maintaining confidence, prompting overseas Chinese to invest on the mainland. Indeed, China made large investments itself in Hong Kong companies and, the day after the 1987 stock market crash, it invested about $300-million to bail out shaky Hong Kong financial institutions as a demonstration of its support of Hong Kong's economic system. Tian'anmen shattered this confidence. Whether economic confidence can now be restored before 1997 depends on the extent of political reform in Beijing and the installation of the reformers to power well before 1997.

The effective settlement of the Hong Kong question by fully and unequivocally applying the concept of "one country, two systems" is essential to any hope of reunification with Taiwan. Taiwan has been offered reunification terms more favorable than those provided to Hong Kong. Taiwan will be a Special Administrative Region and will keep its social system and lifestyle unchanged. It may also continue its external economic and cultural exchanges, and foreign investment there will be protected. More liberal trade opportunities for Taiwanese business in China add to the pressure for Taiwan to put reunification ahead of ideology. Prior to 1989, the process of reconciliation between Taiwan and the mainland had begun with indirect trade, scientific exchanges and thousands of family journeys to native Chinese places from Taiwan.

Increasingly neglected by the United States, Taiwan's "orphan" status will not make its life easier in a protectionist world where managed trade and government-to-government deals on market access are gaining ground. While Taiwan has continued to stoutly resist China's entreaties to reunify, notwithstanding the Tian'anmen incident the momentum for reunification from the "ties that bind" amongst Chinese people are perhaps stronger than in any other culture. Three million mainland families have 13-million relatives in Taiwan (out of a 19-million total population) and Taiwanese tourists added an estimated $3-billion to China's foreign exchange coffers in 1988 alone.

Taiwan also needs China's resources. The island is faced with an acute shortage of land and there is a growing local environmental opposition to industrial and infrastructure projects. China is ready to provide oil, coal and other raw material at "domestic" prices, co-operate with Taiwan in developing East China Sea petroleum, expand duty-free imports from Taiwan, and give Taiwan businesses preferential access to factory sites and cheap labor pools on the mainland.

While the economic success of Chinese people in Southeast Asia is sometimes resented (in Malaysia, for example), that very success should leave no doubt that a unified China would modernize its economy and, with its huge resource base, economically outmatch not only the rest of East Asia (including Japan) but also the world.

Political Reforms

The absolute priority given to economic modernization and political reunification is reinforced, Tian'anmen again notwithstanding, by a widely recognized need for political reforms. As the 4-STEP process has proceeded, economic reforms have understandably affected the very foundation of central state power. The rural and enterprise-responsibility system has reduced the arbitrary power of the Communist Party and its agents while expanding the areas subject to individual decision and economic forces. In the political arena, therefore, Chinese leaders have been endeavoring to rationalize, legalize and institutionalize the structures of the state and the Party and to effectively separate the Party from day-to-day government and management of the economy.

In 1966, ignorant of and isolated from the world, the young "Red Guards" of Mao's closed China heeded his call for "Cultural Revolution," shouting hate slogans about all they were told to hate. In 1987 and again in 1989, fully aware of the world but ignorant of democracy, the next generation of Chinese youth took to the streets of its own initiative to throw the party's Orwellian slogans back in its face. The former "Red Guards" cheered them on. The hard-line patriarchy became the focus of the hate as the people's revolution came full circle. The young people, the intellectuals, and the reformers throughout the party bureaucracy and its related organizations (that is, throughout the entire economy) are the 4th-Wave revolutionaries of modern China. Essentially inspired by the reforms of Zhao Ziyang, Secretary General of the Communist Party until the Tian'anmen incident, they have long ago thrown out Mao's little red book of slogans in favor of Alvin Toffler's *The Third Wave* and its call for participatory democracy. These people are creating a new revolutionary paradigm for China in the 21st-Century.

The Tian'anmen incident highlights the competing socio-political visions of China's three adult generations: the old hard-line gerontocracy; the middle-aged reformers, and the young idealists.

The so called hard-liners are the out-of-touch gerontocracy of Chinese politics and social values. These old men are victims of Mao's closed-door China. But despite Deng's repeated attempts to remove them (and what he has called their "ossified thinking") from political influence, he has not only failed to do so but still relies on their support for his open-door economic reforms. Consequently, although most members of this group essentially do not hold any official posts, they form an old patriarchal, autocratic clique that still controls the country's politics. Living in the past, they are stubbornly but naively still fighting Mao's communist revolution. Hence, ideologically, they have now entirely lost the support of the masses — who are inspired by Deng's new revolution to get rich — and will not be able to govern effectively or for long. True, they currently have a tight grip on the military, and their nominee, Li Peng, is the Premier who imposed martial law in Beijing. They have outmanoeuvred Deng and mounted a "palace" *coup d'état*. But this can only be short-lived. The clique itself has an average age of 83 and is totally out-of-touch with global economic and political realities. Now hated by the masses, this regime has lost "heaven's mandate" to govern and is doomed by the ticking of the clock.

At the other extreme are thousands of student and intellectual radicals who wish to "democratize" China. However, except for a few dissident intellectuals such as Fang Lizhi, virtually all of this group do not even know how Western democracy functions. While half of China's population is under 30 years old and could possibly join some mass uprising, the vast majority of them are poorly educated and are too concerned with the struggle of daily life in the countryside. Along with their parents they care little about the pendulum of politics in the Forbidden City of Beijing which, it seems to them, has swung too and fro in power struggle after power struggle for centuries. Of course, the more ambitious young people have flocked to the coastal cities where relative economic affluence serves as a beacon which awakens political aspirations. There they campaign for freedom of speech, press and assembly. However, what they — and the outside world — do not realize is that Deng struck these freedoms out of the Chinese constitution in 1980, essentially in return for the old guard's political support of his economic reforms.

Deng himself is totally opposed to any form of Western democracy. While he has actively campaigned for political reforms since 1986, these would be along the lines instituted by Gorbachev in the Soviet Union, with multiple candidates but a one-party system. Deng maintains that further "liberalization" would have to be deferred for another 10 or 20 years, presumably until after the death of the old guard, including himself. In any event, it must be realized that the Chinese government at large, including the "reformers," believe in the supremacy of the Communist Party and will not adopt Western democracy. The repeated government campaigns throughout the 1980s against "bourgeois liberalization" make this clear. These campaigns are not directed at Westernization in general — which is welcomed in modernizing the economy — but at Western forms of democracy. According to Deng, Western democracy not only rejects socialism (from which China will not swerve) but causes political fractionalism which impedes concerted economic modernization.

Instead, Deng has advocated and implemented a large degree of restructuring in the political system. Apart from the old hard-liners at the top, government ministries and factories across China have been revitalized, from top to bottom, by the training and appointment of tens of thousands of reform-minded cadres in the 40-to-60-year age group. This politically centrist group represents the next revolution in Chinese political ideology. It is not yet strong enough at the central government level to dislodge the old guard, but the seeds of real political reform — 10 or 20 years ahead, as Deng says — have been sown. As the old generation dies off, this middle-aged group will gain in critical mass and finally find itself free to re-invent China's polity and society.

The reformers recognize what the oldsters and the youngsters do not — but what Marx and Lenin taught — that the old and socially obsolete regime is increasingly divided and afraid of the masses. This can only reinforce the legitimacy of the reform group which, in turn, should be able to unite the mass population behind its platform for change once it comes to power. Indeed, the masses are already on board. It is only a matter of time before the reformers gain their "mandate from heaven" to rule for the next generation — bringing meaningful political reform to China in the 21st-Century.

This has in large measure been accomplished at the provincial levels and below and, in theory, the Communist Party Congress in late-1987 accomplished the same goal at the central government level. Moreover, by mid-1988, the swing to liberalization was so strong that, despite intense pressure from hard-line leftists, *Red Flag*, the venerable theoretical journal of the Communist Party for 30-years, was closed down and replaced by *Seeking Truth* whose editorial mandate is to focus on economic reform and political democratization. As the Party's control over economic resources continues to weaken, the matters subject to political decision will decrease and the idealism in official ideology will diminish. In turn, this will reinforce economic reform and will make it essentially impossible to stop: once economic gains are realized, they will have to be protected politically.

China is also experimenting with increased levels of participation in the political process. While not yet nation-wide as in the Soviet Union, in selected towns and villages multiple local government candidates now stand for one position, with voting rights being extended to non-Party members. These experiments, started in 1985, are proving successful and are to be gradually expanded to other centers. China's political problem, of course, is a huge 800-million peasantry of which about half are still illiterate and most of the remainder have only recently gained access to education and would not yet constitute an intelligent voting population. Thus, while Hong Kong (which has had no elections under British colonial rule) may begin an electoral process under the agreement with China by 2012, and while Taiwan (which has had a one-party system since 1949) only allowed the formation of a second party in 1988, any nationwide move to democracy in China will not likely occur for at least a couple of decades.

In the interim, China will probably have to maintain the authoritarian system that has been in place under Deng's autocracy since 1978. However, by moving the Party out of the day-to-day running of the country, a system of political and economic dualism is modernizing the economy and protecting economic rights. This enlightened approach drove the economic success of South Korea, Singapore and Taiwan and has been meeting with similar success in China. Three or four decades hence, China's economic progress and reunification will no doubt result in distinct shifts towards full participatory democracy. This must occur if economic progress is to be sustained.

Finally, as discussed, China will re-invent communism into a form of "socialistic entrepreneurialism." Entrepreneurialism is being fostered to counteract bureaucracy. A 1987 article in the Chinese *Economic Daily* pointed out that the lack of entrepreneurs was slowing the progress from a centrally planned economy to a more market-oriented one. The article called for "large numbers of entrepreneurs, in the real sense of the word" to run thousands of enterprises across the country in place of government appointed enterprise leaders. The article attributed "low returns on investment, slow technological progress and the enterprises' lack of flexibility as all directly attributable to the practice of having government officials run enterprises." Government officials, the article flatly stated, are not entrepreneurs, and it concluded that the management of the enterprise must be separated from its ownership. This is now rapidly occurring.

China's next generation of reformist leaders feel that valuable time was wasted in the Mao era and are eager to get on with the task of restructuring the nation into a modern member of the world community. Internationally, they want to forge extensive economic ties with Japan, and to improve and stabilize its still basically adversarial relations with the U.S.S.R. China has thus tried to balance its slowly growing ties with the United States with improvements in diplomatic relations with the Soviet Union. At the same time, China is able to offset its growing economic relations and trade deficit with Japan through a rapid expansion of barter trade with the Soviet Union and its Eastern European neighbors. In this way, China reduces its vulnerability to (or its dependence upon) any single major power in the Pacific Rim. As well, it avoids being subordinate to (or allying itself with) any superpower. By these means, it may determine an autonomous or distinct role for itself.

If China sustains rapid economic growth over the next 25 to 30 years it will alter the global security relationship in the 21st-Century nearly as fundamentally as the emergence of the United States and the Soviet Union did in the 20th-Century. In the meantime, the Chinese strategy is to obtain trade and economic benefits from the Soviet bloc without sacrificing any political independence. As China continues to prosper, the gap between it and the U.S.S.R. will narrow significantly. For example, if China continues to grow by 8% per year through the 1990s, while Soviet growth averages 3%, China's economy will increase proportionately, from roughly one-sixth to one-third the size of the Soviet economy by the year 2000.

China's improving technological and economic capability is already encouraging Moscow to seek better relations with Beijing. For the time being, of course, the international setting permits a concentration upon economic development for all countries and Gorbachev has agreed to withdraw almost all its troops from the Chinese border. China can therefore enjoy a stable environment in East Asia for the foreseeable future.

Although the urge for reunification demonstrates that China is driven both by a sense of nationalism and a determination to become a major actor in world affairs, like Japan it intends to regain its former greatness through economic growth, based on the import of foreign technology and ideas, not on military strength or expansionism. After full reunification, by about 2020, China's per capita income will have risen to the standard of middle-income countries.

By then, it will also be increasingly obvious that the real strength of the ongoing Japanese success, economic as well as scientific, will be drawn increasingly from its links with China. As the next 57-year long-wave economic cycle matures in the 2040s, Japan will be a waning economy like the U.S. today. By

2049, the 100th-Anniversary of the founding of modern China by Mao, and the 70th-Anniversary of the launching of the modernization drive by Deng, China will have caught up all developed countries except Japan in terms of per capita income. It will be on the verge of becoming the unchallenged economic super-star of the latter half of the 21st-Century.

G-Force P-7
Third World Solidarity

"To those people in the huts and villages across the globe, struggling to break the bonds of mass misery, we pledge our best efforts to help them help themselves — for whatever period is required; not because the Communists are doing it, not because we want their votes, but because it is right."
— John F. Kennedy

Their future is our future. What happens in the scores of mega-cities and millions of villages across the world over the next few decades will determine the fate of us all. I have concluded that the Western "empire" is in techno-economic decline and that the 21st-Century belongs not to the U.S., Western Europe or even to Japan, but to China, which today is a developing country. Where does this leave the rest of the Third World?

Potential for Self-Reliance

The population dynamics of the planet are focussed on the Third World, where 80% of all people currently live, and where 90% will live in future. While this poses tremendous and varying problems, it also presents tremendous economic opportunities if the basic needs of this fast-growing population are to be met. Various forms of education and the transfer of technology and investment are the keys to enabling the vast populations of the planet to solve their own problems, no matter where they reside.

Beyond that, the only way to help backward countries — and hence the only way the advanced countries can enjoy an equitable share of the expanding global economic pie — is through understanding technology transfer, global wealth creation and its distribution. Businesspeople, economists and politicians are only just beginning to comprehend this. Companies around the world are turning more and more to the joint-venture transfer of production line technology, and this trend is expected to continue as they see the dazzling potentials of developing the Third World marketplace.

But this might not be enough. The vast majority of the developed countries still remain blind to their own enlightened self-interest. The Third World should remain skeptical that it can rely on the developed countries to wake up. After all, Kennedy's pledge of three decades ago has not been fulfilled. The Third World must, like China, try to forge its own pathway to economic self-sufficiency and political independence.

The first step to self-sufficiency and self-reliance is to get out of debt. While the Western countries are about to witness a "Mini-Depression," much of the Third World has been in a full-blown Depression throughout much of the 1980s, the result of unserviceable debts. Since 1982, in the hope that some miracle will transpire, the West has rescheduled $600-billion of debt into a mountain of $1.3-trillion. This endless dallying has trapped the Third World in backwardness and stalls global economic progress. The scenario is all too reminiscent of the 1930s. After about 1927, the capital outflow to the rest of the world from New York and London, then the two biggest lenders, began to dry up. This resulted in almost 80% of all outstanding loans to Latin America being in default by the mid-1930s.

The debt problems of developing countries in the late-1980s have similarly been magnified by a collapse in the flow of new loans. The world's investment capital has instead been going to finance the U.S. trade deficit and enhance the American standard of living, creating a fool's paradise in the West and a living hell in the debtor countries. As in the late-1920s and early-1930s, agriculture is depressed worldwide, causing increasing global disparities in income and wealth. As living standards drop in the agriculture-dependent Third World, the increasing concentration of income in the West (through another reverse capital flow from the Third World to New York) is only intensifying the crisis and will force many countries into debt default.

The coming "Mini-Depression" will make it almost impossible not to eliminate the global financial imbalances. The relative economic success of the Third World — and its geo-political allegiance — depends on whether and when the debts get written off. Ineffective debt-for-equity swaps and other schemes, or further delays in restructuring the international financial system, will result in severe social unrest, toppling many Third World governments in favor of socialist or dictatorial successors. This could set back global economic progress by 50-years. If the problem is solved quickly, we will all advance rapidly.

Pathway to Independence

To retain its hard-won political independence, however, the Third World must also achieve technological and economic self-sufficiency and political maturity.

The key to technological self-sufficiency is higher education and research capability. According to World Bank statistics on lower-middle-income Third World countries, the number of 20 to 24-year-olds enrolled in higher education rose from 3% of the population in 1960 to 10% by 1982, while for upper-middle-income countries the increase was from 4% to 14%. To put this in perspective, as recently as 1960 Japan had only 10% of the same age group enrolled in higher education. By 1982, therefore, all of these countries were only 22-years behind Japan in higher education. In 1989, it was estimated that the Third World was only 18-years behind the West.

On this basis, the Third World will have caught up in higher education by the year 2000. Moreover, despite an ongoing brain-drain to the West, there has been a shift towards science and engineering education in developing countries. In India, for example, where 9% of the 20-to-24-year-old group are in higher education, the pool of scientists and engineers has increased from about 190,000 in 1960 to 2.4-million in 1984 — exceeding the counts in both the United States and the Soviet Union. Clearly, the potential for new technology in the more advanced developing countries is high. Their main problem, as anywhere else, is how to make more effective use of the scientific and engineering skills they have and are creating — and how to quickly diffuse the technology throughout the economy.

Although the Third World is gaining increasing shares of global manufacturing output, the real key to economic self-sufficiency is revealed by new patterns of global trade. The traditional view that the Third World can export only products that are either labor- or resource-intensive is no longer valid because the developing countries are dramatically increasing their mutual trade. During the 1970s, the exports of developing countries grew faster than the exports of the rest of the world. Even in the 1980s, when the growth of Third World exports to the world marketplace declined, exports between developing countries continued to rise.

The United Nations Industrial Development Organization (UNIDO) believes that mutual trade among the developing countries will become even more of an engine of growth in the decades ahead (because of its comparative advantage over exports from the West), thereby increasing Third World incomes. UNIDO has forecast that the proportion of Third World imports supplied by the Third World itself will have risen from 25% in 1979 to 34% in 1990. By 2000, the Third World will be importing 52% of its own needs from other Third World countries (see Table 11). Once it becomes collectively more self-reliant, with the help of Western governments and corporations, the Third World will provide the necessary impetus for renewed expansion in the global economy at large.

Most of the Third World countries that have gained political independence during the last 40-years are in a process of political maturation. Most of the Third World, of course, is still a 1st-Wave society, and this is reflected in its "immature" political structure. Until after World War II, most Third World countries were colonies of Northern empires such as Britain, France, Spain, Portugal and the Netherlands. Rarely was any form of governance system left in place by the colonizers. There are now more than 160 independent nations, and, since gaining their political independence, they have been struggling to find ways

Table 11
Increasing Third-World Self-Reliance

(% of Imports from Third World)				
Selected Items	1970	1979	1990 (est.)	2000 (fcast.)
Food	27 %	30 %	41 %	50 %
Textiles	27	39	59	68
Clothing	35	54	72	83
Leather	18	32	57	70
Wood, etc.	43	52	68	82
Paper, etc.	10	16	30	43
Chemicals	7	11	21	31
Glass, etc.	18	22	33	42
Iron & Steel	1	13	22	33
Non-Ferrous Metal	27	36	43	54
Electrical Machinery	5	12	23	37
Scientific Equipt	5	12	26	39
All Manufacturing (avge.)	14 %	25 %	34 %	52 %

Source: UNIDO; forecast GEODEVCO

to govern themselves. And this has taken place during a period of unprecedented social change (especially population growth and urbanization), as well as rapid technological modernization, frequent economic turbulence and geopolitical change in the world at large. Inevitably, the Third World will experience continued political turbulence for some time.

The Soviet Union in particular is trying to exploit this turbulence by developing many Third World trade links with the hope of creating new political dependencies. Both superpowers have adopted a geo-strategic approach to foreign aid (see Fig. 26) in attempts to win allies in the Third World. The big worry is that this aid competition would serve Soviet interests, not those of the Third World or, ultimately, of global peace.

The Soviet Union and its allies used to refer to aid as a Western sweetener — part conscience money, part bribe — designed to oil the wheels of an exploitive North-South economic system. Now, the U.S. is retrenching its economic aid activities, and the Soviet Union is extending aid rapidly and geo-strategically. Moscow recognizes better than Washington the potential econom-ic and political gains to be made, especially if Washington continues to antagonise many in the Third World. Moscow learned during the cold war that aid conditional on political support was antagonistic. Egypt is a good example.

Most Soviet aid goes to build infrastructures, particularly in the energy and steel sectors, and to train technicians and engineers. Moscow's basic foreign pol-icy interest today is to have a full-blown presence in various regions and to court young states that are "traveling the capitalist road" (Argentina and Brazil, for instance) as well as the oil-producing nations of the Persian Gulf with their market-oriented economies and strong political ties with the West. This approach, endorsed at the 1985 Communist Party Congress, seeks to exploit the "contradictions" or conflicts of interest between capitalist-oriented Third World states and the United States (and other developed Western countries).

Fig. 26 Superpower Foreign Aid Competition

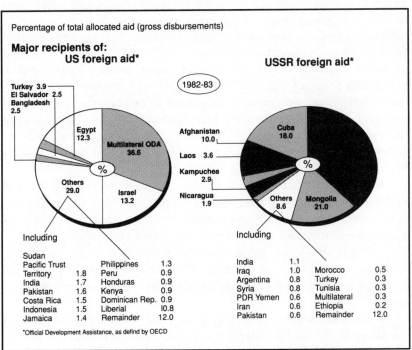

Percentage of total allocated aid (gross disbursements)

Major recipients of:

US foreign aid*

1982-83

USSR foreign aid*

Turkey 3.9
El Salvador 2.5
Bangladesh 2.5

Egypt 12.3
Multilateral ODA 36.6
%
Others 29.0
Israel 13.2

Afghanistan 10.0
Laos 3.6
Kampuchea 2.9
Nicaragua 1.9

Cuba 18.0
%
Others 8.6
Mongolia 21.0

Including

Sudan
Pacific Trust Territory 1.8
India 1.7
Pakistan 1.6
Costa Rica 1.5
Indonesia 1.5
Jamaica 1.4

Philippines 1.3
Peru 0.9
Honduras 0.9
Kenya 0.9
Dominican Rep. 0.9
Liberial 10.8
Remainder 12.0

Including

India 1.1
Iraq 1.0
Argentina 0.8
Syria 0.8
PDR Yemen 0.6
Iran 0.6
Pakistan 0.6

Morocco 0.5
Turkey 0.3
Tunisia 0.3
Multilateral 0.3
Ethiopia 0.2
Remainder 12.0

*Official Development Assistance, as defind by OECD

Sources:OECD and U.K.. Foreign and Commonwealth Office; reprinted with permission from *South* magazine (January 1987).

Third World Outlooks

To the extent that the Third World nations are able to develop their economies and forge links amongst themselves, they will enhance their political maturation process and increase their independence from their old imperial parents and from the two superpowers. While space does not permit an assessment of the prospects of 100+ nations, let me briefly review the specific outlook for two of the biggest (Brazil and India) and the general outlook for Latin America, Africa and the Middle East region.

Africa: Too Many Tribes

With a population of 600-million, the whole of Africa generates no more GNP than Canada's 27-million, and one-quarter of it comes from South Africa. With a population of 900-million expected by the year 2000, poor access to education, little or no modern technology, and an immature political system still driven by divisive tribal aspirations, Africa's deteriorating economy can only worsen, at least in the short term.

Tribal antagonisms still tear at the arbitrary borders drawn by colonial European mapmakers. Several hundred tribes inhabit Africa, each with its own territory. The war in Angola, for example, is caused solely by tribal conflict, antagonized by Cuban and South African interference. Indeed, the Republic of South Africa encourages tribalism (a form of divide and conquer) to ensure it is not overwhelmed by a combined black opposition, and so it keeps a grip on power. This policy, of course, is not sustainable in the modern world; its ultimate failure will cause the regime to be smashed by its foes as they aspire to genuine political maturity and participation. Though not in imminent danger of collapse, the undercurrents of revolution are growing and, in time, the South African government will crack. A military junta may first replace it, and a Marxist outcome is ultimately probable.

A huge debt problem, in proportion to GNP, also looms over all eastern and southern Africa, and the entire continent is a long way from the path to economic recovery and sustained growth. Most African countries have experienced a steady erosion in their already mediocre standard of living since the early-1970s; despite some improvement since 1985, real GNP per capita is now lower than a decade ago for most countries. Without a much slower population growth, whatever economic progress is made in national income growth will be useless.

While much Western aid has been poured into Africa, ever since the 1960s the Soviet Union has increasingly established a durable African presence by undertaking major agricultural and other modernization projects in countries such as Morocco, Yemen, Angola, Libya, Sudan and Madagascar. Marxism-Leninism has taken root, and there are now more than a dozen African states that espouse Marxism or some related form of scientific socialism. The Soviets claim that socialist-oriented countries now account for more than a quarter of

Africa's total population. Most of the other countries have military regimes. Only three African countries (Senegal, Botswana and Mauritius) allow their people to choose their leaders. There would therefore seem to be little to stop the African continent from further economic decline and a steady entrenchment of socialism, with most countries falling into the Soviet camp in the next two or three decades.

But it does not have to turn out that way. Caught up in perennial crisis since Sudan and Ghana initiated the wave of political independence in 1957, few nations adopt a long-term perspective in Africa. Recognizing the need to broaden the policy agenda beyond its current stalemate, the Nairobi-based African Academy of Sciences is sponsoring an R&D policy study called Africa 2057. While preliminary results forecast a ninefold increase in agricultural production, population will have topped 2-billion, and per-capita GNP will reach only $3,800 by 2057. While I think this is much too pessimistic an outlook, on this basis a prosperous future for Africans is at least 100-years away.

Middle East: Sovietized Islam

Moscow has mastered the "Muslim Card," not Washington. That card will continue to be played as the Soviet Union continues with its goal to control the Middle East. Gorbachev's 1989 withdrawal from Afghanistan is part of a strategy designed to shape the political environment more favorable to a continued Soviet presence. Even with the complete Soviet military evacuation, about 5000 Soviet advisers remain in Afghanistan to support the Soviet-backed government, and since 1979 about 75,000 Afghan children have been indoctrinated into Marxism in the Soviet Union.

Afghanistan is also economically tied to Moscow, with all of its energy coming from the Soviet Union and about 75% of its exports going to the Soviets — most of which cannot be diverted elsewhere because they are produced by joint-Soviet ventures. Another Soviet venture generates 80% of the electricity in Afghanistan. In late-1988, when the Soviet deputy foreign minister also took on the post of Ambassador to Afghanistan, he immediately announced a $600-million donation to the U.N. Aid Fund (half its budget) to be used in guerrilla-held areas. One aim is to build solid relations with the guerrilla leadership. There is thus no abandonment of the Soviet goal of imperial domination. Rather, the key objective is to insulate the Afghan resistance from external sources of supply, and the principal Soviet target is Pakistan.

The Soviets are trying to take Pakistan out of the war, to make it vulnerable to political influence. The target audience is a Pakistani public and government increasingly weary of the social and economic burden of hosting 3-million Afghan refugees. The Soviet Union has also supported separatist in the arid province of Baluchistan, which covers 40% of Pakistan's territory but has only 5% of its people. In 1985, the then-leader of the Afghan regime called for the "reunification" of the ethnic Pushtuns and Baluchis in Pakistan "with their brethren" in Afghanistan, arguing that this "sacred land" had been "left in the hands of the British colonists and their inheritors." Baluchistan gets huge sums of Western aid, primarily because its tribesmen threaten, unless bribed, to turn to the Russians.

Gorbachev thus helped to increase Pakistan public support for 1988 election winner, Benazir Bhutto, who wants to reach a quick agreement for repatriation of the Afghan refugees. To accomplish this, however, Bhutto will be increasingly dependent on Baluchistan and Moscow. Yet, only weeks after the election, Baluchistan's chief minister dissolved the local assembly to call a fresh provincial election aimed at weakening Bhutto — and hence Pakistan's chances of political maturity.

Similar tense situations exist in Iran and Turkey, where there are another 2-million Afghan refugees. Since the Khomeini takeover in Iran, Moscow has signed numerous economic accords with Iran, and Soviet-Iranian trade more than tripled between 1979 and 1987. Throughout the north of Iran, the Soviets have been building infrastructures to expedite trade and Soviet traffic — and military invasion if necessary. A direct Soviet rail link to the Indian Ocean now goes through Iran, and an Iranian gas pipeline has been converted to carry oil from the Persian Gulf to Baku in the U.S.S.R. Soviet influence has also spilled over into NATO's vulnerable southern flank, where both Greece and Turkey are now on much better terms with Moscow than with Washington. One of the main growth areas of Soviet foreign trade since 1987 has been with Turkey, through the opening of yet another Soviet gas pipeline. Russia also controls Syria, where joint Soviet enterprises account for all the phosphorous-processing and the production and refining of oil. And Syria controls war-torn Lebanon.

The biggest prize of all is Saudi Arabia. Moscow has frequently honored Saudi requests to cut back on oil production so that OPEC can still function. The recent establishment of full diplomatic ties now enables Moscow to benefit from the kingdom's influence on Muslims all over the world, because of its guardianship of Islam's most important holy places. In turn, this moderates the attitude of Soviet Muslim populations towards the Soviet regime itself. Saudi Arabia itself, despite U.S. support, is an extremely fragile, monarchic, dictatorial regime, which, despite its riches, has a majority of its people living in poverty. The "Mini-Depression" will cause world oil prices to plunge, which could topple the Saudi regime within a decade. Thereafter, I believe the Soviet Union will control all Middle Eastern oil territory — and the Persian Gulf and the Red Sea.

India: Too Many Divisions

India's 800-million people face massive obstacles to progress. India is now the Third World's sixth-biggest borrower ($52-billion in 1989) and could owe $70-billion by 1995, according to the World Bank. While average per-capita GNP is less than $300, India is not all poor. Unlike China, the country has a growing urbanized middle class of about 200-million with an average annual income of close to $2,000. This represents a large consumer market with distinct potential. The country's labor rates average only 25-cents-per-hour in manufacturing, offering an attraction to foreign multinationals. India is also a rapidly industrializing and, with a major high-tech center in Bangalore focussing on computers, software, biotechnology and aerospace, is trying to modernize.

Nevertheless, the world's largest parliamentary "democracy" is under severe pressure to change. The country is in the grip of a series of intensifying polarizations — between rich and poor, government and people, majority community and minorities, and between the urban and rural masses. Unlike homogenized China, perhaps there are too many Indias: six main religions, 16 languages (comprising at least 1400 dialects) and innumerable castes.

Menacing racial divisions threaten India with a real break-up. One of these could occur in the southern state of Tamil Nadu, where a political error over Sri Lanka could send Tamil Nadu towards secession. The worst problem is in Punjab, India's richest state, which borders on both the Hindu heartland and the still-distrusted Pakistan. Sikh terrorists have killed several thousand people in recent years in the Punjab, and violence has escalated every year since 1984, when Indira Gandhi was assassinated by her own Sikh bodyguards. Ethnic parties govern several states — among them Assam, Andhra Pradesh and Tamil Nadu — and others are gaining ground almost everywhere in India.

Unfortunately, the ruling class has become attached to the status quo, and any change that would significantly shift power and resources to the deprived 80% was bitterly and often successfully resisted by the Gandhi dynasty. Consequently, the Gandhi-run Congress Party fell from favor. Nehru built India's dominant Congress Party around secularism (which in India means religious tolerance) and the championship of "the poor and down-trodden." Indira Gandhi made the Congress Party a tired monster, full of people hanging onto power for power's sake. Under her son, Rajiv, the Congress Party (which has not held an internal election of officials since 1973) is now even more firmly in the control of the corrupt, the self-seekers and the time-servers.

Rajiv Gandhi does not embody any concept of the Indianness of his mother or grandfather and is widely considered the inept heir to an elite dynasty, not one of the masses. The Congress Party thus has lost touch with the people who first put it in power, and it has inevitably lost their trust. In addition, a new generation of voters — 50-million became eligible in 1989 with the lowering of the voting age from 21 to 18 — are unlikely to act out of traditional loyalty to the Gandhi name. As it is, the party has won only one state election since 1983 and now rules only seven of the country's 15 larger states. Opposition governments in eastern and southern India have been routinely dismissed from office by Gandhi proclamations.

The next round of changes are likely to come through struggle from the bottom rather than from dynamic leadership, which seems totally lacking. The struggles of the coming decades will be increasingly violent and bloody, and there may be little to stop India from becoming a socialist country. The opposition parties, led by the pro-Moscow Communist Party of India, have formed a coalition, which made a remarkably strong showing at the 1989 election.

Communists, in coalitions, already head the governments of two states, Kerala and West Bengal, and the Chief Minister of West Bengal is a prominent long-time communist.

Captured in the emotive word *swadeshi* ("from our own hand"), India already has small-s socialism in its heart and blood. This has been encouraged by four decades of links with Moscow, usually siding with the Soviets against the West and playing a lead role (spurred by Moscow) in the so-called non-aligned (but leftist) nations movement.

Moscow is also arming India to the teeth and the country now spends at least 20% of its budget on defense, again blocking its socio-economic progress. India now has a nuclear-powered Soviet submarine fitted with missiles, several long-range Soviet bombers and MiG jets and is getting two Soviet nuclear reactors. Thousands of Soviet military advisers are in India, and Moscow's fleet regularly visits key Indian ports. Moscow is also pushing India to export arms to other Third World countries and to play a strong-arm role, as in Sri Lanka and the Maldive Islands, throughout the subcontinent. In early-1989, India signed a deal to lease a fleet of civilian airliners — complete with flight crews — from Moscow for its domestic and international traffic, thereby giving Soviet pilots free access to all airspace now entered by Air India. The planes are equipped with remote sensing and surveillance technology.

Rewarded by Gorbachev with the Order of Lenin, Gandhi made the same mistake China once made: he brought India much too close to the Soviet Union, condemning India to economic backwardness and inexorably leading the country into Soviet hands. It does not have to be so. But for the star of India to rise again, its new leaders must initiate political reforms, dilute their dependence on Moscow and push ahead with industrial modernization programs.

Latin America: Too Many Debts

Latin America is perhaps the biggest conundrum of the Third World. Will it become capitalist and join its northern neighbors? Or will it drift further away from the maturing American economy and into the arms of the other super-power? Or can it go its own way and prosper like Southeast Asia? The potential is there. South and Central America plus the Caribbean has a combined population of about 400-million and an overall average GNP per capita of about $2,000, thanks to rapid economic growth throughout the region from the early-1960s to the late-1970s.

The 1980s, however, brought a prolonged economic crisis. Burdened by a foreign debt of more than $420-billion, Latin American household incomes have fallen every year since 1979. On the other hand, political instability during the early-1960s and pervasive authoritarianism through the 1970s were replaced by a strong regional turn towards democratic politics in the 1980s. The key issue in the 1990s and beyond is whether truly democratic politics can be consolidated throughout Latin America despite the economic crisis, which will prevail and become more severe until the debt problem is adequately dealt with.

The short-term outlook is not promising. Even in Venezuela, which, along with Costa Rica, is the most stable democracy in Latin America, falling standards of living have created antagonisms among former allies and have weakened public trust. The Costa Rican peace plan for Central America fell on deaf ears in the Reagan White House, and Washington has blissfully ignored the debt crisis so that more than one-third of Latin America's export earnings are devoted to interest payments. During the first six years of the 1980s, Latin America transferred approximately $150-billion (in loan service payments) to the industrialized countries, an amount equal to almost 5% of the region's total product for that period, sharply reducing the funds available for investment, which has fallen by 25% since 1980.

This does not bode well for democratic capitalism. Throughout Latin America and the Caribbean, labor and social unrest is growing. In countries as diverse as Argentina, Brazil, Mexico, Jamaica, Ecuador, Barbados, Peru, Bolivia and the Dominican Republic, incumbent governments have been defeated or severely weakened since the mid-1980s, largely because of prevailing economic conditions. Latin leaders cannot continue telling people to tighten their belts without providing some hope that relief is in sight. Domestic pressures are mounting to stop all payments on the debt, and defaults are becoming more politically appealing.

Prompting internal social unrest, the debt is unifying the Latin American nations against the West, particularly the United States, to whom most of the money is owed. Oblivious, Washington has been confident that Latin America's largest economies will revive after a strong dose of further austerity and the institution of Reaganomic capitalism. For decades America has blithely assumed that Latin "Americans" are grateful to the United States and has expected inter-American relations to become more cordial as a result.

In reality, many Latin Americans are dissatisfied and apprehensive and see no end to the region's economic distress or little evidence that the United States will help relieve it. Latin Americans increasingly find Washington an obstacle to progressive reform — they hear the United States preaching economic discipline abroad, but see it running up unprecedented budget deficits at home. As economic and social conditions further deteriorate in Latin America, insurgent movements will become more appealing. A further prolonged depression will push some countries in an extreme populist direction.

Latin Americans also fear that Washington's intense focus on combating communism in Central America will not only damage that region but will also have a polarizing effect throughout the hemisphere. Contra funding is annoying to most Latin Americans. As long as the underlying U.S. aim in Central America is simply to remove the Sandinistas from Nicaragua, diplomatic initiatives to forge regional peace have little or no chance of success. The security and stability of the western hemisphere, including that of the U.S., is automatically much more threatened by the economic and social problems in Mexico and South America than by the civil wars in Central America. The fundamental threats are overwhelming debt, poverty, inequality and unemployment, which, if not addressed, lead to guerrilla movements and civil wars.

Of course, in the absence of corrective U.S. action, the Soviets will support insurgency. They wish to develop long-term, state-to-state relations and economic ties. Latin American countries are often willing to reciprocate in order to gain greater room to maneuver against the United States, and Moscow is currently defeating Washington for the hearts and minds of Latin Americans by providing economic assistance. Anxious to assert their independence from the U.S. and move beyond the rigid anti-communism of the conservative military regimes they replaced, the new governments are looking for new options.

Moscow has been quick to accommodate them. In 1987, the Soviet foreign minister became the first Soviet leader to visit South America, with major stops in Argentina, Brazil, Uruguay, Cuba and Mexico. Several Latin American leaders have made return trips to Moscow. The Soviet's long-time proxy in the hemisphere, Cuba, recently resumed diplomatic ties with Uruguay, Ecuador, Bolivia and Brazil, and Moscow has diplomatic relations with all countries except Paraguay and Chile. While the Soviets have little other than political support to offer the Latin nations in the way of relief from their burdensome debt, they are expanding trade links and initiating projects such as power plants in exchange for coffee, sugar, cotton and other commodities. Gorbachev is intent on cultivating strong ties in anticipation that American capitalism will not cure Latin America's problems and, hence, socialism will seem more attractive — as almost occurred in Mexico in 1988.

As it strives to be the master of its own fate, in 1988 Latin America agreed to convoke a special conference on debt "in defense of the region's right to development" and to ultimately "integrate their countries, economically and politically, as soon as possible" to avoid social and political turmoil. In 1988, the "Club of Rio" debtors' cartel (also called the Group of Eight) — which had been informal since 1984 — was formed by Argentina, Brazil, Colombia, Chile, Peru, Uruguay, Venezuela and Mexico to create a "solidarity" position on the debt issue.

The hard fact is that U.S. policy is not effectively addressing this crucial issue and is thus imperiling the future economic prosperity of all the Americas. As Latin American markets have contracted, since 1979 the United States has lost $30-billion in exports per year — $300-billion in the last decade — compounding the U.S. trade deficit and eliminating about 300,000 American jobs. The Latin American crisis also compounds the problems of illegal immigration and illicit drugs. This mutual self-destruction can be reversed if Washington bites the bullet on the debt and assumes a greater sensitivity in helping its Latin neighbors achieve their own economic and political aspirations. Once this occurs, Latin America will resume its path to prosperity — and political independence.

Brazil: Not So Latin

Brazil has the best prospects. Unlike its "Latin" neighbors, it does not get so caught up in the heavy emotions of everyday life and takes a longer view. The only Portuguese-speaking state in Latin America, Brazil is also the most populous (150-million) and is the only real regional power (GNP of $300 billion). Moreover, it has considerable ambitions. Until the debt crisis, it was the fastest-growing national economy in the world and was widely expected to become a major power by the 21st-Century. It should still be viewed with this prospect in mind.

With its strengths and abiding desire to become a modern post-industrial nation, Brazil will push ahead once the debt is dealt with. Notwithstanding the uproar over the burning of the Amazon forest to clear land, Brazil is the Third World's major source of lumber and paper. The country also produces more manufactured goods than Hong Kong, South Korea, Singapore and Taiwan combined. By the year 2000, Brazil could be the world's third-largest auto manufacturer and the fifth-largest aircraft manufacturer; it has also launched its own computer industry in order to become a major microcomputer producer.

Brazil is also getting into the space age — with Soviet help. The Soviets in 1987 "offered" (that is, requested) to launch Soviet rockets in Brazil, and a Brazilian communication satellite will be launched by a Soviet rocket in 1990. It will be assembled in Brazil, by Soviet and Brazilian personnel, sent aloft from Brazil's new launch site in Rio Grande do Norte state. If such collaboration continues, the U.S.S.R. will gain a southern hemisphere space center — and, potentially, another major and prosperous Latin American ally.

Politically, Brazil's infant democracy is staggering under a $120-billion foreign debt, and the (Marxist) Workers' Party gained landslide victories and captured the mayors' seats in 36 cities in late-1988. The party is a strong contender in future federal elections.

Third World Solidarity

Despite its economic and political challenges, the Third World seems determined to not allow itself to be dominated by what it sees as U.S. imperialism. Unwittingly or not, however, the Third World is in danger of being successfully seduced by the Soviet Union into marriages of convenience. Of course, there tends to be a loss of economic sovereignty everywhere in the world as national economies become more subject to foreign economic trends and growing trade links that make national policies less effective. Collectively, however, the growing intradependence of the Third World does create a growing independence from the superpowers and the developed countries. This emerging Third World solidarity, as it continues to gather momentum, is the best hope that the developing world will be able to shake off both the Soviet Union and the United States — as with its colonizers before — and thereby allow its economies to prosper.

A major solidarity step was the 1987 creation of the South Commission to study the whole question of economic co-operation between Third World countries, to recommend needed institutions, and to formulate a course of action most likely to produce beneficial results in dealing with the developed Northern countries. An independent body, with members drawn from the Third World under the chairmanship of Julius Nyerere, president of Tanzania, the South Commission plans to "move the idea of South-South co-operation from concept to concrete implementation within a long-term economic development framework." Such integration through economic and geo-political co-operation, around issues such as debt, strengthens the hand of the Third World in trade and finance negotiations with the North. It also takes the Third World further along the path to political maturity in its constituent states.

The concept of Third World trade self-reliance took concrete shape in 1988 with the Global System of Trade Preferences agreement, which gives the Third World its own preferential trading system. Almost 50 countries signed the agreement, including all the major Third World economies. The South Commission has also issued a statement on the Third World's debt crisis. It calls for a reversing of the current net transfer of money from the South to the North, and for structural reforms to the world financial system. Indeed, the Third World has initiated plans for the creation of its own central bank (to be called the South Bank) whereby members could opt out of the currently North-dominated IMF/World Bank framework, unless this can be restructured to meet the needs of all countries.

These initiatives continue to change the old patterns of dominance and disadvantage. Despite the stubbornness of the North in refusing to change world economic institutions and the patterns of trade, the South increasingly finds itself able to assert its independence. Indeed, to avoid dominance by one or other of the two superpowers, the South must continue to forge its own intradependence. As Canadian international corporate diplomat Maurice Strong observes: "It is only a question of time before the South will find the leadership it needs to challenge the industrialized North on a collective basis."

The desperate economic conditions of the Third World are rapidly producing a sense of solidarity. The Third World does have levers of power at its disposal: these countries take 40% of U.S. exports of manufactured goods and 45% from Japan. Increasingly, the South realizes that they will only prosper as independent nations if they organize themselves and fight. Support is growing for the idea that the Third World will never move out of its trough unless it imitates the tactics of Mahatma Gandhi and collectively refuses to co-operate with the industrialized world until it is given a better deal. The North must realize that the only way to resuscitate its economies is to liberate the potential buying power of the Third World marketplace so that those economies can flourish.

Every G-Force has a bearing on the fate of the vast majority of people in developing countries, far removed from our daily attention. Our response to the challenge of Third World self-sufficiency will establish whether the 900-million of what the World Bank calls "the absolute poor" falls, or increases even further. If their problems are not addressed, then, except for Mexico, China and the developing parts of East Asia, most of the rest of the Third World will drift. Under such a threat to our common global heritage, traditional definitions crumble: the Third and other Worlds must be merged into One World. The fate of the Third World cannot be separated from that of the rest of humanity. The task is to bring the mutual interest and common impulses of humankind together. We must enable Third World political systems to become more participatory and governable so that the 4-STEP process of economic development can flourish in an environment of global peaceful co-existence.

G-Force P-8

Informed "Partocracy"

"Any people anywhere, being inclined and having the power, have the right to rise up, and shake off the existing government, and form a new one that suits them better. This is a most valuable, a most sacred right — a right, which we hope and believe, is to liberate the world."
— *Abraham Lincoln*

The quest for global freedom is shaking politics at its roots. In an information society, people are increasingly less satisfied with mere material goods. Their chief desire is for self-realization and personal growth, and for participation in decision-making and the management of the economic, social and political system. The political system in the Third World will continue to mature towards more participatory forms of government, and all true kingdoms and dictatorial regimes must ultimately reform. The political system in the Western information society must also change to participatory democracy ("partocracy") if it is to survive. Much of this G-Force is driven by the baby boom generation of knowledge workers — a new political class increasingly demanding a political platform for post-industrial policies. With millions of home computers at their disposal, citizens of the future will be able to understand both the nature and the implications of the problems arising on any issue. The spread of computers will change politics in capitalist and communist societies alike, educating voters about the issues and providing for more intelligent electoral outcomes and increased electoral participation.

Beyond Kingdoms & Dictatorship

In countries with one-party or dictatorial systems, of course, the problem of public participation is very real. China currently has a great advantage over the Soviet Union: the economic reforms instituted to date have gained widespread support, and decentralized decision-making has motivated managers and workers by slowly but gradually democratizing the management of the economy and the working environment. The overwhelming majority of China's population has a direct stake in the continuation of these reforms, and the workers and peasants would be relatively happy with a paternalistic, benevolent dictatorship. While millions of Chinese clearly feel that political reforms should move the country towards a Western democratic system, this could bring chaos to a generally backward, peasant society if instituted too soon. In any event, the present regime is dogmatically opposed to the multi-party "balance of powers" political system of the West because it would pull economic decision-making in different directions and slow down economic progress. Although growing numbers of Chinese will seek political participation in the future, in the interim the Communist Party is experimenting with voting for multiple candidates in selected towns and cities. In the Soviet Union, political reforms are progressing more rapidly, but politics is still a matter of imposition by the Party on the citizenry that *perestroika* is to their benefit, even though economic results are slow in coming. Such one-party "democratic dictatorships" are, of course, no more democratic or participatory than the monarchies they replaced. Political reform must occur sooner or later.

All forms of dictatorship ultimately fall. With the evolution of statehood in the West, we witnessed the continuing decline of the kingdom. Some ruling monarchies still exist, as in Jordon or Saudi Arabia, and a few self-anointed elites, such as Gandhi in India, still rule as if by the divine right of kings by means of authoritarian or dynastic regimes. The major autocratic regimes now at greatest risk include those of Iraq, Saudi Arabia, Nigeria, South Africa, India, Mexico, Chile, Burma, and South Korea. Unless greater public participation and democracy is restored to these regimes, they will fall like those of the Shah (Iran), Marcos (Philippines), Duvalier (Haiti) and Zia (Pakistan).

Once the masses feel that the "ruler" cannot carry out his obligations — as they perceive them to be — a new political belief system that offers a new order spreads like wildfire. Political scientist and sociologist Sebastian de Grazia observed that this often occurs during economic depression, when expectations are so frustrated that a sense of confusion results. Then comes a loss of orientation, a sense of personal alienation amid disintegrating social structures. Once a majority of the adult population feels this, faith in the ruling entity dissolves and belief in the entire political system falls apart. In time, a solidarity movement starts and an ideology for the whole political community begins to emerge. This brings harmonic integration of the society with clear-cut values and direction, defining the role of each member of the community. With the "Mini-Depression" about to sink the Third World even further economically, we can expect many such transitions.

The transition will be to either a totalitarian regime or a democratic alternative. This process is neither complex nor novel, yet how it unfolds determines the political outcome, affects global balances of power and moves the world's governing systems closer to global and participatory ones. The period of unrest prior to the fall of an authoritarian regime can last 10-years or longer and will be marked by a series of events that creates serious internal tension. For example, the dictator may pursue outright Westernization of social and political policies, or persecute anyone opposed to his policies; the nation may suffer a severe financial crisis; there may be an abrupt political crackdown; there probably will be rising political patronage throughout the entire period; political arrests will be made; able technocrats will be dismissed; elections will be rigged; and funds will be misappropriated. We have all seen elements of this in the Philippines under Marcos, Iran under the Shah, Pakistan under Zia, and it occurs today in Mexico, Chile, India, Burma and South Korea.

If an autocrat continues to maintain tight control over the basic instruments of power, such as the military and the economy, he may survive despite the unrest. If the situation continues to deteriorate, however, the dictator will eventually lose his legitimacy with those who really control the instruments of power (the military officers or the middle class) and the country will go into a second period of steep decline. Once legitimacy with these key elements of power has been lost, the dictator's demise is almost inevitable. A military crack-down might be effective during earlier stages, but when large coalitions form against him and the military's reliability is in question, violent repression generally results in an even more tumultuous transition.

In such a revolution, in which most institutions of the old society collapse along with the autocrat, the transition generally is violent. A revolutionary leadership that is ruthless and single-minded, as in Iran, will eventually take over. If the transition takes place within an institutional setting inherited from the old society, there is likely to be a more stable outcome. New political leaders will emerge to run the revolutionary government, and elements of the former military leadership will either share power or acquiesce to civilian leadership, as occurred in the Philippines when Aquino replaced Marcos. The new leadership is usually much more pragmatic than ideological.

Another type of transition, of course, is revolution by *coup d'état*, where the military, as the dominant institution, offers the only possibility of political change. Coups and countercoups will occur until a dominant figure appears. Finally, a dictator might depart the scene through managed stages where he sees the need for a peaceful transition of government and where he plans for it through a process of gradual liberalization. As recent history has shown, except perhaps in Spain, this initiative hardly ever occurs.

Whatever the scenario, the type of system that emerges from such a revolution depends on factors such as: the prior existence of a democratic tradition or a supportive role model; the institutional foundation for the development of democracy; and the orientation and capabilities of the new leadership. Where these factors have co-existed, democracy has tended to prevail after a revolution. On the other hand, where the dictator did not allow opposition parties to exist, where the middle class was small, or where religious and military institutions held extremist rather than centrist views, transitions in countries formerly ruled by dynasties do not have a good chance of yielding democracies.

These scenarios will continue to play themselves out on the world stage as development proceeds across the six waves of socio-economic progress.

Socio-Economic Aspirations for Political Reform

In the mass-production-oriented 2nd-Wave industrial era, material satisfaction reduced the demand for participation in politics. In the 4th-Wave information society, where the demand for self-fulfillment becomes the motivational force, the process of satisfying social demands finds culmination in the production and utilization of information, the selection of action and the attainment of set goals. People's desires change direction as objectives are attained; their demand for participation in decision-making and the management of the economic, social and political system becomes stronger. The political system in the information society must change to partocracy if it is to survive.

The more advanced and educated they are, the more people want to participate in making decisions that affect them, and not just elect decision-makers. At the same time, at least in the West, there is a rising demand for political accountability; people want another lever (other than voting) over their political leaders. This is reflected in political activism. People used to identify on the basis of religion and occupation but they now have multiple identities and loyalties. With the rise of special interest groups and federations of different issues movements, formerly inclusive organizations, such as political parties and trade unions, are less effective in meeting this need. With the move to self-reliant values, and with increased emphasis on independence, there is a trend away from dependence, bureaucratization, regulation, and government control of any kind. Political manipulation of the justice system is under attack — witness the 1987 hearings to find a politically representative and publicly acceptable appointee to the U.S. Supreme Court, or the 1989 march in support of its 1973 pro-abortion decision.

Instead, there is a movement towards organization based on self-government and decentralization. Although centralized bureaucracy is not about to disappear, its growing limitations are clear. Since the French Revolution, generations of social theorists have been predicting an inexorable march towards an ever more powerful, liberty-destroying, centralized nation state. They have been proven wrong. We are witness to the devolution of political power within both capitalist and communist nation states.

Much of this is driven by the worldwide social movement of the baby boom generation, which increasingly demands a political platform of post-industrial policies. From California to China, there is an emphasis away from large-scale economics to entrepreneurialism, from sunset 1st- and 2nd-Wave industries to sunrise 3rd- and 4th-Wave industries, from investment in infrastructure to investment in human capital through education, from confrontation to co-operation, from self-sufficiency to global interdependence, from nationalism towards globalism.

In short, this new generation of voters — in Western countries and elsewhere — is looking for a new generation of leaders that cares more about solving problems than debating party ideology. Party politics is being superseded by issue politics, and the major political issue today is between the keepers of the old order, who want to maintain the status quo, and those wanting a new, more participatory society.

Knowledge workers, intellectuals and students are the major instigators of these social dynamics. The 4th-Wave Information Age is based on the production and distribution of knowledge. As the principal activity of our time, the knowledge-creation process is also the governing principle of organization structure, and knowledge itself is the chief source of power. The creators of this knowledge are the growing millions of intellectuals, scientists and knowledge workers of all kinds — some 40% of the work force already in North America and Japan. This group or class of workers includes scientists, teachers, academics, students (learning *is* work) and educational administrators, journalists and other media professionals, social workers, psychologists, baby boom lawyers and doctors, computer programmers, entrepreneurs, city planners, bankers, stockbrokers, financiers, institutional executives, civil servants and government bureaucrats. They all make their living from knowledge and ideas, often using computer technology.

The noted economist Joseph Schumpeter believed this burgeoning 4th-Wave knowledge class to be hostile to capitalism because of their critical or adversarial nature and because available jobs do not satisfy their aspirations. He also believed their powers of articulation and their ability to coalesce ideas into group points of view would enable them to determine the terms of public debate and ultimately to replace capitalism with socialism. The Chinese intellectual on the other hand wants to replace communism with socialism or outright capitalism. Neither group will succeed because none of the three ideologies still exists in pure form, nor are they restorable in the Information Age. Instead, we will get a form of socialistic entrepreneurialism and a new set of socio-economic ethics.

The recognition sought by knowledge workers in the West is largely denied to them. Crass commercial activity and productivity still yield only traditional capitalistic rewards. Fourth-Wave workers are critical of the old bourgeois society, shunning the traditional 2nd-Wave identities offered by church, workplace or trade union, or neighborhood or family. Instead, a sense of community is achieved through shared interests in global issues — say, disarmament, environmentalism, feminism and social justice. Their concerns are with global spirit, multiculturalism, global village and global family, reinforced by their identification with universal rather than in-group values. Traditional capitalism provides no common purpose or coherent theory of distributive justice; religion offers no reason. Politically, participatory democracy is the only vehicle for the self-actualization of their neo-socialistic desires.

Irving Kristol, a devout neo-conservative, believes that this new knowledge class has "the power to shape our civilization." This power stems from their access to strategic occupations and strategic knowledge, their politically significant skills and resources, and the lack of an effective opposition to their viewpoints. Their power manifests itself in stressing non-materialistic satisfactions, government social programs, and hostility to military spending. Knowledge workers believe that the state should determine the distribution of resources, but that this need not involve state ownership or equality of condition. Their social policy ideals tend to range from neo-socialist to neo-liberal, while in economic policy they range from neo-liberal to neo-conservative.

As mentioned, these wide-ranging political tendencies have essentially destroyed the standard ideological notion of party politics. There are still many die-hard conservatives and liberals, but their parties now exist in name only. It is the party of the day that most effectively tackles the issues of the day, that garners most public support. Today those issues may be socialist, tomorrow they may be conservative. Knowledge workers have already exercised immense political power by forcing political parties to address popular issues such as ecology and disarmament, regardless of political stripe. Their dissatisfaction with representative democracy will, sooner rather than later, bring participatory democracy fully to the fore.

Technological Move to Real-Time Global Democracy

In the past, technical difficulties made it impossible for large numbers of people to participate in policy-making at any level of government. Today, the communications revolution is changing traditional political processes and is forcing us to devise new political theories. Democracy is not dead, but some of our ways of practicing it are obsolete. Communication satellites and home computers are fast creating an environment where citizens of the future will be able to participate not merely once but repeatedly, enabling them to comprehend more deeply, from many angles and from a long-term perspective, both the nature and the implications of the problems arising on any issue.

Personal Computers

Between 1979 and 1988, the number of computers in North American homes grew from zero to more than 15-million. Every year, 25-million personal computers are produced worldwide, and about 40% of them end up in homes. The 1990s will see another explosion in home computer use; by the year 2000, 100-million PCs could be in home operation. Each successive computer generation will be more advanced, easier to use and more powerful in many senses.

PCs "empower" their users to create, manipulate, store, receive and transmit information and knowledge, thereby providing independence from traditional media. Computerized access to electronic news media brings a greater volume of information, at a faster rate, to consumers who have greater ability to control, understand and analyze its messages. Personal computers can provide people with power over their governments — to monitor the activities of government and politicians and to tap into the world's many databases that affect government decisions.

Satellite Dishes

The proliferation of satellites is also transforming politics and governments. In medieval Europe, most people knew little about ideas circulating in the world beyond what their village priest told them. In more recent times, Europe did not learn of Abraham Lincoln's assassination until three weeks later. John F. Kennedy's sad demise sent the whole world into stunned silence within an hour.

Today, the whole world is becoming a satellite dish, where everything that is knowable is known instantly and collectively. Nothing can be hidden. The state can try to control television, as it does in many countries, but it can only regulate signals that come from within its borders. Satellite transmission does not recognize such antiquated barriers. Signals sent to small in-home satellite dishes (that by the year 2000 will be no larger than a dinner plate and as easy to hide as a book) cannot be jammed except at an inestimably huge cost. Repressive governments will fall as opposition candidates, who perhaps never have a say on their own countries' television, are interviewed abroad — as happened in the 1988 Mexican presidential campaign — and then beamed home to the local voters. Similarly, if the South African government banned the film *Cry Freedom* in the morning, global broadcasters would compete to show it in the afternoon.

News Media

No longer is a political event limited by the distances voices can be heard. Nor is a politician limited by the distance that can be traveled on a horse, by train, or even a plane in a single day. Political perceptions are not delayed by the time necessary to transport the news. News travels instantaneously. Government perception of public reaction no longer depends on the upward flow from the grassroots constituent through to the elected politician. The new emerging political order *is* the communications infrastructure. Political and communications systems are now two sides of the same coin. Political influence, as defined by the limits of the communications system, is now instantaneous, and the governing system is too cumbersome to keep up.

Political orders are now communications orders, and the political party that cannot communicate cannot govern. Imagery and the 15-second commercial-like quote or "sound bite" are what count: the news issues of the day transcend the party politics of it all. As Marshall McLuhan forecast, whatever is "hot" gets the most play. In this environment, the media severely foreshortens the horizon of government to the crisis of the present — or to yesterday's "news." Like politicians, the media needs to focus much more on the long term.

At the same time, future democratic processes do not have to be hampered by the present one-way nature of mass communications. While fireside chats by political leaders are valuable, 3rd-Wave politicians had to be "actors" if they were to maintain their image of credibility. An actor in the White House was inevitable, and we have become spectators (not participants) in the drama of the government of our affairs.

While the character of the system has changed, we have been increasingly excluded from it. For example, voters at large do not choose their representatives; they are chosen by close friends who nominate them for election. If citizens voted for the candidate of their hearts, there would be a wide scattering of votes. In reality, the choice of each voter is limited to a very narrow field of candidates who are championed by groups, committees and organized minorities. Majority decisions could be called an electoral farce. Once elected, the representative tends to forget the constituents (until the next election) and joins an oligarchical party that suffocates every basic democratic principle. The masses essentially never rule. And, whereas the news media is destroying the antiquated political process by better informing (if only briefly) the citizenry about the issues, it has not helped to put a more participative system in place by educating the electorate about issues.

Electronic Voting

This trend to trivialized politics can be changed. Because of increased news coverage and access to information, the vast majority of citizens are overwhelmed with information and do not understand the political issues. During the 1988 American presidential primaries, an extensive study by the University of Utah found that most Americans who were eligible to vote could not name more than four of the twelve candidates, nor the position of those candidates on any more than three issues.

In actual elections, of course, only 40% of eligible American voters even bother to register to vote, and only half of those actually vote. (By comparison, voter turnout in other Western countries, in their last elections, was: Belgium 95%, Australia 94%, Italy 89%, Denmark 86%, West Germany 84%, Israel 79%, U.K. 75%, Japan 71%, Canada 69%, France 65%.) Because they feel disenfranchised, Americans do not bother to understand the issues or to get to know the candidates from whom they are forced to select a winner.

The more uninformed electors are, the more poorly are they represented. Indeed, the University of Utah study found that less than 1% of the electorate felt equipped to vote intelligently. Those who still vote do so according to party, name recognition, personal appearance, or on the basis of the sex, race or religion of the candidate. Voting is thus haphazard and mindless.

Clearly, this is no way to govern a town, city, province, nation — or the world. If we are to have candidate representation, then at least we must know the issues and the positions of all candidates on these issues. In short, we must make it possible for all citizens to vote intelligently. Whereas apathy, passivity and spectator-like noninvolvement invite a leader's abuse of power, intelligent constituents should produce intelligent leaders.

The University of Utah studied what might constitute intelligent political voting and how computer programs might be used to enhance the process. A computer voting model, which is individualized to the needs and values of the average voter, was tested in the 1986 mid-term electoral race in Utah, using all candidates in the state's capital district. Through extensive interviews, a panel of experts evaluated the candidates on 60 of the most important issues. On voting day, voters were asked to write down for whom they had voted (so they would remember the names of the candidates they had selected). After the election, these voters completed a questionnaire, which ascertained their position on and the importance they attached to each of the 60 issues. The computer compared this information with the views of the candidates, who were then ranked by how well they represented the values of the voter on each issue. This computer analysis was presented to each voter, along with another questionnaire which asked them how this evaluation, had they received it before the election, might have caused them to vote differently.

The results confirmed that the voters had not voted intelligently in the election. Indeed, only 15% said they would vote the same way again. Of the 85% who would have voted differently, 23% would have changed their vote in two of the nine electoral races, 46% would have voted differently in three races, and 16% would have changed their vote in four of the nine electoral contests. In other words, the voting intelligence of the public can be dramatically raised with an inexpensive piece of computer software.

We might expect political candidates as well as special-interest groups to start providing customized versions of such software to enlighten voters. In turn, as computerized voting is seen to be effective, the major parties will find it necessary to communicate their real position to the electorate. Minority parties will also start to receive equal voter consideration. It has also been shown that the use of simple "yes-no" programs, which enable electors to vote from home (as occurs in The Woodlands, Texas), increases electoral participation from 50% to almost 90%. With such electronic voting systems, intelligent voting by everyone can become a reality. Political power will then spread to a wider base.

That still leaves us with nonrepresentation by candidates who are forced on us by elites. There are, however, a variety of electoral processes that must become more widespread so that we can all express our own opinions on the major issues. The use of public opinion polls (fully published) by political parties, referenda, ballots, and so on, will eventually lead to one-issue electronic voting, and ultimately to total real-time electronic voting in elections from our armchairs at home — with instant results nationwide — in a two-way interactive communications environment. Government policy would then reflect public opinion, which would not change whimsically as it often does today, but would evolve gradually as public knowledge grew.

While despotic governments could use such systems to fix electoral outcomes (as in Mexico in 1988), computers can also be used to overcome the same problem. During the heavily contested 1986 Philippine election between then-president Marcos and Corazon Aquino, an independent poll-watcher's group used computer disks encoded with original voting results as evidence of the tampering by the Marcos regime.

Finally, these trends will increasingly lead us to question governmental bodies originally designed to facilitate citizen involvement. During the next 60-years, parliaments will either disappear or justify their existence on some other show biz grounds, just like the ruling monarchs did.

With the worldwide spread of education, information/knowledge, and information technologies, the aspirations of the masses to decide their own fate is growing in intensity. Over the duration of the 4th-Wave society (1990-2050), this G-Force will gradually transform political processes in the West into a true "partocracy" of real-time electronic participation of/for/by the people early in the 21st-Century. Politics also will increasingly be democratized in maturing communist and Third World societies and all dictatorial and one-party systems will ultimately disappear as the 4th-Wave information revolution spreads.

G-Force P-9
Globalized Governance

"The whole international system is in a state of crisis, and the cohesions —
political, economic, social and otherwise — that have held it together are
coming unstuck at an alarming rate."
— *Soedjatmoko, Rector,*
U.N. University, Tokyo

The planet is not being governed. Overwhelmed by the social, technological, economic and geo-political G-Forces at work, the lack of a global government system is exacerbating the problems which such a system could solve. The vacuum is causing us to miss the huge opportunities to foster global welfare. Despite all I've written, without global political integration — with full participation by nation states and citizens at every level — the quality of life will deteriorate worldwide, probably resulting in a catastrophic global war.

The nation state is now ineffective in managing the global village. As the world shrinks, nationalism is the juvenile delinquency of a maturing global civilization. The individual nation state — even acting in consort with a few others — is increasingly powerless to manage not only international issues but even its own affairs. This can readily be seen in economics and finance, energy, food and in any other major geo-system. In these geo-systems, it is essential that the nation state give up its authority and sovereignty to a higher global level of governance.

The problem, of course, is that no adequate global governing system exists. The United Nations, once ahead of its time, is now distinctly behind the times. What was conceived as a "league of nations" is not in league with the future; it is fragmented against the G-Forces of change and made impotent by the superpower veto. Future global governance demands a powerful corporate nucleus and a planetwide network of participatory cellular units designed to harmonize with the G-Forces it must govern. Such globalization is inevitable. Indeed, it is the final step in the 4-STEP process of reinventing the world.

Global Economic Integration

Throughout the industrialized nations of the West in the 1980s, there has evolved a growing urgency for new policies to strengthen national economies and improve competitiveness. When relying on trade policies to improve competitiveness, governments are essentially attacking the symptoms of rapid change without addressing the causes. If every nation acts to limit imports and boost exports, the ultimate result will be global economic contraction. In reality, trading activity is evolving from the national to the global level, and protectionism is beside the point. Ironically, the new foreign-owned plants in the United States, for example, are relatively more able to withstand intensified competition because of their state-of-the-art production technologies. Such technological innovation cannot be stopped by protectionism or a revival of economic nationalism. Policy-making is also being overrun by the pace of scientific change. For example, new material sciences make it possible to meet a need by creating a new material, making it atom by atom. It is no longer necessary to dig materials out of the ground to make products.

Similarly, accelerating advances in computer and telecommunications technology provide enormous economies of scale in supplying services and transferring technology across natural boundaries. Geographic distance is eliminated in a real-time world. As China has learned, and as Gorbachev has acknowledged, a relatively rigid, centrally managed economy has great difficulty keeping pace. In this environment, even government-to-government negotiations on specific issues, particularly those aimed at official management of trade flows (whether bilateral or multilateral through GATT), become increasingly irrelevant. Explicit economic nationalism is more difficult for governments to practice, and the ability of any single nation to control trade or the transfer of technology will inevitably diminish over time. A degree of sovereignty will have to be yielded in order to obtain greater multilateral co-operation.

Even the global system of multinational corporations is changing. We are leaving behind the era where one country was able to exert a primary influence over each multinational corporation. These companies are now slipping away from home country control. Their economic web is constantly rewoven to match international trading realignments. We are now entering an era of binational, trinational and regional economic systems that will likely prevail for a couple of decades. In this environment, multinational corporations must be regulated multilaterally. The public and private sectors will also have to co-operate in leading the way to post-industrialism in such an environment.

In the end, rather than being a competitive factor, money will be the greatest motivator for political integration. One of the most powerful forces for geostrategic integration has always been economics. The most familiar integrated organizations today are common markets, like the EEC or COMECON, in which member states consolidate all or part of their economic activities. The very function of the common market is to raise economic potential through policy co-ordination, by eliminating barriers to trade, and implementing a single economic policy whereby everyone can benefit.

Such economic co-ordination tends to be followed by social integration or the transforming of national preferences into a loyalty to the larger political community to which the individual nation state then belongs. This is now occurring in Western Europe with a slowly emerging sense of "Europeanness," which the EEC hopes to firmly establish with the final elimination of all trade barriers and the creation of a common European currency by 1992. At the same time, a Western European parliament has been in place for several years and is an increasingly trans-European governance system where all West Europeans vote and where transnational political decisions are growing in importance.

As boundary lines fade and countries gravitate economically and politically from one orbit to another, a parallel series of economic trading blocs is emerging. As the global economy disintegrates during the "Mini-Depression," this process of economic trading integration will be reinforced. International economic conditions will become more difficult, and trade offensives of debtor nations will increase as they find themselves more restricted in Western markets

Despite more frequent consultations, trade frictions between Western countries will increase, and the international financial system will become more unstable as a result of the need to continually restructure unserviceable debts. International trade will contract. Nations and companies will be forced to structure even more complex barter transactions than before, to be able to secure a supply of essential materials; markets for internationally traded consumer goods will be seriously dampened. In some cases, this will lead to food riots, urban unrest, and the virtual shut-down of industrial sectors that run out of markets or raw materials. Political change will ripple around the world, sometimes violently.

Ultimately, the governments that survive the short-term economic and political disruptions of the early-1990s will reorient their national economic structures towards greater self-sufficiency and closer ties with the members of their emerging preferential trading blocs. Like the EEC, in desperate anticipation of this coming global trade contraction and subsequent political realignment, the U.S. in 1988 signed free trade agreements with Israel and Canada, and is discussing a new one with Mexico.

Several other economic trading arrangements exist in the communist bloc and the Third World. And they are all integrating further. In mid-1988, the 10-member COMECON bloc (U.S.S.R. and its Eastern European satellite states) decided to create a fully integrated market and approved the collective concept of an "international socialist division of labor" for the years 1991 to 2005. The Contadora Group of eight Latin American nations also agreed in 1988 that "Latin American integration in economics and politics must be achieved as soon as possible." In the Third World at large, 48 countries agreed in 1988 to form the Global System of Trade Preferences (GSTP) among themselves, ignoring neoclassical economic advice from the West — and from institutions like GATT, controlled by the West.

During the late-1990s, the international environment will continue to be dominated by the North American, West European, COMECON, and Japanese preferential trading blocs. Each trading bloc will contain a complementary balance of industrial capacity, raw materials and scientific expertise. Unaffiliated nations that are rich in raw materials will be eagerly sought by the various trading blocs. China, Latin America and most of the Third World nations will not yet be strongly affiliated with any of the principal trading blocs — although Japan is assiduously trying to capture China into its economic orbit. Japan has also recognized that the relative decline in U.S. economic power is gradually rendering the existing GATT system obsolete. In the Pacific, in addition to the ASEAN group, Australia and New Zealand will form a free trade area by 1990, likely followed by a single currency, a common labor market, a single legal system and, ultimately, by political union. In a move to foster greater economic cooperation in the Pacific, Japan is spearheading the creation of the Pacific Economic Co-operation Conference (PECC) as a trading bloc of all Pacific nations, including North and South America.

During the first decade of the 21st-Century, four main trading blocs in the world will continue to evolve. One will be North America (U.S., Canada, Mexico) and some of its major trading partners: Central America, the Caribbean, Israel and possibly Saudi Arabia. The biggest and fastest-growing trading group will be in the South Pacific and will comprise Japan, China, ASEAN, Australia and New Zealand. The Soviet bloc plus India and some other major Third World countries will constitute another bloc. The EEC will try (but fail) to expand ties with resource-rich former African colonies but will increasingly trade with Eastern Europe. As we move beyond the year 2000, the EEC will merge with the COMECON bloc in a unified Europe. The common markets in Africa, the Middle East and Latin America will continue to evolve in and through their GSTP group as the major trading bloc of the South, although many of these Third World countries could eventually be aligned with the Soviet Union.

The continuation of these separate trading relationships well into the 21st-Century, however, is not probable, even though the leaders of most countries involved continue to speak today as if it is. They simply do not recognize any fundamental long-term flaws in their structure. Each of these blocs is, by nature, protectionist. Continued economic prosperity depends on ever-expanding global trade. Consequently, regional blocs can only be preludes to the formation of a single global trading market. As we move into the second and third decades of the 21st-Century, tariffs and trade barriers between countries tied to the major political groupings will evaporate. Free trade within the blocs will further encourage and facilitate today's trend towards "global product mandating," where multinational corporations assign responsibility to local subsidiaries for the design, development and global marketing of selected products. In the 21st-Century, multinationals will become even more global than today and must be able to trade freely across blocs. In short, trading blocs must also become global.

Such lifting of bloc protectionism is to be expected as the world economy booms during the 21st-Century. Freer trade will encourage yet more global industrial innovation, new investment and economic modernization. This will have a favorable long-term effect on real incomes, growth and employment in all countries worldwide. The continued liberalization of world trade has been a major source of global prosperity since the 19th-Century. Exports of manufactured goods from the developing countries have grown rapidly since World War II and these countries as a group have continually increased their access to world markets. If world trade is allowed to become more intertwined, these countries will grow and prosper further and a global economic trading system will eventually evolve.

The realities of and the benefits accruing from global interdependence will, as with "Europeanness" in Europe, foster a feeling of "globalness" in the world at large. Through the integration of our economies, and the creation of a governing system able to manage the global economic modernization process, we will create a model for global political government. The EEC already serves as a good model. Its parliament will gradually gain more legislative power over the transnational affairs of its sovereign members.

Multi-Polarity Transcends Nationhood

The nation state itself is becoming ineffective in world affairs. Its situation is like the monarchy in England at the time of the American Revolution. In London, the members of the court — and of parliament — took it for granted that power still resided in the king. However, underneath the monarchic system, the "new world" patriots in America were looking for a new kind of power based on freedom and self-government. So it is with the individual nation state in the "new world" as we enter the 21st-Century. The modern world cannot be governed from 160 scattered capitals, or even by a small Western clique of nations, and the global citizenry knows it.

The basic driving force for global integration is a human one. Prerequisites for global social assimilation are mutual tolerance (if not embrace) of cultures, a commonality of foreign policy goals, and generally cordial contacts of governments and respective nationals. Integration of the global economy is also bringing expectations of mutual benefits. Competition is giving way to co-operation, eliminating more differences and bringing about greater understanding between different values and beliefs. As well as the desire to establish economic links, historic cultural ties are a powerful force for political integration — witness the moves for the reunification of China (with Hong Kong, Macao and ultimately Taiwan), North and South Korea, and East and West Germany. This latter step will eventually bring about the total integration of all of Europe.

Every traveler, every global businessperson and every international politician is aware of the evolving multi-polarity. Much that happens across international boundaries is far removed from issues of national sovereignty and intergovernmental negotiations. Many of the questions that we have to decide, then, are matters that concern all humanity — global issues that know no national boundaries, and the settlement of which directly affects the lives of all persons. Mass social and, hence, political attitudes are thus being nurtured around various global issues. In the shrinking global village we are increasingly seeing a sharing of common values, especially among educated people, on such subjects as pollution and disarmament. With an increasing movement towards a "global community consciousness" (to use Japan's words), nationalistic attitudes are beginning to recede.

We must also remember that international transactions occur on a people-to-people basis, even when between two governments or foreign corporations. Such contacts also contribute to the quality of co-existence, either directly (by improving individual perceptions and tolerances) or indirectly (by affecting wider inter-governmental relations). In this way, increasing private contact is bringing about global contact and stability. It promotes changes in attitudes, perceptions and tolerance, and enlightens outlooks among peoples. This evolving international pluralism is taking national governments out of the spotlight in international transactions.

As well, whereas mass industrialization brought about mass anxiety and a crisis of individual identity in Western society, exacerbated by World War II and several major wars since, the new post-industrial implosion of society is bringing about the reverse effect on a transnational basis. Individual responsibility within a global context is returning. The necessary transfer of loyalty from nation state to global community is occurring. People are beginning to see the benefits of a global family.

In the evolving multi-polar world, the prospects for peace and participatory global governance are much brighter. The two superpowers are trying to govern the world, but they account for only 10% of humanity, and none of us is represented, not even the majority viewpoint in their own populations. Once we have three major powers of more-or-less equal strength, the power of the first two is automatically reduced by one-third. With four powers, the strength of each of the first two would be halved; with five powers it would be reduced by 60%, and with six powers it would be only one-third of its original strength (see Figs. 27 and 28). In short, we will soon have the opportunity to reduce the combined global power of the two major protagonists to only a third of their present level — closer to their 10% share of population.

Such multi-polarity forces a more realistic worldview on the major players, cutting them down to size, forcing them to forge alliances and to collaborate. Moreover, in such a world there will be no superpowers and no veto power. Consensus will have to be achieved. That will force the creation of various global

Fig. 27   Incipient Global Multi-Polarity (1965-90)

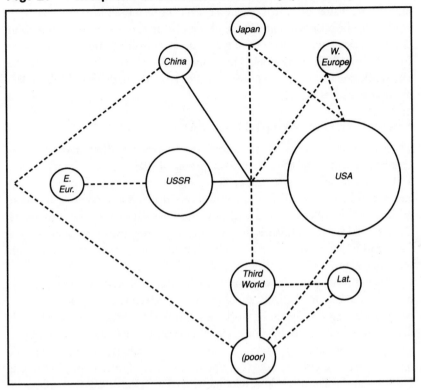

Fig. 28   Global Multi-Polarity by 2000

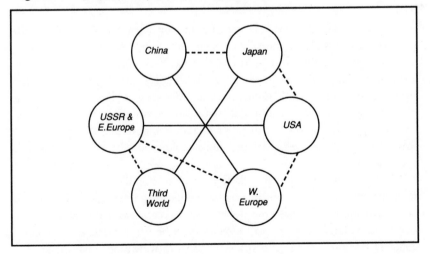

Sources: Adapted from Walter S. Jones, *The Logic of International Relations*, 6th Edition, pp.310-11;
Copyright 1988 by Walter S. Jones. Reprinted by permission of Scott, Foresman and Company

frameworks through which to forge a consensus. Global governance will no longer be a matter of heated debate or arrogant dismissal; it must be actively worked for because without it none of the players can participate. Those who don't participate will be left out of global decision-making; they will be barred from the future. To veto global governance is to condemn yourself — to the same exclusion that such veto power has affected others in the past. Multi-polarity turns the tables entirely.

State-Centric World Disorder

The present arrangement of international institutions is a reflection of the state-centered world, with the multi-polar group of major powers at its center. Today's world political system may be represented by a series of concentric circles (see Fig. 29) in which the superpowers are the largest in power and closest to the center in influence. In this system, the superpower has greater influence on world affairs (an influence that is increasingly negative) than international organizations, such as the U.N., which wield minimum influence even though they are the most central to the future of world affairs.

Even if — with the rise of Japan and China, and the relative waning of U.S. power — the U.S. and U.S.S.R. should become more equal in such a multi-polar world, to attempt to govern the world through an elite of such nation states will not be an effective mechanism for global governance, and social development will not be optimized. In addition, of course, this multi-polar structure could revert to one of bipolarity between superpower blocs. For example, if Western Europe and the Third World (excluding China) drift into the Soviet sphere of influence, the others would be forced to form a counterbalancing group. Multi-polarity therefore yields only fragmented nationalism and global nongovernance.

Of course, the fundamental concept of the sovereign state — that is, a territorial entity that is constitutionally independent and hence eligible for membership in international society — is one that has been positively welcomed by societal groups and elites in the Third World. The number of nations has increased from only 51 in 1945 to more than 160 today, and they maintain a jealous attitude towards their nation state status. At the same time, the Third World countries are starting to think that, in a currently ungoverned world, each state may have to fend for itself, such as in unilateral decisions by Peru or Venezuela about debt payments.

Increasingly, nation states must find a way to stop the anarchy of a multitude of disjointed, even conflicting national policies and strategies. The planet is now ungovernable. To make the global system governable, and to learn how to govern it, national policies and strategies must be harmonized and become a coherent body of policies and strategies of worldwide scope and impact. For this to happen, national politics must acquire a new dimension so as to flow naturally into, and form part of, global politics.

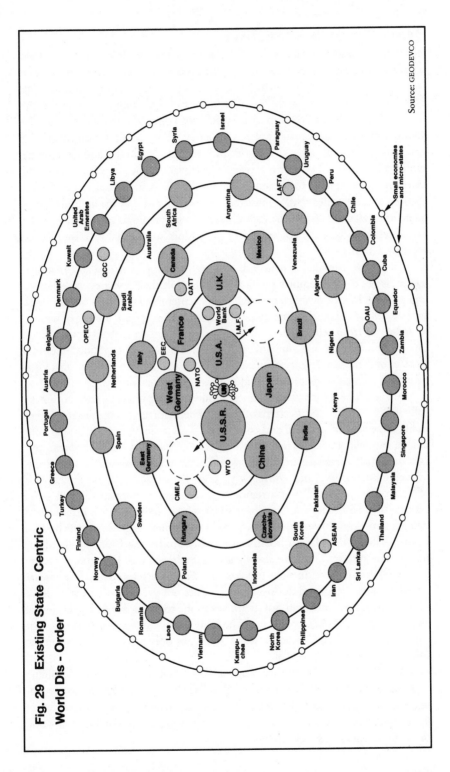

Fig. 29 Existing State - Centric
World Dis - Order

Source: GEODEVCO

Move Towards Globalism

It is impossible to prescribe an ideal world that would satisfy everyone's criteria of perfection, but the peoples of the world do share a common future. The future offers a new arena in which the world's peoples can find reconciliation. Nations that stand adamantly opposed today can find common ground in the future; there is room and opportunity for everyone. World solidarity on the vital questions of human survival is not merely a lofty ideal, it is an overriding necessity. People all over the world, in both the developed and developing world, are concerned with major issues of the planet. The peoples of the world increasingly recognize, for example, the futility of basing national security on theories and doctrines that, if implemented, would result in the annihilation of all nation states. The era of the nation state has clearly run its course and yet the world seems to lack the collective will or wisdom to marshal its resources for effective action.

Of course, convincing nation states to relinquish power to a supernational system is not easy. It requires political actors to shift their loyalties, expectations and political focus towards a new and larger center. National societies are made from the bonds of patriotism, loyalty, historic mythology and a sense of national difference from other nations. But now we are forging global bonds, a sense of common heritage and similarities. And while political integration requires a transfer of some sovereignty over external policy to common international institutions, it does not require any relinquishment of internal policy.

As mentioned, such political integration is starting to occur rather dramatically in Western Europe. Citizens of the EEC countries now vote at four levels of politics: local, state, national and continental. This promotes transnational links among national political systems. As well, the EEC itself has established a significant diplomatic presence around the world in several capitals and has representatives who observe and confer with several international organizations. Western Europe is still not a regional governance system in the full sense because the constituent countries have so far refused to merge their political and defense structures. Nevertheless, the present economic integration is the basis of future political integration because it steadily erodes the foundations of the nation state system. There are also signs of European integration in the security sector, where integration now follows the Warsaw Pact and NATO alliances. Although fully integrated decision-making does not yet exist even within these bodies, there are concerted Soviet moves afoot to bring about a merging of Warsaw Pact and NATO countries. The economically integrated Europe of the early part of the 21st-Century is likely to see not only political integration but full security integration as well.

As in Europe, and despite occasional friction with Sikhs, Tamils and Shiites and various other tribal disturbances, antipathies among peoples are slowly fading, and an integrated world society is evolving. Integration is now a matter of public will, not one of state power, and the increasingly felt desirability of world order demonstrates its inevitability.

It used to be and sometimes still is thought that the objective of a world government movement was to centralize political authority in order to avoid war. As Europe is showing, this is no longer the case. The need is not so much to avoid war — or to bring about peace. Rather, the paramount need today is to manage the planet in a geo-strategic way in order to turn problems into opportunities and maximize socio-economic development. When this is done, war will disappear from the vocabulary, and peace will be taken for granted.

Through geo-strategic planning and management of a global government system, a proper analysis of threats and opportunities would lead to constructive action in every sphere. Such a global government system will not deprive the individual state of power. On the contrary, as a global actor and full participant in the governing of the planet, the nation state will gain *more* authority and responsibility, not less.

This ultimate level of maturity and civilization will only occur when we evolve to a true system of global governance for the single global tribe. Skeptics will dismiss this as a dream, but I think not. Societies that don't change stay primitive. Mature societies become civilizations. Never have we had as great a capacity, intellectually and materially, to shape our destiny. Never have our motivations and aspirations for unity been so strong. Never have the opportunities been greater. Indeed, their achievement *requires* global governance.

Re-Inventing the United Nations

Admittedly, our attempts at global governance have faltered. But there is a basic system in place. Its weaknesses are reflected in the fact that we have yet to effectively govern the world's oceans, its polar regions, its atmosphere, its natural resources or its land mass in general. Essentially, however, the inadequacies of the United Nations system are products of the inadequacies of our own nation state system — the unwillingness of nation states to relinquish the kind of authority to the higher international community that is needed to deal with the increasing number of global issues that can only be dealt with at an extra-national level.

The United Nations and its family of organizations have become the unwilling defenders of the status quo, at the behest of their veto-wielding founders. The root cause of the failure of the U.N. and other international organizations to meet our aspirations is the nationalistically based disagreements among their members on the goals and purposes of such global frameworks. Indeed, the future of the United Nations is in jeopardy because of the hostility of some Western governments to its necessary Third World orientation. The United States under Ronald Reagan demonstrated time and again its distaste for the United Nations and for true multinational co-operation, and, as worrying as anything else, the U.S. showed its unwillingness to be part of a system of international order based on rules such as the International Court of Justice. The same criticism, on different issues, can be leveled at Israel, the Soviet Union and other countries from time to time.

Such vetos are no use unless they are backed by mass popular will and supported by economic resources. In a multi-polar world, there is no veto. International relations have entered a phase where decision-making on issues of vital concern to all countries can no longer be the prerogative of a small group of countries, however powerful they may be. The democratization of international relations is an imperative necessity of our times. It will lead to the realization of the unfettered development and genuine independence of all nation states.

The United Nations, or something like it, as John F. Kennedy said, is "our last best hope." Indeed, the very widely held frustrations with the U.N.'s failings demonstrate the hunger for global governance. Psychologically, as social scientist Kenneth Boulding has pointed out, all that is required is to "create the psychological foundations of a world society where people in Maine feel the same degree of responsibility towards the people of Japan or Chile or China as they feel towards California. This is pretty small, really, but it was apparently enough to create the United States." In today's world, not even the largest nation state can go it alone. Those that try will be left behind, which is what is happening to the United States today.

Instead, the goal must be co-operative global governance through consensus, designed to maximize global social development. As the 4-STEP process of global change takes us across the six waves of social development, this overriding aim must become crystal clear even to those most resistant to institutional change. Indeed, it will finally dawn on them that their enlightened self-interest has become a matter of how to further the collective interest.

Such enlightenment is not new; it has occurred many times and should serve as a source of encouragement to renewed efforts at global governance. There is a growing list of achievements in global governance: weather forecasting, curing diseases, civil aviation control, radio-wave allocation, ozone agreement, Antarctica claims, outer-space access, sea law, arms control, terrorism. In other words, the world can co-operate when it needs to; we can pool national sovereignties in order to achieve a larger global purpose.

Numerous United Nations' conferences, general assemblies, and security council meetings have paid lip service to the complexity and inter-relatedness of future development. Its many agencies have tended to pursue their own projects in isolation, and have become bloated with bureaucratic staff members and research fanatics, with resultant massive duplication of effort and waste of resources. The U.N. suffers from narrow, old fashioned, ossified thinking. It lacks innovative youthfulness, leadership, and vision.

What the world needs is a sense of global purpose, and an agreement and a commitment to a necessary global framework for governance; to reinvent existing global governance systems or to replace them. The characteristics of our time are vastly different than when these entities were first organized. They were created by human imagination and they can be reinvented by human imagination. They must be revamped to meet the challenges and grasp the opportunities of the 21st-Century.

386

The U.N. must be dramatically restructured to mirror the 4-STEP process of global social development that it is to govern. The U.N. central body, the General Assembly, should become a "Central Global Governance Council" (see Fig. 30) with four subordinate "Co-operation Councils":

- **Social Co-operation Council,** which would manage the Social G-Forces of change and thereby incorporate such U.N. organizations as the World Health Organization and UNESCO. The council's mission would be to minimize human needs and maximize human aspirations.

- **Technological Co-operation Council,** which would manage the technological G-Forces of change to maximize global innovation, would incorporate international organizations (not now in the U.N.) like IATA but would also require new organizational subunits to facilitate global technology transfer, outer-space co-operation, and so on.

- **Economic Co-operation Council,** which would manage the economic G-Forces of change across all six waves of the global economy. It would incorporate a new Global Central Bank (proposed in the Economic Section) as well as such existing U.N. organizations as UNIDO.

- **Political Co-operation Council,** which would replace the U.N. Security Council and take on the governance of the planet, with separate subunits for disarmament, peace, law, law enforcement, human rights, and the management of oceans, environment (now done by UNEP) and outer-space.

As such a planetary network of geo-strategic governance evolves it must, of course, become fully democratic in terms of voting (one country, one vote; no veto) and funding (relative to GNP). Funding would come from the proposed Global Equalization Tax system and Global Central Bank. Furthermore, the entire organization should be geographically decentralized around the planet, following the existing example of the United Nations Environment Program based in Nairobi, to Third World locations. No part should be kept in New York.

In this proposed structure, all countries, especially the superpowers, will finally be placed not at the center but at the periphery of world affairs because they will surrender much of their authority and sovereignty to the transnational government and the agencies that it guides. The superpowers will not be excluded from the system. Indeed, they will be the primary stakeholders with major vested interests in its success, and in its effective management. All states, regardless of size or economic power, will have essentially an equal influence on world affairs under such an infrastructure. Each subcouncil would also have, say, four regional councils in which all governments in that region are participants.

Delay in creating such a new structure will not serve the larger global purpose. The cost of change in terms of missed opportunities is inversely proportional to the delay. What is at stake is not the survival of this or that

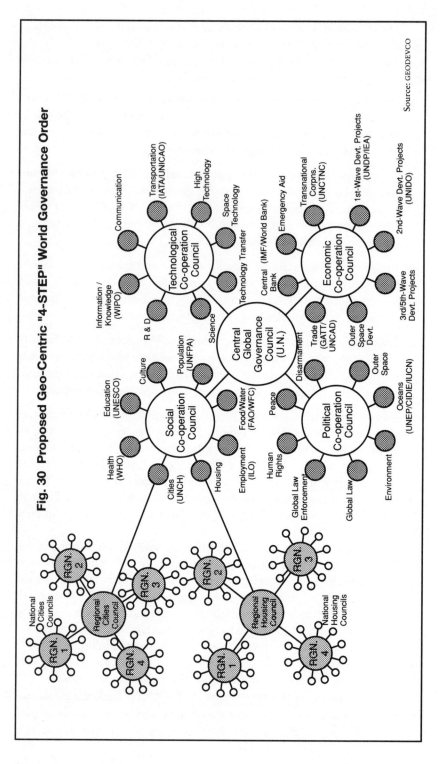

Fig. 30 Proposed Geo-Centric "4-STEP" World Governance Order

Source: GEODEVCO

organization. Nor is it, as some would alarm us, the survival of humanity. What is at stake is the opportunity to provide humanity with all those things it has in common to which it rightfully aspires. Global social development must be effectively managed so that it will not falter, but so that global peace and prosperity can be realized.

A true sense of purpose, then, requires a new mindset. We can only restructure our political and institutional systems if we change the mental structures of their administrators. The question is not whether we need global government but what form it should take. The great weakness of the present system is that it is state-centric. The geo-centric vision of planetary government, where the greatest amount of power would instead be vested in a transnational global authority, is no longer a utopian dream — it is an absolute necessity.

Geo-Strategic Action Leadership Needed

Clearly, the social, technological, economic and political disequilibrium of the present global situation cannot be allowed to continue unattended. Despite the opportunities staring us in the face, the planet is in a mess. The chaos and its cause — political neglect and astonishing mismanagement — is deplored by billions of unsatisfied people. Our desire to enhance the human condition and the state of the planet is in danger of being thwarted by the bungling ineptitude of nationalistic career politicians. Today's top political leaders, as Sir Shridath Ramphal of the Commonwealth Secretariat has observed, are "so highly placed that they miss what happens in the world beneath." They cannot be allowed to remain so cushioned from reality that they fail to perceive the necessary long-term character of global social development.

Our leaders must come to understand that all problems conceal massive opportunities. To turn the tide, two fundamental acts of political will are indispensable. The first imperative is to stop the anarchy of a multitude of disjointed, even conflicting, national policies and strategies. This will not happen overnight, because of ongoing rivalries and lack of a global governance framework. However, this is all the more reason why national priorities have to be harmonized into a coherent body of global policies and strategies of worldwide long-term scope and impact. As the Planetary Information Economy evolves, the enlightened self-interest of even the most ardent state-centered nationalist must inevitably lead to a globalization of world affairs.

We need, simply and plainly, to make the global system governable and to learn how to govern it in a way that solves problems and maximizes opportunities during the next 60-years. Despite the serious state of discord prevailing internationally, we now possess the necessary factual, intellectual and psychological elements needed to equip the world polity and shape public opinion to approach crucial issues in a way that will liberate humankind from the self-imposed shackles of nongovernability. The common interest overwhelms any other consideration. Global unity and prosperity depend on it. This second imperative requires all of us to perform extraordinary deeds. Then we really can reinvent the world by 2050 — and manage the G-Forces of change to the advantage of our common destiny on Earth in the millenia beyond.

Conclusion:

Grasping the Promise

Conclusion:
Grasping the Promise

*"To those fully alive, the future is not ominous but a promise;
it surrounds the present like a halo."*
– John Dewey

The future is bright. There are no unmanageable problems in the world, only an abundance of geo-strategic management opportunities. The so-called problems are but massive opportunities to improve the state of the planet and the quality of life of all its inhabitants. Humanity is coming to the conclusion of a long twilight struggle to find its proper place within the harmonic balance of the natural environment: sustainable global social development, peace and prosperity.

Banishing Gloom and Doom
The G-Forces of change clearly show us that this human future depends on an orderly evolution of the 4-STEP process, and there is no reason why we should not accomplish our goals.

Throughout our history we have achieved remarkable progress. In 1978, Buckminster Fuller estimated that "in this century alone we have gone from less than 1% of humanity being able to survive in any important kind of health and comfort to 44% of humanity surviving at a standard of living inexperienced or undreamed of before." That percentage has increased since 1978, and I am sure that by the year 2050 we will have looked after everyone else. We will achieve this wealth not by recollecting our past accomplishments, not by wringing our hands about today's problems, but by taking individual responsibility for our collective future.

All the gloom and doom reports about the state of the world and its environment are, quite frankly, dead wrong. As Herman Kahn pointed out, because of increases in knowledge, the Earth's "carrying capacity" has increased so

393

much that the term no longer has any useful meaning. The world of the future will indeed be less polluted, less vulnerable to resource depletion and more ecologically stable. The problem of human sustenance has eased rather than grown more difficult over the centuries. Improvement in food supplies per capita over the last three decades have been remarkable. Better forest management, including the implementation of reforestation projects, makes massive deforestation unlikely. There is not a problem of physical resource or food scarcity or disappearance of water. All that is needed is better management.

Of course, we are living in an unstable age, but, as Alfred North Whitehead observed, the great ages have been the unstable ages. Indeed, Yoneji Masuda says that as we move into the next century, we are building what he calls a "computopia." He says that the historical monument of this society will be merely a few one-inch-square microchips stored in a small box. But, he says, "that box will store many historical records, including the record of how 5 billion world citizens overcame the energy crisis and population explosion; achieved the abolition of nuclear weapons and complete disarmament; conquered illiteracy; and created a rich symbiosis of God and man without compulsion of the power of law, but by the voluntary co-operation of the citizens to put into practice their common global aims."

To attain these global aims, lots of things must change. Though the G-Forces of change are hard at work in the world around us, personal change is, as we all know, never easy. If a change is a small one, individuals and organizations usually make the necessary adjustments. If the change is major, we react with uncertainty, fear, disorientation, confusion and loss of equilibrium as we try to adapt under pressure. But we cannot resist. Confucius said, "Only the supremely wise and abysmally ignorant do not change." The Chinese have a sophisticated understanding of the crisis of change. In their written character symbol for "crisis," they combine the images of "danger" and "hidden opportunity." This expresses a philosophy that change, though dangerous, also holds the promise of new opportunities.

In today's rapidly changing world, the need to adjust usually develops during a crisis. Our first response to crisis is to deny change and distort information relating to the true nature of the crisis. Though we acknowledge the need to change, we tend to convince ourselves and others that it isn't really necessary, that the problem will pass — or the opportunity will come of its own accord. When changes pour in, we often react in a knee-jerk way, demonstrating our incapacity to cope in a world we increasingly see as unpredictable, confusing, contradictory and overwhelming.

The opposite reaction is to recognize and grasp the opportunities presented by change. Instead of trying to lay blame for the various problems, we might learn to see the situation geo-strategically and to realize that change is no longer incongruent with a new understanding of reality. With this mindset, even major disruptions and their accompanying discomforts can be seen as necessary to the adjustment process. Problems become a challenge to conquer, not a dilemma to avoid. Signals of crisis serve as a motivation to anticipate and adapt to the change and thereby generate new opportunities.

No matter how we react, change is always under way. If it is managed appropriately, geo-strategic opportunities will emerge. If it is ignored or mismanaged, the consequences can be extremely dangerous. The central problems today facing Western civilization — and hence the world — are rapidly accelerating changes that cannot be managed in old ways. Established Western institutions — which still dominate the world — respond to the threat of change by fighting to remain the same. Western society has been speeding down a path to self-destruction — taking the world with it — by sticking to the old ways of doing things without regard to the G-Forces in the surrounding global environment.

To merely continue with ad hoc ways of muddling through periodic global crises or attempting to "solve" global problems is insufficient. That is not management at all. It is mismanagement. In today's world, the only constant is change itself, and there is no precedent for the many wide-ranging decisions faced daily by policy-makers and managers. We simply cannot cope with the 4th-Wave world if we continue to use values and leadership styles of the 2nd-Wave Industrial Era. Institutions formed earlier this century find themselves threatened by complex changes now under way. The very success of their earlier achievement is what makes them inadequate now. The world of the late twentieth century is quite different. The world of the twenty-first century will be dramatically different.

No established global institution in our society can now realistically believe itself adequate to the challenge ahead. Any that do are simply misleading themselves by denying that "resistance to change" exists within them. Their very resistance to change is causing the rest of us to lose faith in the stability of the world because *we* recognize that these established institutions *are* inadequate to the challenges they face. We must increasingly recognize the feasibility of reinventing these institutions or in developing new, stable ones to replace them. If individuals and organizations are to respond to instability and uncertainty, if they are to come to grips with changes and manage the future effectively, they must feel secure. The only constructive response is to understand and thereby feel at ease with the G-Forces of change — to flow with them, to tap their power, to manage them.

G-Force Management

We are always being presented with views and forecasts about the future, but few of us do anything different than we were doing yesterday. The future is not a spectator sport. As a geo-strategic planner, consulting futurist and businessman, one of my own slogans is "It's not what will happen, it's what you do about it." As Coleridge put it, "in today already walks tomorrow" — and we had better plan for it or suffer the consequences.

By understanding the G-Forces of change and the opportunities they present, we can be confident in our attempts to initiate and manage more change. By being in control of our destiny through the taking of concerted action, we can also retain a sense of identity and self-respect.

The reinvention of institutions will not be easy. One of the basic obstacles is inertia. Culture can be very resistant to change because organizations such as the U.N., the IMF and the World Bank reach a point where they develop a fixed image of the way of the world and of who they are and what they should be doing. This organizational culture of our value system can dominate and overcome the strongest will to change.

Global leaders must set a long-term global agenda — a "Mission Statement for planet Earth" — and bring about the essential co-operation of nation states (and global corporations) to create an institutional framework for grasping the promise of the future. Geo-centric governance is a necessity, not an option.

National leaders must recognize that territorial boundaries are increasingly meaningless and that nationalism is a sign of global immaturity. They must envision a globally oriented mission statement for their own nation and start to shed political responsibility both upstream to the global governance system (for global matters) and downstream (for national matters). Nations must then do everything possible to foster a transfer of citizen "loyalty" from the nation state to the global system, focussing on the collective economic benefits it will bring. Local governments must think and act both globally and nationally but serve the people locally, taking on socio-economic responsibilities from the national government. All governments should plan *beyond* the next election (why not?) and govern as if people mattered, through participatory democracy.

Corporate leadership also is a continual, instinctive exercise in foresight. Geo-strategic planning and management is a matter of understanding the uncertain future in order to take appropriate new actions. Executives are detectives of G-Forces, agents of change and architects of geo-strategic opportunities. Business managers must realize that their purpose is not to manage the past but to manage the future. They must spend 80% of their time planning, thinking, being innovative and securing the future — or the future will manage them and they will spend 100% of their time on the present.

The leaders of global corporations must, like Thomas Bata of Bata Shoe Corporation, recognize the immense business opportunities that lie behind every world problem. They must build truly "geo-strategic opportunity development corporations" which have the creative courage to invest in the problems of the world, solve them profitably and, at the same time, create a substainably prosperous economic order for all our children's children. Perhaps more than government, the world's major corporations have the capacity to move the necessary resources, capital and management skills to develop the indigenous business talents of the Third World.

Certainly, together with government, they can bring desperately needed economic development to poor nations and thereby restore a sustainable socio-economic global balance so that we can all prosper in peace. They should therefore try to create mega-conglomerates (such as a Global Food Megacorp, a Global Water Megacorp or a Global Housing Megacorp) to solve these global problems once and for all. Manufacturers should also decentralize their activities to the Third World through joint ventures, co-production agreements and technology transfers. Bankers must come to recognize that they need the orderly global market that a Global Central Bank and a global currency unit would bring, and they should be leading the task of creating it. As well, of course, Western banks must write off the full 100% of all outstanding Third World debt — and do it now.

Perhaps more than any other sector, the 4th-Wave information sector has the outstanding potential to solve all global problems, across all six waves of society, and create abundant opportunities and wealth. The info-structure must be so designed that it will redistribute this wealth and serve as a framework for effective geo-strategic management at all levels of global society. Electronic technology has the long-term potential to eliminate almost all forms of work and create a 5th-Wave leisure society of affluence and well-being. As distributors of information, the media should learn to tell the "global story," to explain anticipated outcomes of events (tomorrow's "news") and use its info-power to connect us into a "global community consciousness." The leisure/tourism sector also has the opportunity to foster global transculturation and help make that "global community consciousness" a living reality. The arts and entertainment, of course, are our "universal language," and they offer us an array of truly rich cultures. Television broadcasters must put the vision back into television — and make it a global vision. The advertising industry should stop persuading people to destroy the planet (through the mindless consumption of scarce or environmentally destructive products) and recognize the constructive global role that positive persuasion can play.

The managerial challenge for all of us is to reorient ourselves and our social organizations so that we and they are capable of continuously and consciously undergoing change and renewal. In other words, we must invent and develop institutions that are "learning systems" — that is, systems capable of bringing about their own continuous transformation — by learning about the G-Forces and their managerial implications.

Education itself will undergird all our efforts at reinventing the world. Our success or failure in any endeavor will depend on the skills we are able to bring to the task. Education must constantly strive to be ahead of the future, for its purpose is to maximize human potential over the long term. Civilization can no longer stumble along only hazily aware of where it is heading. Educators should teach their students about everything in this book — and others like it — so that we can develop generations of people with the necessary skills to create their own future.

Collective Revolution

We must also learn that we are all members of one family, and we must make that fact an essential part of our planetwide reality. All parents should strive to foster a "global family" mindset within their own family by, for example, eating international foods, sampling international culture, arts and entertainment and getting to know people of different cultures. This is a beginning on the path to ridding our world of prejudice and apartheid. We must realize that there are no sex roles; rather, we must strive to create supra-sexual family arrangements and working partnerships. Parents should try to create an "electronic cottage" environment at home and become an information-oriented family, investing in the children, for they are the global future.

Young people should expect — and demand — a better global inheritance. At the same time, they should be encouraged to decide and plan their own contribution to the future of the new world we are going to create. People everywhere must think globally and futuristically. We must learn to "think community," not as individuals, and cultivate values of humility, self-sufficiency, self-discipline, benevolence, innovation and responsibility to the planet. Working in concert, under carefully and futuristically organized conditions, we have powerful levers that *can* "move the world."

We are party to the biggest revolution in history — and revolutions always go forward. We are in a crucially important period of transition, and when you are in the eye of the storm, it is often difficult to see the direction the storm is heading and to appreciate its real dynamics. We must not let the storm overwhelm us. The present turmoil and confusion are quite natural under the circumstances of the major shifts that are occurring. Yet this huge storm of turmoil presents the greatest opportunity for revolutionary change.

In such revolutionary upheavals, it is possible to achieve absolutely anything and everything. That is exciting. While the global future changes before our eyes like a kaleidoscope, geo-strategic thinking provides us with a geoscopic vision with which to objectively survey events. It also provides us with a closer understanding of the directions of the G-Forces of change and how we can take actions to bring about a constructive revolution of global affairs.

As the century closes, we have the power to move forward into the bright new future that awaits us. We must start afresh, with geo-strategic thinking about the possible. We must stop being confused and confounded, stop being "hypnotized" by the perpetuated myths and misrepresentations of our so-called leaders and their power brokers. We must disturb the status quo. It is time for us so-called followers to wake up, to take the lead, to show ourselves that we are capable of forging the bonds of our common destiny. The implications of this book lead to certain recommendations, based on the realities of present-day circumstances, of what we can and must accomplish. Though we may disagree on the details and the priorities, we must begin now — together — to reinvent the world.

What needs to be done — and can be done — is not a utopian dream; it is the plain common sense of what has to be done — as plain a necessity as plowing a field to sow a crop, or as the need to put gasoline in the car. It is necessary, and what is necessary is never a risk. We must dare to dream, for courage leads to global freedom. We cannot and will not remain where we are.

As Shakespeare wrote: "There is a tide in the affairs of men which, taken at the flood, leads on to fortune." The G-Forces across the six waves of progress have never looked more favorable. We all want a better future. That is our common ground. As friends of the future, our common aspirations will break down the boundaries that keep us in the past, creating a barrier-free global community of which we all will be proud.

To paraphrase John F. Kennedy, let us see what *together* we can do to build a sane world after all: a world free from want and fear. All this will not be finished in our own lifetime on this planet. But let us begin. The torch has been passed to a new generation of global villagers. United, there is little we cannot do in a host of co-operative ventures of a grand global alliance to reinvent the world.

Remember, destiny is something we create.

Bibliography and References

My mind has repeatedly been stretched by the ideas of other writers. As discussed in the Acknowledgments, the works of numerous authors and organizations have been drawn upon in compiling this book. The main sources have been noted within the text; additional sources are gratefully acknowledged here.

— Overview —

General Global Futures Texts

Bell, D., *The Coming of Post-Industrial Society: A Venture in Social Forecasting* New York, Basic Books, 1973.

Brown, L.R., et al, *State of the World Report*, Washington, Worldwatch Institute (Annual Reports 1984–89).

Feather, F., ed., *Through the 80's: Thinking Globally, Acting Locally*, Washington, World Future Society, 1980.

Feather, F., & Mayur, R., eds., *Optimistic Outlooks*, Toronto, Global Futures Network, 1982.

McLuhan, M., *Understanding Media: The Extensions of Man*, New York, McGraw-Hill, 1965.

Masuda, Y., *The Information Society as Post-Industrial Society*, Washington, World Future Society, 1981.

Naisbitt, J., *Megatrends: Ten New Directions Transforming Our Lives*, New York, Warner Books, 1984.

Toffler, A., *The Third Wave*, New York, Bantam Books, 1981.

Toynbee, A., *The Industrial Revolution*, Boston, Beacon Press, 1956.

Wells, H.G., *The Outline of History*, Vols. 1–3, New York, Triangle Books, 1940.

Geo-Strategic Management/Action Leadership

Bennis, W., & Nanus, B., *Leaders*, New York, Harper & Row, 1985.

Cleveland, H., *The Knowledge Executive: Leadership In an Information Society*, New York, E.P. Dutton, 1985.

Feather, F., "Geo-Strategic Thinking... And Its Courageous Application to Planning," *Planning Review*, Winter 1985.

Feather, F., "G-FORCES of Change and the Geo-Strategic Management Era (1990–2050)," *Business Quarterly*, Spring 1989.

Kanter, R.M., *The Change Masters*, New York, Simon & Schuster, 1983.

O'Toole, J., *Vanguard Management: Redesigning the Corporate Future*, New York, Doubleday, 1985.

Ohmae, K., *The Mind of the Strategist*, New York, Penguin, 1983.

Pascarella, P., *The New Achievers*, New York, Macmillan, 1984.

Peters, T., *Thriving on Chaos: Handbook for a Management Revolution*, New York, Alfred Knopf, 1987.

— Section "S" —

Social Motivation — General

Maslow, A.H., *Motivation and Personality*, New York, Harper & Row, 1954.

Yankelovich, D., *New Rules: Searching for Self-Fulfillment in a World Turned Upside Down*, New York, Bantam Books, 1982.

Population Dynamics

Heller, P.S., & Hemming R., "Aging and Social Expenditure in Major Industrial Countries," *Finance & Development*, December 1986.

Thurow, L.C., "Why the Ultimate Size of the World's Population Doesn't Matter," *Technology Review*, August/September 1986.

UNFPA, *State of the World's Population*, New York, United Nations, Annual Reports, 1984–89.

UNICEF, *State of the World's Children*, New York, United Nations, Annual Reports, 1984–89

Food and Water

Dover, M.J., & Talbot, L.M., "Feeding the Earth: An Agroecological Solution," *Technology Review*, February/March 1988.

Feather, F., "Future Food: Agri-Business Trends," speech to Ontario Ministry of Agriculture Conference, 1985.

Ferguson, B.K., "Whither Water? The Fragile Future of the World's Most Important Resource," *The Futurist*, April 1983.

Graff, G., "What's New in Agricultural Biotechnology," *New York Times*, November 8, 1987.

Kay, R.L., "Please Do Drink the Water," *World Monitor*, April 1989.

Middleton, N., "Space Age Control of an Ancient Plague," *South*, September 1988.

Health

de Young, H.G., "Homing in on Healthcare," *High Technology*, August 1985.

Foss, L., & Rothenberg, K., *The Second Medical Revolution: From Biomedicine to Infomedicine*, Boston, Shambhala, 1987.

McLeish, J.A.B., *The Challenge of Aging*, Vancouver, Douglas & McIntyre, 1983.

Platt, J., "The Future of AIDS," *The Futurist*, November/December 1987.

Steinbrook, R., "AIDS: A Global Assessment," *Los Angeles Times*, August 9, 1987.

Jobs/Careers

Blanchard, F., "Global Effort Needed to Create Jobs," *Global Futures Digest*, Fall/Winter 1983/84.

Enzer, S., *Working Our Way to the 21st Century*, Los Angeles, Univ. of California Press, 1985.

Feather, F., *Tomorrow's Best Careers*, Toronto, Global Management Bureau, 1987.

Housing/Cities

Horst, S.A., "Adobe: New Look at a Centuries-Old Building Material," *Christian Science Monitor*, April 17, 1986.

Jacobs, J., *The Economy of Cities*, New York, Random House, 1969.

Perera, J., "Pressing Ahead With a Housing Solution," *South*, November 1987.

Sexual/Race Relations

Colwill, N.L., *The New Partnership: Men and Women in Organizations*, Palo Alto, Mayfield Publishing, 1982.

Feather, F., *Supra-Sexual Entrepreneurialism for the 1990s*, Toronto, Global Management Bureau, 1987.

Joekes, S., *Women in the World Economy*, New York, Oxford Univ. Press, 1987.

Kynch, J., "How Many Women Are Enough?" *Third World Affairs*, 1986 edition.

Lenz, E., & Myerhoff, B., *The Feminization of America*, Los Angeles, Tarcher Publishing, 1985.

Masini, E.B., "Women as Builders of the Future," *Futures*, August 1987.

New Internationalist Cooperative, *Women: A World Report*, New York, Oxford Univ. Press, 1985.

Parrish, J.B., "Are Women Taking Over the Professions?" *Challenge*, January/February 1986.

Sargent, A.G., *The Androgynous Manager*, New York, Amacom, 1983.

Seligmann, J., et al, "Ruckus Over Rotary Women," *Newsweek*, August 9, 1987.

Sivard, R.L., *Women ... A World Survey*, Washington, World Priorities, 1985.

Sowell, T., *The Economics and Politics of Race: An International Perspective*, New York, Quill, 1983.

Vetterling-Braggin, M., ed., *Femininity, Masculinity and Androgyny*, Totowa, NJ, Littlefield, Adams, 1982.

Culture/Values/Beliefs

de Blij, H.J., *Human Geography: Culture, Society, and Space*, New York, Wiley, 1982.

Feather, F., "Electronic High-Tech Culture," speech to Chinese Society for Futures Studies, Beijing, 1986.

Kirk, R., "Historical Consciousnesss and the Preservation of Culture," *The World & I*, January 1989.

McCrum, R., et al, *The Story of English*, New York, Viking, 1986.

Medhurst, K.N., "Catholicism and Radicalism in Latin America," *Third World Affairs*, 1986 edition.

Parrinder, G., ed., *World Religions*, New York, Hamlyn, 1983.

Soedjatmoko, "Values in Transition," *Washington Quarterly*, Fall 1986.

Worsley, P., *The Three Worlds: Culture and World Development*, London, Weidenfeld & Nicolson, 1984.

Education

Feather, F., *The Future of Education*, Toronto, Global Management Bureau, 1987.

Lambert, R.D., "The Educational Challenge of Internationalization," *Washington Quarterly*, Summer 1987.

Livingston, D., "Educational Software," *High Technology*, September 1986.

Marchello, J.M., "Education for a Technological Age," *Futures*, October 1987.

Schultz, T.W., *Investing in People: The Economics of Population Quality*, Los Angeles, Univ. of California Press, 1981.

Shane, H.G., & Tabler, M.B., *Educating for a New Millennium*, Bloomington, Phi Delta Kappa, 1981.

— Section "T" —

Technological Innovation — General

Kranzberg, M., & Pursell, C.W., Jr., *Technology in Western Civilization*, Vols. 1–2, New York, Oxford Univ. Press, 1967.

Kuhn, T.S., *The Structure of Scientific Revolutions*, Chicago, Univ. of Chicago Press, 1970.

Simmonds, W.H.C., "The Ripple of New Technology," *Business Tomorrow*, December 1980.

Leisure Society

Feather, F., "Planetary Playground: Globetrotting Into the 21st Century," speech to International Travel Congress, 1986.

Feather, F., "The 5th-Wave Leisure Society," *Leisure & Lifestyles*, 1987.

Gill, C., *Work, Unemployment and the New Technology*, New York, Polity Press, 1985.

Leontief, W., & Duchin, F., *The Future Impact of Automation on Workers*, New York, Oxford Univ. Press, 1986.

Robertson, J., *Future Work: Jobs, Self-Employment and Leisure After the Industrial Age*, New York, Universe Books, 1985.

Rojek, C., *Capitalism and Leisure Theory*, London, Tavistock, 1985.

Schwaninger, M., "Forecasting Leisure & Tourism: Scenario Projections for 2000–2010," *Tourism Management*, December 1984.

Productivity and Efficiency

Hickman, C.R., & Silva, M.H., *The Future 500: Creating Tomorrow's Organization Today*, New York, New American Library, 1987.

Johnstone, B., "Robots to the Rescue," *Far Eastern Economic Review*, December 31, 1987.

Marsh, P., *The Robot Age*, London, Sphere Books, 1982.

Roscow, J.M., ed., *The Global Marketplace*, New York, Facts on File, 1988.

Intellectual Property Rightsechnology Transfer

Branscomb, A.W., "Who Owns Creativity? Property Rights in an Information Age," *Technology Review*, May/June 1988.

Deihl, L.W., "The Transferability of Management Technology to Third World Countries," *Akron Business & Economic Review*, Fall 1987.

Festa, D., "The U.S. Threat to Shut Off the Flow of Technology," *South*, August 1987.

Gray, H.J., "Technology's Global Role in Industrial Transition," *Global Futures Digest,* Fall/Winter 1983/84.

Hemphill, S.R., "Copyright Technology: Are We Asking the Right Questions?" *High Technology Business,* August 1988.

Makin, K., "Secrets Can't Be Stolen, Supreme Court Rules," Toronto *Globe & Mail,* May 27, 1988.

Potter, R.B., "If Someone Steals a Secret, Has a Theft Been Committed?", Toronto *Globe & Mail,* September 22, 1988.

Saeed, S.M., *Managerial Challenge in the Third World,* New York, Praeger, 1986.

U.S. Congress, *Intellectual Property Rights in An Age of Electronics and Information,* Washington, Office of Technology Assessment, 1986.

Micro-Electronic Revolution

Deken, J., *Silico Sapiens,* New York, Bantam Books, 1986.

Evans, C., *Mighty Micro,* London, Hodder & Stoughton, 1980.

Feigenbaum, E.A., & McCorduck, P., *The Fifth Generation: Artificial Intelligence and Japan's Computer Challenge to the World,* Reading, Addison-Wesley, 1983.

Henson, D., *The New Alchemists: Silicon Valley and the Micro-Electronics Revolution,* New York, Avon Books, 1982.

Wilson, J.W., "Superchips: The New Frontier," *Business Week,* June 10, 1985.

Telecommunications Networks

Didsbury, H.F., ed., *Communications and the Future,* Washington, World Future Society, 1984.

Diebold, J., *Business in the Age of Information,* New York, Amacom, 1985.

Fawer, L., "Shaping the Future of Global Networks," *Business Week,* June 1, 1987.

Feather, F., & Mayur, R., *Communications for Global Development,* Toronto, Global Futures Network, 1984.

Macrae, N., *The 2024 Report,* London, Sidgwick & Jackson, 1984.

Marchand, D.A., & Horton, H.W., *Infotrends,* New York, Wiley, 1986.

Williams, F., *The Communications Revolution,* New York, Mentor, 1983.

Japanese Techno-Leadership

Botkin, J., et al, *The Global Stakes: The Future of High-Technology in America,* New York, Penguin Books, 1984.

Davis, N.W., "Japan's Profit Motive Blasts Into Orbit," *Far Eastern Economic Review,* August 13, 1987.

Goldmann, M.I., "The Shifting Balance of World Power," *Technology Review*, April 1987.

JETRO, *Focus Japan*, Tokyo, 1984–1989, various issues on various topics.

Lee, O.Y., *Small Is Better: Japan's Mastery of the Miniature*, New York, Kodansha International, 1984.

Masuda, Y., *The Plan for Information Society*, Tokyo, Japan Computer Usage Development Inst., 1973.

O'Neill, G.K., *The Technology Edge: Opportunities for America in World Competition*, New York, Simon & Schuster, 1983.

Rubinger, B.F., "Windows on Japan," *High Technology*, August 1986.

Tatsuno, S.M., *The Technopolis Strategy*, New York, Brady Books, 1987.

Wood, R.C., "The Language Advantage: Japan's Machine Translators Rule the Market," *High Technology Business*, November 1987.

Wysocki, B., "Japanese Now Target Biotechnology," *Wall Street Journal*, December 17, 1987.

High-Tech Frontiers

Bowen, K., "The Superconducting Sprint," *High Technology Business*, September 1987.

Dembo, D., et al, "The Biorevolution and the Third World," *Third World Affairs*, 1985 edition.

Drexler, K.E., *Engines of Creation*, Garden City, Anchor Press, 1986.

Harman, W., & Rheingold, H., *Higher Creativity*, Los Angeles, Tarcher Press, 1984.

Hellerstein, D., "Plotting a Theory of the Brain," *New York Times Magazine*, May 22, 1988.

Hunt, M., *The Universe Within*, New York, Simon & Schuster, 1982.

Prentis, S., *Biotechnology: A New Industrial Revolution*, New York, Braziller, 1984.

Rumelhert, D.E., et al, *Parallel Distributed Processing: Explorations in the Microstructure of Cognition*, Vols. 1 & 2, Cambridge, MIT Press, 1987.

Targ, R., & Harary, K., *The Mind Race*, New York, Random House, 1984.

Tyson, P., *The Omni Book of High-Tech Society 2000*, New York, Kensington Publishing, 1985.

Economics of Information Technolgy

Changlin, L., "On the Philosophical Nature of Information," *Social Science in China*, Autumn 1986.

McHale, J., *The Changing Information Environment*, Boulder, Westview Press, 1976.

Morehouse, W., "The New Levers of Global Power: Science and Technology in the International Political Economy," *Third World Affairs*, 1985 edition.

Servan-Schreiber, J.J., *The World Challenge*, New York, Simon & Schuster, 1981.

— Section "E" —

Economic Modernization — General

Didsbury, H.F., ed., *Global Economy: Today, Tomorrow, and the Transition*, Washington, World Future Society, 1985.

Hawken, P., *The Next Economy*, New York, Random House, 1983.

Henderson, H., *Creating Alternative Futures: The End of Economics*, New York, Putnam, 1978.

Economic Shift to Pacific

Downton, E., *Pacific Challenge*, Toronto, Stoddart Publishing, 1986.

Hofheinz, R., Jr., & Calder, K.E., *The Eastasia Age*, New York, Basic Books, 1982.

Holloway, N., "The Land of the Soaring Assets," *Far Eastern Economic Review*, December 3, 1987.

Myrdal, G., *An Approach to the Asian Drama: Methodological & Theoretical*, New York, Vintage Books, 1970.

Oborne, M.W., & Fourt, N., *Pacific Basin Economic Cooperation*, Paris, OECD, 1983.

Prestowitz, C.V., *Trading Places*, New York, Basic Books, 1988.

Scalapino, R.A., "Asia's Future," *Foreign Affairs*, Summer 1987.

Smith, M., *Asia's New Industrial World*, London, Methuen, 1985.

Thompson, W.I., *Pacific Shift*, San Fransisco, Sierra Club Books, 1985.

Veit, L.A., "Time of the New Asian Tigers," *Challenge*, July/August 1987.

Woronoff, J., *Japan's Commercial Empire*, Armonk, NY, M.E. Sharpe, 1984.

Industrializing the Third World

Bata, T.J., "Beyond Borders," interview in *Canadian Business Review*, Autumn 1986.

Brandt Commission, *Common Crisis: North-South Cooperation for World Recovery*, London, Pan Books, 1983.

Norris, W.C., *New Frontiers for Business Leadership*, Minneapolis, Dorn Books, 1983.

Strong, M.F., "Vast Economic Opportunities in Third World," *Global Futures Digest*, Fall/Winter 1983/84.

UNCTC, *Transnational Corporations in World Development*, New York, United Nations, 1983.

Wells, L.T., *Third World Multinationals*, London, MIT Press, 1983.

Collapse of World Financial System

Beckman, R.C., *The Downwave: Surviving the Second Great Depression*, New York, E.P. Dutton, 1983.

Bergsten, C.F., "Economic Imbalances and World Politics," *Foreign Affairs*, Spring 1988.

Feather, F., *Global Eco-Crisis*, Toronto, Global Management Bureau, 1985.

Forrester, J.W., "Economic Conditions Ahead: Understanding the Kondratieff Wave," *The Futurist*, June 1985.

Kindleberger, C.P., *Manias, Panics and Crashes: A History of Financial Crisis*, New York, Basic Books, 1978.

Miller, M., *Coping Is Not Enough: The International Debt Crisis*, Toronto, Oxford Univ. Press, 1987.

Moffitt, M., *The World's Money: International Banking from Bretton Woods to the Brink of Insolvency*, New York, Simon & Schuster, 1983.

Toffler, A., *The Eco-Spasm Report*, New York, Bantam Books, 1975.

U.S. Senate Committee on Foreign Relations, *U.S. Economic Growth and the Third World Debt*, Washington, U.S. Govt. Printing Office, 1986.

Van Duijin, J.J., *The Long Wave in Economic Life*, New York, Allan & Unwin, 1983.

Planetary Information Economy (PIE)

Drucker, P.F., "The Changed World Economy," *Foreign Affairs*, Summer 1987.

Drucker, P.F., "The Poverty of Economic Theory," *New Management*, Winter 1987.

Feather, F., "The New Bottom Line: Managing the Information Age," speech to Society of Management Accountants, 1985.

Johnson, H.T., & Caplan, R.S., *Relevance Lost: The Rise and Fall of Management Accounting*, Boston, Harvard Business School Press, 1987.

Levitt, T., "The Globalization of World Markets," *Harvard Business Review*, May/June 1983.

Lewis, H., & Allison, D., *The Real World War: The Coming Battle for the New Global Economy*, New York, Coward, McCann & Geoghegan, 1982.

Schiller, H.I., *Information and the Crisis Economy*, New York, Oxford Univ. Press, 1986.

Energy

Broad, W.J., "Soviet Studies Satellites to Convert Solar Energy for Relay to Earth," *New York Times*, January 3, 1987.

Goldenberg, J., et al, *Energy for a Sustainable World*, Washington, World Resources Inst., 1987.

IIASA, *Energy in a Finite World: Paths to a Sustainable Future*, Cambridge, Ballinger Publishing, 1981.

Miller, A.S., et al, *Growing Power: Bioenergy for Development and Industry*, Washington, World Resources Inst., 1986.

Miller, J., "The Sun Rises on the Energy Market," *South*, December 1987.

O'Keefe, P., et al, "The Future of Energy Consumption in the Third World," *Third World Affairs*, 1986 edition.

Natural Resources/Recycling

Goldoftas, B., "Recycling: Coming of Age," *Technology Review*, November/December 1987.

United Nations, *Our Magnificent Earth*, New York, United Nations, 1982.

World Resource Institute, *World Resources: 1986*, New York, Basic Books, 1986.

Global Environment

Barney, G.O., *The Global 2000 Report to the President*, Washington, U.S. Gov. Printing Office, 1980.

Comrie, D.C., "New Hope for Toxic Waste," *The World & I*, August 1988.

Conservation Foundation, *State of the Environment: An Assessment at Mid-Decade*, Washington, D.C., Conservation Foundation, 1984.

Kahn, H., & Simon, J.L., *The Resourceful Earth*, New York, Basil Blackwell, 1984.

Myers, N., ed., GAIA: *An Atlas of Planet Management*, Garden City, Anchor, 1984.

Rowland, F.S., "Can We Close the Ozone Hole?", *Technology Review*, August/September 1987.

Rubinoff, I., "A Strategy for Preserving Tropical Rainforests," *Ambio*, XII:5, 1983.

UNEP, *State of the World Environment*, New York, United Nations, Annual Reports, 1984–89.

World Commission on Environment & Development, *Our Common Future*, Oxford, Oxford Univ. Press, 1987.

Communism/Capitalism

Brzezinski, Z., *The Grand Failure: The Birth and Death of Communism in the Twentieth Century*, New York, Scribner's, 1989.

Halal, W.E., *The New Capitalism*, New York, Mentor, 1989.

Heilbroner, R.L., "Does Capitalism Have a Future?" *New York Times Magazine*, August 15, 1982.

Sen, S., "China's View Is Test for Economics," *China Daily*, June 18, 1987.

Theen, R.H.W., "On a Modern Concept of Socialism," *The World & I*, January 1989.

Wang, Z., & Chen, D., "Breakthroughs in Traditional Economic Theory," *Beijing Review*, September 7, 1987.

Wren, W., "Comparing Two Communist Paths to Reform," *New York Times*, September 6, 1987.

Xinhua Agency, "Let Entrepreneurs Run the Factories," *China Daily*, August 6, 1987.

Xu, J., "Reunderstanding Capitalism," *Beijing Review*, November 20, 1988.

Zhang, P., "Develop Social Productive Forces," *New China Quarterly*, January 1988.

Zhao, A., & Wu, M., "Ten Theoretical Questions Facing Reform," *Beijing Review*, August 22, 1988.

Disarmament-Development Link/Peaceful Uses of Outer-Space.

Brandt, W., "Peace and Development," Third World Lecture, 1985.

Marsh, P., *The Space Business*, London, Penguin Books, 1985.

Mayur, R., & Feather, F., *Space for Third World Development: One Giant Leap from the Cradle of Poverty*, Bombay, Global Futures Network, 1982.

Moore, P., *The Next 50 Years in Space*, New York, Taplinger, 1978.

O'Neill, G.K., *2081: A Hopeful View of the Human Future*, New York, Simon & Schuster, 1981.

— Section "P" —

Political Reformation — General

Curtis, M., ed., *The Great Political Theories*, Vols. 1–2, New York, Avon, 1981.

Kennedy, P., *The Rise and Fall of the Great Powers*, New York, Random House, 1988.

Disarmament

Bailey, G., *Armageddon in Prime Time*, New York, Avon Books, 1984.

Caldicott, H., *Missile Envy*, New York, Bantam Books, 1985.

Dyson, F.J., *Weapons and Hope*, New York, Harper & Row, 1985.

Frank, J.D., "Prospects for World Peace: Sociopsychological Considerations," *American Journal of Social Psychiatry*, Spring 1985.

Greenwald, G.J., & Slocombe, W.B., "Economic Constraints on Soviet Military Power," *Washington Quarterly*, Summer 1987.

Horelick, A.L., *U.S.-Soviet Relations*, Ithaca, Cornell Univ. Press, 1986.

Huan, G., *Sino-Soviet Relations to 2000*, Washington, Atlantic Council, 1986.

Leibstone, M., "A Strapped U.S. Defense Budget," *Strategic Review*, Summer 1987.

Melman, S., *The Permanent War Economy: American Capitalism in Decline*, New York, Simon & Schuster, 1985.

Palme Commission, *Common Security: A Program for Disarmament*, London, Pan Books, 1982.

Rivkin, D.B., "SDI: Strategic Reality or Never-Never Land?", *Strategic Review*, Summer 1987.

Sallot, J., "An Accidental Nuclear War Is As Big a Worry As One Started Deliberately," *Toronto Globe & Mail*, December 7, 1987.

Schell, J., *The Fate of the Earth*, New York, Avon Books, 1982.

Thompson, E.P., ed., Star Wars: *Science Fiction Fantasy or Serious Probability?*, New York, Penguin, 1985.

U.S.A./Mexico/Canada

Fundacion Javier Barros Sierra Ac, *Workshop Mexico 2010: Views From Abroad*, Mexico City, 1985.

Kotkin, J., & Kishimoto, Y., *The Third Century: America's Resurgence in the Asian Era*, New York, Crown, 1988.

Lasch, C., *The Culture of Narcissism: American Life in an Age of Diminishing Expectations*, New York, Warner Books, 1979.

Menon, R., *Soviet Power and the Third World*, New Haven, Yale Univ. Press, 1986

Peterson, P., "The Morning After: America Is About to Wake Up to a Painful Economic Reality," *Atlantic Monthly*, October 1987.

Reich, R.B., *The Next American Frontier*, New York, Times Books, 1983.

Sanders, S., *Mexico: Chaos on Our Doorstep*, Lanham, Madison, 1986.

Schlesinger, A.M., *The Cycles of American History*, Boston, Houghton Mifflin, 1986.

Stoga, A.J., "If America Won't Lead," *Foreign Policy*, Winter 1987.

Thurow, L.C., "A Briefing for the Next President," *New York Times*, August 21, 1988.

Vidal, G., "The Future Is Asiatic: The Fast Fall of U.S. Empire Based on Money," *Toronto Globe & Mail*, February 28, 1986.

Wasserman, H., *America Born and Reborn*, New York, Bantam, 1985.

Westlake, M., "What If the Japanese Want Their Money Back?" *South*, September 1987

Perestroika and Glasnost

Brzezinski, Z., *Game Plan*, Boston, Atlantic Monthly Press, 1986.

Cohen, S., *Sovieticus: American Perceptions & Soviet Realities*, New York, W.W. Norton, 1986.

Dizard, W.P., & Swensrud, S.B., *Gorbachev's Information Revolution*, Boulder, Westview Press, 1987.

Feather, F., *Go, Go, Gorbachev & The New Russia: Outlook to the Year 2000*, Toronto, Global Management Bureau, 1985.

Gorbachev, M., *Perestroika: New Thinking for Our Country and the World*, New York, Harper & Row, 1987.

Gorbachev, M., *A Time for Peace*, New York, Richardson & Steinman, 1985.

Hajda, L., "The Nationalities Problem in the Soviet Union," *Current History*, October 1988.

Lemonick, M.D., "Surging Ahead: The Soviets Overtake the U.S. as the No.1 Spacefaring Nation," *Time*, May 11, 1987.

Lewin, M., *The Gorbachev Phenomenon*, Los Angeles, Univ. of California Press, 1988.

Luttwak, E.N., *The Grand Strategy of the Soviet Union*, New York, St. Martin's Press, 1983.

McGwire, M., "Soviet Military Objectives," *Brookings Review*, 1987.

Marantz, P., "Soviet New Thinking and East-West Relations," *Current History*, October 1988.

Morrison, D., ed., *Mikhail S. Gorbachev*, New York, Time Books, 1988.

Piotrowski, J.L., "A Soviet Space Strategy," *Strategic Review*, Fall 1987.

Shtromas, A., "The Soviet Union and the Challenge of the Future," *The World & I*, January 1989.

Strmecki, M., "Gorbachev's New Strategy in Afghanistan," *Strategic Review*, Summer 1987.

USSR, Govt. of, "Soviet Foreign Trade," *Foreign Trade*, Moscow, Fall 1987.

Wilson, A., & Bachkatov, N., *Living With Glasnost: Youth and Society in a Changing Russia*, London, Penguin, 1988.

Europe

Hahn, W.F., "The Endgame in Europe," *Strategic Review*, Fall 1987.

Heisbourg, F., "Europe at the Turn of the Millennium: Decline or Rebirth?" *Washington Quarterly*, Winter 1987.

Knight, R., "A New German Nationalism in the Age of Gorbachev," *U.S. News & World Report*, January 23, 1989.

Kraus, M., "Soviet Policy Toward East Europe," *Current History*, November 1987.

Laurent, P.H., "Eureka, or the Technological Renaissance of Europe," *Washington Quarterly*, Winter 1987.

Lopez-Claros, A., "The European Community: On the Road to Integration," *Finance & Development*, September 1987.

McAdams, A.J., *East Germany and Detente: Building Authority After the Wall, Cambridge*, Cambridge Univ. Press, 1985.

Samielson, R.J., "Stagnation in Europe," *Newsweek*, October 19, 1987.

Japan

Abegglen, J., & Stalk, G., *Kaisha: The Japanese Corporation*, New York, Basic Books, 1985.

Curtis, G.L., *The Japanese Way of Politics*, New York, Columbia Univ. Press, 1989.

Hayashi, Y., ed., *Perspectives on Post-Industrial Society*, Tokyo, Univ. of Tokyo Press, 1980.

Imai, M., *Kaizan,* New York, Random House, 1986.

Japan Research Institute for Peace & Security, *Asian Security, 1986,* Tokyo, Brassey's Defense Publishers, 1986.

Kahn, H., & Pepper, T., *The Japanese Challenge*, New York, William Morrow, 1980.

Kato, H., "Japan 2000," *Futures*, December 1985.

Kohayashi, K., *Japan: The Most Misunderstood Country*, Tokyo, Japan Times, 1984.

Morse, R.A., "Japan's Drive for Pre-Eminence," *Foreign Policy,* Winter 1986.

Trevor, M., *The Japanese Management Development System*, Wolfeboro, Frances Pinter, 1986.

China

China 2000 Research Group, *China in the Year 2000*, Beijing, Science & Technology Documents Publishers, 1984.

China, Govt. of, *Guide to China's Science & Technology Policy,* Beijing State Science & Technology Commission, 1986.

Deng, X., *Fundamental Issues in Present Day China*, Beijing, Foreign Languages Press, 1987.

Hillkirk, J., "Tapping China for Software," *USA Today*, October 14, 1987.

Ma, H., *New Strategy for China's Economy*, Beijing, New World Press, 1983.

Oksenberg, M., & Lieberthal K., "Forecasting China's Future," *National Interest,* Fall 1986.

Schell, O., *To Get Rich Is Glorious: China in the 80s*, New York, Pantheon Books, 1984.

World Bank, *China: Socialist Economic Development*, Vols. 1–3, Washington, World Bank, 1983.

Yang, D.J., "The Next 'Asian Miracle' May Be Underway — in China," *Business Week*, November 2, 1987.

Yang, P., *New Thinking on China's Economic System Reform*, Beijing, Sanlian, 1988.

Third World

Binnendijk, H., "Authoritarian Regimes in Transition," *Washington Quarterly*, Spring 1987.

Crossette, B., "Gandhi: His Luster Dimmed," *New York Times*, April 22, 1989.

ECA, *ECA and Africa's Development, 1983–2008*, New York, United Nations, 1983.

Fagen, R.R., *The Future of Central America*, Stanford, Stanford Univ. Press, 1983.

Fukuyama, F., "Gorbachev and the Third World," *Foreign Affairs*, Spring 1988.

Gawad, A.A., "Moscow's Arms-for-Oil Diplomacy," *Foreign Policy*, Summer 1986.

Gupta, B.S., "India: A Survey," *South*, January 1987.

Katz, M.N., *Russia and Arabia: Soviet Foreign Policy Toward the Arabian Peninsula*, Baltimore, Johns Hopkins Univ. Press, 1986.

Lowenthal, A.F., "The U.S.A. and South America," *Current History*, January 1988.

Mujal-Leon, E.M., "Perspectives on Soviet-Latin American Relations," *Washington Quarterly*, Fall 1986.

Munslow, B., ed., *Socialism in Africa*, London, Zed Press, 1985.

Olshanji, A., "East-South: Reciprocal Effort Is Needed", internal paper, Intl. Inst. for Economic Problems of the World Socialist System, Moscow, 1987.

Ramphal, S.S., "The Third World: A 25-Year Retrospective and Prospective," Keynote Address, Third World Foundation, 1985.

Smith, C., "Militarization and Conflict in the Third World," *Third World Affairs*, 1985 edition.

Tuan, B.A., "Let's Stop Appeasing India," *The World & I*, September 1988.

Tulchan, J.S., ed., *Latin America in the Year 2000*, Reading, Addison-Wesley, 1975.

Turok, B., "The Dynamics of African Marxism," *Third World Affairs*, 1986 edition.

Valkenier, E.K., *The Soviet Union and the Third World*, New York, Praeger Publishers, 1983.

Watt, W.M., "Muslims and the Third World," *Third World Affairs*, 1986 edition.

Participatory Democracy

Bezold, C., ed., *Anticipatory Democracy: People in the Politics of the Future*, New York, Random House, 1978.

Dogan, M., ed., *Pathways to Power: Selecting Rulers in Pluralistic Democracies*, Boulder, Westview Press, 1989.

Innis, H.A., *The Bias of Communication*, Toronto, Univ. of Toronto Press, 1981.

Mill, J.S., *Utilitarianism, Liberty and Representative Government*, New York, E.P. Dutton, 1951.

Smith, G.W., & Debenham, J., "Intelligent Voting Systems," *The Futurist*, September/October 1988.

Global Government

Brown, L.R., *World Without Borders*, New York, Random House, 1972.

Feather, F., "The U.N. as a Global Futures Network," paper to UNA conference, 1981.

Fuller, R.B., *Operating Manual for Spaceship Earth*, New York, E.P. Dutton, 1978.

Jones, W.S., *The Logic of International Relations*, 6th edition, Cambridge, Scott, Foresman, 1988.

Reich, R.B., "Beyond Free Trade," *Foreign Affairs*, Spring 1983.

Schon, D.A., *Beyond the Stable State*, New York, Random House, 1971.

Strong, M.F., "The Way to Only One Earth," *Policy Options*, July 1986.

Ward, B., & Dubos, R., *Only One Earth*, New York, W.W. Norton, 1972.

Index

G-FORCE (see under "G")
4-STEP (see under "F")
1st-Wave (see under "F")
2nd-Wave (see under "S")
3rd-Wave (see under "T")
4th-Wave (see under "F")
5th-Wave (see under "F")
6th-Wave (see under "S")

Abortion, 88-9, 368 (see also Birth control; Population)
Acid rain, 249 (see also Environment)
Activism (see Political activism)
Aerospace industry, 237, 295, 312, 322, 338-40, 361 (see also Outer-Space; 6th-Wave)
Afghanistan, 317, 355
Africa, 354-5; 24, 36, 42, 202, 315, 378 (see also specific countries)
Aging, 27, 298, 329 (see also Life Expentancy; Retirement)
Agricultural Age/Revolution, 170-1
Agriculture, 35-43, 343 (see also Fertilizer; 1st-Wave; Food; "Green Revolution"; Irrigation)
Agro-forestry (see Reforestation)
AIDS (Acquired Immune Deficiency Syndrome), 55-57
Air India, 358

Airline industry, 260
Alberta (Canada), 304
Aluminum, 238
Amalgam process, 239
America (see U.S.A.)
American Express card, 74
American Telephone & Telegraph (AT&T), 146
"Amexicana", 293-307, 318 (see also Canada; Mexico; U.S.A.)
Andropov, Yuri, 310
Angola, 36
Apple Computer Company, 93, 101
Appropriate technology, 107, 133-4
Aquaculture (see "Blue Revolution")
Aquarian Conspiracy, 89
Aquino, Corazon, 367, 374
Armaments (see Disarmament)
Artificial Intelligence, 118, 122, 138, 339

Arts, 396-7 (see also Culture)

Asia (see specific countries)

Association of South-East Asian Nations (ASEAN), 186, 333, 378 (see also specific countries)

Atlantic "Sunset", 177-8, 185-90

Atlantic trade, 186

Australia, 224, 228, 321, 378

Authoritarianism/Autocracy, 344, 346, 358, 366-7 (see also Dictatorship; Monarchy; Oligarchy)

Automobiles/Automobile industry, 125, 153-4, 189, 237-8, 259, 361

Baby-Boom Generation, 301, 304, 311, 314, 323, 329, 345, 365, 368-70 (see also Knowledge "Class" of Workers)

Bailouts (corporate), 113, 180

Baluchistan (Pakistan), 355-6

Baltic republics (U.S.S.R.), 311, 324

Banks/Banking, 202-8; 171, 178, 180, 185, 187-8, 305, 397 (see also Global Central Bank; International Monetary Fund; International financial system; World Bank)

Barter trade, 205, 377 (see also Free trade; GATT Trading blocs)

Bata Shoe Corporation, 124, 196-7, 396

Bata, Thomas J., 396

Batra, Ravi, 221

Behrman, Jack, 261

Belgium, 315, 321

Beliefs, 87-94 (see also Spirituality; Values)

Bell Communications Research (Bellcore), 153, 259

Bellini, James, 322

Bhutto, Benazir, 77, 356

Biosphere (see Environment)

Biotechnology, 55-56, 153, 157-8, 164-6, 240-1, 252, 276, 331, 338, 339-41 (see also Cloning; Genetics)

Birth control, 88-9 (see also Abortion; Population)

Blacks, 82-4, 301-2

Blue Cross, 119, 147

"Blue Revolution" (in aquaculture), 41-2

Blumenthal, Michael, 204

Boeing Aircraft Company, 146, 216

Bohm, David, 162

Boulding, Kenneth, 386

"Brain Drain", 134

Brain power, 95-102, 258 (see also Holographic Mind)

Brain research, 159, 161-3

Brain/sex differences, 81 (see also Supra-Sexuality)

Brandt Commission, 210

Brandt, Willy, 323-4

Brazil, 361; 10, 38, 42, 230, 246, 250, 327

Bread-winner, 73, 79-80

Britain (see U.K.)

British Broadcasting Corporation (BBC), 101, 161

British Columbia (Canada), 304

Brzezinski, Zbigniew, 332

Budget deficits (esp. in U.S.A.), 202, 273, 287, 296-7, 299, 303, 319-21, 348, 359 (see also Debt)

Bureaucracy, 265, 267, 282, 312

Burke, Edmund, 21

Bush, George, 199, 203, 204, 263, 296-298, 302

Business (see Corporations)

Business cycles, 199-201 (see also Long-wave cycle; "Mega-Cycle")

Business Schools, 74

Business Week magazine, 185

Caldicott, Helen, 285
California, 82, 301
Cambodia (Kampuchea), 317
Canada, 303-5; 3, 27, 32, 35, 43, 119, 224, 228, 258, 264, 293, 377, 378
Cancer, 54-6, 167
Cangene Ltd., 166
Capital Iron & Steel Co., (China), 78
Capitalism, 257-69; 181-2, 286, 299, 309, 342, 358, 359, 368, 369 (see also Free Enterprise; Market economy; Socialistic Entrepreneurialism)
Carbon dioxide emissions (see Environment)
Carnegie-Mellon University, 118, 127
Catholicism, 88-9, 311-2 (see also Spirituality)
Central/State Planning, 260-8, 313-4, 337, 346, 376 (see also Communism; Government intervention; Industrial strategy)
Ceramics (see New materials)
China, 335-48; 9, 25-6, 29, 30, 32, 33, 36, 38, 40, 51, 55, 70-1, 78, 96, 121, 127, 165, 187, 219, 224, 230-1, 246-7, 250, 260, 265-9, 287, 288-9, 298, 314-5, 317, 365-6, 369, 379; Bourgeois liberalization, 345; Cultural Revolution, 336, 344; Four Modernizations program, 335; Gerontocratic leadership, 344; Great "Green" Wall, 247; Open Door policy, 266-7, 344; Red Guards, 344 (see also Confucianism; Deng Xiao-Ping; Hong Kong; Macao; Mao Ze-Dong; Taiwan; Zhao Zi-Yang)
Chinese people, 82, 343, 369, 394
Chlorofluorocarbons (CFCs), (see Environment)
Chrysler Corporation, 113, 258
Churchill, Winston S., 98
Cities (see Mega-Cities)

City management, 65, 71-2
Clarke, Arthur C., 106
Cleveland, Harlan, 6, 21
Cloning, 40, 166 (see also Biotechnology; Genetics)
Club of Rome, 21, 151, 218
Coal (see Energy; Fossil fuels)
Collective interest, 9, 20, 386 (see also Co-operativism; Self-interest)
Colonialism, 196-7, 257-8, 312, 322, 351, 354, 361 (see also Political independence; Third World)
COMECON 329-25; 224, 258, 376-8 (see also specific East European countries)
Commodities, 203, 209, 216, 360
Common markets, 91, 376-7, 378 (see also Economic integration; Free trade)
Communications (see ISDN; Telecommunications)
Communism, 257-69; 181-2, 309, 344, 359, 388-9 (see also Central/State Planning; Marxism; Socialism; Socialistic Entrepreneurialism)
Commuting (see Telecommuting)
Comparative advantage, 123-4, 195, 210-1, 351
Competition, 123, 154, 257-60, 265, 376, 379
Computer literacy, 159, 314
Computers, 42-3, 47, 71, 93, 98-101, 110, 113, 118, 139, 153-7, 159, 172, 219, 294, 302, 313, 331, 338, 361, 365, 369, 370-1
Conference Board of Canada, 119
Conference on Security & Cooperation in Europe, 321
Confucianism, 85, 156-7, 185, 264, 337, 394
Conservatism (political), 299, 370
Construction materials/methods, 66-7
Contadora Group, 377

Continental Illinois Bank, 258
Control Data Corporation, 147
Co-operation, 20, 244, 257-62, 269, 273, 303, 369, 376, 379, 385, 386, 396-7 (see also Collective interest)
Copyright (see Intellectual property rights)
Corporation for Open System, 146
Corporations, 260, 264, 351, (see also Geo-Strategic corporations; Multinational corporations)
Corruption, 263, 330
Costa Rica, 359
Cottage industry (see Electronic Cottage)
Council on Superconductivity, 155
Creativity (see Brain power; Geo-Strategic Thinking)
Cuba, 360
Cultural hearths, 91
Cultural mixing, 91-4 (see also Marriage; Supra-Racialism)
Culture, 87-94; 72, 379, 397 (see also Arts)
Culture "gathering", 93
Currency (see Banks/Banking; Global Currency; ECUs; Japanese yen; SDRs; U.S. dollar)
Curriculum, educational, 97-100 (see also Education; "Future Basics")
Cycles, 7 (see also Business cycles; Long-wave cycle; "Mega-Cycle")

Dams, hydro-electric, 51-2 (see also Hydro-electricity; Irrigation)
Death, 21 (see also Fatalism)
Debt/Debt Crisis, 113, 179-80, 194-5, 202, 206-7, 209, 263, 267, 296, 299, 318; Debt rescheduling, 202-3, 350; Third World debt, 8, 178, 188, 203, 289, 294, 298, 305-7, 334, 350, 354, 358-60, 397; Debtors' Cartel, 209,
360 (see also Budget deficits)
Decentralized workplace (see Telecommuting)
Defense spending (see Military spending)
Deforestation, 36, 237-8, 245, 254, 277 (see also Environment; Reforestation)
de Grazia, Sebastian, 366
De-industrialization, 127-8, 184, 230, 249 (see also Industrialization)
Delors, Jacques, 322
Democracy, 323, 345, 358-9, 366-7, 370-4 (see also Partocracy)
Deng Xiao-Ping, 265-9, 317, 335-7, 342, 344-5, 348 (see also China)
Denison, Eward, 171
Depression, economic (see Great Depression)
d'Estaing, Valéry Giscard, 265
Developing countries (see Third World)
Development (see 4-STEP process)
Dictatorship, 290, 323, 350, 365-7 (see also Authoritarianism/Autocracy; Monarchy)
Diet, 35 (see also Nutrition)
Diminishing returns, 113
Disarmament, 271-7; 285-92; 184, 319-21, 331, 394 (see also Military spending)
Disarmament-Development Link, 288
Disease (see Healthcare)
Distance education (see Education)
Division of Labor, 313 (see also Globalized Labor)
Divorce rate, 80 (see also Family; Marriage)
Drexler, Eric, 163-4
Drucker, Peter F., 7, 123, 181
Drugs (narcotic), 297, 360
Duvalier, Jean-Claude ("Baby Doc"), 366

Eastern Europe (see COMECON and specific countries)

East Germany, 312, 315, 320, 324, 329 (see also German reunification)

Eastman Kodak Company, 146

East-West Axis, 319, 334 (see also Superpowers)

Ecological deficits, 243-4

Ecology (see Environment)

Economic growth, 218-9, 221 (see also Growing "PIE")

Economic integration, 305, 376, 379, 384 (see also Common markets; Political integration; Social integration)

Economic power, 185, 188 (see also Geo-Political power; Global economic ranking of nations)

Economics, 180-3, 257-69 (see also Information Economy)

Economies of scale, 124, 376

Economist magazine, 341

Economy, global (see Global Economy)

Education, 95-102; 159, 198, 272, 274, 299, 338, 349, 350-1, 396 (see also Creativity; Curriculum; "Future Basics"; Knowledge; Life-long Learning; Literacy; Training/Re-training; Universities)

Educational enrollment, 96

Educational television, 97, 101

Efficiency (see Productivity)

Einstein, Albert, 163

Elections (see Partocracy)

Electoral fraud (see Electronic voting)

Electronic Cottage, 119, 147, 398 (see also Telecommuting)

Electronic mail, 147, 274

Electronic shopping, 147

Electronic voting, 372-4 (see also Partocracy)

Electronic workstation, 146

Eliot, T.S., 98

Elites, 282, 322, 330, 357, 372-3

Ellsworth, Henry, 106

Employment (see Job creation; Work)

Employment restructuring, 1, 171-2

Energy, 225-33; 274, 277, 329, 333, 394 (see also specific energy forms)

Energy-efficiency, 237

Energy-intensity, 225-9, 249, 329

English language (as universal language), 93, 303, 321, 339

Entertainment (see Arts; Culture)

Entrepreneurialism, 180, 198, 258, 261, 264-5, 268, 302, 315, 322, 346, 368 (see also Socialistic Entrepreneurialism)

Environment, 243-55; 183, 210, 237, 274, 301, 343, 393; Carbon dioxide emissions, 248-9; Chlorofluorocarbons (CFCs), 253-4; "Greenhouse" effect, 43, 164, 247-9; Global Ozone Agreement, 253-4; Ozone layer, 244, 253-4; Global Environmental Monitoring System (GEMS), 252 (see also Deforestation; Ecological deficits; Reforestation; UNEP)

Environmental ethic, 254

Ershov, Endrei, 312

"Eureka" program, 323, 332

European Currency Unit (ECU), 208-9, 318, 379 (see also Global currency)

European Economic Community (EEC, 310-5; 163, 224, 258, 303, 305, 328, 376-7, 379, 384; Council of Ministers, 322; Parliament 323; Sovietization of, 323-5 (see also specific Western European countries)

European Free Trade Association (EFTA), 321 (see also specific member countries)

European Gas Pipeline, 320-1
"Europeanness", 323, 377, 379
Exurbia, 72 (see also Mega-Cities)

Facsimile (FAX) copiers, 147
Family, 25, 80, 398 (see also Divorce
rate; Supra-Sexuality)
Fang Li-Zhi, 345
Fatalism, 87 (see also Death)
Fathy, Hassan, 68
Feldstein, Martin, 296
Feminist Movement (see Women's
Movement; Supra-Sexuality)
Ferguson, Marilyn, 89
Fertility (see Population)
Fertilizer, 39, 165-6, 253 (see also
Agriculture; Food)
Feudalism, 282, 335
Fiber Optics, 140, 149, 313
5th-Wave Economy/Society, 3, 16-18,
39, 93, 106, 112 117-122, 169, 181,
217, 283, 291, 322, 341, 397
Financial Services Industry, 171 (see
also Banks/Banking)
First Global Conference on the
Future, 79
1st-Wave Economy/Society, 1, 9, 17,
24-6, 57, 76, 87, 93, 111-2, 146, 169-
70, 216, 282-3, 304, 310, 314, 340-1,
368 (see also Agriculture)
Flexible manufacturing, 127, 171
Food, 35-43, 110, 388 (see also
Agriculture; Fertilizer; Irrigation;
Nutrition)
Ford, Henry, 120, 171
Ford Motor Company, 113
Foreign aid, 188-90, 208-10, 253
Foreign investment, 186-90, 295, 306,
316, 332-3, 349
Forestry (see Deforestation; Reforest-
ation; Environment)
Fossil fuels, 179, 206, 231, 225-8, 249,

343, 346, 356 (see also Energy)
Foundation for International Development, 29
4-STEP process, 4-5, 24, 33, 91-2, 99,
106, 109, 115, 118, 122, 236, 244-5,
257, 267, 281, 283, 306, 310, 317, 327,
330, 335, 343-4, 363, 375, 386-7, 393
4th-Wave Economy/Society, 2, 8, 16-
18, 39, 57, 64, 93, 96, 105, 112, 114-5,
117, 144, 146, 169-74, 180-3, 204,
209, 213-24, 235, 257, 265, 283, 297,
299-302, 314, 322, 328, 341, 368-9,
374, 395-6 (see also Information
Economy/Society; High-technology; Knowledge; Planetary Information Economy)
Freedom, 15-16, 286, 345 (see also
Global Freedom)
Free Enterprise, 260, 262, 266 (see also
Capitalism; Market Economy)
Free trade, 258, 307, 321, 334, 377,
378-9 (see also Barter trade; Com-
mon markets; GATT)
France, 321
French Revolution, 368
Fuller, R. Buckminster, 5, 233, 235,
240, 393
Fundamentalism, 87 (see also
Spirituality)
"Future Basics" (educational), 98-99
(see also Curriculum; Education)
Future Shock, 57-58,
Futuribles, Association Internationale
(France), 88
Futuristic thinking, 7, 398 (see also
Geo-Strategic Thinking)

G-FORCE (defined), 1
G-FORCE Management, 395-7 (see
also Geo-Strategic Management)
Gandhi, Indira, 357
Gandhi, Mahatma, 362

Gandhi, Rajiv, 357-58, 366
Gas Research Institute, 240
General Agreement on Tariffs & Trade (GATT), 133, 179, 376, 378 (see also Barter trade; Free trade; Trade blocs)
General Electric Company, 146
General Motors Corporation (GM), 113, 127, 132, 144, 146, 168
Genetics, 39-40, 141, 165-6, 339-41 (see also Cloning; Biotechnology)
Geo-Centric Governance, 387-9, 396 (see also Global governance)
Geo-political power, 219-24, 233, 255, 281-4, 327 (see also Economic power; Global economic ranking of nations; Superpowers)
George Washington University, 56
Geo-Strategic Action Leadership, 9, 219, 389-90 (see also Leaders/Leadership)
Geo-Strategic Corporations, 123-4, 261, 396-7 (see also Corporations; Multinational corporations)
Geo-Strategic Management, 10, 207, 244, 385, 393, 396
Geo-strategic mind, 5-6 (see also Geo-Strategic Thinking; Holographic mind)
Geo-Strategic Planning, 10, 159, 261-2, 298, 386, 396
Geo-Strategic Thinking, 5-6, 81, 288, 294, 309, 315, 394, 398
German reunification, 324-5 (see also East Germany; West Germany)
Glasnost (see U.S.S.R.)
"Global Central Bank", 207-10, 387, 397 (see also International Monetary Fund; World Bank)
Global civilization, 22, 94
"Global Community Consciousness", 327, 333-4, 380, 397
Global Competitiveness Council (U.S.), 152
"Global" currency unit, 205, 208-9, 397 (see also ECU; Japanese yen; U.S. dollar)
Global economic ranking of nations, 222-4 (see also Economic power; Geo-political power)
Global economy, 184, 297 (see also Global market)
Global Environmental Monitoring System (GEMS, (see Environment; UNEP)
"Global Equalization Tax", 205, 208-9, 387
Global forces of/for change (see G-FORCE above)
Global freedom, 16-18, 365, 399 (see also Freedom)
Global governance, 206, 245, 255, 281, 375-90 (see also Geo-Centric Governance; United Nations)
Global Information Utility (GIU), 149, 154 (see also Information Utility)
Globalism, 5, 94, 286, 379-80, 384-5
Globalized labor, 63-4, 377 (see also Division of Labor)
Global market/supermarket, 7, 124, 216, 258, 260, 315, 378 (see also Global economy)
Global Ozone Agreement (see Environment)
Global product mandating, 123-5, 196-7, 378-9 (see also Multinational corporations)
Global System of Trade Preferences (GSTP), 362, 377-8
Global television, 92 (see also Culture)
"Global Tribe", 290, 385 (see also Globalism; "Global Village")
Global thinking, 6, 99, 398 (see also Geo-Strategic Thinking)
Global values, 87

"Global Village", 5, 18, 21, 92-3, 129, 143, 281, 286, 289, 369, 375, 380 (see also Globalism; "Global Tribe")

Global Warming (see Environment)

Gorbachev, Mikhail S., 9, 20, 265-9, 287, 309-18, 320, 324, 345, 355, 358, 360, 376 (see also *Glasnost; Perestroika;* U.S.S.R.)

"Gorbymania", 324

Government intervention, 263, 302 (see also Central/State Planning)

Grant, James, 37

Gray, Harry, 131-2

Great Depression, 201, 206, 268 (see also "Mini-Depression")

"Great Recession", 180, 194, 201

"Greenhouse"effect (see Environment)

"Green Revolution" in agriculture, 35-36

"Group of 7", 205 (see also OECD)

"Group of 8", 360 (see also Debtors' Cartel)

Growing "PIE", 213, 217, 218-9, 222, 349 (see also Economic growth; Planetary Information Economy)

Harman, Willis, 91, 288

Harmonic globalism, 94

Harvard Business Review, 262

Harvard University, 157

Hawaii, 3

Hawken, Paul, 170

Hayashibra Company, 157

Hazardous waste, 244, 249-51 (see also Waste disposal/recycling)

Health & Welfare Canada, 54

Healthcare, 53-58; 77, 157, 167, 272, 274 (see also Pharmaceuticals; Tele-Medicine)

Hepatitis, 155-7

Hewlett-Packard Company, 339

Hickman, C.R., 124

Hierarchy of needs, 4, 6, 16, 105, 169, 194, 216, 255, 327, 329-30, 349

High-technology, 137-42, 143-50, 151-9, 161-8 (see also Biotechnology; Computers; Microchips; New materials)

Hispanics, 82, 301 (see also Supra-Racialism)

Holistic health (see Healthcare)

Holographic mind, 161-2 (see also Brain; Geo-strategic mind; Inner-Space)

Honecker, Erich, 324

Hong Kong, 196, 336, 340-3, 346, 379 (see also China)

Household water usage, 47

Housing, 65-72, 274 (see also Mega-Cities)

Hubbard, Barbara Marx, 79, 81

Human capital, 183, 197, 210, 274 (see also Intellectual capital)

Human rights, 84

Human relations (see Supra-Sexuality; Supra-Racialism)

Human resources (see Human capital)

Hungary, 264, 267, 315, 324, 337

Hydro-electricity, 228, 230-1, 233, 249

Imperialism (see Colonialism)

India, 356-8; 4, 10, 26, 30, 36, 60, 96, 246, 316, 366, 378 (see also Gandhi, Rajiv)

Individualism, 84-5, 87, 90, 262, 303

Industrial Age/Revolution, 72-3, 100-1, 119, 171, 245, 257 (see also 2nd-Wave)

Industrialization, 191-8 (see also De-industrialization)

"Industrial Nostalgia", 184, 219-21

Industrial rationalization, 146

Industrial strategy, 159, 298, 328-9 (see also Central/State Planning)

Industrial water usage, 47
Info-globalization, 10, 143-50
Information, 213-24; 3, 10, 93, 114, 169-74, 181, 204, 207, 265, 289-91, 294, 328, 338, 368
Information Economy/Society, 5, 105, 114, 169-74, 180-2, 213-4, 235, 265, 341, 365, 396 (see also 4th-Wave; Planetary Information Economy)
Information "gathering", 93, 173
Information industry, 213-5
Information-intensity, 170-3
Information, power of, 172
Information rich-poor gap, 114-5, 173
Information Utility, 143, 149, 154, 327 (see also Global Information Utility)
Inner-Space, 6, 161 (see also Brain; "Global Community Consciousness"; Holographic mind)
Innovation, 3, 18, 161, 287 (see also Productivity; Technological innovation)
Institute for Security & Cooperation in Outer Space (ISCOS), 273
Institute of Water Economics, Legislation & Administration, 51
Integrated Pest Management (IPM), 250-2
Integrated Services Digital Network (ISDN), 144-6, 304 (see also Telecommunications networks)
Intellectual capital, 95 (see also Human capital)
Intellectual property rights, 129-31 (see also Knowledge Transfer; Technology Transfer)
Interdependence of nations/national economies, 181-2, 204, 294, 315, 334, 369, 379
International Business Machines Corporation (IBM), 74, 153, 185
International Court of Justice, 385

International Energy Agency (IEA), 231
International financial system, 195, 199-211, 297 (see also Banks/Banking; Global Central Bank; International Monetary Fund; World Bank)
International Labor Organization (ILO), 59-60
International Maritime Satellite Organization (INMARSAT), 149
International Monetary Fund (IMF), 28, 179, 181, 184, 188, 190, 204-8, 305, 362, 396 (see also Global Central Bank; World Bank)
International Telecommunications Earth Satellite Organization (INTELSAT), 149
International Tropical Moist Forest Reserve System, 246
International Wheat Council, 36
I.P. Sharp Network, 144
Iran, 19, 89-90, 109, 293, 312, 356, 366-7
"Iron Curtain", 323
Irrigation, 46, 247-8 (see also Dams; Water)
Islam, 88-90, 294, 311-2, 355-6 (see also Spirituality)
Israel, 47, 377, 378, 385
Italy, 229, 315

Jackson, Jesse, 263, 301-2,
Japan, 151-9, 327-34; 3, 8, 9, 40, 63, 66-7, 78-9, 119-20, 139, 141, 163, 187-90, 204, 207, 224, 228, 239-40, 252-3, 264, 276, 287, 294, 297, 299, 303-5, 313, 316, 321-2, 330, 336, 337, 343, 347-8, 351, 362, 369, 378, 382; Declining Industry Act, 329; Global Industry & Culture Institute, 333; Human Frontier Science Program,

Japan (cont'd)
159, 276, 332; Industrial Structure Council, 159; Industrial Technology Council, 159; Leisure Development Center, 120; Protein Engineering Research Institute, 157 (see also Global Information Utility; "Technopolis Strategy")
Japanese yen, 208-9, 330 (see also Global currency unit)
Jews, discrimination towards, 82
Job creation, 63, 306 (see also Employment)
Jobs (see Work)
Job sharing (see Work sharing)
John Paul II (the Pope), 88
Joint ventures, 131-4, 152, 186-7, 259-60, 269, 349, 397
Junk bonds (see Debt)
Just-in-time inventory, 153-4

Kahn, Herman, 24, 393
Kaufman, Henry, 296
Kennedy, John F., 83-4, 168, 272, 293-4, 301, 303, 371, 386, 399
Kennedy, Paul, 295
Khomeini, the Ayatollah, 312, 356
King, Martin Luther, 83
Knowledge, 216 (see also Education; 4th-Wave; Information)
Knowledge "Class" of workers, 173-4, 302, 311, 329, 365, 369-71
Knowledge-intensity, 151
Knowledge transfer, 96, 109, 129-36, 182-3, 197 (see also Intellectual property rights; Technology Transfer)
Kohl, Helmut, 324
Kondratieff, Nikolai, 199, 201
Kondratieff Wave (see Long-wave cycle; "Mega-Cycle")
Kristol, Irving, 370

Labor (see Work)
Labor-intensity, 60, 109, 121, 136, 329, 351
Labor unions (see Unions)
Labor mobility, 321 (see also Globalized labor)
Language, 93 (see also English language)
Lasers, 46, 54, 152, 153, 315, 338
Latin America, 358-61; 88, 202, 378 (see also specific countries)
Leaders/Leadership, 9-10, 206, 284, 291, 297, 305, 327, 333, 369, 396 (see also Geo-Strategic Action Leadership)
Lebanon, 294, 356
Leisure, 3, 16, 117-122, 169, 170, 330, 397 (see also 5th-Wave; Leisure ethic)
Leisure Development Center (see Japan)
Leisure ethic, 18, 120
Lenin, Vladimir Ilich, 267, 310, 345
Liberalism (political), 263, 265, 370
Life expectancy, 29-30, 340 (see also Aging)
Life-long Learning (see Education)
Lima Target, 194-7
Lincoln, Abraham, 83, 371
Literacy, 77-8 (see also Education)
Local government, 71, 281
Lockean Pillars, 262 (see also Capitalism; Free Enterprise)
Long-term focus, 155, 157, 298-9, 315, 328
Long-wave cycle, 3, 7, 113-4, 159, 179, 182-3, 199-201, 207, 219, 224, 347 (see also "Mega-Cycle")

Macao, 336-7, 341-2, 379 (see also China)
Machida (Japan), 240
Magna International, 264

Malaysia, 246, 327, 343

Malcolm X, 83

Male-Female relationships (see Supra-Sexuality)

Malnutrition, 54 (see also Healthcare, Nutrition)

Management (see Geo-Strategic Management)

Manila (Philippines), 68

Manufacturing, 178, 197, 295, 341, 351, 397 (see also De-industrialization; Industrialization; Robots/Robotization; 2nd-Wave)

Manufacturing Value Added (MVA), 194-6

Mao Ze-Dong, 336, 348

Marcos, Ferdinand, 19, 210, 306, 366, 367-74

Market economy, 260-4, 265-8, 313, 337, 346 (see also Capitalism; Free Enterprise; Open economy)

Marriage (see Divorce rate; Family; Supra-Sexuality; Supra-Racialism)

Marshall Plan, 261, 319

Marx, Karl, 181, 269, 345

Marxism, 263, 265-69, 311-2, 337, 354-5, 361 (see also Communism; Socialism)

Masini, Eleonora, 79

Maslow, Abraham, 16, 18

Massachusetts Institute of Technology (MIT), 125, 163, 296

Masuda, Yoneji, 5, 107, 149, 172, 394

Materialism, 90-1, 154, 307, 330, 370

Mayur, Rashmi, 148

McClelland, James, 162

McHale, John, 114,

McLuhan, Marshall, 5, 32, 93, 98, 107, 143, 172, 289-90, 371-2

Media (mass), 92, 371-2, 397

Medicine (see Healthcare; Pharmaceuticals)

Mega-Cities, 65-72, 349 (see also City management; Exurbia)

"Mega-Cycle", 199-201, 207 (see also Long-wave cycle)

"Mega-Depression", 206, 219, 262 (see also Great Depression; "Mini-Depression")

"Megatrends", 1

Mensch, Gerhard, 111

Metaphysics, 90-91 (see also Holographic mind; "Global Community Consciousness"; Psychic abilities; Spirituality)

Mexico, 305-7; 8, 37-8, 203, 206, 293, 303, 360, 363, 374, 377-8

Microchips, 137-42, 154-5, 167, 313, 322 (see also Computers)

Microwave ovens, 110-1

Middle East, 355-6; 46, 203, 315, 325, 378 (see also specific countries)

Migration, 30, 71, 91, 341, 360 (see also Population)

Military industrial complex, 274-5, 291, 294

Military spending, 270-7, 285-92; 113, 183, 190, 204, 210, 233, 254, 297, 319-20, 330-1, 358, 370; "Conversion" to civilian purposes, 271-7, 289, 314 (see also Disarmament; Strategic Defense Initiative)

Miniaturization, 140-1 (see also Nanotechnology)

"Mini-Depression", 201-4; 179-80, 206, 211, 219, 226, 262, 268, 275, 287, 297, 298, 309-10, 315, 318, 350, 356, 366, 377

Minorities (see Supra-Racialism)

Monarchy, 282, 379 (see also Authoritarianism/Autocracy; Dictatorship)

Money (see Banks/Banking; Global currency unit)

Money supply, 201-2, 208, 263 (see also Reaganomics)

Moscow Institute of Avionics, 233

Moscow State University, 93

Motivation (see Hierarchy of Needs)

Motorola Corporation, 339

Multiculturalism (see Supra-Racialism)

Multinational corporations, 123, 125, 196-7, 261, 356, 376, 378-9; in Third World 125-7 (see also Geo-Strategic Corporations)

Multiple cropping (see Agriculture)

Multi-Polarity (geo-political), 284, 379-82

Mumford, Lewis, 91

Music, 93

Nakasone, Yasuhiro, 276

Nanotechnology, 163-164 (see also Miniaturization)

Napoleon, 132, 252

Nasser, Gamal Abdel, 293

National Aeronautical & Space Agency (NASA), (see U.S.A.)

Nationalism/Nation state, 109, 181-2, 197, 204-5, 281, 284, 294, 369, 375, 376, 379-83, 389, 396 (see also Geo-Centric Governance; United Nations)

National security, 288-9

National Technological University, 101

Natural gas (see Energy; Fossil fuels)

Natural resources, 235-41, 394

Negev Desert, 43

Nehru, Jawaharlal, 357

Nepal, 246

Netherlands, The, 229

New Jersey, 239

Newly Industrialized Economies (NIEs), 328 (see also Third World)

New materials, 66-7, 153, 159, 166-7, 235, 236-7, 274, 313, 331, 338

New York (city), 19, 32, 82, 239, 302, 387

New York (state), 239

New York Stock Exchange, 185

New York Times, 238

New Zealand, 378

Nicaragua, 359

Nigeria, 30

Nippon Electric Company (NEC), 185

Nobel Prizes, 302

Non-aligned nations, 358 (see also Third World)

North Atlantic Treaty Organization (NATO), 204, 319-20, 324, 325, 384

North Korea, 332, 379

North Sea Oil, 322, 325 (see also Energy; Fossil fuels; U.K.)

Nuclear Arms Reduction Agreement, 289 (see also Disarmament)

Nuclear fission energy, 226, 231

Nuclear fusion energy, 231

Nuclear Risk Reduction Centres, 291 (see also Disarmament)

Nuclear weapons, 285, 289-90, 330 (see also Disarmament)

Nutrition, 35-7, 54, 340 (see also Healthcare; Malnutrition)

Nyerere, Julius, 362

Oak Ridge National Laboratory, 165

Oceans, as resource, 241, 249

Oil (see Energy; Fossil fuels)

Oligarchy, 306

Ontario (Canada), 239, 304

Open University (U.K.), 101

Opportunistic thinking, 9 (see also Creativity; Geo-Strategic Thinking)

Opportunity development, 173 (see also Geo-Strategic Corporations)

Oregon, 304
Organization for Economic Cooperation & Development (OECD), 35, 190 (see also "Group of 7")
Organization of Petroleum Exporting Countries (OPEC), 179, 206, 327
Orwellianism, 286, 344
Otis Elevator Company, 216, 226, 356
Outer-space exploration, 3, 6, 158, 167-8, 271, 272-4, 317 (see also Aerospace industry)
Outer-Space Economy, 331-2 (see also 6th-Wave)
Ozone layer (see Environment)

Pacific Economic Cooperation Conference (PECC), 333, 378
Pacific "Sunrise", 177-8, 185-90, 301, 316
Pacific trade, 185-6
Pacific Rim, 186, 204, 213, 304, 325, 334, 341, 347, 378 (see also specific countries)
Paine, Thomas, 168
Pakistan, 355-6, 366-7 (see also Bhutto, Benazir; ul Haq, Zia)
Pan American Health Organization, 57
Parallel distributed processing, 162 (see also Brain; Computers)
Parliamentary systems, 376
Partocracy (participatory democracy), 365-75; 83, 281-4, 325, 330, 344, 346, 357, 396 (see also Democracy; Electronic voting)
Patents (see Intellectual property rights)
Paternalism/Patriarchy, 77-9, 336, 344, 366 (see also Authoritarianism/Autocracy)
Peace (see Disarmament)
People Power, 15, 284, 290-2

Pearson Commission, 210
Perestroika (see U.S.S.R.)
Perez, Carlos, 209
Pharmaceuticals, 153, 165-6 (see also Biotechnology; Healthcare)
Philippines, The, 19, 88, 306, 332, 366-7, 374
Philips Electric Company, 339
Photonics (see Fiber Optics)
"Pioneer 10" space probe, 167
Piotrowski, John, 317
Planetary consciousness, 8 (see also "Global Community Consciousness")
Planetary Electricity Grid, 233
Planetary Information Economy (PIE), 213-24; 182-3, 257, 258, 260, 267, 337, 389, (see also 4th-Wave; Information Economics)
Planetary production site, 7, 123, 125, 178, 191
Planning (see Geo-Strategic Planning)
Poland, 88, 312, 324
Political activism, 368-9
Political independence, 351 (see also Colonialism; Third World)
Political integration, 184, 305, 375, 384 (see also Economic Integration; Social integration)
Political maturity, 351
Political reform, 306, 312, 330, 335, 336, 343-7
Political representation (see Elites; Partocracy)
Political reunification, 268, 341-2, 343, 347, 379
Political revolution, 366-8
Pollution (see Environment)
Population, 23-33; 36, 195, 349 (see also Migration)
Population growth, 24, 25, 32, 183, 191, 245, 352, 354

Population imbalance, 17

Population management, 32-3, 70-1

Population "Spike", 24-5

Post-Industrialism, 1, 73, 184, 204, 219, 221, 228, 236, 262, 267, 314-5, 322, 376 (see also 3rd- , 4th- , 5th- , and 6th-Wave)

Poverty (see Rich-Poor Gap)

Pribram, Karl, 161-2

Princeton University, 232

PRI Party (Mexico), 306

Production (see Manufacturing)

Productivity, 18, 28, 123-8, 169, 183, 195, 211, 295, 298, 314 (see also Innovation; Technological innovation)

Professions, service, 75

Protestantism, 298, 328, 334, 376, 378 (see also Spirituality)

Psychological drives (see Hierarchy of Needs)

Psychology, 162 (see also Hierarchy of Needs)

Psychic abilities/phenomena, 163

Quality control, 158

Québec (Canada), 303

Race relations (see Supra-Racialism)

Rafsanjani, Hashemi, 312

Ramphal, Sir Shridath, 389

Reagan, Ronald, 20, 83, 184, 202, 258, 262-3, 286, 294, 296-7, 301, 322, 359, 386

Reaganomics, 184, 190-6, 199, 295, 359 (see also Budget Deficits; Debt; Money supply)

Recreation (see Leisure)

Recycling (see Waste disposal/recycling)

Reforestation, 39, 166, 245-7, 394 (see also Deforestation; Environment)

Religion (see Catholicism; Islam; Protestantism; Spirituality)

Religious dogma, 88

Remote working (see Telecommuting)

Republican Party (U.S.A.), 302

Research and Development (R&D), 132, 152, 183, 216, 259, 295, 329, 330, 355; in Third World, 134, 304, 312 (see also Innovation; Technological innovation)

Resistance to change, 394-5

Resource-intensity, 181, 235-6, 329, 351

Resources (see Natural resources)

Retirement, 62-3, 99 (see also Aging)

Rich-Poor Gap, 134, 221, 222, 301-3, 306, 333, 357, 359, 362 (see also Information rich-poor gap)

"Ripple Effects" of technology, 109-11

Robinson, James, 209

Robots/Robotization, 66, 127, 140, 152, 153-4, 171, 313, 331 (see also Manufacturing; 2nd-Wave)

Roman Catholicism (see Catholicism)

Roosevelt, Theodore, 252

Rosin, Carol S., 273

Rosso (Mauritania), 68

Rotary International, 76

Rumelhart, David, 162

Rushdie, Salman, 312

Russia (see U.S.S.R.)

Rwanda, 39

Sahara/Sahel, 248

Salinas, Carlos, 307

Samurai Warriors, 291

Sanitation, 49-50, 240-1 (see also Waste disposal/recycling)

Satellites, 42, 149, 273-4, 304, 340, 361, Satellites (cont'd) 370-1 (see also Outer-Space; Tele-

communications)
Saudi Arabia, 356
Schell, Jonathan, 22, 291
Schools (see Education)
Schumpeter, Joseph A., 199-201, 369
Schlesinger, Arthur, 299
Schultz, George, 287
Sears, Roebuck & Company, 147
2nd-Wave Manufacturing Economy/
Society, 1,17, 57, 77, 87, 111-2, 127,
144, 162, 169-70, 216, 236, 245, 257,
280-1, 295, 297, 306, 314, 334, 341,
368-9 (see also De-industrialization;
Industrialization; Industrial Revo-
lution; Manufacturing; Robots/
Robotization)
Self-interest, 6, 20, 85, 386, 389 (see
also Collective interest)
Semi-conductors (see Microchips)
Senegal, 39
Service sector (see Professions; 3rd-
Wave)
Seth, Satish, 33
Sex drive, 23
Sex research, 81
Sexual roles (see Supra-Sexuality)
Shah (Pahlavi) of Iran, 8, 17, 109, 294,
366-7
Short-term focus, 155, 157, 299
Silicon, 235 (see also Microchips)
Silva, M.H., 124
Singapore, 196, 230, 346
6th-Wave Outer-Space Economy, 3,
16, 17, 18, 42, 106, 112, 169, 181, 217-
8, 271-7, 281, 331 (see also Outer-
Space; Satellites; Space industry)
Smith, Adam, 62, 95, 262
Social Change, Axis of, 16
Social integration, 377 (see also
Economic integration; Political inte-
gration)
Socialism, 263, 266-8, 301-3, 323, 337,

345, 350, 355, 358, 360, 369 (see also
Communism; Marxism)
Socialistic Entrepreneurialism, 257,
264-5, 269, 293, 302, 328, 346-7,
369 (see also Capitalism; Com-
munism)
Socialist International, 323
Social responsibility, 260, 264
Social security, 27-8
Socio-economic development (see
4-STEP process)
Software (see Computers)
Soil/Soil erosion, 247, 249, 277
Solar energy, 228, 232-3
Solow, Robert, 171
South Africa, Republic of, 82, 353, 371
South Bank, 362
South Commission, 362
South Korea, 230, 332, 346, 379
Soviet Union (see U.S.S.R.)
Sowell, Thomas, 82
Space industry, 168, 273-4; Space
Plane, 158, 317, 332; Space Shuttle,
158, 167, 304, 317, 332; Space
Station, 317, 331 (see also Outer-
Space; 6th-Wave)
Spain, 323, 367
Special Drawing Rights (SDRs), 205
(see also Global currency unit)
Spirituality, 87-94, 311, 357, 369-70
(see also Beliefs; Values; and specific
religions)
Sri Lanka, 356, 358
Stanford Research International, 120
Statistics Canada, 119
Steel industry, 124-5, 238, 272
Steel, Ronald, 294
Stockman, David, 297
Stock market crash (of 1987), 185, 201,
262, 343
Stone Computer Corporation (China),
339

Strategic Defense Initiative (SDI/"Star Wars"), 109, 271, 272-3, 276, 287, 288, 290, 291, 332 (see also Military Spending)

Strategic planning (see Geo-Strategic Planning)

Stress, 57-8 (see also Future Shock)

Strong, Maurice, 362

Sumitomo Bank, 189

"Super-Boom", economic, 180, 211, 213, 286

Superconductivity, 140, 155, 167, 231-2 (see also Energy; Transportation)

Superpowers, 284, 285, 288, 291, 298, 347, 352, 361, 362, 375, 380-2, 387 (see also Multi-Polarity; Nationalism; Veto Power; U.S.A.; U.S.S.R.)

Super-Sonic Transport plane, 275

Supra-Racialism, 73-85, 89, 91, 301 (see also Blacks; Chinese; Cultural mixing; Hispanics; Jews)

Supra-Sexuality, 73-85, 87 (see also Women)

Supreme Court of Canada, 130

Sweden, 47, 118, 231, 321

Switzerland, 22, 253, 321

Syria, 356

Taiwan 336-7, 339, 341-3, 346, 379 (see also China)

Taxation, 202, 295, 297, 321 (see also Global Equalization Tax)

Taylor, Gordon Rattray, 161

Teachers (see Education)

Technological innovation, 5, 105, 111, 152, 169, 183, 216, 376 (see also Innovation; Productivity; Research & Development)

Technological revolution, 111-2 (see also 4th-Wave; High-technology)

Technology diffusion, 125, 313

Technology forecasting, 109-110

Technology management, 135-6

Technology, "Ripple Effects" of, 109-111

Technology Transfer, 109, 129-36, 191, 210, 260-1, 304, 329, 333, 349, 376, 397 (see also Knowledge Transfer)

"Technopolis Strategy" (Japan), 151-3

Teikoku Research Bank, 78

Telecommunications networks, 143-50, 313, 315, 333 (see also ISDN; Satellites)

Telecommuting, 63, 72, 119, 146-7 (see also Electronic Cottage)

"Tele-frustration", 147-8

Tele-learning (see Education)

Tele-medicine (see Healthcare)

Telephone, 144-9

"Tele-prosperity", 144-7

Television, 92-3, 282, 289, 397 (see also Educational television)

Thinking skills (see Geo-Strategic Thinking)

Third Wave, The (the book), 1-2, 17, 267, 344

3rd-Wave Service Economy/Society, 1-2, 57, 111, 112, 146, 169, 217, 282, 283, 337, 341, 368 (see also Professions)

Third World, 191-8, 349-63; 2, 4, 8, 16, 19, 24, 27, 29-30, 36-41, 48-51, 53-4, 60-1, 63, 67-71, 76-8, 96-7, 107-9, 124-27, 131, 133-6, 147-9, 178-9, 188, 203, 219, 221, 224, 230-1, 246, 249, 274, 286-9, 298-9, 303, 312, 329, 331, 333-4, 338, 340, 368 (see also Colonialism; Debt; Debtors' Cartel; Non-aligned nations; Political independence; South Bank; South Commission)

3-M Company, 168, 250

Thurow, Lester, 24, 296

Tian'anmen Square incident (see

China)

Time magazine, 89, 297

Toffler, Alvin, 1, 2, 57, 93, 147, 265, 267, 344

Tokyo, 239

Tokyo Stock Exchange, 178, 185

Toronto, 304

Toshiba Corporation, 156, 163

Totalitarianism, 366

Tourism, 121, 304, 397 (see also 5th-Wave; Leisure)

Toxic wastes (see Hazardous waste; Waste disposal/recycling)

Toyota Motor Company, 132, 153, 189

Trade blocs, 258, 379-81 (see also Free Trade; GATT; Protectionism)

Trade unions (see Unions)

Training/Retraining, 159, 197 (see also Education)

Translation systems, 138-9 (see also Language)

Transnational corporations (see Geo-Strategic Corporations; Multi-national Corporations)

Transportation, 167, 231-2 (see also Automobile Industry; Space Plane; Superconductivity)

Tribalism, 354

"Trickle Down" economic theory, 184, 196, 322

Tropical Forests Action Plan, 246 (see also Reforestation)

Trudeau, Pierre Elliott, 305

Tufts University, 93

ul Haq, Mahbub, 211

ul Haq, Zia, 210, 366, 367

Unemployment, 59-64, 171-2, 321-2, 360, (see also Employment restructuring; Job creation; Work sharing)

Union of Soviet Socialist Republics (U.S.S.R.), 309-18, 319-27; 9, 43, 78, 203-4, 224, 241, 265-9, 271-2, 287-89, 294, 298-9, 303, 331-2, 340, 345, 347, 351-2, 354, 356, 360-1, 366, 376, 382, 385; Expansionism, 309-10, 315-8; *Glasnost*, 309-12, 318; *Perestroika*, 309-18, 366; Sovietization of Europe, 323-5 (see also Andropov, Yuri; Baltic republics; Gorbachev, Mikhail S.)

Unions (labor), 64, 304, 306, 322, 328

Unisys Corporation, 204

United Kingdom (U.K.), 321-3; 229, 263, 264, 294, 296-8

United Nations (U.N.), 385-90; 24, 210, 282, 305, 375, 396; Children's Fund (UNICEF), 25, 37, 52, 54, 272; Development Program (UNDP), 52; Educational, Scientific & Cultural Organization (UNESCO), 41; Environmental Program (UNEP), 42, 245, 249, 252; Food & Agriculture Organization (UNFAO), 36, 38, 41; Fund for Population Activities (UNFPA), 25-6, 33, 41; General Assembly, 387; Industrial Development Organization (UNIDO), 124, 194, 351; International Drinking Water Supply & Sanitation Decade, 51; Security Council, 387; Water Conference, 51 (see also Geo-Centric Governance; Global governance; International Labor Organization; World Health Organization)

United States of America (U.S.A.), 293-307; 3, 6, 10, 26, 29, 35, 52, 64, 82, 184, 189-90, 203, 205-7, 224, 228, 230-1, 246, 252, 258, 263-4, 271-2, 286-7, 290, 315, 319, 321-2, 327-8, 331-2, 340, 341-3, 347-8, 350-1, 359, 362, 368-70, 376-9, 382, 385-6; Agency for International Development (AID), 25; U.S.-Canada Free Trade (cont'd)

United States of America (cont'd)
Agreement, 258, 305; Center for Disease Control, 56, 344; Central Intelligence Agency (CIA), 36, 293, 314; Chamber of Commerce, 119, 133; Congressional Committee on Science & Technology, 163; Department of Agriculture, 43; Department of Defense, 155-6, 163, 275; Department of Labor, 62; as debtor nation, 202-3, 293, 295, 296; dollar, 206, 208-9; economic decline of, 189-90; elections, 83, 298, 301, 372-3; Federal Reserve Board, 205; Forest Service, 246; International Trade Commission, 133; National Aeronautical & Space Agency (NASA), 40, 158, 168, 261, 273, 275, 304; National Institute of Allergy & Infectious Diseases, 56; National Institute of Genetic Medical Science, 165; National Oceanic & Atmospheric Administration, 248; Office of Technology Assessment (OTA), 155; Public Health Foundation, 56; Supreme Court, 76, 368; (see also "Amexicana", Bush, George; Budget deficits; East-West Axis; Reagan, Ronald; Reaganomics; Superpowers; Voter registration)

United Technologies Corporation, 131

Universities, 97, 99-101 (see also Education)

University degrees earned by women, 74-5

University of California, 165

University of Illinois, 163

University of Minnesota, 67

University of Nebraska, 56

University of North Carolina, 261

University of Oregon, 46

University of Utah, 372-3

University of Waginingen, 41

Upper Volta, 42

Urbanization, 68-70, 244, 352 (see also Mega-Cities)

Urban management (see City management)

Utah, 373

Value added (see Information Economy; Manufacturing Value Added; Wealth creation)

Values, 18, 87-94, 121, 369, 379 (see also Beliefs; Hierarchy of Needs)

Vancouver, 304

van Dam, André, 262

Veblen, Thorstein, 121

Venezuela, 202-3, 209, 298, 359

Very Large Scale Integrated circuits (VLSI), 155, 338, 339 (see also Microchips; Computers)

Veto power (of superpowers), 284, 375, 380-2, 385-6 (see also Superpowers)

Vietnam, 294, 332

VISA Credit Card Company, 146

Vocational training (see Training/Retraining)

Voice-activated technology, 138-9, 339

Voter registration, 83, 372 (see also U.S. elections)

Voters, 346 (see also Electronic voting; Partocracy)

War, 285-7, 290, 375, 385

Warsaw Pact, 325, 384

Wasserman, Harvey, 299

Waste disposal/recycling, 50, 165, 235-41

Waste-to-Energy plants, 240

Water, 45-52, 394

Water conservation, 48

Water cycle, 43

Water pumps, 49-50
Water purification, 50, 253
Water Research Centre (U.K.), 51
Waves of change (see 1st-, 2nd-, 3rd-, 4th-, 5th-, and 6th-Wave)
Wealth creation, 11, 114-5, 120, 131, 169-74, 177, 180-1, 182-3, 213-24, 349, 397 (see also Information)
Wellness (see Healthcare)
Welfare state economy, 263, 304
Western Europe (see European Economic Community)
West Germany, 10, 47, 229, 264, 297, 320, 322, 324-5, 379
Wheeler, Raymond, 7
Whitehead, Alfred North, 394
Wild-Card Events, 8
Wind power, 228, 231 (see also Energy)
Women's Movement, 73, 301, 302 (see also Supra-Sexuality)
Women politicians, 75-76
Women military officers, 76
Women, Third World, 76-8
Woodlands (Texas), 373
Work, 59-64 (see also Employment; Job creation)

Work Ethic, 117, 121 (see also Leisure Ethic)
Working hours/Work week, 117-8, 195
Work sharing, 61-6, 118-9
World Bank, 37, 52, 70, 96, 179, 184, 188, 202, 204-9, 230, 305, 327, 350, 363, 396 (see also Global Central Bank; International Monetary Fund)
World Health Organization (WHO), 20, 49, 53-4, 56
World Resources Institute, 229
Worldwatch Institute, 238, 252, 253, 276

Xerox (China) Inc., 339

Yamaichi Securities Co. Ltd., 187
Yangtze River, 51
Yellow River, 247
Young, Andrew, 302
Youth, 398

Zhao Zi-Yang, 344
Zimbabwe, 39

About the Author

Frank Feather is a leading consulting futurist, lecturer and writer on global trends and their strategic implications for executive decision makers in business, government and education.

Since 1981, as President & CEO of Geo-Strategic Opportunity Development Corporation (GEODEVCO), Toronto, he has consulted on global economics/finance, international trade, technology transfer, strategic planning, corporate development, global marketing, and human resource development. His roster of FORTUNE 500 clients includes numerous global corporations such as ARCO, Ciba-Geigy, IBM, Northern Telecom, Shell, and Touche Ross. He has been active in the American Management Association and the Canadian Institute of Management.

He has also consulted to world bodies such as the International Monetary Fund, the World Bank and the United Nations, as well as several agencies/departments of the governments of the United States, Canada, Mexico and the People's Republic of China. He was Special Advisor on international technology and economy to the leading think tank of the State Council (the cabinet) of the Chinese government from 1986 to 1988 and presently is Research Fellow to the Zhejiang Institute of Asia-Pacific Studies, Hangzhou, China.

Prior to founding GEODEVCO, Frank Feather accumulated 22-years of senior executive planning and business experience with three of the world's major international banks: first with Barclays Bank in the United Kingdom; then with the Toronto-Dominion Bank and the Canadian Imperial Bank of Commerce in Canada. This corporate experience included senior positions in international banking, domestic banking, corporate planning and business lending. He holds qualifications from both the British and Canadian Institutes of Bankers.

A leader of the international futures movement, Mr. Feather served as Chairman & Director-General of the First Global Conference on the Future held in Toronto in 1980. With 5400 attendees, 1000 speakers and 400 sessions over five days, this is still the largest futures conference ever held. In 1980, with Dr. Rashmi Mayur, he co-founded the Global Futures Network, now based in Bombay, India, as a non-profit organization which brings futuristic ideas to the global socio-economic development process. He is also a member of the World Future Society, the World Futures Studies Federation, and the Society for International Development. As a promoter of global change, he is an avid student of brain science research, sociology and psychology, and is a Fellow of the World and American Associations of Social Psychiatry.

Mr. Feather has also been active in the field of education. He undertook graduate business studies at York University, Toronto, and as an Adjunct Professor later taught graduate students there. He is a Fellow of Norman Bethune College at York. He has also taught at the community college level and is an active speaker to the educational community in North America.

As an accomplished and sought-after public speaker, Mr. Feather has given over 350 speeches to a wide variety of international conferences and seminars and is now represented by The Leigh Bureau in Princeton, New Jersey. He is also widely published on strategic management, socio-economic change, and global trends, and his articles have appeared in numerous books, journals and magazines. He has edited two books: *Through the 80s* (1980) and *Optimistic Outlooks* (1982). *G-FORCES Reinventing the World* is his first authored work.

Frank Feather was born and raised on a small farm in Yorkshire, England. He emigrated to Canada in 1968 and has lived in Toronto ever since. He has two daughters from a previous marriage and is now married to Tan Min (Tammie Tan), a native of China.